The Pacific Islands

The
Pacific Islands

THIRD EDITION

DOUGLAS L. OLIVER
Illustrations by Sheila Mitchell Oliver

University of Hawaii Press
Honolulu

Maps 1–4 originally appeared in *Oceania: The Native Cultures of Australia and the Pacific Islands* (1989, 2 vols., Honolulu: University of Hawai'i Press), by Douglas L. Oliver.

00 99 98 97 96 95   6 5 4 3 2

Library of Congress Cataloging-in-Publication Data
Oliver, Douglas L.
   The Pacific Islands / Douglas L. Oliver ; with
illustrations by Sheila Mitchell Oliver. — 3rd ed.
     p.   cm.
   Bibliography: p.
   Includes index.
   ISBN 0-8248-1233-6
   1. Islands of the Pacific. I. Title.
DU17.056   1989   88–38668
990—dc19   CIP

University of Hawai'i Press books are printed on acid-free paper and meet the guidelines for permanence and durability of the Council on Library Resources

Contents

Cataclysm

Illustrations and Maps

Unless otherwise indicated, the illustrations of native artifacts were sketched by Sheila Mitchell Oliver from objects in collections at the Peabody Museum, Harvard University.

Preface

The first edition of this book was published by Harvard University Press in 1951. A second edition, copublished by Harvard University Press and the American Museum of Natural History/Doubleday & Co. in 1961 (and reprinted by the University of Hawaii Press in 1975 and subsequent years), constituted a revision only to the extent that it provided a chronicle of events up to 1960. The present edition, like the first, terminates the book's narrative at 1950 but contains extensive revisions and additions, based on the large and continually increasing number of historical and anthropological writings about the Pacific Islands published since 1960. In fact, the quantity of such writings has become so dauntingly large that I was reluctant to attempt another revision and was persuaded to do so only at the urging of some colleagues who continue to make use of the 1961 edition in their teaching despite its many obsolescences. Thus it is to them, and especially to Thomas Harding, that I owe principal acknowledgement for the appearance of this third (and definitely final!) edition. (Acknowledgements for assistance in preparing the earlier editions are listed therein.)

Help of other kinds has been provided by this edition's dedicatees: to Harry Maude, for his inspiring, generous, and unpretentious deanship of Pacific Islands history; and to Philip Phillips, for his perdurable friendship.

THE ISLANDERS

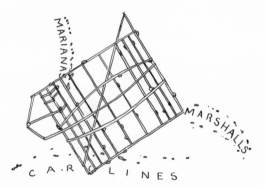

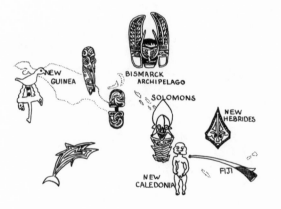

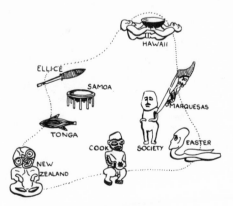

CHAPTER ONE

The Islands and the Islanders in Pre-colonial Times

There are more than ten thousand Pacific Islands, ranging from tiny coral islets to vast New Guinea, which is as large as Texas and contains mountains fourteen thousand to fifteen thousand feet high. Just before the first contact with Westerners, the Pacific Islands were inhabited by about three and a quarter million people whose ancestors had migrated from Southeast Asia, some of them forty thousand to fifty thousand years ago. At that earliest stage of settlement, the ocean gaps between Southeast Asia and New Guinea (the westernmost Pacific Island) were somewhat narrower than they are today, as a result of a lowering of sea levels brought about by the freezing and impounding of much of the earth's waters during that most recent Ice Age. As a result of that same worldwide lowering of ocean levels, the shallow sea bottoms between New Guinea and Australia were exposed off and on for thousands of years so that the lands were united into a single continent, which geologists have named Sahul (see Map 1). Archaeology has demonstrated that Australia was first settled at least as early as New Guinea and likely from

This chapter is a brief summary of the author's *Native Cultures of the Pacific Islands,* Honolulu: University of Hawaii Press, 1989.

Map 1. Sunda and Sahul (shaded areas now submerged) (drawn by Lois Johnson)

some of the same sources in what is now eastern Indonesia. But during the following millennia the peoples of the two land masses, which were only periodically united, diverged from one another both physically (i.e., genetically) and culturally and were almost totally separated about ten thousand years ago when that final Ice Age ended and sea levels rose to their present heights. (Since then the only contacts, and those few and transient, between the native peoples of New Guinea and Australia have been by New Guineans living in the islands of the Torres Strait.)

The pioneer settlers in New Guinea found a climate cooler than today's and hence somewhat different types and locations of vegetation and animals. About ten thousand years ago, however, those natural elements began to become as they were when Western colonization commenced, which leads to the question of what those elements were, not only in New Guinea but in all the other environments into which the Islanders eventually settled. The question is relevant because although physical environments do not directly, necessarily, shape mankind's cultures, they do provide limits to what humans can do, especially in the case of the Pacific Islanders, with their Stone Age technologies.

Understanding of the numerous kinds of natural environments found in the Pacific Islands must begin with some knowledge of their underlying bases, which consist of portions of three tectonic plates, the huge sheets of rock sixty or so miles thick on which the earth's lands and seas are based, and which float on a thicker layer of magma. The numerous separate plates that make up those sheets move about continuously over the magma. When adjoining plates move apart, the magma flows up through the gaps to build mountains. When they collide one of them pushes under (subducts) the other, creating great ridges and troughs. And when they grind past each other the resulting friction produces cracks, and hence earthquakes, in the adjoining plates.

The Pacific Islands are based on three adjoining plates: the vast Pacific Plate in the east, which consists mainly of basalt, and the Philippine and Indo-Australian plates in the west, which consist of continental-type rocks such as granite and slate (see Map 2). At its western edge the westward-moving Pacific Plate subducts the other two, thereby forming mountainous ridges and deep ocean trenches, accompanied by continuing vulcanism and earthquakes. Meanwhile, the magma underlying the Pacific Plate continues to flow up through its weak spots (faults), thereby adding to the existing archipelagoes.

Another great rock-forming element in the tropical Pacific (excluding New Zealand, which is outside the tropics) is coral, a hard calcareous substance made up of the skeletons of certain marine animals and plants that attach themselves to rocks or to the shells of dead predecessors, thereby building up solid structures of varied shapes. The animals (the polyps) involved in this process can survive only in warm, clear, sunlit waters. Thus, as the sea level rises and falls in relation to a coral-encrusted shoreline, so does the zone of coral formation. And as a result of the many changes in shoreline level, dead coral reefs are to be found on the slopes of the islands, in some cases as much as four thousand feet above or below present sea level.

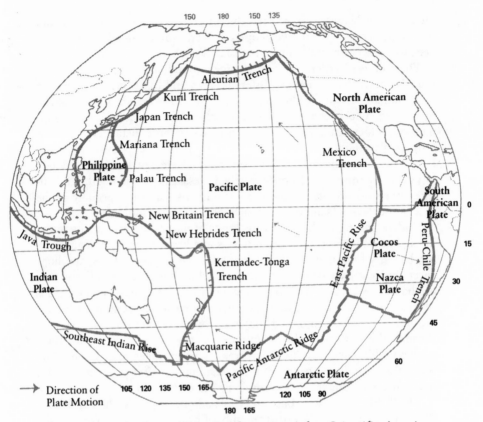

Map 2. Tectonic plates of the Pacific region (after *Scientific American,* June 1979:166) (drawn by Lois Johnson)

The rock-forming processes just described have served to build three main types of islands in the Pacific:

continental ones, such as New Guinea, New Zealand, Guadalcanal, New Caledonia, and Viti Levu (one of the Fiji islands), all of which are located on the Philippine or the Indo-Australian plates, and which consist of continental-type rocks with intrusions of volcanoes and, except for New Zealand, shoreline deposits of coral.

volcanic islands, which consist chiefly of volcanic products and which include all those based on the Pacific Plate (e.g., Hawaii, Tahiti, Upolu, Ponape) and many based on the Philippine or Indo-Australian plates (e.g., Manam, Kolombangara).

coral islands. In many locations dead coral constitutes the only parts of an island above sea level, either in the form of a low, narrow atoll islet (e.g., those of the Marshall islands) or of a higher flat-topped "pancake" island (such as Nauru, Makatea, and Angaur).

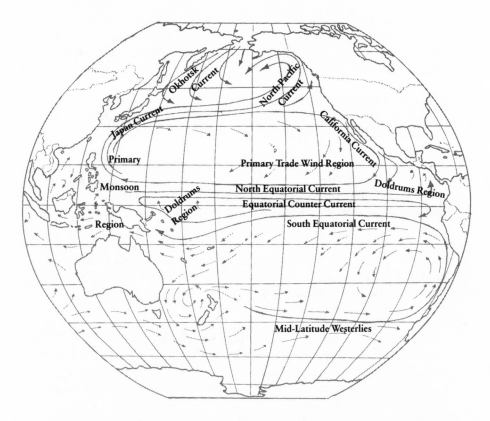

Map 3. Ocean currents and surface winds of the Pacific region (drawn by Lois Johnson)

Winds, rainfall, and ocean currents have also served to shape the Pacific Islands and their vegetation, and of course the lives of their human inhabitants.

Two vast whorls dominate seawater movements in the Pacific. The one north of the equator flows clockwise, the one south of it counterclockwise. The southern segment of the northern whorl flows from the American side to the Philippines before it is turned north, except east of the Hawaiian and the Mariana islands, where parts of it are deflected from its east-west course. Some of the northern segment of the southern, westward-moving, whorl also flows unobstructed as far as Australia, but much of it is deflected southward by the numerous intervening islands. In between the two major whorls flows the Equatorial Countercurrent in a Pacific-wide band from the Caroline and the Gilbert islands all the way to Panama (see Map 3).

Islanders living in places brushed by the currents were influenced by them in two ways. Indirectly, the currents served to determine what species of ocean-borne plants and animals an island received from elsewhere. More directly, the currents served to facilitate, or to impede, boat travel between islands, with all the cultural and social consequences that such interactions made possible.

Apart from New Zealand, nearly all of the inhabited islands are within the tropics, and their year-round temperatures are high. However, surrounded as they are by the ocean, few places among the tropical islands experience the very high summer temperatures that occur in the Temperate Zone. Also, the temperatures in many of the Pacific Islands are tempered by offshore winds. And although most of those tropical islands undergo some seasonal change in climate, these changes result mainly from variations in wind and rainfall.

Surface wind patterns around the islands are few in number and fairly regular in occurrence. North of about latitude 25 N and south of about latitude 27 S the strong mid-latitude Westerlies blow almost continuously year-round. Between them prevail four kinds of wind patterns: trade winds, monsoons, doldrums, and typhoons.

Trade winds dominate the eastern parts of the tropical Pacific. Those north of the equator blow from the northeast and are strongly felt as far west as about longitude 165 W; those south of it blow from the southeast and spend their main force before reaching that far west. The Pacific trades blow in every month of the year but do so more uninterruptedly and steadily during the period from May to September.

More seasonal winds, or monsoons, take the place of the trades in the western third of the Pacific. During the Asian winter, winds are pushed out from there to the south and east, and the direction is reversed during Asia's summer. During the Asian winter the winds in the western Pacific islands are more variable and sometimes stormier than the winds from the east, and tend to bring more rain.

The largest areas of doldrums lie between the two trade wind zones and extend as far west as the Solomons, where the monsoonal pattern takes over. As their name signifies, doldrums are characterized by low wind velocities; they are also marked by high humidity, much cloudiness, and by even, year-round high temperatures.

Typhoons (hurricanes) occur throughout much of the tropical Pacific but do so most frequently and violently in the areas shown on Map 3. The high winds and torrential rains that constitute typhoons are devastating and life-destroying even in our modern era of advance-warning communications and massive rescue operations; they doubtless destroyed whole populations of Islanders in the past. Like explosive-type volcanic eruptions and unheralded tsunamis (tidal waves), they were an unavoidable hazard to many Island peoples.

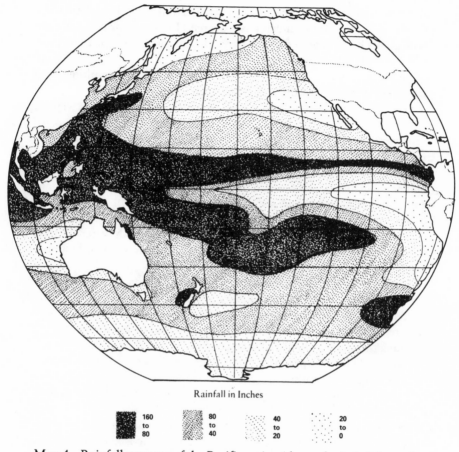

Rainfall in Inches

| 160 to 80 | 80 to 40 | 40 to 20 | 20 to 0 |

Map 4. Rainfall patterns of the Pacific region (drawn by Lois Johnson)

Rainfall in the Pacific Islands is marked by wide variability (see Map 4). Generally speaking, most islands near the equator experience year-round high rainfall, averaging 80–160 inches annually; the islands farther north and south receive about half that amount and on a more seasonal basis. On the other hand, there are several equatorial islands in the central and eastern Pacific that receive virtually no rainfall at all (e.g., Canton, Enderbury) and some others (such as the southern Gilberts) that receive none for months at a time. Farther west, where monsoonal winds take over, the rainfall follows a more regular, seasonal pattern, complicated however by the mountainous terrain found on some islands. Precipitation may also vary among islands in the same archipelago and on different sides of the same island.

Another factor that served to determine the kinds of plants growing on Pacific Islands when humans first settled them was an island's distance from Asia, since most of their plant genera derived from there. (Australia was also a source but to a much lesser degree.) In other words, since most of the plants had "migrated" by water, many of them "dropped out" during the journeys from west to east.

The diversities in soil, moisture, terrain, and so forth resulting from various combinations of the above factors resulted in a number of different types of natural plant complexes, of which the major ones were as follows.

Seacoast or *strand*. This complex, which is present on nearly every tropical Pacific Island (and indeed throughout insular Southeast Asia as well) is usually confined to very narrow areas and contains only a small number of genera, including casuarina, barringtonia, hibiscus, pandanus, Indian almond, and the extremely useful coconut palm (which, however, is found mainly where it has been planted by man). Common to all these plants is the capacity to thrive in salt or brackish water; in fact, they owe their wide distribution to the ability of their seeds to be borne long distances in the ocean without loss of viability.

Mangrove forests. This complex includes "true" mangrove trees, terrestrial ferns, and epiphytes (air plants); in other words, plants specially adapted to growth in mud flats partly or totally covered by salt or brackish water. Such plants thrive along shores protected from wind and wave and along the swampy banks of tidal creeks.

Swamps. Several types of swamp vegetation occur in the Islands, either in large and pure stands (as, for example, along the course of the Sepik River in New Guinea) or interspersed among other complexes, including some at very high altitudes.

Lowland rain forests. Throughout the "continental" lands of the western islands and on most of the mountainous volcanic islands of the central and eastern Pacific this was the most widespread type of vegetation complex. Forests of this type are characterized by large numbers of different plants, including huge trees festooned with vines and ferns.

Montane or *subtropical rain forests*. Under similar conditions of atmospheric moisture, the vegetation of the lowland rain forest is replaced by other species on lands of higher altitude or greater distance from the equator. The plants of this complex differ somewhat from island to island but in general consist of only two levels of vegetation, in place of the three to five found in their lowland forest counterparts.

High montane cloud forests. In New Guinea this complex replaces the montane rain forest at about six thousand feet; in other islands where it occurs (not many) the transition from rain forest to cloud forest takes place at lower altitudes. In this chill, wet atmosphere there is generally a single-story canopy, and the dominant trees are temperate-zone ones such as myrtles and rhododendrons, festooned with mosses and liverworts and ornamented with orchids.

Alpine. Above the usual cloud level the climates of the highest tropical islands become dry and sunny, and the mossy forests change, first into shrubby woodland and higher still into tussocky grasses and herbs. Patches of such vegetation occur at the summits of the highest mountains in the Solomons, but large indigenous stands of this kind of vegetation occur only in New Guinea and in the Hawaiian chain.

Grasslands and *savannah woodlands.* Vegetation complexes of this type now occur widely in the Pacific Islands, either indigenously, as a result of insufficient rainfall, or as a result of continuous burning of the original forest by humans. The largest of these areas are on New Guinea (e.g., in the Highlands and south of the Fly River). Smaller stretches are located on the leeward sides of some of the large islands, such as Guadalcanal, New Caledonia, Viti Levu, and Hawaii. And even smaller but nevertheless extensive stretches of it occur on Easter Island and on some other islands of the Hawaiian chain.

And then there is New Zealand. The two principal islands of this archipelago extend north and south some 745 miles and comprise about ninety-six thousand square miles of land, which is larger than the total land area of all the other islands occupied by Polynesian-speaking peoples before Western contact. Even the northernmost tip of New Zealand, at latitude 34 S, is well outside the tropics, and the southern tip of the archipelago's South Island is only 23 degrees from the Antarctic Circle, all of which resulted in a variety of climates (and of vegetation) ranging from semitropical (where four-fifths of its indigenous peoples lived) to one too cold to permit the thin scattering of residents to garden.

Turning now to the kinds of animals found on the Islands when humans first reached them, here again the factor of distance from Asia (and secondarily, from Australia) was critical. Thus, none of Asia's larger land vertebrates reached any of the Islands, and of the smaller vertebrates present, although New Guinea contains seventy-two genera of indigenous mammals, Tahiti had only rodents (and even they may have been introduced, unwittingly, in Islanders' canoes).

Distance of course was not an absolute obstacle to the truly oceanic birds (such as gulls, terns, noddies, albatrosses, and shearwaters), nor to some far-flying land birds (such as the golden plover, which migrates annually from Alaska to Hawaii and beyond). And although freshwater fauna tended to be influenced by the same rule of distance that governed terrestrial fauna, the distribution of saltwater fauna was determined by conditions of other kinds, including currents, water temperature, undersea topography, and coral formations.

Finally, mention must be made of two other fauna that affected many Pacific Islanders in very important ways. One was the malaria-bearing anopholes mosquito, which infested most islands from New Guinea to the New Hebrides. The other was the filaria-bearing mosquito, *Aedes*

polynesiensis, which infested a chain of islands stretching from New
Guinea to eastern Polynesia.

Such were the natural environments of the Pacific Islands when
humans first settled on them, during a span of time that began (on New
Guinea) forty to fifty millennia ago and ended (in Hawaii) about A.D.
750. Next to consider are the physical features of those migrants and the
kinds of cultural baggage carried with them. (Much of the following is
speculative, but not wildly so.)

Those earliest migrants were dark brown to black in skin color and
curly to frizzly in hair form. They derived from peoples who lived in
small bands that were scattered from Timor and the Moluccas westward
into mainland Southeast Asia and northward into the Philippines (that is,
throughout most of ancient Sundaland). Their stone tools were made
mainly by flaking and they subsisted by hunting and gathering wild animals and plants. Reflecting the wide scattering of their bands, their languages must have been numerous and exceedingly diverse; such is the
case with those now spoken by most of their descendants on New Guinea
and several nearby islands, although some linguists perceive enough similarities among most of them to assign them to a single language family,
labeled Papuan. And they must have had watercraft of enough size and
stability to ferry families across the sixty or so miles of open ocean that
has always, during the span of human existence, separated Sundaland
from Sahul.

(What is said here about the first settlers on New Guinea applies
equally to the source and technology of those who first settled in Australia but, as remarked earlier, in the course of time the descendants of the
two streams of pioneers moved increasingly apart, in their ways of life
and in their genes.)

The Sundanoids (i.e., the descendants of the earlier streams of New
Guinea settlers) eventually dispersed throughout New Guinea and into
the Bismarck and Solomon archipelagoes. And for many millennia they
continued to subsist by hunting and gathering (including fishing, for
those near seas, rivers, and lakes). Then, beginning about nine thousand
years ago the revolutionary techniques of horticulture spread from the
west into the settlements of the Sundanoids (as much perhaps by contact
as by new immigrations) so that food growing largely replaced food
hunting and gathering nearly everywhere. Also accompanying food
growing was the raising of pigs. Some of the early Sundanoid settlers may
have brought chickens and dogs with them (there were none in the
Islands before humans arrived), but the first evidence of pigs coincided
with the first signs of horticulture (which appeared archaeologically in
the New Guinea Highlands).

Sundanoids may have continued to drift into New Guinea from the west for thousands of years, but beginning about five thousand years ago humans of a different physical type entered the Islands, bearing a different type of language along with several other distinctive cultural traits. They differed physically from the Sundanoids in having lighter skin color, straighter hair, rounder crania, and flatter faces—they were members of the Mongoloid race, whose original domain extended throughout central and east Asia (and some of whom eventually populated the Americas). Peoples of Mongoloid race spoke a variety of tongues, including Chinese, Japanese, and Austronesian. The latter family of languages originated in southeastern China or Formosa; people speaking it, here labeled Austronesians, eventually migrated far and wide: into the Philippines, Indonesia, the Malay Peninsula, coastal Indochina, even Madagascar—and what is important here, into the Pacific Islands.

Austronesians entered the Pacific Islands by two separate routes. One stream, probably from the southern Philippines-northern Moluccas, ended up in the Mariana islands and Yap (and possibly Nauru). The other, following more southerly routes, moved along the northern coast of New Guinea, through the Bismarck Archipelago, and down the chains of islands to New Caledonia. Note that "stream" implies just that: these movements, and especially the southward ones, would doubtless have been made by successive generations of migrants over scores or even hundreds of years. And although the islands settled by the northern (i.e., the Marianas and Yap) streams seem to have been previously uninhabited, many of those along the southern routes were already inhabited by peoples of Sundanoid physical features speaking Papuan languages. Over the course of time some of the latter peoples retained both their (Papuan) languages and their (Sundanoid) physical features, while others adopted Austronesian traits into their languages and cultures but few if any Mongoloid genes, and still others fused both their languages and other cultural traits *and* their genes with those of the newcomers. And while those movements and changes were taking place, some other fleets of the newcomers dared the unknown and sailed farther east. Many canoes were doubtless lost in the hundreds of miles of empty sea, but enough of them survived to establish colonies from which their descendants went on to colonize all of the remaining habitable islands between (and including) New Zealand, Easter Island, Hawaii, and the Marianas—movements that were completed within about two thousand years and by at least two different streams. Some of these seafarers went first to the northeast, more than likely from the Solomons or the New Hebrides to the Gilbert islands, and from there successive generations of their descendants went on to colonize the Marshalls and the Carolines (except for Yap, which had already been settled by descendants of the Marianas-Yap pioneers).

More certainty, and much more publicity, attaches to the southern branch of these seafarers. For, after colonizing the Fiji islands (from the

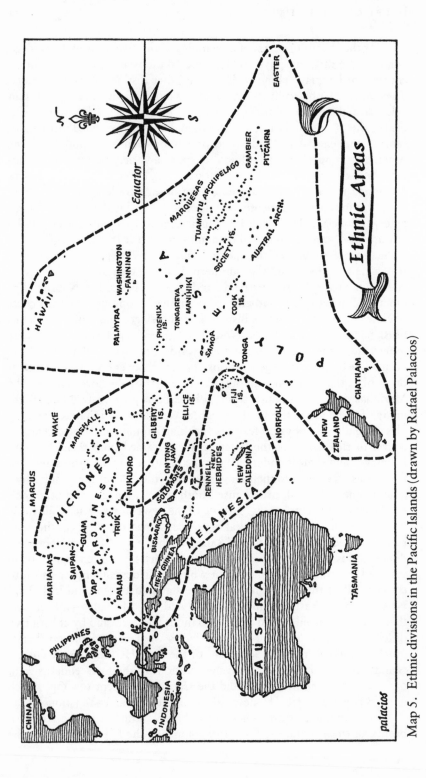

Map 5. Ethnic divisions in the Pacific Islands (drawn by Rafael Palacios)

New Hebrides) in about 1500 B.C., successive generations of them went on to colonize the vast triangle of islands now called Polynesia (from Greek, "many islands"), by which label its peoples and their languages are now known (see Map 5).

And speaking of such labels, there are several good reasons for lumping all so-called Polynesians under the same name: all their languages are closely interrelated (more closely, say, than the several Germanic tongues), their physical features are on the whole fairly similar and closer to those of the Southeast Asian Mongoloids than to those of their Sundanoid neighbors, their religious concepts and practices are much alike, their kinship units resemble one another in structure, and so on.

A second label popularly applied to an aggregate of Pacific Islands, and their inhabitants, is Micronesia (from Greek, "small islands"), which has come to be identified with the Marianas, the Carolines, the Marshalls, and the Gilberts (plus Ocean Island and Nauru). Most of the islands linked together under this label are indeed "small," and the languages spoken in all of them except the Marianas, Yap, and Nauru are indeed closely interrelated (not, however, as closely as those of Polynesia). Moreover, large numbers of these Islanders belong to kinship units constituted in the same way (i.e., by matrilineal descent). But the aggregate as a whole falls short of the cultural homogeneity that characterizes the Polynesians.

As for the rest of the Pacific Islands, from New Guinea to New Caledonia and Fiji, the common label of Melanesia (from Greek "black islands") that map-makers apply to them and their native inhabitants refers more to the inhabitants' skin color than to anything else, and to that not entirely correctly (i.e., it is only in the northern Solomons that skin colors are truly black; elsewhere in Melanesia they range from light to dark brown). Although it is true that all Melanesians practice horticulture, the same is true of Polynesians and Micronesians—and most other peoples of the world. And as for the languages spoken by the Melanesians, they differ both in family (i.e., between Papuan and Austronesian) and between branches of the same family, to an enormously wide degree.

But let us forego the fruitless search for broad regional labels and consider the many ways in which Islanders were living their lives at the times when Westerners first "discovered" them—first, their kinds of boats and seafaring skills; for without boats they would not have been there to be discovered.

As mentioned earlier, a simple raft or a bark or dug-out canoe would have sufficed to transport Sundanoids to New Guinea, and similar watercraft could have carried migrants from New Guinea to New Britain and New Ireland. However, the next habitable islands, Buka and Bougainville, were over 100 miles farther on; to reach them would have required larger and more stable craft, which were in fact developed by enlarging and adding an outrigger to existing dug-out canoes. Equipped with these, people could and evidently did move farther south and east as far as San Cristobal, and with a few more improvements, to New Caledonia, which was and remained the end of *that* line.

The next phases of migrations into the Pacific (to the Marianas, the Gilberts, and Fiji) involved open-sea voyages of about 500 miles and required even larger canoes, equipped with sail. Such improvements continued to be developed to the point of enabling some Islanders to travel distances of up to 1,890 miles (which is the shortest distance between Hawaii and the Marquesas, the source of Hawaii's first settlers). At the peak of their development the largest of the Islanders' boats had double hulls and carried up to 500–600 persons. (For comparison, the largest of the Viking boats carried no more than about 200 persons and achieved nonstop open-sea voyages of no longer than about 500 miles.) Such achievements, in size, or in seaworthiness, or both, took place mainly in Fiji, in Polynesia, and in parts of Micronesia. (Although "Micronesia" is troublesome as a label for many other cultural traits, it is appropriate in this context.) Elsewhere in the Islands the boats were smaller and of numerous kinds (e.g., rafts, with or without sails; simple dugouts, with or without sails; canoes built of planks; canoes with outriggers on both sides; and so forth), and many inland peoples had no boats at all.

Islanders used their boats for many purposes, including among others fishing, going to their gardens, and visiting nearby places to trade or wage war. In addition, many of them had through time used them for deliberate, long open-sea voyages to destinations either known or unknown. Reasons for such voyaging included trade, conquest, escape from enemies or from starvation at home, even, in some instances, a desire for adventure. Numerous other long voyages had doubtless taken place involuntarily (i.e., in boats drifting while lost at sea). Some writers have asserted that even the most isolated of Pacific Islands had been colonized in this way, an opinion that has been challenged by recent studies of patterns of currents and winds. But it is the deliberate voyaging to known destinations that has aroused most scholarly interest. And because there can be no doubt about the adequate steerability and carrying capacity of some types of Island canoes, the question becomes: did any Islanders possess enough knowledge to *navigate* successfully over long distances of open sea?

The answer to this question is, of course, yes, and the procedures used nearly everywhere divided such a voyage into three stages. The first consisted of heading the boat in the known direction of the destination by lining up landmarks at the place of departure (e.g., mountain peaks, capes, tall trees); the second of maintaining the desired direction through the open seaway to the third stage, the actual "finding" of the destination (i.e., to within sight of islands known to adjoin it; or by signs such as land-produced ocean swells, land-based fishing birds, cloud colors reflecting vegetation or lagoons, and so forth). On long open-sea voyages it was the second stage that presented the greatest difficulties and encouraged the most ingenious solutions. During this stage, which could have lasted up to three or four weeks on some routes, the most commonly utilized direction markers were wind (and wind-generated waves), sea swells of known shape, currents of known speed, plus sun and, especially, stars. In this brief account it is not possible to catalog the numerous ways in which those markers were utilized. Suffice it to say that the knowledge they evinced, of meteorology, ocean topography, astronomy, and so forth, must be judged as being among the highest intellectual achievements of the Pacific Islanders, knowledge that in some societies could only be acquired through lengthy study in navigation "schools" and through years of apprenticeship to master navigators.

The three and a quarter million or so Islanders alive when Westerners first met up with them were distributed very unevenly over their Islands' half million square miles of land. Densities ranged from two to three per square mile (in some mountainous parts of New Guinea and New Zealand) to 1,000 to 1,600 per square mile (on some atoll islets of the Carolines). In some places the dwellings of a community were widely dispersed, in others densely concentrated (in some cases in "apartments" of a single longhouse). Houses varied greatly in size and shape. In a few places dwellings and other buildings were built on foundations of stone, but the buildings themselves were there and elsewhere made of plant materials, wood, leaves, vines, and plant cordage fiber.

At this point it will be useful to introduce the reader to a few important terms and the ways they will be used throughout this book.

The first one is household, which refers to the group of persons sharing a dwelling (and, as we shall see, usually other things and activities as well). Throughout the Islands most households were composed of a man, his wife (or wives), and their offspring. Other fairly common types of households included the above plus a grandparent or two; a widowed parent and his or her offspring; any of the above plus one or more other relatives. Households composed of a single individual were quite rare; the Islanders' food economies rendered solitary subsisting next to impossible. (Households were everywhere the basic social unit for producing and processing as well as consuming food, and the production [and often processing] of what was considered to be a satisfactory diet required nearly everywhere the conventionally defined labors of both men and women.) A household's dwelling was, also nearly everywhere, the place where all of its members regularly slept, although in several societies the adolescent boys of a neighborhood slept in a house of their own (to separate them from their female relatives) and were joined there frequently by the neighborhood's married men.

The second term requiring precise definition (and consistent usage) is community, which will be used to label any distinct cluster of households whose members shared enough sentiments of their own unity, and of difference from other communities, to dispose them to interact among themselves in relatively peaceful and cooperative ways, and to settle disputes among themselves by means short of unbridled killing. In many places community members also joined together to work, to fight outsiders, to feast, or to engage in religious rites. Pacific Island communities ranged in size from about twenty persons to a thousand or so, and in spatial separateness from almost total isolation (as on some small islands and in some forest fastnesses) to virtual junction with like units (as on some densely populated atolls).

The third term to be introduced at this point is society, the social unit made up of persons who resided in adjacent communities and who shared, more or less distinctively, a common culture (i.e., a common set of premises, values, and practices, including usually a common language). In some cases a single, usually very isolated, community constituted a whole society as well, but in most cases a society contained two or more communities. Unlike single communities, some societies were riven, occasionally or chronically, by warfare; however, for the members of any one society the behavior of co-members would have been comprehensible, no matter how personally obnoxious it may have been. Throughout this book, *a people* will be used to refer to all members of any one society.

Other technical terms (or, rather, common English terms used technically) will be introduced as this chapter proceeds, but those just specified will suffice for now.

Most Islanders between childhood and senility spent more of their waking hours on food than on all other activities combined—producing it, processing it, conserving it, discussing it, and so forth—and in some societies bartering it, or "giving" it away to win public acclaim.

The practice in most Island societies was one large meal a day, usually in late afternoon, with snacks in between. Nearly everywhere that main meal consisted of a large portion of one or two cultivated staples (e.g., breadfruit, sago, bananas, taro, yams, sweet potatoes); a smaller portion of some leafy vegetable; a condiment (e.g., salt, nuts, crushed insects); and whenever available, which was infrequent in many places, a portion of animal flesh (e.g., fish, pork, wild game).

Peoples differed widely in what they could or chose to produce and therefore in what they ate: for example, sago in New Guinea's swampy riverine areas; sweet potatoes in New Zealand and the New Guinea Highlands; breadfruit, taro, and other root crops in lowland forest areas; rice in the Marianas (the only place where a cereal crop was grown); and on some coral islets, flour from the fruit of the pandanus palm, the only starchy staple they could grow.

Where root crops were grown (which is to say, in most of the region's societies), the tools employed were nearly everywhere the same: stone or shell axes or adzes for clearing and sharp-pointed sticks for turning turf and digging holes. Unlike some other agricultural methods, whereby seeds are scattered over uniformly prepared ground, Islanders used mainly cuttings, which were planted one by one. On the other hand, techniques of soil preparation and watering varied widely. One extreme was represented by the many peoples who practiced long-fallowing, which involved little or no clearing or soil preparation or artificial drainage and replanting intervals lasting many years (i.e., due to soil exhaustion, real or imagined). The other extreme was represented, for example, by some peoples of New Caledonia and of the New Guinea Highlands, who were able to use the same site over and over by carrying out measures such as terracing, drainage ditching, soil turning, and composting. Another relatively high level of technology was exemplified by irrigation, the peak of which was developed by the Hawaiians, who constructed (on the island of Kauai) a stone and clay aqueduct "ditch" over twenty feet high. The consummate application of technology, however, was located on some soilless atolls of the central Pacific, where pits were dug into the coral fundament and filled with decaying vegetation and soil from nearby islets (brought in canoes) to grow otherwise ungrowable root crops.

Pigs were raised throughout almost all of Melanesia and on many islands of Polynesia, but nowhere in Micronesia. But even where they were domestically raised their numbers were so few that they were eaten, usually, only at feasts (and usually after having served as highly valued objects of exchange). Dogs were also kept by many peoples and eaten by a few of them, but were more typically used for help in hunting game. Chickens were also present in many societies but survived mainly by scavenging; their flesh was seldom eaten, their eggs almost never.

Hunting wild game occurred mainly in New Zealand and in New Guinea and nearby islands, the only areas where large-enough game actually lived. For fishing, however, most Islanders were much better supplied, thanks to the encompassing ocean and in some places rivers, lakes, or streams. There were, however, some communities (e.g., in the mountains of New Guinea) where marine life was so meager that no fishing at all was done. In contrast, there were many coastal and some riverine communities where fishing was done every day and where fishing tools and techniques were highly diversified and practiced with consummate skill.

Wide differences in natural resources and in cultural practices made for wide dissimilarities in peoples' diets—which raises the question: how satisfactory were those diets in terms of modern nutritional standards? In fact, the question is unanswerable: not only do modern specialists disagree over those standards, but such standards as there are have been deduced from studies of populations (mainly industrialized ones) with life-styles too different from those of the Islanders to make comparisons sensible. The only general response to the question is the finding that single individuals, perhaps, but no Island *peoples* encountered by Westerners in their pristine native state were known to be dying out as a result of malnutrition.

We turn briefly now to the beverages drunk by Islanders: water was the principal one and in most societies the only one. Whenever coconuts were available, the tangy juice of the unripe nut provided a between-meals snack, and on a few islands in Micronesia natives also drank a toddy prepared from the sap of the coconut palm. The only other beverage drunk by Islanders (and that not everywhere) was *kava,* a narcotic infusion of the pulverized root of a pepper-family plant, *Piper methysticum.*

Although tobacco was being grown and smoked by many New Guineans when Westerners first met them, the plant, which is American in origin, had spread into New Guinea in post-Columbian times from Portuguese settlements in the Moluccas.

A more ancient import from Southeast Asia was betel-chewing. It involved three items: the nut of the *Areca catechu* palm; the leaf, bean, or stem of the *Piper betle* vine; and slaked lime, made of either seashells, coral, or mountain lime. The mixture was chewed like plug tobacco and eventually expectorated. The nicotinelike properties of the nut, combined with other properties of the mixture, produce a general feeling of well-being, including a diminution of hunger and fatigue, without impairing consciousness. By the time of Western contact it had spread no farther east than the New Hebrides.

Before leaving the subject of food it is pertinent to inquire whether any Islanders also ate one another. The answer is yes, although cannibalism was not as widespread as many Western travelers reported, and such ingestion was in many societies not done for nourishment but for one social purpose or another—e.g., to display grief for a dead relative by eating (i.e., joining with) part of him; to imbibe some of a dead person's powers or skills; to render a consummate insult to a dead enemy (i.e., by devouring part of him). Nevertheless, there are many credible accounts of Islanders having killed and eaten humans for gustatory pleasure, examples having ranged from the practices of some peoples who ate only those enemies killed in their wars, to some Fijian chiefs whose aides were kept busy supplying their ovens with human flesh, including that of some of their own hapless subjects.

From "cannibal isles" to "love in the South Seas": Like cannibalism, Hollywood-style, under-the-waving-palms-type "love" was far from pervasive among Pacific Island societies. To begin with, culturally programmed attitudes towards sex varied widely. To Tahitians, for example, coitus was as pleasurable and natural as eating. (Obesity was in fact erotically attractive, having been deliberately induced by systematic gorging to increase an individual's sexual desirability.) In contrast, to the New Guinea Mae Enga sexual intercourse was considered dangerously debilitating, especially for males, who were obsessed with what they considered to be the magically pollutive effects of menstrual blood. Or consider the residents of Manus Island (north of New Guinea), who shunned sex not through fear but through disgust towards it and all other genital and anal excretions. The conventional attitudes of most other Island peoples, however, were in between those extremes, having been perhaps nearer the Tahitian than the Mae Enga or Manus attitudes.

Island peoples varied also in other aspects of sex—for example, in their coital techniques; in their attitudes concerning when sex life should begin (e.g., at the onset of puberty, or not until physical maturity) and end (e.g., never, or at the beginning of "old age"); when spouses should abstain (e.g., never, or during menstruation or before a newborn is weaned); and, most important, who could have sex with or marry whom. With one or two exceptions, all Island peoples forbade sex (and hence marriage) between father and daughter, mother and son, and sister and brother. (The most notable exceptions to these proscriptions occurred in Hawaii, where brother-sister marriage sometimes occurred among the nobility to enhance the noble rank of their offspring.) In addition, all Island societies discouraged (from absolute prohibition to mild disapproval) sex (and marriage) between a person and one or more of some other categories of relatives (e.g., with all of a mother's, or father's, sisters; with all clan mates), the categories having differed with a people's overall kinship structure.

Sometime during his (or her) life nearly every Islander became "married." What "marriage" consisted of differed from one society to another, but everywhere included at least: publicly approved sexual cohabitation, the sharing of labor and subsistence goods in a common household economy, and the co-parenting of the woman's progeny born during the union.

In only a few Island societies did a man obtain a wife by genuine (as contrasted with simulated) capture. In others a man sometimes obtained a wife (usually a second one) by inheritance (i.e., by succeeding to a dead brother's widow). But even in those societies, and in all others, the most common method of establishing a marriage was by contract, usually between the families of the couple and usually formalized by an exchange of goods. (Note well: although in many societies the tangible goods handed over by the side of the husband exceeded those received from the bride's side, the latter were *not* thereby regarded as "chattels" in the ordinary sense of the word.)

Mention above of a man's "second wife" leads to the topic of polygamy. I know of no Island people who had religious or ethical rules against polygyny (i.e., one husband, more than one wife), although because of demographic and other factors few families in any society were polygynous. Polyandry, on the other hand, was exceedingly rare; a few peoples (mainly in Polynesia) tolerated a married woman having an extra lover or two, but only one (the Marquesans) practiced the institution of secondary husbands.

Islanders differed widely in their beliefs about the way children were reproduced. In at least two societies the fetus was believed to be implanted entirely by some supernatural agency; in all the rest, coitus was considered necessary for conception, although peoples differed widely about the nature of the process. Some thought the father's semen to be the activating element and the mother's womb a mere receptacle. Others held the reverse idea. But most believed both parents to be essential for a conception (e.g., the mother for the fetus' blood, the father for its bone). And in all cases such beliefs assumed the assistance of spirits to be essential to the process.

Once a child was born, biologically, most Island peoples considered it necessary for it to advance to full maturity (marriageability, political adulthood, and so forth) through well-defined stages, including, in many cases, protracted initiation rites for males. The latter were especially conspicuous in parts of New Guinea and the New Hebrides, where boys underwent years-long segregation, physical hazing, and indoctrination. For girls the analogous rites, where they existed, were less grueling and consisted usually of segregation at the time of first menstruation.

Old age in Island societies was also defined, culturally, in many different ways, as was the treatment accorded the old: in some societies with high respect and privilege, in others tolerance and sustenance, in a few contempt and neglect.

As for death, the ways in which it was explained and ceremonialized were no less diverse than were beliefs about the fate of what survived, if anything, of the mortal remains. Suffice it to say that, except for the very old and decrepit, all deaths were believed to be due to the intervention of spirits, either acting on their own or at the behest of a human enemy of the deceased. As for ceremony, that varied, from immediate disposal of the corpse (usually out of fear), to weeks- or months-long funerals involving exhibition of the corpse, one- or two-stage inhumation (or cremation), and lengthy periods of mourning (lasting for the spouse in some cases a year or more). Truly, no aspect of Island cultures was as diverse as were the ways of dealing with death.

From dying we back track to fighting.

As in most human societies, conflict occurred more frequently within communities than between them, but it is the latter kind of conflict now referred to, and more specifically that in which groups of community mates banded together to use physical measures to inflict bodily harm on their "foreign" enemies. Islanders also used solely religious measures to harm their enemies, domestic and foreign, but it is physical attack (clubbing, spearing, piercing, and so forth) that is our present concern.

The most widespread and impelling kind of reason that led Islanders to engage in "foreign" fighting was to avenge real or imagined wrongs against themselves or other members of some social unit to which they belonged. The nature of such "acts of war" varied from one society to another but in most included homicide, serious bodily injury, abduction or seduction of females, theft, and insult. Other reasons for fighting that prevailed in some societies included status enhancement (e.g., the killing of a foreign enemy, with or without taking his head, was essential for attaining full manhood in some societies); economic (e.g., the capture of enemies for their labor or their flesh); and religious (e.g., the capture of enemies for sacrifices).

The most widely used offensive weapons of the Islanders were spears, clubs, axes, and bows and arrows. Of more limited distribution were slingstones (mainly in eastern Polynesia), daggers, swords, cutting rasps, knuckle-dusters, and strangling and tripping cords. Although bows and arrows served as weapons in Melanesia, throughout much of Polynesia they were used only for hunting or sport.

Reports agree upon the deadly accuracy of Island slingsmen but are less complimentary about Islanders' effective use of arrows (which were unfeathered) and throwing spears. In fact, most serious (in contrast with sportive) fighting was done with cutting, jabbing, and striking weapons, particularly clubs and axes.

The only weapons used exclusively for defense were shields, and those in only a few societies. Instead, reliance was placed on dodging (in which some men were highly adept), on parrying (with clubs, spears, and axes), on protective garments (in many societies, helmets; in a few, plaited-cord armor), and, of course, on magic and other religious measures. In addition, in some societies whole communities were situated, deliberately, in defensible locations or fortified with walls and camouflaged traps.

The types of warfare waged were not everywhere the same. Some peoples engaged in, say, hit-and-run raids and ambushing, others in pitched battles and all-out extermination, others in sportive but lethal contests, and still others in three or four of the above, suiting the type of action to the reason behind it.

And in all the above, the physical measures undertaken were commonly reinforced by religious ones (e.g., magic was employed to empower one's own weapons or to neutralize the enemy's; prayers and sacrifices were addressed to tutelar spirits; and so forth).

Religious measures by themselves were also used by Islanders to harm their enemies, both domestic and foreign. These included spirit invocation, telepathy, witchcraft, and several forms of magic. And although few if any such actions actually achieved the desired result, it was common belief that they did so, which, in understanding Island cultures, is the important thing.

It should not be concluded from this résumé that Islanders spent much of their lives actually fighting one another. On the other hand, the fear of, or the fervor for, warfare were perennial among many peoples. Moreover, in perhaps the majority of their societies, "normal" relations between neighboring communities were latently hostile, and almost the only institutions that served to mitigate that hostility were kinship, which will be discussed later on, and intercommunity exchange, to which we now turn.

The transfer of objects or services was a component of all relationships among Islanders: giving between parents and children; taking between enemies; lending between neighbors; and bartering or buying and selling between members of different communities, which is here called "trade."

The most straightforward example of Island types of trade occurred when several members of two communities met regularly, at neutral and established locations, to exchange traditionally defined goods: say, fish (by coast dwellers) for vegetables (by inlanders). The latent conflict that characterized most such markets was in many cases solved by "silent trade," whereby the opposing traders did not meet face-to-face. Instead, one side deposited its goods at the prearranged place and withdrew, leaving the other side to collect them and leave their payments in place; the sanction that kept the trade going was the parties' mutual satisfaction with the values of the objects exchanged.

A variation occurred in some places where several members of one community traveled regularly, on foot or by boat, to some distant but traditionally associated community to barter their products for goods not available at home. Another, more widespread, variation took place in the form of individual traders who traveled far from home bartering their wares; not, however, to any and all prospective customers but to designated trade partners (who were not only dependable buyers but who guaranteed the otherwise vulnerable traders hospitality and protection as well). And speaking of "buyers": although most of this and other kinds of trade among Islanders consisted of barter (of one kind of consumable object for another) there were many areas, especially in Melanesia, where consumable objects such as pigs, pottery, and weapons were exchanged for "money" (i.e., for shells and other objects that were not ordinarily "consumed," except perhaps for occasional ornamentation).

In several areas, mainly in Melanesia, trading was also conducted by individuals or by groups of middlemen. One of the most wide-ranging examples of the latter took place in the Vitiaz Strait, north of New Guinea's Huon Peninsula. There, through the regular trading voyages of the residents of one small cluster of islands, about 150,000 people, living in numerous small communities and several different societies, were linked together into a single trade network.

The kind of trading discussed so far focused on the objects bartered or bought and sold. There was, however, another widespread form of inter-community exchange that focused not on the objects themselves but on the social relations established or maintained through the exchange: a form of transaction labeled "gift-exchange" because the objects were "given" rather than bartered or bought and sold (although given with the expectation that in due course they would be matched with a return gift). In some areas (e.g., in the New Guinea Highlands and the northern Solomons) such transactions were conducted as contests and involved huge numbers of pigs and other forms of wealth. In fact, winning such contests (by "giving" more to a rival than the latter could reciprocate) constituted a principal way of achieving political leadership in such societies (where leadership by inheritance was only weakly developed).

A somewhat different form of gift-exchange took place among the numerous islands off New Guinea's southeastern tip. There, pairs of individuals (many of them residents of different islands) exchanged "gifts" of valuable shell ornaments and used the occasion for bartering as well.

Different again was a kind of exchange that took place in the Caroline Islands. There, every two or three years a fleet of about twenty large canoes visited the island of Yap to engage in several kinds of transactions. The expedition started out from atolls seven hundred miles east of Yap and was joined by additional canoes from atolls along the way. Each canoe represented a single community and carried both official "gifts" and items for barter. The gifts were presented as "tribute" to the heads of the Yapese clans that claimed figurative ownership of the donors' home islands, an ownership whose origin is unknown but that may have been an invention by the tribute payers to guarantee their privilege to visit Yap (which produced goods not found in the smaller home islands and which provided sanctuary when their home islands were, as they sometimes were, devastated by typhoons).

So ends this résumé of the principal life-maintaining activities of the Islanders. Because of lack of space I cannot dwell on the many ways in which the Islanders ornamented and added pleasure to their lives: their decorative arts, their "oral literature," their music, their dancing, their games, and so forth. From that omission, however, it should not be concluded that such activities were absent or were unimportant to them, or that they were the same everywhere. For, here again, Island peoples differed widely, both in the cumulative prominence of all such activities and in the kinds engaged in. Thus, although some peoples decorated only themselves (e.g., with feathers or paints or tattoos), others devoted much effort and considerable talent to decorating the objects they used. And some gave much time to dancing and theatricals without accompaniment, but others delighted in music making with arrays of instruments.

The rest of this chapter will be concerned with the social relations of the Pacific Islanders before Western contact. We shall be looking at the same peoples, who were doing the things already described (gardening, marrying, fighting, and so forth), but our focus will now be on the social relationships involved in those activities. Needless to say, no two Island peoples conceptualized their multifarious relationships in exactly the same ways; nevertheless, they do form patterns few enough to permit some classifying and summarizing. Two such patterns have already been touched on, namely, households and communities, both of which involved common residence—the one in a domestic homestead, the other in a compact village or cluster of hamlets. Ties of kinship (i.e., consanguinity) or affinity (i.e., relationship by marriage), or both, existed among all members of most households and among many members of all communities, but households and communities per se were based not only on kinship or affinity as such but on common residence.

Most surveys of this kind begin with some discussion of that allegedly universal type of social unit, the family. Something like what most English speakers conceive to be a family was to be found in all Island societies, but in so many variants that they can be best understood in context of the many other kinds of institutions that served to shape them. One of the most determinative and widespread types of those institutions was that based on common descent.

Descent refers to the concept whereby a person is identified as being related to an ancestor or ancestress through his (or her) parent, that parent's parent, and so on back to that ancestor. Based on this concept, a descent unit (hereafter labeled a *clan*) is a social unit (either a group of interacting persons or a conceptualized category of persons, and in some cases, spirits) formed exclusively or mainly through descent. In most Pacific Island societies clans were, next to households, the most important type of social unit; among other characteristics possessed by them, such units in most societies were the corporate owners of all or most of the land within a society's borders. On the other hand clans differed, from society to society, in several significant respects.

First, they differed in composition. In some of them membership was based on descent through males (i.e., patrilineal descent) in others through females (i.e., matrilineal descent), in still others through either males or females (i.e., ambilineal descent), although in most of the Island societies having ambilineal clans individuals tended to affiliate more closely to their father's clan. Societies in which all clans were patrilineal were located in New Guinea (where they predominated), in the south-eastern Solomons, the central and southern New Hebrides, New Caledonia, the Loyalty Islands, Fiji, and in one society of Polynesia (Tikopia). Those in which all clans were matrilineal were located throughout the Marshall and Caroline islands, in New Britain and New Ireland, the northern Solomons, Guadalcanal, parts of the New Hebrides, the Massim area (east of the southeast tip of New Guinea), and along some stretches of the New Guinea coast. And those in which all clans were ambilineal were concentrated in the Solomon islands of Malaita and Choiseul, in the northern Gilberts, and throughout most of Polynesia. (In addition, there were a few such societies scattered through New Guinea.)

In addition to the above, there were a few societies (e.g., Yap, Wogeo, northern Ambrym, and Pukapuka) in which both patrilineal and matrilineal clans functioned (i.e., every individual belonged to both kinds and inherited different rights and obligations from each). And finally, there were a few societies, mainly in New Guinea, that had no clans (as herein defined).

Island clans differed not only in composition but in span. In some societies the ancestor or ancestress from whom members traced their common descent went back only three or four generations, hence the genealogical span of the clan was narrow and the membership small. At the other extreme were some societies in which there were only two clans (i.e., where all of its people traced descent from one or the other of two remote [and usually mythical] ancestors [or, in most cases, ancestresses, because in the Islands most such units happened to be matrilineal]).

In the cases of clans of wide span, some segmentation usually prevailed. Thus, in those societies divided into only two clans, each was usually segmented into subclans, and those into sub-subclans (i.e., lineages), consisting, for example, of the matrilineal descendants of a common great-grandmother. And in such a situation it was quite characteristic for an individual to share his (or her) most important rights (e.g., those having to do with land use and work cooperation) with lineagemates, and only common worship (i.e., of the common clan ancestress) with clanmates outside his lineage.

The clans of Island societies also differed with respect to their bearing on a member's choice of spouse and, more generally, of sex mate as well. Most clans that were unilineal (either patrilineal or matrilineal, exclusively) were exogamous: a person was forbidden to marry a fellow member—and was at least discouraged from having extramarital sex with him or her. In addition to the social disapproval and other human-applied sanctions that attended violations of such rules, there were usually religious ones as well (e.g., spirit-caused sickness or other misfortunes). In societies divided into numerous distinct clans of narrow span such prohibitions were not especially constraining, but in those having, say, only two clans, an individual's choice of mate was limited to about one half of all otherwise accessible persons. In societies having non-unilineal (i.e., ambilineal) clans the choice of spouse (and of casual sex mate) was constrained not by clan membership as such but by closeness of kinship. That is to say, a person was forbidden to marry anyone to whom he or she was related, through either parent, closer than, say, a third or fourth cousin. In contrast, in many societies with unilineal clans, a male was *encouraged* to marry a first cousin: a mother's brother's daughter, or a father's sister's daughter, or either one of the two.

A fourth way in which Island clans differed from one another lay in the political role they played in community life. In some societies that role was inconsequential but in many others the senior members (the headmen) of a community's clans were ipso facto the community's political leaders as well.

And finally, Island societies differed with respect to the importance of their clans in the religious lives of their members. In some societies the spirits associated with clans were only vaguely identified and were secondary to other kinds of spirits; in others a clan's tutelar spirits (including apotheosized ancestors and mythically consanguineal animals [i.e., totems] were the principal objects of a whole community's veneration and worship).

To round out this résumé of kinship-based social units: individual Islanders (like individuals elsewhere in the world) tended to maintain more or less close relationships with kinsmen of both parents, regardless of clan membership. For example, relatives (both kinsmen and affines) of both parents were likely to assist a person in times of need and to attend a person's rites (of birth, marriage, death, and so forth). Indeed, in a few Island societies (mainly in New Guinea) bilateral units of this kind were the only enduring social aggregates outside of households and communities.

We turn now to some other types of social units that were prominent in many Island societies, beginning with those in which membership was based on common gender or proximate age, or both.

In nearly every Island community its youths and adult males tended to congregate informally and more or less regularly, to gossip, to work together, and so forth. And in many Island societies all of the adolescent boys, several at a time, underwent formal initiation into "manhood" by means of periods of seclusion (i.e., from all females) accompanied by instruction (e.g., in fighting, religious "secrets," etc.), by physical and psychological hazing, and in many cases by circumcision or some other kind of genital surgery. In addition, there were several societies, mostly in Melanesia and the western Carolines, in which youths and men of all ages banded together into exclusively male, usually secret "clubs." (Clubs of females also existed in a few Island societies but they were far less active or influential in community life.) Entry into a male club usually involved either grueling initiation, or costly fees (e.g., pigs, shell valuables), or both.

In some societies (e.g., in New Britain) the men's clubs were focused on the veneration of one or another spirit. And in at least one society (Tahitian) there was a societywide club, called *Arioi,* that concentrated its activities on one particular spirit (the war god, 'Oro), but unlike clubs elsewhere in the Islands this one admitted females into its membership.

In addition to those based on common residence, on common descent, on gender, on common age, and on shared religious worship, there were in one or another Island society social units of some permanence based on common occupation (e.g., fishermen, temple functionaries), but these were relatively small and not widespread. So instead of dwelling on the latter, or on a few other unusual and narrowly localized types of social units, we turn to the phenomenon of Islanders' governance: to the question of what kinds of groups constituted their autonomous political units, or tribes, and the related question of who were their "chiefs"?

The answer to the first question is fairly straightforward. In most Island societies each community was politically autonomous however few persons it happened to contain (the number having ranged from twenty or thirty to up to a thousand). In a few societies in Melanesia, and in many more in Polynesia, two or more communities were drawn together to form larger than average-sized tribes, but elsewhere each community constituted a more or less independent political unit of its own (i.e., one whose "chief" was subordinate to no one elsewhere). As for who those chiefs were, the answer is much more varied.

In communities centered around one or two clans the individuals who exercised most authority over community affairs tended to be the headmen (i.e., the senior members) of those clans. I write "tended to be" with good cause, because of the circumstance that the de facto political leaders of many such communities were individuals other than the clan headmen. Thus the question becomes: by what avenues other than inherited succession could some men achieve chieftainship?

Depending upon their traditional preoccupations, Islanders held expertise in them in high respect: in some places expert gardeners, in others successful fishermen, in others skilled navigators, in others victorious warriors, and so forth. In only a few societies, however, was technical expertise as such a sufficient warrant for achieving chieftainship. Nor did personal wealth (e.g., in pigs or fine mats or shell valuables) assure its owner political authority; unless, that is, it was used in ways to win friends and supporters (e.g., by making loans or giving feasts or purchasing advancement in men's clubs) or to overcome opposition (e.g., by employing henchmen or sorcerers). In fact, in many societies (especially but not only in Melanesia) men were able to achieve chieftainship without themselves owning large amounts of wealth and without possessing expertise, except for skill in managing the labor and possessions of others: in other words, through entrepreneurial and managerial skill. Even in societies heavily predisposed to warfare and where aggressive and successful fighters were held in high esteem, political authority was more commonly in the hands of the war managers (the men who organized the financing and strategies of fighting) than of the fighter heroes themselves.

Finally, a few words need to be said about the institution of social class.

The Polynesian practice of stratifying persons by birth into different social classes is well known. In the smaller Polynesian societies only two such classes were demarcated. A good example of this pattern was the society of the small and isolated island of Tikopia, which was divided into an upper class, comprising the senior members (the headmen) of the society's four patrilineal clans and their close kinfolk, and a lower, "commoner" class containing all other Tikopians. And although commoners were expected to show deference to all upper-class persons, especially the clan headmen, that was about the extent of the difference between them. Several commoners were in fact wealthier than most upper-class persons and, in recent times at least, there was no prohibition against interclass marriage. In some of the larger Polynesian societies, however, the stratification was much more rigid and complex. In Tahiti, for example, there were three major classes and some further layering within the upper one. Moreover, marriage there between upper- and middle- or lower-class persons was so rigidly proscribed as to make the former a caste: any issue resulting from sex between an upper-class person and a member of a lower class was killed at birth.

In at least two other Polynesian societies (i.e., Hawaii and Tonga) the class system was even more rigid and complex than in Tahiti (and in a few other small Polynesian societies it was even less rigid than in Tikopia), but some degree of social stratification seems to have prevailed in most of the societies of Polynesia *and* of Micronesia as well. Indeed, the seeds of stratification existed in all Island societies, including those of Melanesia, in which clans had important roles in community governance and in which ideology ascribed high value to seniority by birth.

Such, in broad outline, were the more tangible kinds of social relationships that prevailed among Pacific Islanders when Westerners first appeared on the scene—and by doing so initiated processes that were to loosen or alter some of those relationships and to replace many others with entirely alien kinds.

SOURCES

Alkire 1977; Bellwood 1979; Berndt and Lawrence 1971; P. Brown 1978; Goldman 1970; Harding and Wallace 1970; Hogbin 1973; Howard 1971; Howells 1973; Jennings 1979; Langness and Weschler 1971; Sahlins 1958; Valle 1987; Vayda 1968.

THE INVADERS

CHAPTER TWO

Explorers: 1521–1792

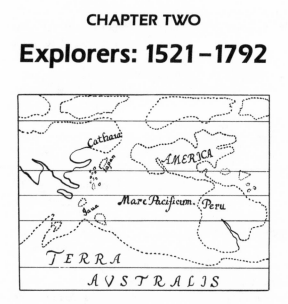

To hail Europeans as discoverers of the Pacific Islands is ungracious as well as inaccurate. While they were still moving around in their small, landlocked Mediterranean Sea or hugging the Atlantic shores of Europe and Africa, Pacific Islanders were voyaging hundreds of open-sea miles in their canoes and populating most of the vast Pacific's far-flung islands. Nevertheless, it is an accepted European conceit to describe the sixteenth, seventeenth, and eighteenth centuries as the Era of Discovery in the Pacific. This era divides conveniently into three periods: the sixteenth century was the Spanish and Portuguese period, the seventeenth the Dutch, and the eighteenth the English and French. The era was brought to a close by the voyages of Captain James Cook, who did such a thorough job of it that, paraphrasing one writer, he left his successors with little to do but admire.

Many factors led the Pacific Islanders to fan out over the Pacific: refuge from stronger enemies, search for more elbowroom, adventurous curiosity, and, perhaps most important, being lost at sea. In contrast, one driving force behind the earlier European voyagers was the search for Terra Australis Incognita, the great Unknown Southern Continent.

The existence of such a continent had been postulated for fourteen centuries before Europeans actually set out to find it. The Roman geographer Pomponius Mela assumed its existence as early as A.D. 50, and a century later the Alexandrian astronomer Ptolemy expressed similar conjectures. But with the cultural split between Eastern and Western (i.e., Roman) Europe, growing out of doctrinal and political differences and widened through the incursions of northern "barbarians," Greek scientific knowledge (including its conceptions of a spherical world and an unknown southern continent) became inaccessible to Western Europe. Those early theories, along with other legacies of Greek science, were again made available to the West through Islamic scholars; misunderstandings of Marco Polo's reports, of about 1295, also gave substance to them, so that scholars of Western Europe, including Albertus Magnus and Roger Bacon, began again to speak of a southern continent. "Logical" reasons were adduced to support the belief; Mercator, for example, held that symmetry and stability *demanded* a large and heavy southern land mass: without that for balance, a top-heavy world would topple!

These theories excited curiosity and led to endless scholarly controversies about the precise location, size, and nature of the unknown continent. Imagination made up for the absence of fact, and the fabled land was generously supplied with great quantities of gold and silks and spices and populated with highly civilized but wretchedly heathen races.

After the Turks shut off Europe's direct overland access to the silks and spices of the Far East, practical Europeans began to search for alternative routes, thereby raising another incentive to explore in the direction of the imagined southern continent (although not specifically for the continent itself). Prince Henry the Navigator of Portugal pressed his countrymen into this enterprise, and by 1498 Portuguese ships had rounded the Cape of Good Hope and arrived in India. By 1511 Portugal's empire was extended to the East Indies, and Malacca had been reached and set up as a colony.

Meanwhile Spain was contesting Portugal's rights to the Spice Islands and was moving westward toward the Pacific. In the New World, twenty-one years after Columbus' discovery, Balboa sighted the Pacific from his celebrated peak in Darien and claimed it, along with all the shores washed by it, for his master, the king of Spain. This action of his, a standard gesture for explorers in those days, was the second claim asserted by Europeans over that vast expanse of water. It unwittingly ran counter to an earlier treaty, the Tordesillas *Capitulación* of 1494, which had divided the newly discovered or still undiscovered parts of the world into a western half for Spain and an eastern half for Portugal, with the dividing line running longitudinally 370 leagues west of the Cape Verde Islands, and which consequently placed the western part of the Pacific within the Portuguese sphere.

In our modern days of exploring task forces, governmental and corporate, it might seem strange that a conjecture as exciting, and possibly as profitable, as the existence of Terra Australis Incognita should have been talked about for so many centuries with so little physical effort made to locate it. But good reasons there were. In the first place, the European ships of earlier eras were poor things, unsuited for long open-sea voyages. It was not until the single-masted vessels and oared galleys were replaced by three-masted vessels that long ocean voyages became feasible.

Another obstacle was the crude state of navigation. Rough compasses and astrolabes helped fix directions and latitude, but the estimating of longitude was not approximated until the invention of the sextant in 1731 and the chronometer in 1735. Before that, voyaging westward and eastward was an uncertain, perilous adventure, and cartography a matter of guesswork.

To those technical difficulties was added the problem of supply. Small ships had neither space nor facilities for carrying the quantities of food and water and cooking fuel believed to be required on long voyages. Nor does it seem that the gallant captains of those earlier times provisioned their vessels wisely, even within the limits of the carrying capacities of their ships. Inevitably, on nearly every long voyage recorded, there came the day when the remaining water stank and when the inadequacies of the food (mainly salt pork and ship's biscuit) resulted in scurvy, leading to disablement or death of all but the hardiest. Little wonder that the usual ship's company was made up largely of waterfront dregs and other men of small consequence; no other sorts could be induced (or impressed) to take on such certain deprivations for such uncertain rewards.

Yet what ships and crews lacked in fitness, the captains of some of them made up for in courage or zeal. The history of Pacific exploration during most of this era of discovery is less a chronicle of concerted national efforts than an account of the heroic attempts of a handful of dedicated individuals carrying out their missions against official inertia at home and terrible hardships at sea.

Spanish and Portuguese Period

The discovery of the Americas was a minor incident for the men whose prime goal was the Great East. Many of them, in fact, considered America an obstacle and sought ways to pierce it with a canal. Others were obsessed with the idea of a natural passage through or around America, if it could be found. Among the latter was Ferdinand Magellan.

Magellan was born in Portugal about 1480 and, like many of his countrymen, spent his youth in the service of the Portuguese fleet then opening up a way to the East Indies around Africa. After Magellan's return to Portugal, a friend who remained in the Indies fired his ambition with accounts of the vast new riches to be found there. But since the king of Portugal would have none of him or his plans, Magellan denaturalized himself and traveled to Spain. There his plan received royal support: he was to seek out a shorter western passage to the disputed Spice Islands and thus establish that they belonged in Spain's rather than in Portugal's half of the world. Magellan's fleet of five ships (the largest only 120 tons) and about 270 men left Spain in September 1519; thirteen months later, after the mishaps and minor mutinies usual for such voyages, its remnants discovered and sailed through the strait that bears Magellan's name. Following upon this remarkable feat, the now reduced fleet accomplished another by sailing across the entire island-strewn Pacific without encountering a single inhabited island until it reached (and thereby "discovered") the Marianas in March 1521. After a short and strife-ridden stay it pushed on and "discovered" the Philippines, where Magellan was killed by some natives. The survivors of the expedition proceeded to the Moluccas, and thirty-one of them eventually reached Spain in September 1522, thereby completing the first circumnavigation. Of the two goals of the enterprise, the western passage was thus found, but proof of Spanish rights to the Moluccas was not demonstrated, and these "Spice Islands" were acknowledged to belong to the Portuguese half of the world.

Few Spanish ships followed Magellan's track; most of the later Spanish expeditions to the East set out from the new Spanish ports in Mexico and Peru. After 1565, galleons established a regular route from Mexico to the Philippines and return, sailing westward in the latitude of Guam and eastward in a wide sweep to the north, taking advantage of the prevailing winds in those latitudes. Along this regular course there were no islands except Guam, which thereby became thoroughly Spanish two centuries before any other other Pacific island was effectively colonized by a European power. Until 1898 Guam and its neighboring islands remained Spanish and altogether separate from the influences that shaped events elsewhere in the Pacific.

Meanwhile, the huge island of New Guinea had been sighted and claimed by both Portugal and Spain while their agents were engaged in rivalry for the trade of the nearby Spice Islands. Some cartographers of that period thought New Guinea to be the northern tip of the fabled Terra Australis Incognita, which continued to intrigue imaginative men, including Alvaro de Mendaña.

In 1567 the viceroy of Peru outfitted two ships and placed them under the command of his young nephew, Mendaña, with instructions to search out the unknown continent, establish a settlement there, and convert its inhabitants to Roman Catholic Christianity. The expedition sailed between the Marquesas and the Tuamotus without sighting either and, after the usual sequence of thirst, hunger, scurvy, loss of life, and near-mutiny, finally reached Santa Isabel in the Solomon archipelago. Mendaña and his crews remained for six months in the Solomons, touching at most of the southern islands of the chain and leaving a trail of pillage and blood. They then returned to Peru, which was reached after a perilous voyage of thirteen months. The charts that they drew of their routes and discoveries, however, were so inaccurate that no Westerner was able to find and identify the Solomons for two hundred years.

For twenty-five years Mendaña haunted the courts of Spain and Peru, trying to secure support for a return to the Solomons, which he considered to be outposts of the unknown continent. In the end he succeeded in enlisting lukewarm support and again set out to establish a colony; the company included wives of some of his officers, along with a few friars.

En route this bizarre assortment of voyagers discovered the Marquesas, tarried long enough to raise their crosses, and then sailed on westward, having slain some two hundred natives during altercations there. The expedition eventually reached Ndeni Island in the Santa Cruz archipelago, where some of the voyagers disembarked with the intention of settling. But the place chosen was a far cry from the gold-rich Paradise they had envisaged, and after a few weeks of illnesses, fights with the inhabitants, mutinous discord, and many deaths, including that of Mendaña himself, the survivors abandoned the settlement and proceeded to Manila.

But even this experience did not discourage Mendaña's pious lieutenant, Pedro Fernandes de Quirós, from undertaking another voyage to search out the fabled continent and convert its millions of heathens. Quirós' zeal was eventually rewarded by royal support, and in 1605 he departed from Peru with three ships. His fleet discovered several islands along the route and reached what was believed to be its hoped-for destination four and a half months after leaving Peru. The name Australia del Espiritu Santo was given to the new discovery, in the belief that it was the long-sought southern continent; it was in fact a large island of the New Hebrides archipelago, four hundred miles southeast of the Solomons. A great religious thanksgiving was held on the site of this New Jerusalem, but the palm garlands had hardly dried out before disillusionment, native hostility, and mutiny caused the settlement to be abandoned. Quirós' ships returned to Mexico, while that of his chief lieutenant, Luis Vaez de Torres, made for Manila. Torres' route, however, lay south, not north, of New Guinea and through the hazardous labyrinth of reefs and small islands that now bears his name, thereby proving New Guinea to be an island and not the northern projection of the still-unsighted southern continent.

Quirós' missionary zeal drove him to continue his petitioning for a new expedition until his death in 1614; and with his demise Spanish ambition for lands and Catholic converts in the South Seas subsided for a century and a half.

Although the sixteenth-century Pacific was very much a "*Spanish*

Lake" (Spate 1979), its waters were for a time also ruffled by a small band of Englishmen.

When exaggerated versions of Mendaña's discoveries in the Solomons reached England, they kindled enthusiasm for an English share of the South Seas' fabled wealth, and during the expansionist mood of Elizabeth's reign an expedition was organized to explore and exploit the riches of the still-unknown but credible southern continent, and to discover and return home by a hoped-for northern passage between the Pacific and the Atlantic. The seaman selected to lead this expedition was Francis Drake, and although his publicly announced mission was as stated, he evidently was secretly authorized (perhaps by Queen Elizabeth?) to do what he subsequently did—to focus on the tangible riches of Spain's Peruvian colony instead of the hypothetical treasures of unknown lands. He left England in 1577, passed through Magellan's strait, and spent four months harrying and pillaging Spain's American ports and Pacific shipping. Then, with his small *Golden Hind* loaded with treasure, he sailed northward to California and beyond and, finding no eastward passage as far north as 48 degrees, returned home via the Philippines and the Cape of Good Hope. Although his feat of circumnavigation and his rich booty made him a public hero, the only geographic discoveries he made were of lands at or near Cape Horn, and, most likely, the main islands of the Palau cluster (where he killed twenty of its natives for petty thievery). He neither confirmed nor denied the existence of Terra Australis Incognita, the search for which continued to spur exploration.

Dutch Period

A greater contrast than that between the Spanish and Dutch South Sea adventures is hard to imagine. Spaniards, and their Portuguese agents, were mainly visionaries seeking new lands and souls for the glory of king and Church; the Dutch were businessmen searching for new resources, trade routes, and markets.

Spain's maritime supremacy was beginning to wane when the Netherlands won their independence in 1581, and it was hastened by England's defeat of the Armada in 1588. After that, Dutch merchants lost little time in forcing their advantage against the weakened Portuguese, and by 1609 the East Indies were theirs.

The Dutch wasted no energies in trying to convert heathens; they demanded more tangible profits, in spices and gold. The strength and weakness of Dutch enterprises lay in the monopoly over Far Eastern trade enjoyed by one faction, the united Dutch East India Company. Financed by wealthy merchants and backed by the Netherlands Crown, this company had exclusive rights to Dutch trade in the Indies, along with sole access (among Dutchmen) to the area by way of the Strait of Magellan and the Cape of Good Hope, a formidable advantage, since those were the only known routes to Asia, including the Indies.

By the second decade of the seventeenth century, Indies-bound vessels of the Dutch were rounding the Cape of Good Hope and, taking advantage of favorable winds, were sailing northeast for four thousand miles before turning north to Java. It was in the course of these voyages that European (i.e., Dutch) ships first touched at the western coast of Australia. Moved by the prospects of new commerce, the company directors in the Netherlands and their managers in the Indies authorized several exploratory voyages, which charted, but only roughly and piecemeal, the southern shore of New Guinea as far east as Torres Strait and the northern, western, and southern coasts of Australia from Cape York to about the middle of the Great Australian Bight—without, however, establishing that it was a single continent.

Only twice during this period was the Company's monopoly circumvented by Dutchmen: the first time by the Le Maires, the second by Jacob Roggeveen. Isaac Le Maire, an independent Dutch merchant and no friend of the Company, succeeded after many remonstrances in obtaining permission from the government to trade in Asia and the Pacific, provided he did not trespass upon the Company's routes of access. Confident of finding new routes, Le Maire's son, Jacob, and an already famous navigator, William Schouten, set out from Holland in 1615 and sailed around the southernmost cape of South America, which they named Hoorn after Schouten's birthplace and which is 230 miles south of the Atlantic entrance to the Strait of Magellan. They then proceeded to sail across the Pacific, discovering en route several inhabited islands in the northern Tuamotus, two of the northernmost islands of the Tongan archipelago, and Alofi and Futuna (which they named the Hoorn Islands). Of their encounters with the inhabitants of several of the islands touched at along the way, some were friendly and others bloody. After eighteen months at sea they reached Batavia, Java, by way of the northern coasts of New Ireland and New Guinea. In port their ship was confiscated by Company officials, who disbelieved their account of having come by a route south of the Strait of Magellan. Jacob Le Maire died on the voyage home, but back in Holland his father, Isaac, finally succeeded in having the new route accepted and his property returned; the latter, rather than their Pacific discoveries, seems to have been the more important issue to him and to the other sponsors of this remarkable expedition.

The Dutch were too occupied in their new Indies empire to follow up immediately the numerous discoveries made by Le Maire and Schouten, but twenty-five years later a more enterprising Indies governor-general, Anthony Van Diemen, secured approval for exploratory voyages, the first to the north, the second to the south and east of the Indies. Abel Tasman, a sea captain in the service of the Company, was commissioned to carry out the latter of the two missions. The quest for geographic knowledge as such undoubtedly played a part in the sponsorship of this voyage, but the ultimate outcome of that knowledge was a hoped-for enhancement of Dutch trade. And more immediately (unlike the inspired Catholic soul-rescuing exhortations that had been addressed to Quirós), Tasman's orders read, in part:

> If [you] visit any land populated with civilized people (as [is] not likely), [you] shall take more account of them, than of the wild savages, trying to get in conversation and acquaintance with the leaders and subjects, informing them, [you] come there to trade, showing the samples of the wares, given for this purpose, as [you] shall be able to see in invoice, duly observing what they esteem, and to what goods [they] are most attracted, particularly finding what wares are among them, likewise about gold and silver, and if [it] is in valued regard by them, representing yourself to be not eager for it, in order to keep them unaware of the value of the same, and if [they] should give you gold or silver in any bartering, [you] must conduct yourself as if [you] did not value this specie, showing copper, spelter and lead, as if these minerals were with us of greater value. (Sharp 1968:32–33)

Beginning in 1642 the expedition's two ships sailed eastward from Mauritius to Tasmania (which Tasman named Van Diemen's Land), then to New Zealand's west coast (where efforts to land were frustrated by native attacks), on to the Tonga Islands (where encounters with the natives were mutually friendly), then westwards and along the northern edges of the Fiji group (where no landings were made and no natives seen). From there the ships sailed northwest past Ontong Java and Green Island, along the northern coasts of New Ireland, New Britain, and New Guinea, and so back to Java. By any other standard the voyage was a remarkable achievement, but in the judgment of the Company directors it elicited only mild thanks. In fact, Tasman was held to have been remiss in not having done more, inasmuch as ". . . no riches or things of profit but only the said lands and apparently good passage were discovered" (quoted in Sharp 1968:311).

For the remainder of the century the Dutch merchants and administrators kept to their factories and plantations in the Indies. From time to time shorter voyages were dispatched to nearby New Guinea and western Australia, but the ruling policy of the Company was reflected in an answer the directors gave to a report on some promising new lands: "It were to be wished that the said land continued still unknown and never explored, so as not to tell foreigners the way to the Company's overthrow" (quoted in J. C. Beaglehole 1966:162).

Only once more did a Dutchman sight and name hitherto unrecorded islands in the Pacific. In 1722 Jacob Roggeveen, unaffiliated with the all-powerful Company, entered the Pacific from the east and subsequently discovered Easter Island, the eastern islands of Samoa, and, from a distance, Borabora and Maupiti. Upon reaching Java, Roggeveen was punished for his temerity in trespassing on Company area by having his ships confiscated.

English and French Period

During the first half of the eighteenth century most exploration of the Pacific was carried out by armchair geographers in their academies in Europe, where the journals and charts of the great voyages of the preceding centuries were pored over and argued about. Some scholars persisted in the dream of a great southern continent, others weighed the prospects of finding a northwest passage to the Orient, and in both cases the controversies fed on ignorance. Indeed, knowledge about the area was so deficient that Jonathan Swift was not challenged when he located his Lilliput and Brobdingnag there.

Almost the only physical explorations carried out at that time were byproducts of the practical occupation of buccaneering. That greatest of privateers, Francis Drake, had long before concluded that real loot from Spanish ships and settlements was preferable to the theoretical treasures of a southern continent. His royally sponsored voyage to the Pacific in 1578–1580 had not solved many geographic mysteries, but it set a noble precedent that Englishmen were still following a century and a quarter later.

Another English navigator, William Dampier, was an accomplished buccaneer with a flair for reportorial writing. Between 1699 and 1711 he made three circumnavigations, during which he learned much that was new about the coasts of New Guinea and harried the Spanish galleons carrying gold and silver from Manila to Mexico. After Dampier, English activity in the Pacific was interrupted by the European Seven Years' War. Within a short time after its conclusion, however, there took place a number of voyages, by four Englishmen and one Frenchman, that transformed European knowledge about the Pacific from fanciful speculation into near exactitude. The men responsible for this accomplishment were, in chronological order, Byron, Wallis, Carteret, Bougainville, and Cook.

By 1754 England and France had commenced again to concern themselves with national honor and opened up their treasuries to promote projects designed to aid (English or French) science and prestige, and incidentally to pick up any unattached lands that happened to be found in the process. Interest was also revived in the possibility of discovering the southern continent; moreover, the hope of locating a northwest passage to the Orient added strong commercial motivation to Pacific explo-

rations. England sent out Commodore John Byron to initiate exploration; he, however, blithely ignored his official directive to search for a
northwest passage and sailed instead through the Pacific to the Marianas
and thence home. While in the Pacific he discovered islands in the northern Tuamotuan, Cook, and Tokelauan archipelagoes.

Soon thereafter the Admiralty sent an expedition of two ships, cap-
tained respectively by Samuel Wallis and Philip Carteret, to search for the
southern continent. After their ships parted company during a storm,
Wallis sailed on to discover Mehetia, Tahiti, Mo'orea, and Uvea (Wallis
Island), while Carteret sighted for the first time Pitcairn, Buka, and the
Admiralty Islands.

Next came Louis Antoine de Bougainville, sent by France to surrender
the Falkland Islands to Spain and to sail through the Pacific to regain for
France, if possible, some of the prestige recently dimmed in her wars with
England. Bougainville followed approximately in Wallis' path to Tahiti,
after which he sailed west to Samoa, the New Hebrides, and on to the
Great Barrier Reef. Turning northeast from there he threaded his way
through the Louisiade archipelago, past Choiseul and Bougainville,
around New Ireland, and thence home via Java.

All these voyages were truly remarkable feats of endurance, and their
reports filled many gaps in the charts of the Pacific (while nourishing
romantic and philosophical ideas about "Noble Savages"). They would
excite even greater wonder than they do had they not been followed by
other voyages that far surpassed in accomplishment any previously
undertaken in the Pacific: the three voyages of Captain James Cook. It is
not possible to speak of Cook in less than hyperbolic language.

Born in Yorkshire in 1728, the son of a day laborer, Cook escaped the
shopkeeper's life that lay before him and went to sea. Later, while in the
navy, he established a reputation as an outstanding navigator and hy-
drographer. At the age of forty he was commissioned by the Admiralty
and the Royal Society to lead an expedition to Tahiti, recently discovered
by Wallis, to observe from that strategic location the forthcoming transit
of the planet Venus, an event of great importance to navigation and
astronomy. In addition, Cook received secret instructions to search for
the southern continent and to stake out English claims to any lands he
might discover anywhere.

The journal of Cook's first voyage (1768–1771) has now become such
a classic that it is almost impertinent to attempt a summary. Nevertheless, for the continuity of this chronicle it will be useful to repeat once
more his list of discoveries after he had successfully completed his mission at Tahiti. They included Raiatea, Tahaa, Huahine, Rurutu, and a
survey of the coasts of New Zealand and of almost the entire eastern
coast of Australia.

During his second voyage (1772–1775) Cook circumnavigated the globe, going close to the Antarctic in a vain search that dispelled, for that era, hopes for discovering a humanly *habitable* southern continent. On this same voyage he revisited several islands seen during his first voyage and made many new discoveries, including islands in the Tuamotus, the southern Cooks, Fatu-huku (Marquesas), Palmerston, Niue, New Caledonia, and Norfolk.

During his third voyage (1776–1779), undertaken partly to seek out a northern passage from the Pacific to the Atlantic, Cook discovered Mangaia, Atiu, Tubuai, Christmas Island, and the Hawaiian Islands. (Claims by some scholars that the latter were first discovered by the Spaniard Juan Gaetano in 1555 have not been credibly documented.) After a visit to the northwest coast of North America his two ships returned to Hawaii, where Cook was slain by theretofore friendly Hawaiians in a confrontation whose causes are still being debated.

Cook's voyages left few new lands to be discovered in the Pacific, and his observations, maps, and charts have not had to be too radically revised. In addition, he kept his officers and crews in good health and fair spirits throughout the hard, years-long voyages. And so skillful was he in his relations with most Islanders that among many of them his name *(Too-te)* was venerated for generations.

The era of major Pacific discoveries ended with Cook. A few other explorers and navigators came after him and added an island or two to the charts (e.g., Aitutaki and most of the Fiji Islands by William Bligh, Rarotonga by Fletcher Christian and his *Bounty* mutineers, the Kermadecs and Penrhyn by Captain Lever in the *Lady Penrhyn,* the Marshalls and the Gilberts by ship captains of those names, etc.), but by 1780 the stage had been set for the traders, the whalers, and the missionaries.

SOURCES

J. C. Beaglehole's *The Exploration of the Pacific,* first published in 1934, remains the best one-volume study on the subject. O. H. K. Spate's three-volume work will cover the same subject and in more detail; the two volumes already published are listed in the Bibliography under Spate (1979, 1983). Explorers of French nationality are the subject of Dunmore (1965) and those of Spanish nationality who traveled to Tahiti in 1772–1776 are the subject of Corney (1913, 1915, 1919). Works on individual explorers are listed below.

Bligh (Bligh 1792; Oliver 1988); Bougainville (Bougainville 1772); Byron (Gallagher 1964); Carteret (Wallis 1965); Cook (J. C. Beaglehole 1955, 1961, 1967, 1974); Dampier (Masefield 1906); Drake (Lessa 1975); La Pérouse (Gassner 1969); Le Maire and Schouten (Spate 1983); Magellan (Nowell 1962); Mendaña (Amherst and Thomson 1901); Quirós (Kelly 1966); Roggeveen (Sharp 1970); Tasman (Sharp 1968); Vancouver (Lamb 1984); Wallis (Carrington 1948).

CHAPTER THREE

Whalers, Traders, and Missionaries: 1780–1850

By the end of the eighteenth century most of the Pacific Islands had been "discovered" by Europeans. From that time onward the islands were pawns in the great chess game of international rivalries; the main moves were made in Europe and America and, to a lesser degree, in Australia and New Zealand.

The Napoleonic Wars gave the islands some respite; Great Britain and France were too preoccupied in Europe to bother about a few islands on the other side of the world. France, more than Britain, was barred from Pacific enterprises because the Royal Navy blockaded France and literally ruled the seas. In fact, after the Napoleonic Wars the Royal Navy played an important role in the South Pacific throughout the nineteenth century, facilitated by its control over the main entrances to the region from stations in the Falklands, India, and the Cape of Good Hope. The Royal Navy was also a factor during the War of 1812 in driving American whalers into the Pacific, unwittingly forcing Americans onto a scene of fishing operations in which their vessels quickly captured and retained predominance.

Yet even with her naval ascendancy Britain did not exploit her opportunities to extend her empire to the Pacific. Her one planned accession during the early phase of this period was in 1788 at Australia's Botany

Bay and its surrounds, which was chosen as a site for a penal settlement
—accession motivated more by a desire to rid herself of undesirables than
to acquire new territory. True, later on Britain took vigorous steps to
consolidate her position in Australia with other colonies, as much to
keep France out as anything else; and the mother country was pushed
into doing this mainly by the clamors of her colonists already in Australia. For very much the same reasons, Britain reluctantly agreed to establish sovereignty over New Zealand, in 1840.

Several factors contributed to Britain's reluctance to extend her sovereignty over the Pacific Islands. One was the Evangelical Revival, which
comprised a system of religiomoral philosophy based upon a reaction
against the Regency and "popery" and upon Protestant standards of
values. The stereotype of an individual proponent of this "Victorian" era
was that of a hard, commercial-minded tradesman who scrupulously
attended church services and vigorously supported good causes. At the
government level Victorianism consisted of an economic-minded bureaucracy, which supported industrialism at home, bringing large profits for
the few (but creating stark misery for many in the working class), while
backing the abolition of slavery abroad and supporting the formation of
mission societies to wipe out heathenism.

Most of the members of the mission societies were of upper-working-
class and lower-middle-class backgrounds, but they contained many
upper-class individuals as well. In fact, many of Her Majesty's Colonial
Office ministers were supporters of the idea of foreign missions, some of
them holding high offices in missionary societies; it has even been
claimed that Britain's colonial policy was formulated out of resolutions
coming from Essex Hall, the site of the annual meeting of mission
societies. That policy was to support missions morally and with naval
force if necessary (though rarely with money), but to stay clear of other
kinds of colonial adventures, including annexation. The arguments
behind that hands-off policy were that colonies cost money, and that
natives should be allowed to develop their own governance, aided, of
course, by advice from British missionaries. The only counters to this
policy were the importunities of nonmissionary colonials and the more
practical necessity of frustrating threats of annexations from other powers, chiefly France.

After her humiliating defeat at Waterloo, France experienced a resurgence of nationalism that persisted until the middle of the century and
that was aimed at restoring national honor, mainly by outdoing her arch-
rival, Britain. This movement reached a peak with the midcentury July
Monarchy and throughout its course was closely wedded to Roman
Catholicism. France sought to bring about this revival by restoring her
prestige as an enlightened nation through scientific expeditions and
through support of the state religion throughout the uncivilized world,

especially in those areas in which English Protestantism was attempting to gain a foothold. Along with these strategies France supported a policy of establishing a worldwide network of "stepping-stone" naval bases to counteract British Singapores and Gibralters. In this endeavor Science, State, Navy, and Church were inseparable. Trade also became a partner, although a minor one.

Elsewhere in Europe nothing much of a political nature occurred to shape events in the South Pacific. Spain was preoccupied with domestic and American affairs and hardly bothered about her possessions in the Marianas and the Philippines. Holland's activities in the Indies were concentrated in Java, leaving little energy or interest for adventures elsewhere. Germany was still split into several states and hence did not possess a unified policy toward the Pacific; on the other hand, several powerful merchants in the Hanseatic League vigorously went after a share of the world's waterborne trade, including the new trade developing in the South Pacific.

Economic more than political events had their repercussions in the South Pacific. One such was the revival of the British whaling industry, stimulated by a generous bounty designed to increase national income and develop a better reserve navy. Another economic stimulus was Europeans' high regard for sea animal furs: Russian court circles were especially extravagant in their demands for fine furs. The first situation led to a vigorous commerce in whale oil; the second to Russian, British, and American fur trading along the western coast of North America. Russians were particularly active, and trading stations of the Russian-American Fur Company extended from Alaska as far south as present-day San Francisco. Their principal rivals were agents of the Hudson's Bay Company and, to a lesser extent, those of American promoters such as John Jacob Astor.

Meanwhile, the vigorous young United States was pushing its frontiers westward in pursuit of its "Manifest Destiny" to establish republicanism from the Atlantic to the Pacific and share in the opulent trade of the Far East. By treaty, Russia was contained within the present southeastern limb of Alaska, and British Canada was pushed back to Vancouver Island and the adjacent mainland. Spain was cleared out of California during the Mexican War, leaving the new port of San Francisco to Americans as a base from which to expand their China trade.

However, Americans were not dependent upon West Coast bases to exploit the China trade. Long before San Francisco became a base, Yankee traders were carrying China silks and teas and porcelains around Africa or South America and back to Boston and New York and Philadelphia, and this trade had a decisive effect upon the Pacific Islands. When the Chinese began to demand more than "Yankee notions" for their wares, European and American traders had to scour the seas for items more to Oriental tastes: for furs, for sweet-smelling sandalwood, for pearl shell, and for gourmets' delicacies. These enterprises brought traders to the shores and islands of the Pacific, and several American fortunes were made by trading Yankee knickknacks to Islanders for sandalwood and other local products that were then carried to Canton and bartered for silks and tea, usually with a fine profit at each turnover. But surpassing all those undertakings in volume and in commercial yield was whaling, which involved hundreds of vessels and thousands of men in the hazardous task of supplying European and American lamps with oil and Western fashions with properly corseted silhouettes.

Whalers began to hunt in Pacific waters as early as 1776, and within a few decades the Pacific became their bonanza. One after another schooling ground was discovered and exhausted before moving on to the next. First was the sperm-whale fishery off the coast of Chile and Peru; then came the dangerous game of hunting in the teeming but exceedingly rough waters between New Zealand and the young colony of New South Wales. This was followed by open-sea whaling throughout the waters surrounding the Pacific Islands. In 1819 new grounds were found off Japan, and in 1833 off Kodiak.

During the peak years, in the 1850s, many hundreds of whaling vessels roamed the Pacific. Americans led the field, then the British, and, far behind, the French. A few Prussian whalers appeared now and then, but not until after the middle of the century did this or any other kind of German enterprise expand in Pacific waters.

Americans, mainly from Nantucket and New Bedford, far outdistanced their rivals in numbers. The American Revolution drove American whalers off the Atlantic, but as soon as the war ended they were at it again and delivering their catches both to home ports and to Britain. British naval supremacy again drove Americans from the Atlantic during the War of 1812, but this time the Yankees moved into the South Pacific and were soon predominant there. For a while the British paid liberal bounties to its whalers, even holding out attractive inducements to Americans to join their fleets. France went even further in attempting to build up its whaling industry. Five vessels were fitted out with the help of generous subsidies and of bounties on catches, and with the assistance of American and British seamen. Moreover, the French Navy was assigned to provide help to French whalers by maintaining discipline abroad and by supplying new replacements and naval stores. It was not unusual for a French man-of-war to stand to near whaling grounds where French whalers were active. Meanwhile, the U.S. government provided no special inducements to its whalers; it did not have to.

The French government also sent several naval scientific expeditions to the Pacific to assist in regaining for France her role as handmaiden of Science, and to help French whalers while doing so. Expedition captains were specifically instructed to remain on the lookout for new whaling grounds and assist their whaling compatriots. These expeditions, and the earlier ones of Bougainville (1767–1769) and La Pérouse (1785–1788), did indeed reflect great credit upon their nation with respect to Science but were not sufficient to bolster French whaling to first rank. Their shortcomings in skilled manpower limited the French to hunting the less strenuous right whale in the safer waters of bays, while Americans and British were roaming the open seas pursuing the ocean-ranging cachalot or sperm whale.

Large whales do not often appear in tropical lagoons, so most of the time the whaling fleets kept to the open seas. But even whalers put ashore sometimes, and when that happened in the Pacific Islands the effect must have been quite stupefying. Picture the scene of a thousand or so lusty fellows suddenly turned loose on an island beach, after months of poor rations, hard discipline, and body-breaking work or mind-numbing tedium—all far away from the sight of women and the taste of rum. Only the pen of Melville could graphically describe it, and the science of genetics cannot even attempt to appraise its more lasting consequences.

Hawaii, Tahiti, and the Marquesas were the first to receive the full impact. Vessels called at their ports during the off season in whaling to replenish their supplies, to recover the health and morale of their crews, and sometimes to render (melt down) and dispose of their oil. It would be intriguing to attempt to calculate how many kegs of rum were drained, how many wedding vows were broken, how many cases of venereal disease were transferred, in those melees.

When the fleets sailed again they usually took with them many of the local natives, who had come aboard in response to various kinds of inducements to replace seamen lost at sea, to scurvy, or to native belles.

South of the equator New Zealand subsequently replaced Tahiti and the Marquesas as the main shore station for whalers, and a large and lively industry in oil rendering developed there. But few islands escaped altogether the visits of whalers. Some, such as Tahiti, Samoa, the Marquesas, and Ponape, were especially popular, partly because of the beauty and hospitality of their women. On the other hand, most of the islands of Melanesia were avoided, for reasons of unhealthiness, inhospitality, and greater distance from the main whaling grounds.

Like their explorer predecessors the whaling ship captains engaged in trading with the natives at their ports of call, bartering knickknacks for the fresh food needed by their scorbutic seamen. Nevertheless, the Islanders were not prepared for the kind of commerce introduced by the agents of the China trade.

The silks and teas and porcelains of China were highly treasured in the fine houses of Europe and America, and the China trade vied with whaling in attracting maritime-minded financiers and adventurers. After a while, however, the mandarins lost interest in the cheap manufactured goods sent them, and the traders were obliged to find more tempting things to barter for the Chinese goods. The shores of North America supplied one answer to the problem, the Pacific Islands another.

The luxuriously soft, warm fur of the North Pacific sea otter found great favor in the court circles of China and of Russia, and agents of the Russian-American Fur Company had by 1780 extended their fur-trading operations from Alaska to California. Five years later vessels of the British East India Company also visited these coasts and stocked up with furs for their China trade. Soon thereafter Boston merchantmen followed suit, and until sea otters, ermines, bears, and even seals were almost wiped out this trade was vigorously pursued. Many of the vessels of this trade were accustomed to stopping in Hawaii to rest and replenish supplies, and on one such visit some sandalwood was spotted and carried along to China for barter. There it was eagerly accepted, so much so that within a few decades there was hardly a stick of sandalwood left in the Islands.

Meanwhile several other Island products were discovered to be marketable in China: trepang (the sea slug used by Chinese gourmets in their soups), pearls and pearl shell, tortoise shell, and arrowroot (coconut oil was more acceptable in Western than in Asian markets).

In addition to the China trade, there developed a demand for some Island products in the new settlements growing up in California and Australia. The penal settlement in New South Wales was so far from self-sufficiency that its governor sent agents to Tahiti to procure salt pork. And in Hawaii there was carried on a lively trade in locally grown potatoes to feed the fur-trading and gold-mining settlements in California. There also developed in New Zealand a trade for timber and flax to supply the New South Wales market; in fact, New Zealand produced goods to suit almost any taste, including that of curio hunters, as exemplified in the following.

The Maori of New Zealand were accustomed to preserving human heads by a painstaking smoking and drying process; the product was exceptionally valued if the deceased's face had been finely tattooed. Western visitors paid high prices for these shriveled specimens, thereby leading to an increase in the practice. It was rumored that some Maori chiefs would permit specially favored Western visitors to pick out heads from among the living, and these would be ready, tattooed and cured, for the customers upon their return.

Throughout the first half of the nineteenth century the trade in Island products was mainly in the hands of British and Americans. The former predominated in and around New Zealand and the latter in Hawaii, both having shared in the trade of Samoa and Tahiti (until the French annexed the latter in 1843). As for Fiji, its trade was from the beginning controlled mainly by Salem (Massachusetts) merchantmen, who were also active in southern and central Melanesia (along with traders from Australia).

At the beginning of the nineteenth century the Western traders had their own way with the Islanders, exchanging calico, mouth organs, dogs, knives, muskets, rum, and the like for cargoes that brought fortunes in Canton. Gradually, however, this one-sidedness gave way as more and more traders began to compete and as Islanders lost their awe for any and everything offered them. The reaction reached a point in some places that the exchanges—wonders to relate—became almost equitable; in Hawaii, for example, some chiefs demanded fully rigged ships in exchange for the diminishing supplies of sandalwood. Of course, the progress toward "fair" exchange did not proceed everywhere at the same rate, and even as late as 1950 Western traders in inner New Guinea could be heard complaining that the natives were being "spoiled" by too openhanded barter.

Mention has already been made of the huge profits regarded as "reasonable" for trading voyages; needless to say, such profits were not always forthcoming. In fact, even for the stay-at-home financiers many voyages returned little or no profit, and some of them ended in total loss, due, for example, to shipwreck, hostile native customers, or market vagaries. And as for the crews that survived the trading voyages, even with the more profitable ones they tended to receive small returns for their hard and hazardous employment.

On larger islands such as Oahu, Tahiti, Upolu (Samoa), Ovalau (Fiji), and the North Island of New Zealand, shoreside trading centers were established to serve as focal points for native suppliers and visiting merchants, and these in time resulted in more equitable and peaceful commerce, mainly because of the presence of competing traders and of more sophisticated and less gullible native customers. But elsewhere and in many other instances some visiting traders chalked up records of chicanery, violence, and evil to equal the blackest chapters of Island history. One record relates how a sandalwood trader held a native chieftain hostage while the latter's subjects filled the ship with wood; then, to render the place unhealthy for competing traders the sandalwooder murdered the chief as he swam ashore (Harrison 1937:142). Multiply this incident several times and add various refinements of mayhem available only to members of technically superior nations, and it is hardly to be wondered at that the natives of some Islands were described at the time as having become "inhospitable." But, as one historian has pointed out (Howe 1984:95), the kind of incident just related was not invariable, nor perhaps even typical: Island trading, as contrasted with outright robbery, was usually a two-way transaction that required a measure of mutuality. And although a handful of glass beads may seem, by ethical Western standards, to have been an inequitable exchange for, say, a hundredweight of sandalwood or a bag of pearl shell, it was not viewed as such in many native eyes; otherwise, such bartering would not have taken place. Moreover, many accounts could be cited of natives attempting, and sometimes succeeding, in deluding the Western traders (with, for example, stones hidden in bags of copra). And one should not overlook the many instances in which Islanders robbed unsuspecting traders of their goods and even of their lives. Nevertheless, when balancing the books on the Western-Islander trading of that period, it seems clear (at least to this writer) that the itinerant Western traders (including Americans, Australians, and others) were more of an affliction than a blessing to the Islanders, despite or perhaps even because of the Western goods they left behind.

Another question to consider when weighing Western-Islander trade relations is, Which Islanders gained, or lost, the most? This question applies especially to some of the highly stratified native societies of Polynesia, whose chiefs pressed their subjects into, say, cutting sandalwood or raising pigs to trade with Westerners and then retained most of the Western goods for themselves. But the question also applies to many of the more egalitarian societies of Melanesia as well, where the inhabitants of coastal communities were able to monopolize trade with the visiting ships and then barter the received goods with inlanders at greatly inflated "prices," or, in many cases, use the firearms acquired from Westerners to harass or wipe out their inland enemies.

Afflictions of another kind were also showered upon some Islands during this period in the persons of beachcombers, those Westerners who landed and remained in the Islands with no purpose in being there other than their ability or wish not to be somewhere else.

The beachcombers were a nondescript lot. Some had escaped to the Islands from the penal settlements of Australia or from the only slightly easier servitude of whaler and merchantman forecastles. And a few of them had been cast on the shores from shipwrecks or been left there after mutinies. But there were many who had gone to the islands purposefully —to seek their fortunes or to avoid some personal problem at home (such as an indiscretion with another man's money or wife). A few islands with more hostile inhabitants managed to escape this plague by killing, and in some cases eating, any hapless Westerner who ended up on their shores, but in many other places the beachcombers managed to survive—some to settle down unobtrusively and become second-rate "natives" (being treated as curiosities or allies or semislaves), others to become active in local commerce and politics to the point, in some cases, of founding mixed-blood dynasties (some of which eventually became the bane of missionaries and of more conventional colonists). In several places they were adopted as advisers by local chiefs, with consequences as bizarre and as varied as the advisers' personalities and political ideas.

Now and then tales got back to Sydney or London about the more sor-

did deeds of beachcombers, traders, and whalers; and such reports managed to stir up some popular as well as official indignation. There was
even good enough official sense to attribute some native ferocity to
revenge for the misdeeds of Westerners. On occasion, British and French
warships cruising in the area would step in and mete out a little quarter-
deck justice to miscreant Westerners, and as early as 1817 the British Parliament passed a police act, which enabled naval officers to take British
mischief-makers to British territory for trial. But years were to pass
before the establishment of colonial governments in the Islands themselves.

While all of the above Western comings and goings were taking place,
not all of the Islanders themselves remained at home, marveling at the
ships of the Westerners and waiting for the treasures they would bring.
Many of them accompanied those ships as crew members on their whaling or trading voyages and remained for years away from home, or ended
up as residents on other islands. (For example, in 1844 almost six hundred Hawaiians were employed on American whalers, and another four
hundred were working at the Hudson's Bay Company station in Oregon
[Howe 1984:101].) Although some of the traveling Islanders had been
kidnapped into service, most of them had gone along willingly, even
eagerly. And when keeping score on some of the inhumanities inflicted
upon Islanders by visitors to their shores, one must include many especially savage acts committed by Islander members of the crews.

Meanwhile another kind of influence was at work in the Islands, for
better or for worse, depending upon the point of view. It was of course
not entirely new. Spanish Catholic missionaries had been active in the
Marianas long before and had attempted but failed to become active in
some nearby Caroline islands. But the kind of mission activity now
referred to differed from that of the Spanish in several respects. It began
in 1797, with the arrival of the British ship *Duff* at Tahiti carrying a band
of London Missionary Society evangelists and craftsmen. These Calvinis-
tic pioneers first applied their persuasions and good works to persons at
the summit of the social and political hierarchy in the district where they
landed, assuming that conversion would follow a *downward* direction.
After eighteen years and many vicissitudes the strategy paid off, and
Christianity became the official religion of a politically united Tahiti (and
Moorea). The progress on Tahiti was interrupted from time by local
strife, but by the 1830s the L.M.S. missionaries had built up strong positions there for themselves and their faith, and had branched out to the
Leeward, the Cook, and the Samoan Islands. One of their leaders, John
Williams, got as far as the New Hebrides—where he promptly acquired
martyrdom.

It is a tribute to the zeal of that L.M.S. band that they were able to fill
so many heathen minds with Christian lessons and cover so many brown

bodies with respectable garments, including the flowing Mother Hubbard dresses that eventually were to envelop Island women nearly everywhere. For, from their sponsors back in England the missionaries received little other than pious exhortation; consequently, most of them had to become farmers or traders to gain livelihoods. This led some of them to acquire substantial interests in island affairs and a few to turn full time to trading or planting.

In the course of their proselyting many L.M.S. missionaries also gained local political power by means of their influence over converted chieftains. It would have been surprising indeed if they had failed to use that influence to frustrate mischievous traders or beachcombers and missionaries of rival Christian sects. But some of them went so far as to regard the presence of *any* other Westerners as inimical to their status (and, they rationalized, to that of their native flocks) so that for a time they and their sponsors maintained constant pressure upon the British government not to permit secular colonization in *their* islands and not to establish colonial authority there.

Meanwhile, other mission organizations became active elsewhere in the Islands. In 1799 the Church Missionary Society, an evangelical movement of Anglicans, was organized in England, whence it moved to Australia and, in 1814, to New Zealand. The early phase of its history in New Zealand was marked by the zeal of its agents to acquire land from the Maori and to agitate against secular colonization and annexation on the part of all nations, including Great Britain.

The Wesleyan Missionary Society was founded in England in 1814 and five years later set up its own station in New Zealand. Soon thereafter it extended its activities to Tonga, and thence to Fiji and the Loyalty Islands.

Protestant missionary labors in the New Hebrides were pioneered by Presbyterians from Nova Scotia, who first encountered fierce opposition from the inhabitants and who succeeded in maintaining their stations only at the expense of several particularly sticky martyrdoms.

In 1841 a third Protestant mission was established in New Zealand, also by Anglicans. A clerical error in the letters patent of its bishop defined his diocese as being from 50° south latitude to 34° *north* and directed him to extend the Gospel to "the Isles of the Pacific" within those latitudes. This might have daunted most men, but not the daring young Bishop George Selwyn. He rallied support in New Zealand and Australia and from a headquarters in Norfolk Island sent courageous missionaries to the New Hebrides and the Solomons, thereby founding the famed Melanesian Mission.

In Hawaii Protestantism was established in 1820 by evangelical Yankee missionaries from the Boston Mission (American Board of Commissioners for Foreign Missions). This band ultimately converted most of the Hawaiians and secured great influence over local affairs; and in due course it spread to the Marshalls, the eastern Carolines, and the Gilberts. Its agents also attempted to convert the Marquesans, but without success.

Despite some doctrinal differences among them, all of the Protestant missions shared a common goal—to extend both Protestantism and "civilization" (of which Protestantism was a fundamental component) to the less blessed peoples of the world, including especially the heathen, barbaric, and depraved Pacific Islanders. In the words of one of the missionaries: "They are in one word the very dregs of Mankind or Human Nature, dead and buried under the primeval curse, and nothing of them alive but the Brutal part, yea far worse than the Brute-Savage quite unfit to live but far more unfit to die, and yet they are the Sons and Daughters of Adam, and destined to live forever" (quoted in Howe 1984:113). Moreover, the "Brutal part" of the peoples the evangelical missionaries set out to convert included not only their heathenism and their immoralities (such as polygamy, infanticide, sexual promiscuity, nakedness—and dancing) but what was perceived to be their laziness and profligacy. Hence to save their souls it was also desirable, indeed essential, to instill in them proper attitudes and habits regarding *work*.

A common commitment to the above goals served to reduce rivalry among the various Protestant missions to a remarkable degree. Each kept to its own bailiwick and respected the staked-out claims of others. The London Missionary Society, for example, disavowed responsibility for Hawaii when it was learned that the Boston Mission was already operating there. All that Christian cooperation vanished, however, when the pope's emissaries appeared on the scene—or rather, appeared for the *third* time on the scene.

The first appearance of Catholic missionaries in the Islands took place in the sixteenth century in the Marianas, as has already been described. Then, the second appearance took place in Tahiti in 1772–1776, when a Spanish expedition out of Peru sought to establish a mission there but without success; the priests disliked the Tahitians so deeply that they scarcely issued from their station. The third attempt, in 1827, was more concerted and in the end more successful.

The nineteenth-century rebirth of Catholic interest in missions to the Pacific Islands came about largely as a result of the Restoration in France. Monarch and Church were united in their desire to combat British influence and Protestant heresy, and the arrangement was mutually helpful. Catholic missionaries carried the French language and accounts of French civilization along with the dogma of the Roman faith; in return, they received the substantive support of an ambitious government and its naval power. There was good reason to hope that France would succeed by missionary work where her efforts in whaling had failed.

A band of Roman Catholic missionaries landed in Hawaii in 1827.

They could hardly have chosen a more inhospitable site for their pioneering, for by then, the granite-willed Boston missionaries who had preceded them by seven years had won over the Hawaiian ruler to Protestantism and, one can be quite certain, had fully warned the Hawaiians against the perils of popery. The outcome was not surprising—the priests were expelled and the Catholic church was unable to establish its mission firmly in Hawaii for many years: until French agents and naval officers had threatened, fined, and actually seized the local government, an action that was however promptly discountenanced by Paris. The almost symbiotic relationship between France and the Church became evident in the demands made by the French agents during that episode; they insisted that both Catholic priests *and French wine* be allowed entry.

Shortly after the initial Catholic attempt in Hawaii the Church broadened her strategy and formulated a grander program for a "Mission d'Oceania," designating two French orders as instruments: the Société de Picpus for the islands in the east, and the Société de Marie for those in the west.

Laying out his campaign like a seasoned admiral, His Excellency the Vicar Apostolic of Eastern Polynesia established a beachhead in the Gambier islands and, after learning the local language, invaded Protestant Tahiti in 1836. History repeated itself, but only up to a point. As in Hawaii, French naval forces seized control of the Protestant-dominated Tahitian government when the latter sought to expel the newly arrived priests, but this time Paris ratified the seizure, thereby establishing a political "protectorate" over Tahiti and nearby Moorea, and thereby legitimizing and assisting the spread of Catholicism throughout most of southeastern Polynesia.

Meanwhile west of there the Marist bishop, after being repulsed in Protestant Tonga, set up a station in the Hoorn Islands and proceeded to establish his base in New Zealand. By midcentury a new start had been made by the Marists in Tonga and stations had been established in New Caledonia, Fiji, Samoa, Rotuma, and Woodlark. Daring but unsuccessful attempts were made even at faraway Rooke Island (near New Guinea) and at Isabel in the still-savage Solomons. And the Marists played active roles in helping to bring about the French annexation of New Caledonia in 1853.

The rivalry between the Protestantism and the Catholicism of that era may be gauged by the fact that, on Bougainville Island, Methodist and Catholic native converts were still burning down each others' chapels as late as 1930, to the considerable embarrassment of their white spiritual mentors. How much higher the feelings must have run earlier, when Protestant and Catholic missionaries had represented rival nations. Of the two, the Catholic missionaries had the stronger support and the closer identity with national interests, but the advantage was perhaps offset by the circumstance that they had to struggle against entrenched Protestantism in many places. In general, Britain was on the side of the Protestants, but this moral support was not often translated into official assistance. The British government had no appetite for more colonial adventures at that time and occasionally slapped the wrists of British missionaries who demanded a stronger show of backing. The correspondence from London to Paris frequently contained stern phrases, but Britain did not assert her "natural" sovereign rights in the South Pacific except in New Zealand, where the value of the prize and the urgent need for authority in that growing outpost of British subjects led her to annex it in 1840, just in time, it happened, to frustrate a French effort to do so.

Britain's policy aimed at maintaining the independence of the South Pacific islands, particularly independence from other powers. For a while, influential mission sponsors at home, as well as missionaries in the field, urged the maintenance of this policy, claiming that native leaders, given proper instruction by Protestant ministers, could eventually order their own lives and affairs, provided of course that they could be shielded from less altruistic influences. Among those influences the Protestant missionaries included not only Catholics in general along with beachcombers and whalers, but also nearly all traders, other would-be colonists, *and* officials, including British officials. (Later on, after more and more foreigners had flocked to the Islands and their settlements had become more and more unruly, the missionaries in the field came around to the view that British government authority might be beneficial after all, but that change of attitude was slow to come.) Meanwhile, the extent of Britain's intervention, beyond the New Zealand annexation, was to maintain naval vessels among the Islands to apprehend British culprits. Consuls were appointed at some places, but it was not unusual for these to be missionaries.

The United States government, with no navy to spare, displayed official concern only for Hawaii, where U.S. citizens were consolidating their spiritual, commercial, and political conquests. The U.S. government did, however, in one instance (1838–1842) devote attention to other areas of the South Pacific by sponsoring a scientific expedition commanded by Commodore Charles Wilkes, which, among many other accomplishments, provided the first detailed accounts of the Gilbert islands and was the first to reach the shores of Antarctica, thereby proving, at last, the existence of a huge Terra Australis, but one grimly different from the one once hoped for.

How did the native Islanders fit into the above dramas (and comedies) of Western efforts to win their souls and obtain their natural resources? Broader effects of those efforts will be described in later chapters, but it will be useful here to depict one scenario that was replayed many times, especially in Polynesia, Micronesia, and Fiji.

This scenario had to do with the nature of native leadership; it began with Captain Cook in Tahiti and it derived from the circumstance that the Westerners of those eras (explorers, traders, and missionaries alike) simply could not assimilate the fact that most Island societies were divided into small, separate, mostly community-sized political entities, each with its own chief, who was about equal in power and influence with all neighboring chiefs. To the Western subjects of kings and presidents there was something politically amorphous, even inconceivable, about such arrangements. Consequently, one of an Island's native chiefs was perceived to be, or was assisted to become, its "king," and thereafter was supported by citizens of whatever Western nation happened to be preponderant there. In time the citizens of another Western nation would appear and suffer real or imagined wrongs at the hands of the "king." Insults would fly, warships would appear, and ultimatums be sent. The pitifully confused "king," cajoled into a partisan role and forced to accept responsibilities beyond his knowledge or capacities, would then petition a Western nation—*any* Western nation—to protect or even annex his unhappy and ungovernable realm. Usually such petitions would be accepted gleefully by the naval officers or official or self-appointed "consuls" on the spot, only to be disavowed by their more scrupulous, or disinterested, superiors at home. Or, if the petitions seemed to be receiving favorable consideration in the home capitals, then correspondence would increase between Paris and London and Washington, and the Island "king" would end up by having his offer politely refused. And so the drama would end, at least for a few more years.

By midcentury the era of missionary "kingdoms" and warship diplomacy was about over, and a new era of more pervasive colonialism and more officially approved annexation was ushered in. The haphazard plunder of Island resources by whalers and itinerant traders began to be supplanted by the more systematic exploitation of planter and resident merchant.

SOURCES

Whalers: H. Morton 1982; Stackpole 1953, 1972.

Traders: Harrison 1937; Hezel 1978, 1983; Howe 1984; Morison 1921; Shineberg 1967, 1971.

Beachcombers: Hezel 1978, 1983; Maude 1964; Ralston 1978.

Missionaries: Berde 1979; Boutilier 1985; Boutilier, Hughes, and Tiffany 1978; Brady 1975; Davies 1961; Ellsworth 1959; Forman 1982; Garrett 1982; Gunson 1978; Howe 1984; Hilliard 1974; *Journal de la Société des Océanistes* 1969; Laracy 1976; Laval 1968; Miller 1985; Oram 1971; Whiteman 1983; Wiltgen 1979.

International context: Brookes 1941; Faivre 1953; Morrell 1960.

CHAPTER FOUR

Planters, Labor Recruiters, and Merchants: 1850–1914

During the sixty-five years preceding World War I political events in the outside world continued to dominate happenings in the Pacific Islands. Throughout the first half of this era Great Britain's policies towards the area remained unchanged despite the declining influence of the evangelical sects. The Royal Navy continued to play a decisive role in the South Pacific but the home government maintained its reluctance to undertake new and predictably costly colonial adventures there; in fact, its disposition was to barter South Pacific advantages for satisfactory settlements in areas nearer home. Ministers like Derby and Carnarvon seemed to know little, and to care less, about the "cannibal isles." In time, however, this indifference was weakened, in response to sharpened criticism from Australia and New Zealand and, more important, in reaction to the growing imperialistic threat from a united and rising Germany.

France for its part continued to exert some influence in the South Pacific through her position in Tahiti and New Caledonia, and the missionary zeal of her Catholic priests did not abate. For the most part, however, France's role was that of a balance in the game of power politics between imperial Britain and covetous Germany.

Germany entered the South Pacific arena with a flourish. Her unifier, Bismarck, did not at first favor colonial adventures, preferring to concen-

trate efforts in building up industrial power in the fatherland; but propo-
nents of world commerce and naval might and colonialism had their way
after 1880, resulting in an about-face in national policy.

Elsewhere in Europe, Russia's earlier influence on Pacific Island
affairs, always slight, was reduced yet further through her losses in the
Crimean and Russo-Japanese wars. The Dutch remained preoccupied
with their plantations in the East Indies, and paid scant attention to their
outposts in western New Guinea. And as for Spain: she was aroused
enough by German commercial encroachments to reassert her ancient
claims over the Carolines, but after the Spanish-American War in 1898,
she was replaced by the United States in Guam and elsewhere in the
Marianas by Germany.

America's drive towards power and influence in the Pacific was interrupted by the Civil War, and by the periodic ascendancies of the Democratic party (which at the time was opposed to territorial expansion). In
the end, however, the Republican Manifest Destiny policies of Seward,
McKinley, and Roosevelt won out against the nonexpansionism of the
Democrats, so that by 1914 the United States had acquired full sovereignty over three Pacific territories, eastern Samoa, Hawaii, and Guam,
along with viable claims to some forty-eight "guano islands" in the central Pacific.

Developments in the Pacific Islands during this era were also presaged
by events that took place in the Far East: by Japan's seizure of Taiwan in
1895 and by her victory over Russia in 1905. The imperialist designs evident in the former, backed by the military-naval might demonstrated in
the latter, should have been an ominous sign to the powers already
possessing Pacific real estate.

Meanwhile, during this same era, China was opened wide to foreign
trade and attracted increasing numbers of foreigners, particularly of the
predatory commercial variety, so that the Pacific was crossed with
increasing frequency by European and American ships. Traffic now
flowed out of the Open Door as well: Chinese coolies and small traders
emigrated by the thousands to every island that would accept them, to
escape the more dismal poverty at home.

But perhaps the greatest foreign influence on the Pacific Islands during
this era was exerted by Australia and New Zealand. By this time those
British colonies had increased greatly in population and wealth and had
matured to dominion status. Their citizens went forth to the Islands in
large numbers, as adventurers, missionaries, traders, and planters. So
numerous and weighty were the ties between these nations and the
Islands that it was with pardonable presumption that their politicians
considered most of the South Pacific to be British, and moreover *their*
British sphere.

Other developments that influenced events in the South Pacific during

this era had to do with communications. The rise of steam navigation led
to a clamor for coaling stations located at strategic points along the
trans-Pacific trade routes. Also, for years before its actual construction
the plan for a canal across Panama increased the interests of major powers in ports of call in Hawaii, Tahiti, and Fiji. And third, the laying of tel-
egraph cables across the Pacific necessitated the establishment of cable
stations en route.

Whaling, which had been so important in the Islands during the first
half of the nineteenth century, reached its peak shortly after midcentury
and then rapidly declined owing to the supplanting of whale and sperm
oil by Pennsylvania oil and of baleen by steel. Moreover, rival industries,
including textile manufacturing in New England and gold mining in California, drained away manpower from whaling, and the Civil War further
thinned out the American whaling fleets. Later, when the Norwegians
and the Japanese took over leadership in the whale fishery, they generally
bypassed the Islands for the Antarctic.

In contrast to whaling, the Islands' copra industry expanded, to supply
soap and edible oils for the growing populations of Europe and America.
Other tropical products that became increasingly popular during this era
were sugar, coffee, cocoa, fruit, vanilla, fibers, and rubber, all adaptable
to the Islands' climates and soils. For a short period the American Civil
War provided a stimulus to cotton growing in some Islands. And more
scientific approaches to agriculture in the Western world created a
demand for fertilizers, leading to vigorous mining of the Islands' guano
deposits. Meanwhile, trepang continued in favor among Chinese gourmets, and pearls and pearl shell continued to fetch high prices in world
markets. In addition, steel manufacturing raised the value of nickel,
chromium, cobalt, and manganese and created a thriving mining industry on New Caledonia, where these minerals were found in quantity.

The most direct effect of all those outside influences upon the Islands
was to introduce or increase the activities there of three types of foreigners: the planter, the labor recruiter, and the large-scale merchant. Of
these, the planter was perhaps the star actor, supplanting in importance
the whalers, itinerant traders, beachcombers, and missionaries of the
preceding half century.

The planter was a new kind of person: unlike the whaler and the
itinerant trader he was not drawn to the Islands as places of refreshment
or sources of native goods, and he was less interested in the Islanders'
souls than in their labor. He was a colonist, there to stay, at least until he
could return in style to Sydney or Liverpool, Bordeaux or Hamburg.
There were, to be sure, some planters already established in, for example, Hawaii, Samoa, and Fiji during the first half of the century, but their
pedestrian moneymaking did not appeal to the other foreigners living in
or visiting the Islands at that time, who preferred obtaining things

already available and making fast turnarounds. In time, however, sandal-wood gave out, and competition increased for the remaining pearls and pearl shell and other local produce. Also, the increased world demand for tropical agricultural products led some speculators in, for example, London, Paris, Hamburg, and Melbourne, to plan more ambitious South Sea development schemes. Some of those ventures did actually material-ize and succeed, but many of them ended in massive failures and in the bankruptcies of their absentee directors. In the end, most of the pioneer planting was done by individuals, having more hope than capital.

Nearly every known tropical plant of economic value was tried out in the Islands at one time or another, but only a few (copra, sugar, coffee, cocoa, vanilla, fruit, cotton, and rubber) have had any real significance there (and the latter two for only short periods of time).

Copra, the dried meat of the coconut, a source of oil for soap, marga-rine, and nitroglycerine, has affected the lives of more Islanders than all other Island products put together. Its production is admirably suited to Island conditions: much of the land and climates there are ideal for the coconut's growth, and even the least westernized Islander can be quickly trained to collect and process it for commercial markets. There have been, and continue to be, several kinds of production enterprise: for example, by individual native producers (who sell their dried copra to nearby storekeepers or itinerant traders), by jointly owned and managed native plantations, by independent Western planters employing native laborers, and by large corporately owned Western firms.

The heyday of South Seas cotton came about as a result of the Ameri-can Civil War. Desultory plantings were tried out before that but large-scale enterprises developed in the Islands only after English textile manu-facturers sought substitutes for their usual American sources, which were cut off by the Union blockade. Fiji was the first Island center of this boom, and while it lasted scores of Western merchants flocked there. Australians were particularly active in encouraging the growing of cotton in the Islands, and there were even a few American adventurers attracted to the Islands by cheap labor and unobstructed markets. South Seas cot-ton was excellent in quality, and the industry prospered until Dixie cot-ton became plentiful again.

Coffee and cocoa also prospered in the Islands for a while, and in some places continue to do so. Before South Seas coffee lost out (tempo-rarily) to Brazilian competition and to local pests, it was produced in large quantities by Western planters who wished to spread out their risks beyond dependence upon copra. New Caledonia, Tahiti, and parts of the New Hebrides continued to produce some after World War I, as did the Kona coast of the island of Hawaii. (It was only after World War II that the New Guinea Highlands became colonized, and its Western-intro-duced but largely native-produced coffee became a large-scale enterprise.) Cocoa was also grown in quantity during this era, and continues to be grown on many islands, both by individual native cash-croppers and by Western-owned and managed firms.

Although sugarcane may have originated in the Islands (specifically, in New Guinea), the large-scale growing of it was to become the Islands' most alien of foreign enterprises.

To the Westerners who undertook to produce sugar for world markets it was apparent almost from the beginning that Islanders were not suited to the kind of organized and steady industriousness required for efficient production, and that laborers had to be sought from elsewhere. Also, in both Hawaii and Fiji, the only Island places where cane growing became important during this era, the industry was monopolized by large firms of Americans and Britishers, so that the local Islanders shared neither in its management nor its profit, except for the rents paid to some of them for use of their lands. This is not to say that Islanders were not affected by the sugar industry; in fact, the immigration of tens of thousands of Asian laborers (Indians to Fiji; Chinese, Japanese, and Filipinos to Hawaii) had profound and continuing effects on island life.

The expanding populations of Australia and New Zealand during this era stimulated the production and export of citrus fruits and bananas in Fiji, Samoa, and the Cook Islands. Fruit growing in these places was mainly in the hands of Islanders, although Westerners handled most of the marketing. In Samoa and the southern Cooks these enterprises continued throughout this era to provide Islanders with funds for purchasing Western goods, which by then had become necessities; but in Fiji banana production almost ceased after Australia erected import barriers at the insistence of her own fruit growers in tropical Queensland.

Accompanying the development of copra, cotton, and sugar, numbers of land speculators were attracted to the Islands, thereby adding to the inventory of rogues inevitable in the annals of most colonial regions. On paper their land deals appear more respectable than the actions of the labor recruiters, because the kidnapping and murder of even a handful of natives look more culpable than the alienation of native land. But in the longer-range view nothing has been so fateful to Islanders as their loss of land. In most places there was not much of it to begin with, and by the end of World War I this essential resource, this basis of all Islanders' existence, had become alienated to an alarming degree.

Whaling played a steadily declining role in Island life during this era but there were booms in other local marine industries. Diving, both for pearls and for pearl shell, became an economic mainstay in several archipelagoes. Indeed, in some atolls of the southeastern Pacific pearling was the only source of income, until the shell beds were exhausted through overfishing. Then the center of diving shifted to the west, to the Torres

Strait, where the beds were also systematically plundered and would have been cleaned out but for the onset of World War I and the temporary abandonment of diving.

The worldwide search for fertilizers sent prospectors to every corner of the South Pacific. First of all, American and British companies quickly cleaned out the guano deposits from the Line Islands in the central Pacific and abandoned them to the seabirds. Somewhat later, deposits of phosphate were discovered and mined: on Ocean and Nauru in the central Pacific, on Angaur in the western Carolines, and on Makatea in the western Tuamotus. Although a few natives were employed in the digging and loading of guano, this enterprise had little lasting effects on Island history. Not so with phosphate mining, which affected native life in several profound ways, as a later chapter will describe.

Meanwhile Western Man's eternal search for gold went on in some of the larger islands of Melanesia, and now and then some grizzled prospector would strike it just rich enough to keep up the hopes of his fellows. Eastern New Guinea, particularly, became a site, and usually a graveyard, for gold-mining enterprises before World War I.

Far more successful, and much larger in scale, were the mining enterprises on New Caledonia, as will be told.

One common feature of all of the Western-owned and managed enterprises just mentioned was their need for manual labor, lots of manual labor—which brings us to consider how some of that labor was obtained.

A handy rationalization that has alternately eased or increased the "white man's burden" in the Islands is that *white men can do no physical work in the tropics.* This notion is fanciful, to say the least. Characterizing the South Pacific climates as "unbearable" would have drawn guffaws from the Pacific-ribboned veterans of World War II who had lived and worked through summers in Chicago or Los Angeles or Brisbane. Nevertheless, the early South Seas planters and their modern successors have always regarded large gangs of Islander or Asian laborers as an indispensable ingredient to agricultural enterprise.

The early South Seas plantations did indeed require large numbers of laborers, and this posed a problem for the pioneer Western planters. In the eastern islands, where plantations were first established, the local Polynesians of that era proved quite unsatisfactory as laborers. In the first place, their life routines had not conditioned them to the relentlessness of organized work under a foreign master, producing things they did not use and for purposes they did not entirely comprehend. And second, their relatively easy subsistence technologies satisfied all their needs, except perhaps for those things they wished to obtain from the Westerners, and their desires for the latter were not impelling enough to overcome their reluctance to engage in steady plantation work. So, at a very early stage in their enterprises, the Western planters in those islands began to look elsewhere for labor.

The Fijians were not quite so reluctant to work on plantations as were their neighbors in Polynesia, but even in Fiji the supply of tractable laborers soon gave out and the planters had to turn to other Islands for the labor to cut their copra and pick their cotton.

Meanwhile in Australia the end of convict transportation created a need for some other source of cheap labor for herding and plantation-type farming. Early efforts to introduce East Indian laborers were unsuccessful, so that employers turned to viewing the Pacific Islands as a source. History reserves for a Mr. Benjamin Boyd the distinction of introducing the first indentured Islanders into Australia; the first shipment, in 1847, consisted of some sixty-five natives from the Loyalty Islands and the New Hebrides.

Various euphemisms have been applied to South Seas labor recruiting, but some honest firsthand observers characterized what they saw as nothing better than slave trading. What they saw worked like this: captains of vessels so engaged would drop anchor in some bay or lagoon at one of the less frequented islands and "induce" islanders to sign contracts committing them to work hard and faithfully at a distant island or mainland plantation; in return for this labor they were to be fed, paid, and eventually sent home again to dwell in power and prestige brought about by their acquired wealth and knowledge of the Western world—a simple and straightforward commercial arrangement, ensuring mutual benefits and spreading Western civilization (the only kind that really mattered) at an accelerated pace.

Unfortunately, it soon became common knowledge that many recruiters were as ruthless a band of slavers as ever shocked an abolition society. A peaceful trader or missionary, returning to some normally hospitable village one day, would be murdered without warning. Inquiries would then turn up the fact that labor recruiters had lately been there inducing local residents to sign on. Some of them were reported to have captured native chiefs and held them hostage until enough of their able-bodied followers had signed on. In a few cases they are known to have delivered their hostages to the sharks and scattered shot at the village to make the place unhealthy for rival recruiters. It is of course possible, even likely, that many islanders signed on willingly, with no more coercion than a few misrepresentations about the rewards of laboring in civilization's elysian fields, not a difficult negotiation for the contractors since the contractees were unable to read what they signed. In any event, the procedures employed in recruiting had many variants, including some that were brutally inhuman.

Having been delivered to their new employers, who paid the recruiters handsome fees, the recruited laborers experienced fates varying according to the characters of their "masters" (for such they were called, and such they in fact were). Arguing statistically, many laborers were doubtless treated decently, recompensed fairly, and returned to their homes on schedule—all the better for their foretaste of the "civilization" that eventually was to change their lives anyway. On the other hand, many of them fared less well, there having been little in the shape of outside authority to enforce contract observance upon the employers. Particularly did many planters become casual about repatriating their laborers upon expiration of contract.

An additional source of much mischief to Island life was the practice of some employers of paying off laborers in guns and ammunition, thereby assisting the Islanders to kill one another more efficiently than was possible when they had to depend upon mere clubs and spears. The promise of firearms was in fact the only one that induced some Islanders to sign on voluntarily. Through these humble beginnings the South Seas arms trade progressed until it became an important aspect of South Pacific commerce. Some sandalwooders, temperamentally well suited to this commerce, became especially proficient in it and were able to supplement their decreasing profits from the dwindling supply of sandalwood by labor recruiting and by the arms and rum trade. In the Solomons some of them went so far as to join with their favored clients in head-hunting forays.

Most blackbirding (i.e., most of the more iniquitous forms of labor recruiting) took place in the western islands, but the central and eastern islands did not altogether escape. In one case, shiploads of natives from Micronesia and Polynesia were taken to Peru and sold at so much a head to the planters there. After a while the Peruvian transactions received so much notoriety that some of the great powers intervened to terminate it (see chapter 7). Blackbirding in the western islands continued much longer, despite the protests of local missionaries and widespread opposition in Australia. In fact, the strongest opponent of South Seas blackbirding was the Royal Navy; naval vessels had to go in and quell native uprisings that their officers knew had resulted from the conduct of blackbirders. But the navy alone could not stop the trade; and the British Colonial and Foreign Offices seemed unable or unwilling to act, stating that the practice was not *slavery*—had not the natives signed proper contracts? Moreover, their officials argued, the islands involved were not under British authority, nor would it be fair to penalize British planters and recruiters while not also controlling the foreign nationals engaged in the same practices.

Despite this inertia there were a few attempts made to mitigate the abuses. For example, the British Consul in Fiji went through the motions of "certifying" that landed laborers had in fact undertaken their contracts

voluntarily, having obtained this critical intelligence by means of inter-
views carried out in pantomime; certifications of twenty-three hundred
natives were thus recorded in 1870, one of the peak years. More effective
was the work done by the Royal Navy, its Australian squadron having
been enlarged to combat blackbirding. British Orders in Council, including the Kidnapping Act of 1872, gave authority to naval officers to track
down British mischief-makers in the Islands and carry them to Australia
for trial. This "government by commodore" was the only effective
authority represented in most of the western islands at that time, and
although it did much practical police work, it was limited by the circumstance that in Fiji the home government could not, and in Queensland
would not, prohibit altogether the commerce in human beings and
thereby attack the abuses at the source.

   In Fiji the abuses were ultimately lessened by Britain's annexation of
that archipelago, after many petitions and counterpetitions. Simultaneously with annexation the British established a high commissioner in
Fiji, with deputies in all the neighboring archipelagoes outside the recognized jurisdiction of other powers. These deputies were granted authority over all British subjects in those no-man's-lands and were thereby enabled to create some semblance of order (inasmuch as most of the
foreigners in such places were British). However, the worst abuses of
labor recruiting were not wiped out until all of the Islands had been
annexed by one or another of the great powers, and until Queensland
legislated against the import of island laborers.

   Throughout the whole of the blackbirding period Queensland had
remained an embarrassment to Great Britain. Any suggestions from London or Sydney or Melbourne that that colony discontinue the use of
island labor were testily answered to the effect that such abuses did not
occur in Queensland, thank you, and that the islanders not only *profited*
by their sojourn in the colony but insisted on undertaking new terms of
indenture rather than return to the barbarism of their home islands!
(Such a stand is not surprising for a colony where some of the most influential men were employers of island labor.) By 1904, however, even
Queensland had seen the light and abolished the import of island labor,
after having imported some 60,819 Islanders. (But, it must be added, the
light reflected in this abolition had its source in growing popular sentiments for a "white" Australia, not in opposition to inhumanities of the
labor trade [Scarr 1968:1–2].)

   British subjects were the principal characters in both the rise and the
decline of labor recruiting, but they were not the only nationals involved
in it. German planters imported laborers from Micronesia, and a few
from Melanesia, for their Samoan enterprises. French colonial officials
discouraged recruiting in their own island dependencies, but were glad
enough to obtain laborers from other islands. Even the Hawaiian king-

dom imported a few Gilbertese to work on the sugar plantations (and coincidentally, to help arrest the decline in the numbers of native Hawaiians), but this experiment failed in both respects. As for the United States, although its officials deplored the practice of labor recruiting in the Islands (there were no U.S. dependencies there at the time!), Washington did nothing tangible toward curbing it.

Following in the wake of the pioneer planters and labor recruiters there appeared in the Islands several large mercantile firms, supplanting the itinerant trader and the small shopkeeper in all but the more out-of-the-way places. By World War I these large firms not only dominated commerce throughout the Islands, but also, by purchase or mortgage, controlled most other commercial activity there as well.

At nearly every Island port one or two traders, more enterprising and better capitalized than others, had emerged as local business leaders and had absorbed most of their local competitors. The next step for many of them was to acquire fleets of schooners to bring in produce from outstation traders. Then, typically, the leading traders would obtain land and start their own plantations, or, as in Hawaii, they would acquire capital interests in existing plantations for which they were serving as agents (called "factors"). Some of these mercantile firms had evolved from modest local beginnings; others were new ventures planned and financed from abroad. Among the latter was the firm of Godeffroy and Son, which quickly pulled ahead of all local rivals and constituted Germany's imperialistic spearhead in the South Pacific.

Johann Caesar Godeffroy was a wealthy merchant and shipowner in Hamburg. His agents established their South Seas headquarters at Apia (Samoa) in 1856; before that Godeffroy ships were carrying passengers to Australia, and Godeffroy branches were located in Hong Kong and Valparaiso. Within a few years of its Apia opening, the firm's agents and affiliates were operating throughout the Islands. In the Marshalls, the eastern Carolines, the Gilberts, and the Ellice islands, they and their successors were not only the only traders but in many places the only Western residents as well. And in places with numerous Western residents, such as Fiji, Samoa, and Tonga, Godeffroy agents outdid their competitors. Moreover, their agents were the first traders to brave the frontier hardships of New Britain, thereby becoming the forerunners of German sovereignty there.

Back of the Godeffroy field agents were German financiers intent upon building up a trade empire to surpass Britain's. In addition to their many British employees in the islands, they sent out educated and able Germans, capable of speaking English and French and representing a different breed altogether from the usual run of Island traders. Fast steamers moved directly between Germany and the Islands, supplemented by lines from Sydney and Hong Kong and by a network of interisland vessels. Godeffroy agents were also able to offer special inducements to planter customers, such as low freight rates, in return for trade monopoly.

Godeffroy itself was eventually liquidated as a result of losses sustained from the French blockade during the Franco-Prussian War, but other German firms promptly moved in and continued Godeffroy's operations, as well as, in some places, becoming their government's official agent. Against such competition the smaller local firms and those based in Australia and New Zealand had stiff going; nevertheless, some of them survived.

French firms, some of them backed by metropolitan capital and possessing large local landholdings, remained paramount in New Caledonia against all competition. In French Polynesia, however, commerce did not become as integrated as elsewhere; Chinese immigrants set up small establishments in nearly every line of business and at every populated center but they were not under unified control.

Godeffroy's initial operations in the Islands did not have government backing; when the company's agents were making their first gains Germany was divided into a number of states, and the impetus for commercial expansion came from financiers in the Hansa cities. Even the unification of Germany did not immediately change this situation—Bismarck was initially opposed to colonialism. In time, however, expansionists had their way, and the German government turned about-face, toward empire and world-girdling naval power.

The first product of this policy change was strong support for German mercantile firms in New Guinea, which led to German annexation of northeastern New Guinea and the Bismarck Archipelago in 1884. A year later the Reich also took possession of the Marshall islands, thereby consolidating politically what the Jaluit Gesellschaft (a Godeffroy affiliate) had already accomplished commercially. Meanwhile, the center of German commerce in the Pacific remained in Samoa, where the ranking German trader was also consul and had the backing of German naval vessels (which had by then become almost as much in evidence as the Royal Navy in the South Seas). Samoa, however, was not so easy to annex as the Marshalls had been: both British and American interests were involved there, and the United States had by then already persuaded its local chiefs to grant her naval rights in Pago Pago (Tutuila), the best harbor in the archipelago. In due course a succession controversy among native Samoans provided the three powers with excuses for intercession, with Germany backing one faction and the British and Americans the other, each power represented by its own warships. A providential hurricane wrecked the American and German warships (the British ones having escaped by the skin of their teeth) before they were able to do more than bristle at one another, so that further international complications were avoided. Then, somewhat shaken by those explosive potentialities, the governments in London and Berlin and Washington agreed to settle their (local) differences by partitioning Samoa, the western part going to Germany, the eastern to the United States. In doing so, however, they failed to consult Australia and New Zealand and, of course, the Samoans themselves. Nor did Britain come out empty-handed, having thereby received a free rein in most of the Solomons and, what was vastly more important to Whitehall, having obtained assurances of German acquiescence for deals then in progress with respect to Egypt and certain African territories.

Germany completed her Pacific acquisitions after the Spanish-American War, when she purchased the Carolines and the Marianas (except Guam) from a vanquished Spain. As in the other cases, this annexation represented an easy transition from commercial to political control—German traders already were dominant in those archipelagoes.

One reason for Germany's steady progress in the Islands was the single-mindedness of their colonial ventures. At the beginning no missionaries were sent out to assist in paving the way; in fact, when German missionaries did appear the German traders and officials asked no favors from them and showed little disposition to give favors to them. Also, there were few Germans in the islands except those directly associated with government or with semigovernmental commercial firms, so that the home government did not have a troublesome public opinion to placate. In a word, Germany's aim was commercial expansion and, later on, political expansion through commerce. The imperial government even left colonial administration in the hands of company officials for a number of years in New Guinea and the Marshalls, and replaced them with career officials only after the companies had failed financially.

Meanwhile Britain was muddling along, acting in the Islands only when moved to forestall actions by Germany or when pressed by popular outcries in Australia and New Zealand. Her reluctance to assume heavier responsibilities was summarized by one government minister who is alleged to have said, "Her Majesty already has quite enough black subjects." Also, Treasury officials scrupled against spending United Kingdom taxpayers' money on enterprises that would bring profit, if any, only to their South Pacific colonials—the Australians and New Zealanders had been unwilling to share the financing of troubleshooting in the islands. In all fairness, however, it should be recognized that the British government had to fry other and larger fish than those occupying South Seas lagoons. Bigger issues such as Kenya and Egypt deserved, and received, first attention, and when swaps were to be made it is not surprising that Samoa and still-unknown New Guinea were passed over for better prizes nearer home.

Yet, in spite of the disinterest of the home government, British influ-

ence continued during this era to remain dominant throughout most of
the Islands. British missionaries consolidated their religious jurisdictions
over Tonga, Fiji, the Cook islands, and Samoa, and pioneered throughout the New Hebrides, the Solomons, and southeastern New Guinea. (In
New Caledonia and French Polynesia, however, they were supplanted by
French missionaries, both Catholic and Protestant.) The Boston missionaries left little unseeded soil in Hawaii, but elsewhere the British (Protestant) missions had clear fields until French and German Catholics moved
northward and westward toward New Guinea. For the most part, the
Protestants undertook no further king-making adventures during this
era, having relinquished this role to merchants and consuls and commo-
dores in non-French Polynesia and having discovered native political
organization to be too rudimentary in Melanesia.

British planters and merchants continued to play important economic
roles in the Islands during this era. Large numbers of them were attracted
to the Islands by the booms in cotton and sugar and copra; and with their
funds thus invested and their interests localized they needed and demanded stable government (preferably British government) to regularize
their land acquisitions and protect their property.

During this era Australia and New Zealand became more directly and
vocally concerned with Island affairs. Individuals, companies, and syndicates invested fortunes in South Seas ventures; and large segments of the
population supported missionary endeavors with personnel and funds
and moral backing. Again and again officials in the colonies urged London to annex whole Island archipelagoes; and in one instance, in Papua,
the colonials took the initiative themselves, only to have their action
vetoed by London. Many Australians and New Zealanders watched with
trepidation Germany's swift progress in Samoa and northeastern New
Guinea, and although they warned the British government of the potential consequences, London went ahead and "negotiated" those areas to
Germany. Understandably, such actions by London aroused fierce resentment in the Australian colonies and were instrumental in stimulating
them to common action, which somewhat later resulted in their federation.

Only once did Great Britain move swiftly and purposefully to acquire
Island possessions. Urged by an intercolonial conference, London obtained possession of a number of pinpoint islands in the central Pacific in
preparation for laying a trans-Pacific cable.

Nevertheless, despite her policy-based reluctance and her indecision,
Great Britain did raise her flag over a number of other islands during this
era. Fiji was annexed in 1874, partly as a result of efforts to control
blackbirding; nearby Rotuma was added a few years later. Papua was
taken in 1884 at Australian insistence and was later handed over to the
newly established commonwealth. The central and southern Solomons

became a protectorate in 1892. The Gilberts and Ellices also became a single protectorate in 1892 and were designated a crown colony twenty-three years later. The Cook Islands and Niue were taken over in 1888 and 1889 and annexed to New Zealand two years later. Tonga, under British influence from the beginning, was brought under closer administrative control, while remaining a kingdom on its own. Ocean Island was annexed, for its phosphate, in 1900. By agreement with France, a joint naval commission was established in the New Hebrides in 1887 and later on transformed into an Anglo-French condominium.

All together, between 1874 and 1906, over 112,000 square miles and several hundred thousand unwitting Islanders were acquired outright by Britain, in what one writer called "a state of absent-mindedness."

During the era now under review the Tricolor also was raised over several Pacific Islands, representing a consolidation of gains already made during the first half of the century rather than a demonstration of continued French colonial vitality. The political climate in metropolitan France, being complicated by troubles in North Africa and by conflict with Prussia, was not conducive to Island ventures. Furthermore, the marriage of Church and State had been dissolved, and the Catholic missions no longer received the official support they had enjoyed during the July Monarchy. This state of affairs was, however, not immediately reflected in the Islands themselves, and for several decades thereafter many Islanders and Western residents in the Islands continued to identify Catholicism with France.

At the beginning of this era, in 1853, as a result of the momentum gained during the preceding years, France annexed New Caledonia, taking it from under the very noses of some British officials who happened to be there at the time. Also, in due course, France's protectorate over Tahiti was superseded by formal annexation, as were her protectorates over the other archipelagoes that now constitute French Polynesia (the Leeward, Austral, Gambier, Tuamotu, and Marquesas islands). Finally, Wallis and Futuna were added, in 1887, culminating the control that the Catholic mission was already exercising.

New Caledonia was constituted a penal colony in 1864 and within two decades over seventeen thousand convicts had been sent there. The political prisoners among them (i.e., those who had supported the abortive Commune) were eventually amnestied and returned to France, but large numbers of run-of-the-mill criminals remained in New Caledonia or escaped to Australia or to other Islands. The metropolitan French government seems not to have objected to those escapes; Australia on the other hand, objected strenuously to the appearance of some of them on her shore: the convicts among *her* founders were at least mainly *British*. Even more indignation was aroused in Australia by France's proposal to send recidivists (habitual criminals) to next-door New Caledonia, and the Australians were not satisfied with the reassurances London was able to obtain from Paris on this score.

Nor were Australians pleased by the prospects of having even more French influence in other islands nearby, a probability that was increased by the actions of Frenchmen in the New Hebrides, where several French plantations and a French military post were established. Annoyance, and annexation fever, ran high in Australia in reaction to these events, but London would proceed no further than obtaining assurances from Paris that outright annexation was not intended, an agreement that eventually crystallized into the form of the condominium already mentioned.

During this era the interests of the United States in the Pacific received a strong stimulus from Commodore Perry's so-called "opening" of Japan. There was even talk at the time of America taking over such real estate as the Bonins, the Luchus (Ryukyus), and Formosa, to serve as outposts nearer to rich East Asian markets, but these ambitions abated during the American Civil War, and Seward's purchase of Alaska did not immediately succeed in reviving the expansionist spirit.

Meanwhile Americans were actively engaged in consolidating their supremacy in Hawaii, not only in mere numbers but in religious, economic, and political affairs as well. American planters united in movements to bring about closer ties with the United States and succeeded in 1875 in pushing through a treaty of reciprocity, which provided stimulus for a spectacular expansion in plantation activity. Some American missionaries, turned counselors, retained their influence over state affairs of the Hawaiian kingdom and steered its leaders through many critical episodes, domestic and international.

Some of those episodes were, in retrospect, fateful for the future of the Hawaiian people; one of them can only be characterized as pathetic. This was the effort of one monarch to delay the inevitable by drawing together his "royal" cousins throughout Polynesia into a federation. In 1880 he went so far as to send a part-Hawaiian emissary to Samoa to help effect a reconciliation between warring factions there and to confer upon Samoa's "kings" the Grand Cross of the Royal Order of the Star of Oceania! Arriving in Apia, the plenipotentiary proceeded to live a life of champagne revelry until resident agents of the Western powers, resentful of his "unwanted interference," forced his recall.

Americans continued to gain in number and power in Hawaii, and in 1893–1894 they deposed the monarch and proclaimed a republic, which they promptly invited the United States to absorb. In due course (in 1898) President McKinley accepted the offer, characterizing it "a consummation"—which indeed it was.

The United States' political interest in the Islands south of the equator was limited to the acquisition of eastern Samoa, as was described earlier. Also mentioned previously was America's annexation of Guam, a prize of the Spanish-American War, the war that effectively ended Spain's political holdings in the Islands. In fact, the only remnant of Hispanic influence left in the South Pacific after 1898 was Easter Island, which had been annexed by Chile in 1888.

From 1900 to the outbreak of World War I the powers refrained from pulling and tugging at one another in the South Pacific, and the Islands enjoyed a measure of stability, at least on the level of international politics. But that does not mean that the Islanders themselves enjoyed a respite from foreigners. Planters continued to extend their holdings along the shores of many Islands and appropriated more and more land. Foreign merchants bound Islanders closer and closer to the money economy by stimulating desires for new kinds of imports and by the fetters of never-ending credit and debt. Missionaries continued their pioneering into the heathen areas, and the appearance of new sects, such as the Seventh Day Adventists and Mormons, fired new mission rivalries. Although these rivalries were not so heated, physically, nor so significant, politically, as they once had been, they did manage to increase the bewilderment of those Islanders forced into choosing among conflicting doctrines. And while all this was going on, government officials in the large western islands pushed further and further into their interiors and brought more and more natives under colonial rule.

With so much foreign supervision and domination exercised during this era, the Islanders themselves lost the last vestige of control over most of their own affairs, and (except in Tonga) even the symbols of their traditional forms of governance were no longer preserved. In return for these losses they did, it is true, acquire such consolations as salvation for their souls, calico for their loins, and canned salmon for their bellies, along with such diversions as cricket or soccer or baseball for the times they were not laboring in unfamiliar jobs to support newly acquired appetites.

SOURCES

Planters: Brookfield 1972; Brookfield and Hart 1971; Panoff 1986.

Labor recruiters: Bennett 1976; Corris 1973a, 1973b; Harrison 1937; Maude 1981; Newbury 1980a; Palmer 1871; Parnaby 1964; Scarr 1968, 1970.

Merchants: Buckley and Klugman 1981; Gilson 1970.

General: Davidson 1967; Daws 1968; Firth 1982; Gilson 1970; Howe 1984; Scarr 1967.

CHAPTER FIVE

Miners and Administrators: 1914–1939

Compared with hurricane-force battles like Pearl Harbor, Tarawa, and Saipan, World War I struck the Pacific Islands with the impact of a zephyr. The changes ultimately wrought in some of them by that first world war were considerable, but the conflict itself in the South Pacific was mild.

Soon after its outbreak Australian authorities rounded up a nondescript crew, shoved them into uniform, and shipped them to New Guinea. These rollicking "Coconut Lancers" landed in the vicinity of Rabaul and quickly subdued the handful of German residents there. Thereupon the Australian commander, a better soldier than a linguist, solemnly proclaimed the change in administration to a crowd of bewildered natives with these historic words: "No more 'um Kaiser; God save 'um King." Military rule remained in force in the former German colony throughout the war, but introduced few major changes in activities there. German planters were allowed to carry on with their enterprises and many German regulations were incorporated in the new laws. The principal effect was a slowing down of economic developments as a result of the disruption of shipping and of uncertainties about the future status of the colony.

On Nauru Island, also a German possession, the Australians took over the administration and confirmed the already effective control of British management over phosphate mining there. Meanwhile a New Zealand force seized control of German (i.e., western) Samoa, in exuberant fulfillment of the Dominion's earlier aspirations there.

Far more consequential was Japan's elimination of Germany in the northern Marianas, the Carolines, and the Marshalls. A Japanese naval force seized control of those islands with speed and a purposefulness that only the myopic Western statesmen, preoccupied with Europe, had failed to foresee.

Throughout the rest of the Pacific things were placid enough during the war, except for a few gentlemanly raids against Allied shipping carried out by the sporting Count von Luckner in the *Seeadler*. Communications were somewhat disrupted everywhere by the shortage of ships, and a few nonessential industries such as pearling were abandoned for the duration. Copra and other strategic commodities continued to fetch very high prices when they managed to reach markets, and there were several local wartime booms. In Hawaii the war was remembered chiefly for its elevating effect on sugar prices and, consequently, upon the economy as a whole.

Some Pacific Islanders actually served on European battlefields; and a Maori battalion distinguished itself fighting alongside the Britons whose fathers their own fathers had fought against a few decades previously.

The victorious Allied powers lost no time in expropriating German properties in the conquered colonies, and most of the German colonists eventually returned home, penniless. The Peace Conference merely confirmed the conquests and made them a little more palatable to the then less imperialistic United States government by assigning the conquered islands (German New Guinea to Australia; German Samoa to New Zealand; Nauru to Britain, Australia, and New Zealand; and German Micronesia to Japan) as trusts or Class C mandates rather than as outright possessions, a distinction that was to prove politically meaningless until after World War II.

Thus, with little fanfare, World War I ushered in a new era in the Islands. By eliminating Germany and introducing Japan, it carried along one step further the process of dividing the area into several imperialistic spheres of interest. Even before World War I Hawaii stood apart from the other Islands by reason of its close ties with the United States; and now, with Japan in possession, the Marianas, the Carolines, and the Marshalls were separated from the rest and integrated into the Japanese Empire. At first, that integration was less evident, inasmuch as Japan joined with Britain, France, and the United States in 1921 in concluding a treaty for reciprocal guaranty of their Pacific territories. And in the following year this treaty was substantiated by agreements to maintain the status quo with respect to fortifications and naval bases in the Pacific. But with the expiration of naval limitation treaties in 1936 those assurances lost even official recognition, and long before that Japan had already sealed off her Island territories. Meanwhile Holland had retained and somewhat strengthened her de facto political control over the western half of New Guinea, which was tied in with Batavia (later named Jakarta) in every important way: administratively, commercially, and evangelistically.

In summary, during the period between the two world wars the Pacific Islands were divided into four very distinct zones: Japanese Micronesia, American Hawaii, Dutch New Guinea, and the Franco-British South Pacific.

The British islands of the last-named zone moved deeper and deeper into the economic and cultural spheres of Australia and New Zealand, with the distant United Kingdom retaining administrative control over some of them but not much more than that. Most shipping lines began and ended at Sydney or Auckland, and wherever Westerners gathered on Island verandas they usually drank Australian or New Zealand lager.

Even the French islands came increasingly within the New Zealand-Australian sphere of influence. French ships continued to ply between them and France, carrying island raw materials and French manufactures (and administrative officials), but cultural and commercial ties with Australia and New Zealand continued to grow.

Copra retained its hold over the economy of this zone despite price fluctuations that would have wiped out most other kinds of prime-production industries. And although many independent planters were forced out during the hard times, their businesses were absorbed and kept alive by the big mercantile firms.

Sugar and pearl shell, along with most other island industries, were also affected by the worldwide depression of the thirties. The smallholders were of course hardest hit; the big companies, with their more varied interests and larger resources, managed to weather the storm and, as just mentioned, to acquire the businesses of bankrupt smallholders.

During the same depression the Islanders themselves learned the hard way what it means to be "civilized." Because most of them (except for those in the heart of unexplored New Guinea) had become more or less dependent upon the Westerners' world for their incomes (earned by selling their labor or their products), they lost the wherewithal to buy the Western goods they had learned to want and need. The result among most of them was a reduction in use of manufactured imports: an altogether desirable regression from the viewpoint of nostalgic romantics, but an unhappy dilemma for the many Islanders who had nearly forgotten, for example, how to beat cloth out of bark or to illuminate their dwellings with coconut-oil lamps.

The depression might have turned back the clock even further had it not been for the discovery of immense deposits of gold in Melanesia and Fiji. The largest find, culminating the lifelong searches of a few hardy pioneer prospectors, took place in the wild unexplored mountain country of eastern New Guinea inland from the Huon Gulf. It precipitated a gold rush that is quite without parallel in modern times and led to the establishment of an industry that did more in ten years to open up the hinterland than agriculture could have accomplished in fifty. Air transport made it possible to build modern towns in country still inhabited by active headhunters, and revenues from gold provided the Australian administration with enough funds to expand its exploration and "pacification" in spite of the copra depression. In fact, gold replaced copra as the territory's richest, most revenue-producing industry. Smaller gold deposits were discovered in Bougainville, Guadalcanal, and Fiji, all of which served to increase Westerners' stake in the Islanders' world.

Meanwhile the rich phosphate deposits on Nauru, Ocean Island, and Makatea were turning out to be treasures of a different kind. The demand for fertilizer increased around the world despite the depression, and these islands were transformed into huge factories for mining and crushing phosphate rock. Because Australia and New Zealand wished to obtain all of their phosphate from these convenient and relatively cheap sources, their governments energetically supported the industry on Ocean Island and Nauru.

Lacking known sources of its own, Australia was even more urgently concerned with locating supplies of petroleum nearby and encouraged exploration throughout eastern New Guinea. This costly search had not produced tangible results before World War II, but it did lead to systematic mapping of some of the hinterland that even the gold prospectors had bypassed.

The airplane was instrumental in completing the appropriation of South Pacific real estate. In 1928 Kingford-Smith completed his epochal flight from California to Australia and set governments to planning trans-Pacific air routes. The United States already possessed a convenient chain of potential runways across the North Pacific—Hawaii, Midway, Wake, Guam, and Manila—and these eventually became bases for Pan American Airways' flights to the Far East. Also, Japan's chain of islands, the Bonins, Marianas, and Palau, afforded easy stages for regular flights from Japan to the Indies. Comparable one-flag chains did not exist south of the equator, so the United States and Britain raced to establish sovereignty over several tiny uninhabited islets that had been earlier cleaned of guano and then abandoned as useless. In 1936 the United States occupied Baker, Jarvis, and Howland Islands, while Britain occupied Canton and Enderbury. The United States also wanted the latter two for links with (eastern) Samoa, but the small American expedition that "invaded" Canton in 1938 found some Britishers already there, whereupon they shared the latter's beer and left it to Washington and London to sort out ownership. This was done in 1939, by establishment of a fifty-year Anglo-American joint administration. In 1940 Pan American began regular flights to Auckland, via Honolulu, Canton, Suva, and Noumea. Other air routes connecting Australia with New Zealand, New Guinea, and Singapore shortened Pacific distances to a degree not experienced, relatively, since large sail-equipped outrigger canoes replaced small paddled dugouts.

While these events were consolidating Westerners' economic control over the subequatorial Pacific, other influences were at work affecting more directly the lives of the Islanders there. The Western world, with some notable exceptions, was tending toward an increasing concern for the welfare of dependent peoples, and these sentiments produced some concrete results in the Islands. Missions and administrations gave more consideration to the Islanders' health, and the Rockefeller Institute supported a wide-ranging campaign against endemic diseases and against ignorance of the principles of good health. The attack on other kinds of ignorance was much less energetic; for the most part what little schooling there was remained in mission hands.

Somewhat more progress was made in connection with administration itself and was inspired by anthropology's better understanding of the cultures of "primitive" peoples. Some government administrations began to encourage ethnographic research, and the Australian administrations of Papua and the Mandated Territory (of northeastern New Guinea, the Bismarck Archipelago, and the northern Solomons) went so far as to add anthropologists to their staffs. Where such innovations took place, which was by no means everywhere, there was the effect of regulating and moderating somewhat Western impact upon the institutions of the Islanders. These developments were timely, to say the least, because some Islanders were beginning to reassert their objections to Western rule. The ensuing strikes and nativistic movements were less violent than some earlier reactions had been, but they were nonetheless embarrassing to governments that prided themselves on their enlightenment and humanity. Adding to the dilemma of the officials in such colonies were the loud protests from many Western colonials against governmental "coddling" of their native wards at the expense of their own profits and caste privileges. In British Melanesia the labor indenture system itself became a subject of heated controversy between Western entrepreneurs and missionaries, with the officials trying to maintain a central position.

Other complications were introduced by the independence movement in India, which stimulated the Indian workers in Fiji to agitate for a larger share of political and economic rights. And distant though Europe was, Nazi Germany's clamor for the return of her colonies had an unsettling effect upon some vested interests in New Guinea and Samoa. But more foreboding than any of these was the inference drawn by some Western officials from the Sino-Japanese conflict and from Japan's little known (and hence "mysterious") activities in her Micronesian outposts.

Most mainland Americans past sixty will remember the Hawaii of the twenties and thirties as a tourists' paradise, sullied only slightly by the ugly racism disclosed in the notorious Massey murder case. To the residents of Hawaii, however, it was a somewhat different story. The economy continued to be based upon sugar and pineapples and remained under the control of a small group of Western owners and managers, but the structure underlying the latter began to show signs of weakness. In the first place, a few powerful mainland U.S. firms successfully invaded the territory's commercial citadel. Also, mainland labor union leaders went to the fields and the docks and organized membership drives; they were flexing their muscles for a showdown fight against the traditional local paternalism when Japanese bombs brought on a larger conflict. Another disturbance to the status quo came by way of the military, who were strengthening Pearl Harbor and laying out airfields and encampments on a scale large enough to challenge the command of the sugar admirals and pineapple generals over territorial enterprises. Finally, as if these indignities were not enough, along came the federal government and imposed quota restrictions on exports of sugar to the mainland, to tie in with international agreements.

It was therefore no surprise when Hawaii's big business about-faced and joined in a popular agitation for statehood, apparently regarding their previous bête noire, the threat from an Oriental majority in the local electorate, as less dangerous than a federal Congress in which they had no votes with which to counter the representatives of rival sugar producers on the mainland.

The United States Congress, which at the time opposed Hawaii's request for statehood (ostensibly because of the numerous people of Japanese ancestry there), also expressed uncertainties about Japan's intentions in the Pacific by holding back on its appropriations for fortifying Guam, which was considered to be too deep inside Japanese Micronesia for effective defense.

Japan's occupation of German Micronesia seems, in retrospect, to have been anything but accidental. Japanese traders had captured the commerce of some of those islands long before October 1914, when their naval squadron seized military control from the handful of German officials there. Even during Spanish times Japanese traders had been active in the Marianas and the Carolines; throughout the years of German control they dominated commerce in both archipelagoes and actually outnumbered all other nonnative residents in the German Marianas. Their infiltration into the eastern Carolines had, however, been halted when the Germans expelled them for illegally selling arms and alcohol to the natives.

After ousting the Germans during World War I, the Japanese moved into Micronesia to stay, and the Peace Conference was confronted with the fact that Britain had, during the war, agreed secretly with Japan to confirm the latter's possession. The objections of the United States were overridden, but to sugarcoat the deal the islands were awarded to Japan as a Class C mandate rather than as an outright possession.

The terms of the mandate pledged Japan to "promote to the utmost the material and moral well-being and social progress of the inhabitants of the territory." Specifically, the terms prohibited slave trade and forced labor, arms trade, the sale to natives of intoxicating beverages, and the establishment of military and naval bases. Further, Japan was required to allow missionaries freedom to exercise their calling and was asked to present annual progress reports to the League of Nations.

Before 1914 the United States depended upon the Guam-Yap-Shanghai cable system as an alternate line of communication to the Philippines and China in case of interruptions in the Guam-Manila-Shanghai line. Before recognizing Japan's authority in Micronesia, the United States insisted upon free access to Yap. This was agreed upon in 1922, but not subsequently honored in practice by Japan.

As it turned out, few if any of Japan's promises were kept. Within a few years Japanese Micronesia was fenced off from outsiders by a wall of official obstructionism. Only a few Western missionaries were allowed to remain, and foreign commerce was totally excluded. To the rest of the world the area became "islands of mystery," with the sinister effect increased by (unsubstantiable) rumors about construction of military and naval bases there. Until 1933, when Japan withdrew from the League of Nations (as a result of the Sino-Japanese conflict), she continued to forward to Geneva annual reports of "native progress" and so forth in the area, but from then on she dropped the pretense of a mandate and held on to the islands as integral parts of her colonial empire. After that the wall closed solidly until it was penetrated by American warships and bombers in 1943.

Meanwhile, behind the wall, Japan moved swiftly to convert the islands into a source, for herself, of needed sugar, phosphate, fish, and copra. Tens of thousands of Japanese, Okinawan, and Korean colonists were brought in to produce those commodities. Nor was Japanese expansion into the Pacific limited to her own colonies. From Palau her fishing vessels moved into waters of New Guinea and the Dutch East Indies. Sampans (some of them officered by naval personnel) turned up everywhere, poaching on other nations' shell reserves and poking into their strategic harbors and channels. While this was going on, Japanese-owned and manned plantations were being developed along the northern coast of Dutch New Guinea, and Japanese trading firms were setting up branch stores and extending the markets for their goods into the sacrosanct preserves of British and French merchants. Most significantly, Japanese businesses secured proprietary interests in some New Caledonian nickel mines and took much of their output. Also, an iron mine owned and manned by Japanese was operated in New Caledonia and the ore sent to Japan. How much of all these enterprises were straight business and how much calculated preparation for aggression remains a problem for historians.

Though geographically and ethnically connected with Australian (i.e., eastern) New Guinea, the Dutch (western) half of that vast island had few links with the rest of the Pacific. Politically it was part of the Dutch East Indies, administered out of Java. Along the coasts were a few administrative and mission stations, and occasionally parties went inland prospecting for oil, but the rate of Westernization proceeded much more slowly than in the neighboring Australian territories. A few Malays penetrated the forested mountains and grassland plateaus hunting for birds of paradise, but most of the interior continued to rusticate in the Stone Age.

SOURCES

On mining see sources for chapter 13. On administrators see sources on separate colonies listed in chapters 7–14.

TRANSFORMATIONS

CHAPTER SIX

The Dimensions of Change

It can be safely assumed that from the times of their first settlements in the Islands the cultures of its many peoples were continually undergoing change: at times relatively slowly, at other times very swiftly—the former as a result of cumulative endogenous alterations (e.g., in the gene pool, in demography, in climate); the latter in response to natural cataclysms, or to contact with foreign objects or ideas (as represented, for example, by the introduction of a new food crop or a new way of initiating young men). It is essential to emphasize these changes, because of the widespread belief among Westerners that most non-Western cultures, and especially those of "primitives," had been frozen into states of immutability before Westerners had discovered and unfrozen them.

With that said, however, it must also be acknowledged that no objects or ideas previously experienced by the Islanders were as alien or as compelling as those introduced by Westerners (and in some places by Japanese). For novelty and effectiveness no new kind of spear was as lethal as firearms, no native despot's corvées as protracted as plantation indentures, no new cult as comprehensive and exclusive as Christianity, and no endemic diseases as devastating as, for example, measles and dysentery.

It has been recently urged, by a representative of the new generation of Pacific Islands historians, that previous writers, including the present one, have for various reasons (including feelings of guilt) presented erroneously one-sided pictures of the Islands' colonial history by dwelling on the effects that Westerners have had on Islanders and by ignoring the active roles some Islanders have played in the interactive process. That the contacts between Westerners and Islanders were indeed two-way cannot be denied. Island spears and clubs unquestionably ended the lives of many Westerners. Island religions did put their imprints upon many local variants of Christianity. Islanders' attitudes and work habits most certainly forced many a colonial employer to revise his management practices, or to obtain laborers from elsewhere. And so on. Moreover, some Island words (e.g., *aloha, mana,* and *tapu*) have crept into Western vocabularies (although with Western meanings). And some Westerners' perceptions of Island ways of living have shaped some Western philosophies, including notions about "noble savages" and "earthly paradise."

Nevertheless, by 1939, when this book's sociological narrative ends, the *cumulative* effects of contacts between Islanders and Westerners (and in some places Japanese) reveal the latter two to have been overwhelmingly preponderant in the cultural and political interchange.

Those changes cannot be summarized by terse generalizations or neat statistics; each island archipelago suffered a different fate. In some their native peoples were, perhaps undeliberately but in fact nearly, wiped out to make room for the foreigners. In others they were permitted to acculturate or die out gradually, so long as they did not interfere with the foreigners' affairs. In still others they were encouraged to survive for reasons that included their usefulness for the foreigners' enterprises. And in a few fortunate places they were "discovered" and then ignored, because nothing they possessed seemed worth taking.

During the four centuries between Magellan and World War II a few rare non-Islanders traveled to the Islands with the object of giving without taking, but the greater number went to exploit, to extract, or to transform. Some took territory for empire outposts and new homes; others used the soil and the climate for producing things wanted in the world's markets; others ripped up ground for minerals or harvested the seas for marine wealth; still others converted the Islanders' bodies into profitable labor or their minds into evangelized soul-stuff. With zeal and energy many foreigners applied themselves so vigorously that their various enterprises became overpowering forces in Island affairs. In some places the avarice for productive land or protective bases set the pattern. In others the preoccupation with copra (or sugar or pearl shell or minerals or souls) dominated Island life, with each enterprise exercising a peculiar influence according to its own objectives, its technology, and its organization. The following chapters will describe those foreign enterprises and will relate the effects they had upon the native peoples in the places in which they took place—up to September 3, 1939, which ushered in the most violent changes of all.

CHAPTER SEVEN
Lives

"All's well that ends well" is a cheerful creed for Pollyannas and a convenient doctrine for historians who pick the right times for their chronicles to end. In the context of Pacific Islands history, if the "end" happens to be dated A.D. 1939 that judgment can indeed be applied to the total number of Islanders alive at that time. For overall, there were probably as many of them alive in 1939 as there were at the time when Magellan crossed their ocean in 1521. Furthermore, if the terminus of the chronicle were to be dated 1989 (which is a half century beyond the scope of this particular book), it would have to be concluded that "things" (i.e., the number of Islanders) were going all *too* well, because by then the native populations of most Island societies were continuing to increase beyond what their economies could support, necessitating in some cases migrations larger and farther than any undertaken in pre-Magellan times.

In this chapter, however, the concern is not with the overall number of Islanders in 1939, or in 1989, but rather with episodes in the post-Western contact histories of certain Island peoples, episodes during which their numbers became so greatly reduced as to threaten their survival (i.e., near-fatal impacts). And although the focus of this chapter is on population numbers it should be kept in mind that the subject of the book as a whole is cultures and that a people's culture changes as the numbers of persons practicing it change. The change may not always occur pari passu, but change it inevitably will. But even if we were to focus on a people's numbers, rather than on their culture, surely it should be of some concern to historians, however committed the latter might be to the "all's well that ends well" doctrine, that the near-fatal impacts suffered by them en route to the well-ending present were distressing to them at the time and therefore deserve some mention in histories about them. Moreover, for the societies of several Pacific islands that underwent near-fatal population declines, the histories, even by 1989, had *not* ended "well."

One such society was that of the Mariana Islands, where the Western conquest of the Pacific Islands began.

Mariana Islands

Two and a half centuries before the unsuspecting natives of Polynesia welcomed Westerners to their shores, the fate of the Chamorro, the native inhabitants of the Marianas, was already sealed. Magellan led the procession in 1521 and left the familiar calling cards: to recover a stolen skiff he burned forty houses and killed seven men, thereby inaugurating what was to become a Pacific-wide formula for calculating how many native lives equaled one Western life (or boat, or garment, or hatchet, etc.). Then came Loaysa, Gaetano, and López de Legaspi, the latter proclaiming Spanish sovereignty in 1564 after having avenged the killing of one seaman by killing and wounding several Chamorro and taking some of them prisoner as well. After 1600 Guam was the official refreshment port for the Spanish galleons that sailed annually between Mexico and the Philippines, but it was not until 1668 that the Spanish made a positive effort to "civilize" the Chamorro; in that year Jesuit missionaries landed and, backed by soldiers, began mass conversions.

As noted in chapter 1, the first settlers in the Marianas reached there about five thousand years ago, having come from the southern Philippines or the Moluccas, or both, and having spoken an Austronesian tongue markedly different from those spoken by those other Austronesian speakers who migrated eastward by routes farther south (and who were to populate Polynesia and most of Micronesia). When the Jesuits began their labors in 1668 they estimated the native population to be about thirty thousand on Guam, plus another thirty thousand to forty thousand in the other islands of the archipelago. The population of 1521 may have been even larger, but there is no way of knowing how much. Beginning in 1668, however, the previous decline, if any, accelerated at a fierce pace until about 1786, when full-blooded Chamorro numbered only 1,318.

The Chamorro before Spanish contact were concentrated on the large southern islands of the archipelago, and Guam, the largest, seems to have been something of a focal point; the natives made frequent interisland voyages in their fine outrigger sailing canoes. Their principal vegetable foods were breadfruit, taro, yams, bananas, coconuts, and rice (these islands were the only ones in the Pacific where rice was grown in precontact times).

Reliable first-hand information on indigenous Chamorro social organization is meager, but has been assembled from works by several writers (e.g., Thompson 1945, 1947; Safford 1902; Spoehr 1951, 1952, 1954, 1957) to form the following rough sketch.

Households were centered around monogamous extended families; polygyny was permissible but not widespread. Communities varied in size from about 20 to 200 residents, the larger ones having been coastal. In later, Spanish, times they resided in nucleated villages and may have done so before that. Each community contained one or more clubhouses, where postpubertal males frequently congregated and where the unmarried ones usually slept. Some (or all?) of a community's older girls were assigned to its clubhouses to serve as companions for the males—a sex apprenticeship that seems to have enhanced, if anything, their value as potential wives.

Beyond this level of local organization the Chamorro communities were grouped into districts (autonomous political units) whose sizes are not documented but which doubtless varied fairly widely in this respect.

Crosscutting the territorial units just listed was one based exclusively on kinship, specifically on matrilineal kin ties. Little has been reported about such units except that they were exogamous and segmented: persons claiming descent through known forebears to a known and fairly recent common ancestress constituted a lineage, and lineages linked by purported, but not necessarily demonstrable, ties of common matrilineal descent composed clans. The accounts do not report the number of such clans, nor their scatter (i.e., did they or did they not crosscut community or political-district boundaries?), but they do indicate that genealogical seniority determined status both within a lineage and among the lineages of any clan. Moreover, it is reported (Alkire 1977:23) that the clans within each political district were also ranked one with another and that the senior man of the highest-ranking clan was the district's chief (*maga* or *maga-lahe*), but no explanation has been offered concerning how a district's separate clans came to be ranked. (In parallel situations in some other societies of Micronesia such ranking was commonly based on priority of settlement or on victory in interclan warfare.) Each district had its chief, so it is reasonable to conclude that each of a district's component communities had its headman, and that that individual was the senior member of the community's senior clan.

In addition, all members of Chamorro society belonged to one or another of its three social classes (castes): nobles *(matua),* commoners

(magatchang), or an intermediate class of "debased" nobles *(atchoat)*—
nobles (and presumably their offspring) who had forfeited their noble
class status by, for example, having offspring by a commoner. Drawing
on parallels with similarly constituted Island societies, it is reasonable to
conclude that class and lineage memberships were linked.

The nobility, it is reported, monopolized deep-sea fishing and interisland trading. Some accounts state that they also monopolized warfare,
but how that took place is difficult to imagine except in medieval-type
chivalrous tournaments. Persons of the noble class were doubtless the
ones to initiate and manage interdistrict fighting, but it would be most
unusual (for Pacific Islanders) if they alone engaged in ordinary combat.
Some reports also imply that the nobility alone "owned" land, but what
that perhaps means is that, as members of a clan's senior lineage they
held residual, but not necessarily undivided, rights to the clan's land.
(That was the situation in all but one or two Island societies constituted
like that of the Chamorro.)

Some writers also describe commoners as having paid obeisance and
tribute to persons of the noble class. That may indeed have been so, and
if so was not different from behavior in several other Island societies
where members of a clan's cadet lineages owed some respect and some
labor and some "firstfruits" or other "taxes" to their clan seniors.

Such are the bare outlines of the culture of the Chamorro, who
received the first and what was to become one of the most powerful and
devastating impacts on Pacific Islanders by Westerners. The complete
story is forever lost, for the only descriptions (hypothetical reconstruc-
tions) of their indigenous culture were made decades after it had become
almost wholly Westernized.

In the first year of their systematic "enlightenment" by Spanish missionaries, about half of the Chamorro were residing on Guam. Conversion was evidently rapid, but was handicapped from time to time by
native revolts. Facilitated by several epidemics brought on by introduced
diseases, the Spanish eventually brought matters under control by concentrating the survivors of the epidemics and the fighting on Guam. A
few Chamorro managed to elude the roundup by hiding out on nearby
Rota, but Saipan, Tinian, and the other islands in the chain were left for
a time to the seabirds. By 1786 the problem of administration had been
further simplified, since there remained so few natives to govern. That
was the low point, but the population that then began to recover in numbers was no longer pure native; there were 1,825 mixed bloods (Spanish-
native and Filipino-native) in addition to the 1,318 full-blooded Chamorro (the Filipinos had been taken to Guam as soldiers and colonists).

Some might argue that this impact had not been wholly "fatal" (i.e.,
while there's life, there's hope), but a reduction from sixty or seventy

thousand to thirteen hundred cannot be dismissed as a minor setback in a population's struggle for survival.

By 1898, when Guam was seized by the United States and the rest of the Marianas were sold by Spain to Germany, the Chamorro population had recovered to about nine thousand on Guam and about eleven hundred on Saipan, Tinian, and Rota, but it is doubtful that there was a full blood among them. Up to that time all of the Marianas had been a single cultural unit under Spanish rule; but after that Guam went one way, under the administration of the United States, while the other islands in the chain became linked with the German and later the Japanese dependency comprising the Carolines and the Marshalls (see chapter 14).

From 1668 to 1898 the Marianas were ruled by Spanish governors, at first responsible to Mexico and after 1821 to the Spanish rulers of the Philippines. The policy (if such existed) seems to have been based on determination to win over and hold the natives to Catholicism, to keep out other imperialisms, and to carry out these objectives as cheaply as possible. (At the beginning there was also the objective of maintaining a port of refreshment for Spanish vessels.) Save for a few British pirates, England never displayed much interest in the Marianas, and the whalers that visited did no great harm—there was little left to harm. A small colony of Americans and Hawaiians flourished on Saipan from 1810 to 1815, and some Japanese traders established commercial operations in the area toward the end of the nineteenth century; but otherwise Spanish influence dominated these islands until 1899 and in fact was, in 1939, still discernible in the physical features and culture of the Guamanians and their Chamorro cousins on Saipan and Rota.

The Spanish governors of Guam functioned mainly as Protectors of the Faith. There cannot have been much incentive in the work of these officials: local revenues were almost nonexistent, home-government support nominal, and the prestige of the post something less than brilliant. Actually the islands were isolated for years at a time, and the governors were reduced to supporting themselves and their staffs by levying food and labor and by engaging in some commerce. At times Guam must have more closely resembled a sleepy Hispanic-American hacienda than a Pacific colony. Meanwhile the Church was supreme: Jesuits, then Augustinians, later Capuchins, and then Jesuits again.

Two hundred and thirty years of Spanish-Catholic rule transformed the Mariana islanders so thoroughly that their Pacific Islander heritage was barely discernible. Physically they became hybrids; their language alone resisted fundamental change and even it became liberally flavored with Spanish and Filipino (Tagalog) words and syntax.

At the end of the Spanish regime the nine thousand or so Guamanians were dwelling in towns, a radical change from the indigenous patterns of residence. The center of their community life was the local church, a far cry from the clubhouse of pre-Western times! Agana, the metropolis, was laid out like a Spanish town, with cathedral and plaza and tile-roofed dwellings. Chamorro land holdings were restricted in extent, although some Spanish governors had restored to them several large tracts that had earlier been allotted to Church and Crown; and of course the decrease in population had relieved some pressure on land. In another respect, however, land tenure had changed from the pattern of pre-Western times: with the movement of and decrease in numbers of residents the old ties between people and their clan and district lands had weakened, and the nuclear family had become the principal land-owning unit. Moreover, by 1898 the government owned one-half of the land on Guam, and a few families of wealthy *mestizos* owned a large percentage of the rest.

Also, the tempo of social life had greatly changed. Instead of rhythms based on planting and harvesting, on feuding and overseas expeditions, and on the heathen rituals undoubtedly associated with clan membership and an individual's progress through life, the Guamanians faithfully maintained the Church's calendar, with daily prayers, strict Sabbaths, and frequent novenas. And horticulture continued to be the basis of their subsistence economy, although maize and sweet potatoes had superseded taro and home-grown rice. And to whatever domesticated animals they had in pre-Western times (probably chickens but not pigs) were added cattle and carabao.

In pre-Spanish times each family doubtless lived near its cultivations. In 1898 family farmsteads continued to be a feature of Chamorro life, but many families had a main dwelling in a town and resided at their farms only during the farming week. Formerly the Chamorro had been skillful fishermen and supplied most of their animal protein in this way, but little of this activity survived; the deep-sea fishing, which had been monopolized by the native nobility, died out completely, along with the skills of manufacturing large sailing canoes.

The changes wrought in other aspects of the Chamorro economy were even greater than those just listed. In pre-Spanish times all save the most privileged of chiefs produced their own goods and bartered only for luxuries. Long overseas voyages were undertaken to obtain choice materials, and (unlike the nearby Palauans) not much use seems to have been made of shell or other kinds of "money" as a medium of exchange. Also, nearly all subsistence and commercial activity was carried out by groups (families, lineages, and neighborhoods), but under Spanish influence many of these were supplemented by individuals: by wage earning and by the production of things to sell for income used in buying imported goods. This latter aspect of change had been quite gradual during the somnolent first two centuries of Spanish rule, but later on was greatly accelerated by the development of the copra industry. In the Marianas the production of copra never exceeded thirty-six hundred tons a year, but on Guam it was until World War II still the major income-producing industry, and production had remained in Chamorro hands.

Early travelers remarked on the complete nudity of the Chamorro—a far, far cry from the layers of Spanish and Filipino garments they later learned to wear. Spanish-Catholic influence also affected native family life. Judge the contrast between the unclothed native girl of pre-Western times and her Catholic descendant. As described above, the former served a lengthy premarital sex apprenticeship in a men's clubhouse; her counterpart of three and four centuries later was guarded from all contact with sex experience and knowledge, always chaperoned, never permitted to attend dances or mixed parties—a virginal and pious member of the local Daughters of Mary. In most other respects, too, the Catholic concepts of marriage and of family relationships supplanted indigenous forms; particularly did the father assume much of the authority formerly exercised by other relatives under the matrilineal system of lineage membership and inheritance.

Along with these changes there disappeared the matrilineages and clans, which had been a fundamental feature of social and religious life. The patterns of land ownership associated with clans were transformed, and the supernatural sanctions behind clan exogamy were supplanted by Catholic rules for choice of mate. The factors of corporate ownership and cooperative work, which had helped to hold lineages together, were no longer in force, and the matrilineal principle gave way to the Western emphasis upon patrilineal descent. And finally, the institution of leadership that had integrated a lineage and ranked it in relation to other lineages of a clan, and of one clan vis-à-vis another, was superseded by a wholly different kind of arrangement.

During the first years of Spanish rule the nobility are said to have welcomed the foreigners and their unusual new religion, but their attitude changed when church membership was also opened to commoners and when their own authority over life and property was curbed by the new Spanish rulers. The revolts that unsettled the Marianas during the first thirty years of determined Spanish rule were inspired and directed by the Chamorro nobility, and in the process of fighting the losing battles their own numbers were greatly reduced. Meanwhile another social class began to emerge as leaders: those Chamorro who had acquired power and influence by supporting and intermarrying with the Spanish. In time these persons were to constitute an exclusive *mestizo* class, living Spanish lives and becoming wealthy and influential landholders and officials.

Eventually the Spanish delegated much municipal authority to the upper-class *mestizos,* so that there developed a large measure of indirect rule, with the Church, of course, continuing to maintain its dominance over the lives of individuals. Some Chamorro became copra producers, even to the point of importing Caroline islanders for labor. Some also established their own stores and service enterprises, but the more energetic Japanese were on the way to dominating Guamanian commerce when Spanish rule ended. The rest of Guam's story, until 1939, will be told later on, in chapter 14.

Aneityum, New Hebrides

The second case of near-fatal impact concerns the island of Aneityum, whose native population of about thirty-five hundred before contact with Westerners was reduced to a total of fewer than five hundred during its early decades of Western contact, and whose survivors, although thoroughly and complacently Westernized, had not begun to recover their precontact numbers even by 1939.

Aneityum, the southernmost island of the New Hebrides, is almost circular and about ten miles in diameter. Ridges from its central massif (2,800 feet high) divide the island into deep, densely wooded, fertile valleys. Very little has been recorded about the indigenous Aneityumese except that they were divided into several "tribes," each with its "chief," that small-scale fighting took place between the tribes except on certain islandwide ceremonious occasions, and that their settlements were small, widely scattered and shifting, in keeping with their practice of long-fallow gardening (moving their dwellings to another site after exhausting the fertility of nearby soils).

Members of Cook's second voyage sighted the island in 1774 but the first landing on record took place in 1830, when a party of Rotumans and Tahitians was put ashore there to collect sandalwood. Their ship left a few days later, after an affray in which five of the natives and two of the visitors were killed. During the following two decades sandalwooders, mostly from Australia, maintained on the island a settlement consisting of twenty or so Westerners. Also during that period unsuccessful attempts were made by two Christian missions, one of them Marist, to establish stations there.

Then, in 1848, Presbyterian missionaries from Nova Scotia arrived to establish what was to become a permanent station, having applied strategies that were successful in fully Christianizing the Aneityumese, and in doing so nearly wiped out those they had Christianized. Unlike some other Western missionaries elsewhere, the two hardy Scots engaged in this mission were interested only in saving their charges from the certain damnation of heathenism as quickly as possible. As one of them wrote: "The Aneityumese . . . are doubtless descendants of Ham. Their traditions are very vague, and of little or no historical value. . . . Houses, canoes, ornaments and weapons show the least possible skill in their form and workmanship. . . . Their deities, like themselves, were all self-ish and malignant" (Patterson 1882:25–32). And to demonstrate their contempt for those deities, and indirectly for the Aneityumese themselves, the missionaries used the large block of stone that represented, or contained, a deity as a doorstop for a mission building.

In pre-Western times the Pacific Islands harbored several diseases that shortened human lives and rendered them painful: malaria throughout Melanesia (except in New Caledonia); filariasis in several islands of Polynesia; and leprosy, yaws, and consumptive illnesses nearly everywhere. Also, in several places natural calamities such as hurricanes and tidal waves served to kill many people prematurely. In addition, the members of many native societies shortened their own lives by such practices as infanticide (for various reasons), widow strangling, human sacrifice, and cannibalism; and most peoples did the same also by intermittent warfare. Moreover, many Island peoples also engaged in practices that served to reduce the natural number of births by postpartum sex taboos (e.g., by postponing coitus until an infant had been completely weaned). In consequence of all these factors, when Europeans first "discovered" them it seems that most Island peoples had reached a point of stability in their numbers, with births and deaths about equal.

In 1854 the two Presbyterian missionaries on Aneityum carried out a rough census and put the Island's population at about thirty-five hundred. How much larger it may have been before the two decades of sandalwooding cannot now be reconstructed, but nothing experienced during those decades could have prepared the Aneityumese for the calamities that were to befall them during the subsequent, missionary, era—calamities in the form of new acute infectious diseases, which some victims survived, thereby acquiring immunities for shorter or longer periods, but that proved swiftly fateful to many others.

The most epidemic of such diseases to be introduced into Aneityum (and many other Islands) during this era were of two types: those (such as measles and influenza) whose infective agents are contained in droplets of saliva and that are spread through coughs and sneezes (and through loud weeping!), and those (such as dysentery) in which the infective agents are spread through the contamination of food and water by bacteria. Spread of the first type requires close and fairly prolonged contact between persons and is promoted by high humidity. Spread of the second type can also be promoted by, for example, flies and contaminated objects.

Despite their island's seasonally high humidity the pre-Western (specifically, pre-missionary) Aneityumese were fairly well safeguarded against droplet-spread diseases. Some of them had doubtless become infected through their close contacts with Westerners at coastal settlements and on ships, but the small, scattered, and relatively isolated hamlets of most of them evidently impeded a wider spread of such diseases. The well-intentioned efforts of the Presbyterian missionaries changed all that. Both of the island's mission stations contained a large church and school; about five hundred natives congregated in each of the former for Sunday services, and from seventy to a hundred in the latter for training to become teachers. In addition the mission established throughout the rest of the island another fifty-four schools along with several chapels, where most other islanders spent hours each day in close interpersonal contact and which teachers from the main stations frequently visited. In other words, the Aneityumese became for the first time joined together into a unified network, a most effective mechanism for communicating the Word of God—and infectious diseases.

In both respects the mechanism worked: by the end of 1860 the entire population had become, nominally, Christian; and in January 1861 measles were introduced onto the island by the crew of a sandalwood schooner and within three to four months one-third of the population had died of it. After that epidemic the survivors became even more assiduous in attending church services and school and thereby became especially vulnerable to an 1866 epidemic of diptheria, which killed about three hundred of them, and to an 1877 epidemic of whooping cough, which killed another one hundred. Subsequent epidemics, mostly of tuberculosis (another droplet-based disease), were so effective that by the turn of the century the population numbered less than five hundred. Such was one consequence of the spread of the Word of the Christian God.

"Slavers in Paradise"

The third case of near-fatal impact concerns not a single island or archipelago but a number of them that may be classed together on account of their inclusion in a single enterprise—the "recruitment" of Islanders to work in Peru, mainly on plantations. (The title of this section and most of the information in it are taken from H. E. Maude's remarkable study published in 1981.) The many inhumanities suffered by the victims of that enterprise require descriptive skills beyond those I possess (and more space than this book will permit); therefore the following résumé consists mainly of statistics, leaving the reader to visualize the actual scenes.

The economy of Peru (politically independent since 1824) depended heavily upon its agricultural exports (e.g., sugar, cotton, olives, grapes, grains), which were grown on large coastal plantations initially worked by African slaves. After that form of slavery was abolished (in 1854) Chinese laborers were imported to fill the gap, but after two years that also was officially curtailed because of its notorious barbarities. But pressure from politically influential planters forced the government to reinstate overseas recruitment, this time under the euphemism of "voluntary immigration," which "welcomed" Pacific Islander "immigrants" as well as Chinese.

Thereafter, between June 1862 and August 1863 (when diplomatic pressures, mainly from France, succeeded in bringing a stop to the practice) some thirty-three ships plied between Callao and islands in the southeastern and central Pacific recruiting "immigrants" (mostly ablebodied males, plus the wives and children of some of them). In the course of this endeavor some 3,634 Islanders were recruited at their home islands. (This number does not include those who were killed resisting "recruitment.") Of the 3,634, 164 escaped or were freed before leaving Polynesia, and 3,125 actually reached Peru; the other 345 died en route (mainly from illnesses caused or aggravated by below-deck confinement, near-starvation rations, and physical brutality). Of those reaching Peru, 1,009 did so subsequent to the official stoppage of the practice and were held on board their vessels pending "repatriation." Many of the 2,116 who had actually landed died shortly thereafter; the others were sold (or in the legal fiction invented for the transaction, their recruitment "contracts" were sold) to prospective employers. The contracts, which were represented as having been voluntarily signed by the (mostly illiterate) recruits, obliged them to work specific numbers of years at set rates of pay, after which they were to be freed to remain in Peru or return home (at their own expense).

Let us interrupt this narrative with a few words about the methods of recruitment. In about 940 cases recruiting was reportedly done without deceit: the recruits "signed" the contracts voluntarily (i.e., made a cross or some similar mark in lieu of signature) after having been given a general but doubtless rosy explanation of their contents. Another 1,111 were persuaded to sign by means of flagrant misrepresentations (e.g., concerning place and type of work, wages, duration of contract). And at least 1,150 were forcibly kidnapped—by luring them aboard ship with gifts, confining them and setting out to sea; or by outright capture, by force of arms, ashore (often accompanied by the killing or wounding of resisters). As for the other 434 recruits still unaccounted for, the compiler of these grim statistics was unable to discover exactly how they were persuaded or forced to sign on.

When word of the enterprise, and especially of its methods of recruiting, reached the French authorities in Tahiti, they outlawed it within their protectorate and captured the recruiting vessels that happened to fall into their hands. Because no islands under direct British protection were involved in the enterprise, Her Majesty's naval vessels in the Pacific chose not to intervene.

Meanwhile, back in Peru, several residents became scandalized by the whole affair: by sight of the physical condition and helplessness of the recruits and their subsequent treatment ashore, and by news from Tahiti concerning the methods of recruitment. Chief among those residents were the French Chargé d'Affaires and the proprietor of a liberal-minded newspaper; the former especially mounted a campaign that moved Paris to persuade the Peruvian government not only to free the Island "immigrants" from their contractual bondage but to finance and administer their repatriation.

As it turned out, the only Islanders that were embarked for the journey home were the 1,009 who had just arrived and not landed, plus 207 out of the 2,116 who had landed earlier and been sold. (Of the remaining 1,909 recruits who had landed, 1,840 are reported to have died within a year or two of landing.)

For the 1,216 homeward-bound Islanders the journey must have begun with elation, which for most of them was not to last. For 1,030 of them died during their repatriation, and of the 186 who survived their island landings, only a few were landed at their *own* islands. To add another statistic to this chronicle of Western greed and Islander death: in addition to the 3,215 Islanders *known* to have died as a direct consequence of the enterprise, another 3,000 or so nonrecruited Islanders are thought to have died as a result of the smallpox and dysentery passed on to them by the returned recruitees. And for a final, ironical twist: for the Peruvian planters, who had started the whole enterprise, it was also a total, albeit only financial, loss; even those few Islanders who managed to reach their purchasers' plantations proved to be too ill or otherwise unadaptable for plantation work.

The statistics so far given relate to the Peruvian recruiting enterprise as a whole; how individual Island peoples were affected by it is revealed in another set of numbers calculated by H. E. Maude (the superb chronicler of this and several other chapters in Pacific Islands history).

By Maude's calculations the heaviest numerical impact of the Peruvian recruiting was suffered by the island of Nukulaelae (of the Ellice archipelago, now named Tuvalu), from whose total population of about 315 were recruited (in this case kidnapped) 250, none of whom ever returned to Nukulaelae—nor as far as I can discover to any other Pacific Island.

Except for Niue, where only 109 persons were recruited (in this case also, kidnapped) out of a total population of 5,021, even the least affected of the recruited islands (Puka Puka) lost one-quarter of its total population. But even those figures do not tell the whole story of the losses: in most cases the recruits were the most able-bodied males and in some cases able-bodied premenopausal females. (In other words, most of a people's productive and reproductive members.) And when calculating the full numerical consequences of this calamitous episode it is necessary to make another subtraction—of the numbers of nonrecruitees who died as a result of the diseases brought back by the repatriates.

As a conciliatory nod to historians of the "all's well that ends well" school, it must be acknowledged that on several of the islands depleted by this scourge, it was not long before their numbers recovered and in some cases increased, but in most such cases, not by means of the same indigenous genes. In fact, in the absence of local males, natives from other islands, along with some ever-helpful Westerners (beachcombers, traders, or seamen), were prompt to substitute for the absent or dead recruitees.

So much for numbers. It would be impractical in the present book to attempt a full assessment of the long-term *cultural* consequences of the 1862–1864 Peruvian episode, but one brief report will serve to suggest their magnitude. The island in question is Rapanui, renamed Easter by its Western discoverers.

Rapanui, the easternmost outpost of Polynesia, consists of some sixty square miles of rolling and generally arid terrain. It was first settled in about A.D. 400–500, probably from the Marquesas or the Gambier islands, or both. Some local traditions suggest one or two subsequent immigrations (of other Polynesians), but for the remainder of their pre-Western history the Rapanuians remained isolated from the rest of Polynesia, and also from everywhere else. (Attempts by some writers, notably Thor Heyerdahl, to derive some traits of Rapanui culture from that of Peru have received little scholarly support.)

Despite the island's aridity it supported a relatively large population, with ample supplies of sweet potatoes, yams, bananas, and so forth. The only domesticated animals to survive the voyage(s) to the island were chickens, which became a focus of domestic husbandry. Another noteworthy feature of the island's culture was its numerous stone images, some of them huge; there is, however, nothing mysterious about them: in style they resemble religious images found elsewhere in eastern Polynesia. They are sculpted out of stone because of the island's lack of large trees; and some of them are large, made possible by the softness of much of the local stone.

From the little that is known about the society's pre-Western social institutions, they resembled those of other eastern Polynesian societies in most of their basic aspects. That is to say, although the people were divided into several distinct, and chronically feuding, political units, they all claimed descent from a single ancestor, the legendary chief of the island's original settlers.

Rapanui was "discovered" by the Dutchman Roggeveen on Easter Day of 1772 (whence its Western name) and subsequently visited by Cook and La Pérouse, but none of these nor any later visitors left detailed descriptions of the traditional culture while it survived—which it seems to have done until 1863–1864, when it was shattered by a population decline of nearly 60 percent, as a result of the Peruvian recruiting episode. (From an 1862 population estimated to have been 4,126, 1,407 persons were taken to Peru, and a further 1,000 died during the epidemic of smallpox brought to the island by the fifteen recruitees repatriated in 1864.) According to the principal authority, Alfred Métraux: "This catastrophe, disrupting the traditional mode of living, created a state of anarchy and confusion. . . . When the missionaries arrived in 1864, they were surprised to meet such complete ignorance of the past, such rudimentary forms of [indigenous] religion, and such disintegration of social organization. They found only the ruins of a civilization" (Métraux 1937:41). Moreover, it was a civilization that never recovered and from whose ruins there eventually emerged a way of life as hybrid as the people that lived it.

SOURCES

Guam: Safford 1902; Spoehr 1951, 1952, 1954, 1957, 1978; Thompson 1947; Tung 1984; Valle 1979.
Aneityum: McArthur 1968, 1974, 1978, 1981; McArthur and Yaxley 1968.
Peruvian slavers: McCall 1976; Maude 1981; Métraux 1937.

CHAPTER EIGHT

Land

Another demonstrably effective way to transform a nonindustrialized people's culture is to take away their land. Especially in the case of most Pacific Islanders, land was a fundament of their social groupings, a measure of their status and self-esteem, and an ingredient of their religious lives. If a single criterion were to be used to test the survival potential of any Island culture it would be: To what extent have its people retained ownership of their land?

No Pacific archipelagoes have altogether escaped the foreigners' quest for land, and in some cases their greed for it was the most characteristic and devastating aspect of culture contact.

Figures relating to how much land the Pacific Islanders had "lost" by 1939 are clouded with semantic uncertainties. Quite apart from the question of Who is a native? (i.e., in terms of genetic composition and cultural commitment), there were differences, some of them very wide, among the region's colonial polities concerning categories of ownership and the inclusion, if any, of native owners in them. In most of those polities there were at least three such categories of land: that "legally" owned by nonnative individuals and corporations, through purchase and registration; that owned by the colonial government; and that left, for want of something better, in the hands of the natives, whether individuals, clans, "tribes," "chiefs," or some other putative entity.

Most government-owned land had been acquired in one or another of three ways. Some had been obtained by seizure (always of course for a good cause!). Other parcels of it had been acquired through application of Western laws (e.g., whereas in most coastal Islander societies lagoon waters and reefs had been owned by adjacent clans, most colonial regimes held them to be state-owned). And some, perhaps most, of government-owned land had been appropriated by defining it to be "unowned"—either after the demise of an individual or family believed to have been its sole owner, or if it appeared at the time to be unused. The assumptions behind such appropriations were in both these cases mostly incorrect: in most Island societies no person died without heirs of some kind; and except perhaps for the most extensive swamps and alpine barrens nearly all land was owned by someone, whether or not it was in continuous use. (For example, in most places the techniques of long-fallow horticulture required five to ten times the area actually occupied by a garden at any one time.) Moreover, at the times when many appropriations were carried out on the basis of the land having been "unused wasteland," the local native populations were much smaller than they had once been and were to become again.

With respect to lands left in the limbo of "native ownership," the colonial administrations followed one or more of several practices. In some colonies efforts were made to survey and register plots in the names of their current owners—whether in the names of persons who *claimed* ownership or of persons whom the officials thought *ought* to own them (such as "chiefs" or "tribes"), even if the people in question did not recognize such entitlements. Moreover, in many such cases, the registration of a parcel carried with it the requirement that its future ownership devolve according to Western laws of inheritance (e.g., with equal portions going to each offspring). In most of the colonies where it was attempted, land registration proved to be physically impossible—a fortunate outcome, because where it succeeded it either encouraged the registered owners to sell out to nonnatives, or it resulted in paralyzing fractionalization and kin conflict. (It should be added that some colonial regimes took measures to discourage or prohibit natives from selling their land to nonnatives, in many cases, however, only after much of it had already been sold.)

The lands held by colonial governments, however acquired, were used by some regimes to benefit their native subjects (as, for example, in Tonga and in the Gilbert and Ellice crown colony); others were used to stimulate economic development (as, for example, in northeastern New Guinea); still others to encourage and assist nonnative colonists (as, for example, in New Caledonia and the Japanese Mandate Territory, where the natives were confined within smaller and smaller reserves).

Other arrangements for the retention or disposal of what had once been entirely native-owned lands will be described in later chapters, but the foregoing discussion will serve to indicate the semantic difficulties involved in trying to generalize about how much of their lands the Islanders had "lost." Suffice it to say, however, that their losses ranged from very small (as in Tonga, the Gilbert and Ellice crown colony, and Dutch New Guinea) to very large (as in New Caledonia, where the native reserves constituted only 19 percent of the island's total area, but where, it should be added, some native individuals also owned registered plots outside the reserves). The remainder of this chapter will be devoted to an account of the colonial experience in New Zealand, where the alienation of native-owned land was perhaps the most important issue in the relations between the indigenous peoples and Western colonists.

New Zealand

In 1939 New Zealand made plans to celebrate the centennial of the Treaty of Waitangi, commemorating the annexation of the archipelago by the British Crown. One and one-half million non-Polynesian New Zealanders congratulated themselves on their progress: fine cities; keen and athletic citizens; excellent wool, butter, cheese, and lamb; a brave new social revolution designed to wipe out poverty and privilege; and a surge of gratifying loyalty to empire at the beginning of a great brother-binding war.

Ninety-five thousand Polynesian Maori (including about twenty-eight thousand mixed bloods) were not so certain they had cause to celebrate. It is true that in 1939 the Maori were beginning to regain something of their former numbers, but only after a century of decline during which the count dropped so low (to forty thousand, in 1900) that one contemporary observed: "The Maoris are dying out, and nothing can save them. Our plain duty, as good compassionate colonists, is to smooth down their dying pillow. Then history will have nothing to reproach us with" (quoted in Sullivan 1940:28).

Looking about them in 1939, the Maori saw their own, specifically *Maori*-owned lands reduced to a sixteenth of the original area, their share in the dominion's wealth exceedingly limited, and their once-proud status subordinate in the dominion's Western-dominated class system. There were, however, a few bright rays on their horizon: they still retained enough of their able leaders, their robust physiques, and their keen minds to effect something of a comeback, provided, of course, the Westerners permitted and encouraged it.

Two wholly different courses have been followed by scholars in reconstructing the history of New Zealand before Western contact; one relies heavily upon native oral traditions, the other on archaeological research.

According to the *traditional* reconstruction, a great fleet of canoes left eastern Polynesia six centuries ago and sailed southwest, their hulls filled with men, women, and children and all their possessions, escaping from crowded islands and continual wars. For many weeks these Polynesian *Mayflower*s voyaged farther and farther out of the latitudes of warmth and usually calm seas. Finally, gaunt with starvation and nearly dead from exposure to the colder temperatures, those who survived beached their canoes on the shores of New Zealand's North Island and set about to colonize it.

During recent decades archaeologists have had to refute the historicity of the Great Fleet tradition. Numerous excavated sites, some eight or nine hundred years old, have revealed the existence of a material culture much like those of tropical Polynesia in many respects, but unlike any others in its focus on hunting (especially of the famous *moa,* a giant, uniquely New Zealand ostrichlike bird, which the Maori hunted to near-extinction within a few centuries of their arrival). In terms of the Great Fleet tradition the *moa* hunters were descendants of Polynesians (and perhaps some Melanesians) who had arrived there long before the Great Fleet, and who were eventually absorbed by the more recent, and technologically superior, Great Fleeters. On archaeological grounds, however, the evidence supports the theory that the way of life found on New Zealand by Westerners, the so-called classic Maori form of culture, was only the evolutionary development of the earlier *moa* hunter or archaic phase.

However, tradition does not need to be true to exercise a commanding influence over a people's concepts, and the Great Fleet tradition will probably continue to provide the Maori with a grand and dramatic explanation of their beginnings.

In any event, there is no question that the immediate source of Maori culture, including the Maori language, was eastern Polynesia. Hence, the first huge task of the earliest immigrants was to adapt their tropical culture to the temperate climate and physical environment of their new home.

The fowl and pigs they probably loaded in their canoes either did not endure the voyage or the new conditions ashore; only their dogs survived, to become, or remain, a valued food. Bananas, breadfruit, and coconut would not thrive in the colder climate, so the immigrants had to depend upon their taro and sweet potatoes, supplemented with the abundant ferns and berries they found in their new homes. Cloth *(tapa)* beaten out of tropical mulberry bark was supplanted by cloaks woven out of New Zealand flax; huge dug-out canoes carved from local timber replaced the plank-built double-hulled canoes that had transported them from their earlier homelands; and their former well-ventilated tropical dwellings gave way to closed huts to keep out the unaccustomed cold.

On the other hand, in the new homeland Maori social culture retained most of its former features while developing some distinctively new ones. Kinship remained the fundamental link among people and between units of people and land. Each household was occupied by a family, and each community (usually housed in a nucleated village) by a clan (a group of families interrelated by ties of common ambilineal descent [i.e., traced either through males or females, but more commonly males]). Clans occupying adjoining territories were usually linked together into political units ("tribes"). According to their official (but not necessarily histori-cally accurate) genealogies, which were carefully and proudly committed to memory, all tribal mates traced descent from some occupant of one of the Great Fleet canoes. And because most marriages took place within the tribe or in many cases the same clan, these larger units were excep-tionally cohesive and enduring.

Chiefly rank followed the eastern Polynesian principle down the sen-ior, and usually the male, line; but in New Zealand chiefs were not as powerful in authority, nor as religiously sacred, as they were in, for example, Tahiti or Hawaii. A Maori chief was indeed looked up to as the most respected of kinsmen, but he tended to give advice rather than orders, and there was a large measure of democracy, by council. Because the chief was usually a tribe's highest-ranking kinsman, the ownership of tribal lands was symbolically vested in him, but not to dispose of at will. Maori chiefs had their relatively larger measure of divinitylike quality, like chiefs in most other Polynesian societies, but there were fewer large-scale tribal religious ceremonies over which they were required, and priv-ileged, to preside.

Mutual assistance within and among neighboring households was the basis of economic security, and many goods were shared. Thus there was no dire poverty, nor was there any need or opportunity for individuals to accumulate large amounts of valued goods; even chiefs subsisted much as did their lower-ranking kinsmen, except when they were able to capture and enslave enemies in war.

Westerners had ample proof of Maori skill and ferocity in warfare. Intertribal feuding was pervasive, and some instances of it were carried out like sporting events, with mutually agreed-on times for fighting and for recouping, and with punctilios in tactics observed even between the bitterest of enemies. So prevalent was warfare that many villages were permanently located with a view to defense and were skillfully fortified. Quarrels over land and women, along with desire for revenge for real or imagined wrongs, kept the Maori perennially warlike and helped to keep their warriors aggressive and physically fit.

Such were the Maori when Captain Cook visited New Zealand in 1769: a strong, vigorous, independent-minded people, who respected no one but kinsmen and who owed no loyalty to aggregations larger than the tribe. Being forthright, most Maori struck back when the early Western visitors killed some of their fellows, thereby acquiring reputations for savagery. In time, however, some of them began to traffic with the Westerners who flocked to their shores for flax and lumber and for recuperation from the hardships of whaling. It did not take long for the Maori to observe that Western blankets were warmer than native cloaks of flax, that metal knives and axes stayed sharper than stone adzes, and, most important, that firearms were more deadly than clubs and spears. The immediate consequence of this form of enlightenment was to transform intertribal fighting from a sometimes deadly but usually limited mode of feuding into exterminating scourges. Also during that early period of contact, a Maori chief traveled to England and returned home intent on becoming a superchief over a supertribe, like the English monarch he had come to admire. This decision added yeast to the ferment, ending up in an intensification of native warfare that devastated Maoriland for two decades, shifting many tribes, wiping out some of them, and killing altogether nearly sixty thousand Maori.

Western traders abetted this slaughter by bartering firearms for flax and food. Deserters from ships and escapees from the New South Wales penal colony even aligned themselves with one or another tribe, and it was a poor chief indeed who could not count at least one Western aide. Add large numbers of visiting whalers to the brew, and it is not difficult to deduce what aspects of Western civilization (including grog and syphilis) the Maori had opportunities to acquire. Meanwhile, they also began to lose their land, but that did not seem very serious at first.

New Zealand's North and South islands together contain over sixty-six million acres, and all of it, from fishing grounds to mountain peaks, was identified with some tribe or other. It is true that only a portion of this vast area was in actual economic use by the Maori, but that did not lessen the value of the whole for purposes as culturally valid for the Maori as are our "tribal" lands (our parks and reserves) for us. For the Maori all the land was "tribal," and inalienable except by tribal consent. The earliest Western settlers learned how stubborn were the natives' full-tribal councils in parting with their land, so they worked directly upon the cupidity of individual chiefs and succeeded in bribing some of them to "sell" tribal territory. Also, during the period of heightened native warfare it became a simple matter for Westerners to "purchase" land from a tribe that had just defeated its true owners. (By native custom, defeat in warfare seldom resulted in loss of land.)

It was during this period of upheaval that missionaries appeared on the scene: first the Anglican-related Church Missionary Society in 1814, then the Catholics, then the Wesleyans. The earliest of them were good and energetic men; that in itself and the contrast they presented with their lay countrymen won Maori respect and converts for them. Contributing, too, was the circumstance that the Maori pantheon was flexible enough to admit new deities, and the Jehovah of the musket-wielding Westerners obviously deserved an important niche. Between 1830 and 1840 Christianity spread with quite amazing speed; it is estimated that half of the remaining Maori were converted during those years to at least its theogonies and rituals. Christianity eventually was to dilute some phases of Maori culture (e.g., by nullifying the supernatural sanctions of chiefly authority and economic routine), but its effects were not so immediate as some other alien influences, which were visibly so destructive as to compel the British government to step in.

There was a very evident need for some kind of authority, and this was recognized by officials in the nearby colony of New South Wales. Meanwhile, in New Zealand, missionaries, honest settlers, and the Maori themselves suffered alike from the acts of many of the Western traders, who went to any extreme to load their ships with flax and spars. At that time also an influential group of British capitalists organized the New Zealand Association to undertake an ambitious colonizing venture, and these men lobbied in Parliament for the establishment of responsible government in the land, for without that their schemes could not materialize.

Despite these pressures the Colonial Ministry compromised its policy against annexations only to the extent of sending out a Resident, with no authority beyond his moral suasion. About all that wretched fellow accomplished was to solidify the Western settlers against him, to move the Maori leaders to assert a pathetic "Declaration of Independence," and to draw more attention to the need for stable government. In the meantime more Westerners moved in and the turmoil increased.

The precipitant came from an entirely different source. A plausible French adventurer, the Baron de Thierry, self-proclaimed "King of Nukahiva, and Sovereign Prince of New Zealand," succeeded in securing official French backing for a colonial enterprise in his princedom. This action so greatly alarmed the British New Zealand Association that its directors took matters into their own hands and proceeded to dispatch their own expedition while the French party was still imbibing farewell toasts. With its hand thus forced the British Government sent out an agent to negotiate with the Maori for annexation to the Crown, despite the howls of protest from France and the United States. (Washington's ruffled feelings were hardly smoothed by the realization that the American consul in New Zealand, who happened to be a British subject, exerted all his influence to secure New Zealand for his native rather than for his official fatherland.)

The annexation Treaty of Waitangi of 1840 turned out to be a document of noble intent but impossible application. It confirmed the Maori in possession of their lands and granted them " . . . all rights and privileges of British subjects"; but it did not take long for the lawyers, acting on behalf of the British colonists, to interpret these guarantees out of existence. For a few years, however, the unsuspecting Maori were too busy acquiring the goods of the new civilization to realize their true predicament.

Instead of tribe fighting tribe, they now all set about with zest to produce and sell and buy. Soon they were supplying all the food consumed in the colonial settlements and even exporting large quantities of wheat and flax. The old subsistence economy gave way in many places to dependence upon money and outside markets (going even further than Christianity in weakening stability and tribal cohesion). But everything went well when demand was strong and prices high, and it took an economic depression to convince alert Maori leaders about their people's vulnerability.

The Waitangi Treaty guaranteed political equity to the Maori, but they were not allowed to vote despite the fact that most of the colony's revenue derived from direct and indirect taxes on Maori property and enterprises. No laws were promulgated for them, as their special circumstances required; instead, they were penalized in terms of English law when colonials objected to their practices. It was not Maori ignorance and indifference that led to their shabby treatment. There developed in due course a higher percentage of (English) literacy among them than among the colonials, and many of the Maori leaders became sophisticated and articulate spokesmen.

Land was the factor that finally moved them to self-defense. Westerners had flocked to New Zealand by the tens of thousands, and nearly all of them demanded land, for farming and grazing, and their elected representatives saw to it that Maori interests did not interfere. The colonial legislature continued, piously, to express support for the Maori principle that held land to be inalienable except by full tribal consent, but at the same time adopted sophistries that enabled individual Maori to sell land to the Crown, and thence to colonists.

These practices led many disillusioned and angry Maori to confederate into a "kingdom" (an entirely novel institution) for better defense of their persons and land. As a result, in 1860, when the government used troops to enforce an unpopular land sale, there was organized reaction. The bloody Maori Wars that these events precipitated lasted for ten years. The fighting set tribe against tribe, caused enormous casualties among both Maori and colonists, nearly bankrupted the young colony, and reduced the Maori to a condition bordering on abject misery. Three million acres of their best lands were confiscated, and their survivors were pushed back into unwanted corners or allowed to drift along in town slums.

With the Maori thus out of the way, the colonists moved ahead vigorously to build the hardy little dominion the world came to admire. Now and then officials paused long enough to call attention to the picturesque qualities of Maori life that had survived or to commiserate with the rapidly declining minority, but for many years nothing substantial was done by the colonists to stay that decline.

The Maori cultural revival that the New Zealanders of colonial descent talked about in 1939 with such pride came about as a result of *Maori* effort. For decades Maori leaders had worked to revive their people's pride in their heritage and to raise their status economically and politically. It was no mean job.

The wars of the 1860s, which so reduced their numbers and land holdings, had also driven many of them into urban pauperism or to marginal rural subsistence, both situations devoid of the *esprit* of former times. The task of the Maori leaders was to resettle their people on the land and persuade them to work into the dominant pastoral and agricultural economy as independent producers, rather than as dependent laborers. At the same time, Maori interests in their old crafts were revived to slow down the Westernization continually going on.

There were many disagreements, among both Maori and colonials, over the goals of the Maori revival. Some voices in both camps wished to shape the Maori into a strong and self-conscious minority of loyal dominion citizens, equal in cultural and economic and political status to their colonial compatriots, but retentive of their Maori identity. Others wished to see both Maori and colonials sharing in a homogeneous culture and pointed to a growing mixed-blooded population as support for their aims and evidence of their inevitability. In the end, however, it was clear to both sides in that pre-World War II debate that whatever identity the Maori might retain would depend upon their ability to hold onto their remaining lands, for without those they would be *Maori* only in shape of head and color of skin.

SOURCES

Bellwood 1979; Crocombe (ed.) 1971; Kawharu 1971; Lundsgaarde 1974; Mol 1964; Sinclair 1980; Sullivan 1940.

CHAPTER NINE

Souls

Whatever else, such as patriotism or self-salvation, may have induced Western missionaries to labor in the Islands, their official, and probably in most cases personal, objective was to rescue native souls, either from the hell or limbo of heathenism or from the somewhat cooler purgatories of rival Christian denominations. The assumption behind all such labor was that Islanders did indeed possess "souls," with which Islanders in general would have agreed.

In every Pacific Island society so far studied most of its members believed each living human to be made up of a body and a separate, typically less palpable, entity, or soul—say, an invisible vapor in the chest, or a hard lump in the abdomen, or a substance in the blood or breath. (Some Island religions postulated two or more souls per body, each with different functions.) Almost as widespread was the belief that a person's soul(s) left his or her body: temporarily, during sleep (hence dreams) or illness, and permanently, when the body expired. Moreover, it was believed by many peoples that some persons (sorcerers and other magicians) could will their own soul to exit their bodies on missions of various kinds, including capturing or harming another soul that was either inside or outside its own body at the time. Much less consensus prevailed concerning the origin of souls: some peoples expressed total ignorance about the matter, others derived them from ancestors, still others attributed their creation to nonhuman spirits, and so forth. Beliefs about the fates

of souls after death varied even more widely: from expressions of ignorance (and unconcern), to elaborate theories involving Final Judgments
and both painful and paradisiacal Afterworlds. Only a few Island religions held that a soul expired with the body; in most of the others it survived for a time as a ghost or as an ancestral spirit—the former more typically malevolent, the latter more typically benevolent.

In addition to the souls of living and deceased humans, Islanders peopled their respective cosmoses with myriad kinds of nonhuman and
never-human spirits: spirits of individual animals and plants and of
whole animal and plant species; spirits of specific and general features of
landscapes and seascapes; spirits of winds and rain, of sun, moon, and
stars; of fishing, hunting, gardening, and so forth, and of specific social
units (e.g., clans, political units, etc.). No two of their hundreds of cosmoses were exactly the same, although some regional patterning among
them did prevail. For example, most of the Polynesian-speaking peoples
included societywide pantheons of relatively powerful deities, along with
the numerous lesser spirits of particular locales; to many New Guinean
peoples the hosts of spirits were as localized and nonhierarchic as the
peoples themselves. At this point, however, a caveat is called for. If the
above résumé has created the impression that the beliefs just listed constituted more or less official *systems* of religious dogma (i.e., cosmologies
known to and accepted by all mature members of this or that society),
then the impression must be promptly erased. In most Island societies,
whatever consensus there was in matters of religious belief was contained
within the boundaries of a single clan or community or group of politically unified communities. And even within those narrow boundaries
there usually were numbers of persons who knew or professed only *some*
of the beliefs expounded ex cathedra by the local sages or religious specialists. In all too many cases it has been the inquiring anthropologist,
and not even the local sages, who has assembled and systematized the
religious beliefs held by one or another of a society's individual members.

Another kind of unwarranted generalizing concerns the *mana* concept.
Several decades ago a missionary-scholar, R. H. Codrington, attributed
to the natives of the southeastern Solomons a belief in a type of pervasive
nonhuman spiritlike power or force, called by them *mana,* which was in
addition to the numerous individualized spirits in their cosmos. Subsequently, lexical cognates of the word *mana* were identified in the vocabularies of other Islanders, especially of Polynesia, and most of these
received translations similar to that given by Codrington (which *may* or
may not have been true), without further inquiry into their precise local
meanings. (In fact, the usage by anthropologists and other writers of the
word *mana* has become as worldwide, and as vague, as the word *democracy.*)

Less obscurity surrounds our understanding of the Islanders' religious practices, which were nearly everywhere much alike, although peoples differed considerably in the frequency with which the various types and subtypes were performed. Western scholars divide them into three major types: magic, petition, and divination. (Needless to say, few if any Islanders would have categorized them in this way.)

Magic comprises practices aimed at controlling events by manipulating spirits and spiritlike forces (e.g., by verbal formulas, by placing some "harmful" substance in a victim's food, by curing a lame leg with a potion containing a fast-moving insect, by harming an enemy by destroying some of his hair, etc.). Petition consists of such actions as prayers and offerings made to a spirit in exchange for the latter's aid. And divination seeks to communicate with spirits to reconstruct past events or to foretell future ones, by means, for example, of omens and other signs, or by communication through a medium (a specialist possessed by a spirit). In most Island societies nearly every adult engaged in some of these practices. In addition, every society contained a few individuals who specialized in one or another of them (e.g., a community's principal crop-growing magician or most credible diviner, or a clan's official priest). However, in most Island societies such specialists worked only part-time at their crafts; in only a few of the more politically unified and socially stratified societies were there any full-time religious specialists, and those were mainly petitioners, or priests (who, typically, performed magic and divination as well).

Much insight into the complexities and varieties of Island religions has been provided by some of the Western missionaries themselves, who concluded, quite correctly, that it was essential to comprehend those religions in order to transform them. But to most of the early missionaries in the Islands the religious beliefs and practices of their charges were senseless heathenish abominations, unworthy of scrutiny or consideration and requiring wholesale uprooting.

In any case, and by whatever means, by the year 1939 about 750,000 Islanders had been at least partly converted from fully heathen into one or another denominational variant of Christian. Spanish priests had initiated this enterprise in the sixteenth century but their field was limited to the Marianas, with a few sorties, largely unsuccessful, into nearby islands. Two centuries then passed before missionaries became active elsewhere in the Islands, beginning with an abortive Catholic mission to Tahiti in 1774 and the more successful efforts of London Missionary Society agents there in 1797. Since that time numerous mission societies, ranging from the Catholic Society of the Divine Word to the Pentecostal Assemblies of the World, and including Anglican, Methodist, Presbyterian, Seventh-Day Adventist, Salvation Army, Mormon, *Utrechtse Zendings-Vereeniging,* and the Japanese South Seas Evangelistic Band, have sent ministers into the Islands to transform the heathen raw material into one or other of the many, and in some respects rival, models of Christian belief and behavior. An adequate and balanced chronicle of them would require many more case histories, both of successes and failures, than this book can provide. Instead, the short account that follows highlights some of the contrasting ways in which the principal missions went about their work and the most important of the factors that helped to shape their results. Following that are résumés of the Christianization of two Island societies, offered not as a representative sample of how Islanders in general became Christianized (for which dozens of case studies would be required) but as an illustration of how varied the process and effects of Christianization were.

It goes without saying that the various denominations that engaged in Christianizing Islanders differed from one another in theology and ritual —how much so I will not attempt to specify. In addition, they also differed in the sweep of their objectives: some aimed only to transform religious beliefs and practices; others to reform social, especially familial, relations as well; still others to do all that plus instilling habits of hard work, thrift, body modesty, sobriety, cleanliness, and other puritanical values as well. And there were times during the endeavors of some missions when its sponsors at home or its agents in the field aimed also at winning subjects for their respective nations, although there were others who wished to see their converts develop nations (Christian nations) of their own.

The South Pacific missions differed also with respect to the characteristics of their missionaries: in their national origins (and hence in their cultural makeup); in their social and educational backgrounds, from barely literate working class to university-trained upper-middle class; and of course in their individual personalities, from humble followers to aggressively enterprising pioneers.

Just as varied were the proselytizing strategies pursued. Some missions fostered the employment of duly trained (or at least duly motivated) native converts, some of whom proved to be highly successful; others trusted their sacred missions only to fellow Westerners. Again, the agents of some missions proceeded as quickly as possible to work through the local vernaculars: to preach and teach in them and to provide Bible translations in them. This proved to be feasible in parts of Polynesia and Micronesia, where languages were more uniform, but less so in Melanesia where, typically, the flock of a single missionary might contain speakers of two or more different tongues. A more fundamental difference in proselytizing strategies, however, lay in the matter of time scale: generally speaking, Protestant missionaries tended to place great emphasis on a revivalistic kind of conversion (a frontal attack on the heathens' beliefs), whereas Catholic missionaries tended to adopt a longer-range view, concentrating initially upon ritual practices and upon the training of children. (Needless to say, the suitability of these contrasting strategies differed with the cultures they sought to change.) Moreover, most of the Protestant missions maintained relatively few Western missionaries in any of their stations, having trained native pastors and catechists to conduct most services, but Catholics depended mainly on direct contact between the Western priest and his parishioners.

To add a few more differences: the Anglican Melanesian Mission sent a schooner, a traveling chapel, to its far-flung adherents instead of maintaining a large Western staff. Mormon doctrine was disseminated by pairs of youths doing a two-year stint before returning to Utah. Congregationalists encouraged their adherents to form independent churches; Methodists insisted on supervision from their central Conference; and, of course, the South Pacific's several Catholic bishops permitted no relaxation of centralized discipline.

Complicating this array of denominational differences was the factional rivalry (not just expression of doctrinal differences but aggressive competition) that some missions encouraged. The earlier Protestant missions, particularly the London Missionary Society and Wesleyans, consented to separate areas of operation or even worked cooperatively in some places. Catholics acted otherwise: to convert a native from Protestantism was almost as worthy as winning the soul of a poor heathen, who, after all, knew no better. Moreover, with many Protestant missionaries the feeling was the same, in reverse. Mention was made earlier of the fierceness of the denominational rivalry in Tahiti and Hawaii, where warships were sent in to back a nation's favored instrument.

Notwithstanding their many differences, just sampled, the creeds taught by the various South Pacific missions were very much alike when compared with the native religious beliefs and values they sought to transform. Moreover, the Westerners seeking to transform them were faced with religions that usually had no concepts for those they wished to teach. For example, picture the chagrin of a missionary working in a society with matrilineal clans had he realized that his charges regarded his "Christ-the-Son" as half-demon because they had been informed that Christ had been conceived by a ghost in the form of a wild pigeon, or that for them a "God-the-Father" was less important, socially, than a "God-the-Mother's-Brother."

Yet what most missionaries lacked in cultural understanding and linguistic fluency they made up for in energy and zeal. For, as noted earlier, by 1939 some three quarters of a million Islanders had been converted—but not wholly, it must be emphasized, nor even mainly, by that energy and zeal. There were in fact several other things that contributed to those conversions (leaving aside the unanswerable question of how profound those statistically reported "conversions" actually were).

It should be noted at the outset that the overriding requisite for conversion was the active desire or the compliant willingness on the part of the converts (of at least *some* of the converts) to be converted. Moreover, in perhaps most cases, conversion was preceded by events that served to weaken peoples' faith in the potency of their own spirits (but not necessarily in the *existence* of the latter nor in the efficacy of all magic).

In many cases the mere sight of Western ships with their white-skinned mariners and wondrous material goods (plus of course the observed deadliness of firearms) was enough to instill doubts about their own beliefs and practices. And later, when more permanent visitors (beachcombers and traders) openly flaunted local religious beliefs and practices with impunity, those initial doubts were reinforced. Additional misgivings were implanted in many native communities by neighbors home again after working on Western plantations and ships, where most of them doubtless lost some faith in their native religions and several even became Christianized. Thus, many Islanders became receptive to Christianity before a missionary ever arrived.

When missionaries did arrive, the outcome of their efforts depended upon other kinds of factors. In many cases the very beachcombers and traders whose prior presence had helped to prepare the ground for conversion now served to impede it (e.g., by persisting in their unchristian ways and by active opposition to puritanical reformers). Also, in several societies the agents of Christianity were actively opposed by native priests, who quite rightly saw them as rivals.

Conversely, there were other factors that served to promote conversion, quite apart from the effectiveness of this or that mission strategy and the skills and energies of individual missionaries. One such was the degree of similarity between Christianity and the local religion. In many of the latter, for example, it was an easy matter to rename the most powerful native deity Jehovah, or to add the latter to an existing pantheon; more difficulties were encountered in religions containing only spirits associated with particular localities or miniscule social units.

In many native societies local politics was instrumental in the conversion process. Thus, in several instances an ambitious or embattled leader accepted conversion in order to employ the resources of the missionaries (their counsel, their prestige, their goods, and so forth, and sometimes their gunboat backing) to win more supporters and defeat their enemies (either those who were still heathen or those who were converts to a different Christian sect). And speaking of gunboats: in many places the natives became more receptive to the presence and the message of missionaries through knowledge of the mere existence of potentially supportive naval vessels.

In addition to the above, many Islanders were led to accept conversion for more personal reasons—e.g., for schooling in a Western language (with the economic benefits thereby gained), for easier access to Western goods and medical help, and for the enhanced prestige deriving from their relationships with Westerners (including in some cases employment as assistant missionaries).

Finally, accident also played a part in conversion in some places. As reported by James Boutilier in his fine study, just when a Tahitian mission teacher was on the verge of converting a Cook Island chief, an assistant of the former was discovered fornicating with the latter's already betrothed daughter, which served to postpone that polity's conversion until years later, when a series of disastrous storms and epidemics ". . . killed off many of the opponents of the new religion and convinced the remainder that this was the way the Christian god punished non-believers" (Boutilier 1985:51).

The early hope of some British Protestant missionaries and of their supporters at home was that they would be able to help shape native societies into strong native states, capable of maintaining independence and stability in a world of large nations and of international commerce. And, as noted earlier, the home government supported that objective because it meant no perplexing new colonial responsibilities and no new expenditures. However, of all the Pacific Island societies only one escaped total annexation and realized partly this pious hope. Tonga, according to its mission friends, exemplified how grace and selfless devotion to the task could transform a feuding array of heathen communities into a unified Christian state.

Tonga

From the decks of a copra boat pulling into Nukualofa, capital of the Kingdom of Tonga, the buildings looked more like Cape Cod than the South Seas. The architectural illusion remained even after stepping ashore, but the pre–World War II Tongans were if anything more officially, and perhaps more devoutly, Christian than their Cape Cod counterparts.

Her Majesty Queen Salote (Charlotte) Tubou, Honorary Dame Commander of the Order of the British Empire, Chief Member of the Free Wesleyan Church of Tonga, was no upstart; she could trace her descent, lineally or collaterally, back one thousand years through twoscore high chiefs of Tonga to the person of Ahoeitu, sacred ruler of Tonga, son of a Tongan woman and the sky-god Tangaroa.

The twenty-five thousand natives of pre–World War II Tonga were closely related, in language and in other aspects of culture, to those of neighboring Samoa. And they shared many cultural traits with their western neighbors, the Fijians. In fact, their ancestors (and those of the Samoans) had migrated from Fiji nearly four thousand years earlier, before the remaining Fijians became differentiated from them by infusions of genes and cultural traits from peoples coming from the west.

The people of Tonga before Western contact had not always been politically unified, but off and on they had attained a higher degree of political unity, and of religious orthodoxy, than either the Samoans or the Fijians.

Tongan society was divided into thirteen clans, each numbering about eighteen hundred members, who traced descent (potentially through either parent but usually through the father) to one or another common ancestors. Moreover, since all of the common ancestors were believed to have been kinsmen, the whole society constituted a single supraclan, which, however, was perennially rift by intraclan warfare.

A thousand years ago one of the component clans became paramount, and its founding chief (so the myth relates) was the semidivine son of the sky-god Tangaroa (a hardworking deity who had sired many heroes in Tonga and elsewhere in Polynesia). For five hundred years this so-called Tui Tonga line of chiefs remained preeminent. Their rule was semifeudal; the ownership of all land in their realm was vested in them, and as semidivine representatives of the gods they were hedged about with awesome restrictions *(tabus)*. In addition to the tribute regularly received, the Tui Tonga chiefs were recipients of great annual first-fruit offerings to the gods, and they caused their subjects to construct huge burial monuments for them in the form of truncated pyramids. Their power over their subjects was absolute and backed by divine sanction.

Within his closely knit chiefly family the Tui Tonga himself was the actual leader and the high priest of a "state" religion, but the characteristic Tongan recognition of women's superiority in ceremonial rank was also maintained—above the Tui Tonga himself in rank (but not in authority) was his eldest sister, and higher still (the highest-ranking person in the chiefdom) was the latter's eldest daughter. To both sister and niece the Tui Tonga owed ceremonial obeisance.

Legend has it that in the fifteenth century A.D. a Tui Tonga delegated to the head of a collateral branch of the chiefly clan the administrative duties of chieftainship, while he himself continued to function as spiritual head of the realm. (An alternative explanation is that the Tui Tonga was forcibly ousted from his governing role and left with only his priestly one.) Then, after a few more generations, the secular authority was redelegated to a third branch of the chiefly clan, which founded a dynasty that in time eclipsed both of its elder branches in temporal power. But the Tui Tonga, carrying office from father to son, remained spiritual leader of Tonga until the thirty-ninth and last one died in 1865. At that time the other leading chiefs of Tonga handed the priestly title to the most powerful secular chief of the time, George I Tubou (whose rise to secular power is mentioned below).

A millennium of feudal-like rule by autocratic demigods does not particularly well fit a native people to receive the doctrines of Calvin and Wesley, and the first earnest but unsuitable Protestant missionaries to tackle Tonga would have had rough going indeed had they arrived at a less opportune moment. Previous Western visitors (Schouten and Le Maire, Tasman, Wallis, and Cook) had tarried long enough among the Tongans to plant seeds of doubt about the indestructibility of the Tongan universe and the infallibility of their gods. Also, during the early part of the nineteenth century it was customary for Tongans to make the "grand tour" in Fiji—trading, serving as mercenaries in the endless Fiji wars, and returning home with a zest for fighting. As a result of these stimulants, contempt for authority *and* divinity flared into civil war, transforming Tonga into a cluster of fortress settlements and wiping out large sections of the populace. Early in this period several Protestant missionaries tried in vain to preach the gospel of peace, but war was too modish, and they failed in their efforts and either departed or died.

In 1830 a young chief of northern Tonga emerged as a dominant leader and decided to sample Christianity. After a Wesleyan-trained Tongan teacher had converted him, he went about the country pulling down idols, manhandling heathen priests, and "converting" all his own subjects before the appearance of a missionary.

This young chief, renamed George I Tubou, then set about to spread the tidings among the still heathen chiefs. Twenty years of intermittent fighting were required for this, and at the end he was in fact and in title King of all Tonga. His methods were at times somewhat drastic; to para-phrase the words of a Methodist historian: He did not consistently exhibit Christian clemency. But he finally won and opened up another market for Bibles, Mother Hubbards, and frock coats. However, his vic-tory had bitter as well as sweet fruits for his Wesleyan advisers: in the course of the wars some French Marist priests arrived and, forbidden to teach in George's territories, were welcomed by some of his enemies, thereby establishing a large Catholic following that has endured to this day.

With his own realm restored to peace, the restless George traveled to Fiji and aided the hard-pressed Thakombau, chief of the small territory of Mbau, to extend his rule over the rest of Viti Levu and his influence over most of the rest of the archipelago. In return, Thakombau accepted George's practical advice and became a Christian himself.

Meanwhile the new Kingdom of Tonga was enjoying the fruits of *Pax missionis*. Wesleyan missionaries were the king's chief advisers, his prin-cipal link with the great outside world. Having won the battle against heathenism, these worthies plunged into the fight for freedom, Anglo-Saxon style, and persuaded the trusting king to establish a constitution, wiping out in one move the legendary thousand-year polity and substitut-ing for it executive government on the English plan. "The *Conisitutone*," wrote one observer, "became thereafter the fetish of the Tongan people. Most of them did not know what it was, but it had been introduced by the missionaries, and was intimately connected, they believed, with its outlandish fellow, *Konisienisi* (Conscience), and in some mysterious way it elevated their country to the level of one of the Great Powers" (Basil Thomson 1894:365). The principal effect of the new order was to place the missionaries in the positions of power from which they had ousted the society's chiefs.

Critics of these missionaries have had harsh things to say about their motives and statesmanship, but no observer has denied them a talent for raising funds. Their appeals were timed to coincide with the sale of copra, and "plate day" became a dramatic substitute for the former first-fruit offerings to the gods. The scene has been described: "A band of men and women would come up together and walk round and round the basin, each throwing in a threepenny piece as he passed. After a few rounds a man whose stock of coins was exhausted would fall out, and the procession continued without him. . . . Then only two were left to circle round each other in a sort of dance, amid deafening applause. At last one of the survivors gave out, and the victor was left alone to stand before the basin and chuck in his coins from a distance. He was the hero of the day" (Thomson 1894:189).

Enterprising Western traders would stand at the church door with a bagful of coins, which they doled out against promissory notes on the next copra crop. One evangelist, Mr. Shirley Baker, a man of many parts, solved the traders' coin shortage by handing coin back to them as one collection plate was filled, in exchange for bills on Sydney.

With most of the Tongans' cash resources thus rendered to God there remained little for Caesar, and tax collections fell in arrears. This, and the fact that a large proportion of the mission collections was sent out of Tonga to evangelize distant heathen lands, caused the Tongan leaders to secede from the Wesleyan Conference (in Australia) and set up their own Free Church. A moving spirit in this schism was the same Mr. Baker, whose evangelical zeal and financial wizardry were equaled only by his political acumen.

In Mr. Baker we have the prime example of the worldly missionary turned loose among an easygoing South Seas people. He became Prime Minister, Minister of Foreign Affairs, President of the Court of Appeal, Judge of the Land Court, Minister of Education, Agent-General, and Medical Attendant to the King. As spiritual font of the Free Church, he moved the king to carry out a war of persecution against Tongans who refused to leave the old Wesleyan Conference. He lived high, wide, and handsome for several years, until he was deported by the British High Commissioner, who, from his post in Fiji, had jurisdiction over all British subjects in the Islands. As one Wesleyan chronicler put it: "We would fain draw a veil over the history of this regrettable period" (Colwell 1914:432).

The king of Tonga continued to reign as an independent monarch, but the affairs of his kingdom became pathetically confused, complicated by the presence of many Westerners and by attempts to administrate the constitutional democratic reforms that conferred political equality upon commoners (who, according to the native religion, did not even have souls). Eventually Britain agreed to protect the independent kingdom and placed an adviser there in the official person of a consul.

Relieved of many tiresome administrative worries, Tongans returned to playing at government and attending church. Meanwhile, their family relationships had not changed much over the years, nor had their subsistence economy. In addition, enough copra and bananas were sold to finance the import of the usual Western goods. Town life became so enticing that the authorities had trouble in inducing people to return to their ancestral acres; and cricket playing became so popular, and so disruptive of practical work, that it was restricted to certain days of the week.

Nevertheless, up to 1939 the Tongans had managed to retain ownership of nearly all of their land, and there was enough of it at that time to meet the needs of the population (already thirty-four thousand and probably larger than it had ever been). Everyone, including commoners, now had a soul, either Methodist or Catholic; everyone's body was respectably covered; and the use of English was improving steadily. Moreover, their old Polynesian gods had been transformed into *tevalo* (devils) and were relegated to subordinate statuses in the Christian Tongan cosmos.

Siuai

For a second case study we go some two thousand miles northwest to the island of Bougainville, in the heart of Melanesia.

About 110 miles long and averaging 30 miles wide, Bougainville is formed of two great ranges culminating in peaks up to eighty-five hundred feet high, including an active volcano. Most of the island is clothed in tropical rain forests and swamps. In 1939 its forty-five thousand indigenes were divided into sixteen language units, half of them Austronesian, the others Papuan. This sketch concerns the Siuai, a people numbering about five thousand, who inhabited the island's wide southwestern alluvial plain. They spoke a single Papuan language and shared many other culture traits, but before Western contact were divided into numerous, mutually hostile communities, each consisting of a few small hamlets. They engaged in a little hunting and collecting but were mainly root-crop gardeners and raisers of pigs.

Siuai society was divided into a number of matrilineal clans, and those into matrilineages. Members of the same clan were forbidden to inter-marry and believed themselves descended from a common (mythical) ancestress, but members of the same clan resided in many different, and sometimes warring, communities. It was at the matrilineage level of clan organization that members united: to assist one another in food getting, to celebrate one another's rites (e.g., birth, marriage, death), and, most important, to own land together (all Siuai land was divided into tracts that were owned corporately by one or another matrilineage). In addi-tion, each matrilineage owned a hoard of shell money, which was used mainly in its rituals. Authority over use of a matrilineage's land and trea-sure, and conduct of its rituals, rested in the hands of its Old Ones, usu-ally its eldest nonsenile members, female and male.

In 1914 Australia took over the administration of Bougainville from Germany and within a few years put an end to native warfare there. Until then the Siuai, like their neighbors, had engaged in off-and-on feuding among themselves: in revenge for real or imagined wrongs, in search of local honor and personal acclaim, and so forth. The leaders in these small but bloody contests were called *mumi;* although daring and fight-ing skill were also honored, the most successful *mumi* were men who organized the raids or battles, and who financed them (by compensating the warriors with pork feasts and other rewards). Some *mumi* were also the Old Ones of their respective matrilineages, but not all Old Ones were *mumi*—leading *mumi* reached their positions through achievement, not seniority alone.

After lethal warfare had been halted Siuai men ambitious for renown and influence switched to fighting with property: to arranging and fund-ing feasts larger than their rivals were able to do. Initially such feasts were given to accompany other kinds of events (e.g., the funeral of a kinsman, the building or refurbishing of the host's clubhouse, the acqui-sition of the services of a demon-familiar). Then, after a man had consol-idated his influence over his neighbors (literally, by obtaining their grati-tude and praise in exchange for his generosity and managerial skill—in other words, after he had come to be recognized as a *mumi*), he under-took, in some cases, to extend his influence over other communities by challenging their *mumi* in property duels. That he did by inviting one of them to become the guest of honor at a feast at which the host showered him with presents of pigs and shell money in amounts calculated to be beyond the latter's ability to reciprocate. If after a year or so the latter was indeed unable to reciprocate, measure for measure, in a return feast, then the original host was deemed to have won, whereupon he went on to challenge other rivals in the same way. It should be noted that the recipient of such "gifts" was not able to use them as part of his repayment —he was required to distribute most of them among the supporters who had accompanied him to the feast. It should also be noted that the renown and influence achieved by a successful *mumi* did not constitute governing authority (such as that enjoyed by victorious, hence feared, war leaders in pre-Western times), but the influence that accompanied success in property duelling after Western contact was, evidently, valued highly enough to induce many Siuai men to devote most of their energies and resources to it.

A third type of leadership in Siuai derived entirely from the colonial regime. When the Australians took over Bougainville (along with New Britain, New Ireland, and northeastern New Guinea) from the Germans in World War I they retained several features of the German system of administering rural native affairs, including the appointment of local officials.

After consolidating small and scattered hamlets into nucleated villages (called "lines" because of their linear streetlike layouts), they appointed two local men as local officials—one as "chief," the other as "interpreter" (i.e., someone fluent in pidgin). An effort was sometimes made to have the local adult males elect their "chief," but in many cases the undisputed local leaders (either the most senior Old One or the most influential *mumi*) chose not to be elected to such an alien and dubious post. Notwithstanding its alienism, and in some cases its enfeeblement by the co-residence of an influential *mumi*, the position of "chief" did have some coercive authority because of its backing by the colonial administration, a circumstance that made it an attractive goal for some Siuai men.

We turn now to the fourth type of leadership position of colonial-era Siuai: the one that is the focus of this résumé.

In 1902 the Roman Catholic Society of Mary set up a station on Bougainville's eastern coast; not long afterward others were established elsewhere on the island, including one in Siuai. In 1920 the Methodist Mission reached out from its Solomons headquarters and also set up a station in Siuai. From then on the two missions operated more or less competitively in this area, and it sometimes seemed that their agents devoted less energy to converting the Siuai from heathenism than in rescuing them from each other's form of Christianity.

By 1939 all Siuai except for a few old men had been converted to one or the other denomination, although conversion ranged from once-a-year to almost daily church attendance and from virtually total ignorance of Christian doctrines to extensive memorization of Biblical texts and strict adherence to church rules concerning, for example, the sabbath and marriage.

In the early days of missionizing, confrontation between the agents of the rival missions was intense. In the words of an Administration official who visited the area in the early 1930s: ". . . the competitive methods employed by the respective mission organizations in gaining converts wherever possible, leads the population into channels of excitement and strong feeling, such as have not been experienced, probably, since the days of inter-tribal warfare" (Chinnery 1924:87). Subsequently this rivalry flared up into actual hostilities, with both factions burning down the other's chapels, but by 1939 the rivalry had cooled to less violent practices.

In terms of doctrine, the Christian God accommodated easily to one of the Siuai's major deities, named *Tantanu* (The Maker), although the attributes of the former were acknowledged to be greater in nearly all respects. Jesus and the Virgin Mary proved to be harder to accommodate; not so the Holy Ghost, which fit easily into Siuai beliefs about avian supernaturals. Likewise adaptable were Christian doctrines about souls and saints, and mission attacks on demons and magic served only to stress what the Siuai already knew—that most demons were indeed dangerous and that magic could be deadly. On the other hand, the Christian concept of sin proved to be more difficult to translate: most converts agreed that it accumulated within a person from his wicked acts and formed a hard round object in the stomach, but there was disagreement about how to deal with it. Catholic converts believed it to be removable by taking Communion; Methodists, knowing no way to remove it, considered it necessary (though almost impossible) to avoid what Mission authorities declared to be "wicked acts."

More far-reaching perhaps than their influence upon Siuai religious beliefs and practices were the effects of missionization on their social relations.

Nearly every line-village had either a Methodist or a Catholic chapel (some had both), presided over by a native Siuai, who held daily services for his local congregation and in some cases conducted short daily classes in rudimentary reading and writing. In addition, the Catholic mission maintained a station in central Siuai, where the Western priest held regular services and from where he made regular rounds to conduct rites of christening, marriage, and extreme unction. His Methodist counterpart resided on the coast some forty miles away, and although he seldom visited the Siuai in the late 1930s, many Siuai boys attended his boarding school, where instruction was considerably more advanced than in the village chapels.

In one-chapel villages its denomination was in most cases the first to have become established there, usually with the consent of the local *mumi* (who, typically, had embraced the denomination opposite to that of his traditional enemies). In the case of most two-chapel villages, the split usually followed lines of kinship and resulted less from doctrinal differences (even when comprehended) than from individual ambition or pique. Thus, one hamlet unit of a Catholic village had become Methodist when its Old One was asked by the Catholic priest not to acquire a second wife. And in several instances, a breakaway congregation had been established by an ambitious individual who had been unable to become a *mumi* or an Administration "chief."

In the late 1930s the Siuai no longer burnt down one another's chapels, but denominational differences were manifested in other ways. For example, marriages were usually intradenominational, and when intravillage disagreements occurred over any kind of issue they often hardened along denominational lines. Moreover, the interdenominational opposition came to pervade general social attitudes: the somewhat more literate and more Westernized Methodists stereotyped their Catholic neighbors as primitive, ignorant, and unwashed—and were themselves labeled arrogant, hypocritical, and apishly Western.

Cargo Cults

Finally, a word must be added about some other forms of religions that developed in the Islands before World War II—religions that contained some elements of Christianity, along with many heathen elements, but that were reactions to other aspects of Westernization as well. Because of several of their common features they have been labeled nativistic movements, but there were many different types of them, ranging from religiously colored political rebellions to apolitical religious revivals. By 1939 the more bellicose of the former and the more positive and ideological of the latter were in abeyance (they were, however, to revive during and after World War II), but two types still recurred. One was the iconoclastic movements, such as the *Vailala* madness of Papua, in which natives, skeptical of their own cultural values yet lacking faith in the new beliefs and unable to obtain the material goods that Westernization seemed to promise, indulged in mass manifestations of hysteria, destroying all symbols of the old order and demoralizing everyday life. A second type was more positive. Like the first type they were also based on prophesies of an end to foreign rule and of the appearance of a ship loaded with cargo, but differed from the first in social form. Far from being anarchic, they developed into new and well-organized institutions that contained elements of both traditional and western cultures (including, in some cases, a native Messiah; in others a well-drilled "army," armed, often, with wooden replicas of rifles). Some of both types were the products of one or another native's prophetic "dream" (whether fraudulent or not would be impossible to judge), and some of both types were doubtless initiated and led by fraudulent opportunists. But whatever the immediate and particular circumstances that gave rise to one or the other of them, and whatever particular practices they resulted in, they were alike in one important respect. They represented efforts (some of them bizarre and most of them pathetic) to cope with the Western things and conditions and ideas that were reaching, in many cases engulfing, them, not the least of which were the doctrines and practices of Christianity.

One such movement occurred (and periodically recurred) on the island of Buka, the northern appendage of Bougainville. The natives of the two islands were similar in many respects, both physically and culturally, and they were parts of the same colonial district under both the German and Australian regimes. The natives of Buka began their contact with Westerners earlier than had the Siuai, just described, but both peoples were served by (or were subjected to) the same mission organizations, Catholic and Protestant. As was discussed earlier, those missions differed from one another in several respects (in doctrines, goals of conversion, methods of proselytization, and so forth) but were alike in one important respect: they were Western institutions, as basically colonial as the Western plantations and administration enclaves; all important decisions were made by Westerners and nearly all mission material resources reposed in Western hands. What indigenization of Christianity there was received its impetus from the natives themselves and in forms that were more than distressing to the Western missionaries and to other Westerners as well. (The following account is adapted from my *Bougainville: A Personal History*.)

Such developments started in Lontis village and were to encompass much of Buka, and to spread to nearby Bougainville as well. In 1913 word reached Westerners on Buka that a resident of Lontis, a pagan named Muling, was attracting a large following by his claim to be able to acquire Western goods through magic, all other kinds of effort to do so having failed. His message fell on receptive ears. Large numbers of Buka men had served as laborers, policemen, mission students, and so forth, and had come to use and want goods that would permit them to live more like the Westerners, whom they at first greatly admired, and whom one report suggests they first believed to be returned ancestral spirits. In any case, the cult swelled to such size that the German administrators, fearful of its disruptive potential, arrested Muling and exiled him to another island.

The excitement aroused by Muling's prophesies died down at the beginning of World War I, under Australian rule, but Muling's fellow Buka Islanders seemed not to have lost their appetite for Western goods and styles of life, so that when the Catholic Marist missionaries began active evangelization on the island they were well received. The missionaries may not have specifically promised material wealth to the natives in return for conversion, but it seems that the latter read such promises into talk about "spiritual rewards." According to one account, inasmuch as Sydney (Australia) was known to be the source of most of the Western goods (the "cargo") that reached Buka, it was also held to be the future abode of the Christianized; in any case, within a few years of the mission's beginning on the island 90 percent of its population had become Catholic.

Meanwhile, Catholic *lotu* (ecclesiastical services) began to serve purposes that the mission never intended. If the *lotu* worked for the missionaries in bringing what they wanted, some natives reasoned, why should it not work for them and bring ships laden with goods? Armed with this argument another Buka man, Pako, initiated a new movement to obtain the desired "cargo." One of the leaders of this new movement was a Catholic catechist, but the principal one, Pako, along with his associate, the repatriated and durable Muling, were pagans; *lotu* had become disengaged from the mission itself, but maintained some of its practices.

Modeling their actions on the mission practice of approaching the divinity through saints, Pako and his associates employed the *lotu* in petitioning their own ancestral spirits for aid in bringing the desired cargo. People refurbished their burial grounds and spent nights there in prayer, and a mood of excitement prevailed in expectation of the arrival of the cargo, which had been prophesied by Pako. Gardening and pottery making ceased (why work when the expected ships would bring all the food and utensils needed?); wharves and storehouses were built to receive the cargo. The movement was a bizarre mixture of new and old, and its members proclaimed themselves to be equal to Westerners. At its peak the cult embraced some five thousand Buka and Bougainville islanders, the largest grouping ever to unite on those islands, and a sign of things to come.

Subsequently, when some cult members attempted to claim goods landed for Westerners the Australian authorities stepped in and exiled the leaders to the New Guinea mainland, where Pako later died. After that the popular excitement abated for a year or two but was stirred up again by another Buka pagan, Sanop, who moved into Pako's residence and began receiving mysterious messages that he identified as coming from Pako's spirit, again promising cargo, but this time ominously anti-Western in tone. Again, however, the cult contained much from Christianity, including the rituals of *lotu,* regular church attendance, and insistance upon monogamy (except for the leaders!). But even though cult members continued to value the ritual powers of the Catholic priests (the local priest baptized two hundred new converts including some Methodists who were visiting the headquarters of the cult, and "Bishop" appeared with "Pako" on the banners of the cult), the cult members otherwise distinguished between their brand of Christianity and the Western mission itself.

This latest version of the cult also spread to northern Bougainville, becoming even more militantly anti-Western. Then, when talk of "liberation" was reinforced by a mass desertion of cult members from their plantation jobs, the administration moved in again. The cult leaders were arrested, along with about one hundred followers, and Pako's house was burnt down. Meanwhile, no cargo arrived to offset the food shortage resulting from the earlier cessation of gardening, and the disheartened cult adherents returned to their ordinary pursuits. With this the Pako-Sanop episode ended, but faith in "cargo" was again revived a few years later, when Japanese ships appeared—but that is another story.

SOURCES

(See also sources for chapter 3.)

Tonga: Gifford 1929; Korn 1978; Lātūkefu 1977; Marcus 1980; Rutherford 1977; Thomson 1894.

Siuai: Chinnery 1924; Laracy 1976; Oliver 1955, 1973.

Cargo cults: Williams 1977; Worsley 1957.

CHAPTER TEN

Coconuts

In 1939 there were about fifty million producing coconut palms in the South Pacific, enough to cover completely three islands the size of Oahu (where the few that actually survived made up for their small numbers by their importance to amateur photographers and the local tourist bureau).

South Seas sugar statistics were far more impressive in tonnage and in money value than those of the South Seas coconut, but sugar's influence was limited to Hawaii, Fiji, and pre–World War II Tinian-Saipan, and only Westerners and Asians benefitted directly from it. In contrast, the influence of the coconut stretched from Truk to Tonga and from Hiva Oa to Hollandia and directly or indirectly affected the life of nearly every Islander throughout that vast area, even including those dwelling in the remote mountain regions of Melanesia, who had never seen a coconut palm until going to work on Westerners' coastal plantations.

Coconut palms require year-round warm temperature, a well-drained soil, and plenty of moisture and sunlight; they grow best in low altitudes near the coast. The palm grows out of the mature fallen nut and requires from eight to ten years to reach the bearing stage. After that it lives for nearly eighty years and bears nuts at the rate of about fifty a year for sixty or seventy years.

The mature nut consists of a hollow kernel of oily white "meat," one-half inch thick, encased in a hard woody shell. Around this is a fibrous husk one-half to two inches thick. The cavity of the unripe nut is filled with a thin "milk," a nutritious and refreshing beverage with a tangy taste. As the nut matures this milk precipitates to form the white meat.

In most Island colonies the coconut had two entirely different kinds of uses: one, as an ingredient in native subsistence, the other as a source of money for larger-scale producers, including those Islanders who grew enough palms to allow sale of the nuts.

To Islanders the milk of the unripe coconut was a prized beverage, the only one on islands that lacked potable water. The meat was scraped from the shell and eaten either by itself or mixed into puddings of taro or yams or sago, or the oil was squeezed from the meat and used as an unguent or a cosmetic or as an ingredient with other foods. The hollowed shell became a flask, the clean-scraped shell a cup or spoon or a material for carved ornaments. Cordage was made from the nut's fibrous husk; furniture, utensils, and building timbers from the palm's tough trunk. Leaves were used to thatch huts or to weave baskets, and even the pith of the palm was eaten when for some reason the palm was felled. In several of the islands of Micronesia, a sugar-rich sap was drawn off by tapping the flower bud and either eaten raw in the form of crystallized candy or allowed to ferment into a mildly inebriating toddy.

From the copra of commerce, which is merely coconut meat removed from the shell and dried sufficiently for shipping, oil was (and still is) expressed to produce margarine, cooking and salad oils, fine soap, and cosmetics. Copra cake, the residue after most of the oil has been expressed, is an important stock food rich in protein. Coir mats and rugs are manufactured from the fibrous husks, and coconut-shell charcoal was formerly one of the best vapor absorbents known, especially valuable for absorbing industrial odors, for recovering gasoline and benzol from the air, and for use in gas masks. In the manufacture of soap, coconut oil plays a unique role; it hardens well, and its highly soluble acids possess exceptional lathering qualities, even in salt water; consequently it is a favorite for toilet and saltwater soaps and for soap chips. And, in addition to all those blessings, consider how empty life would be without coconut pie!

But most of those good things are end products, processed in factories thousands of miles from the Islands where the coconuts grow. With the exception of a few tons of coconuts used in the local manufacture of desiccated coconut, most palm products leaving the Islands do so in the form of copra. To obtain it, mature nuts may be picked from the palm or they may be collected after they have fallen (which is and was the more common practice on commercial plantations). The whole coconut is then split in half and the meat either immediately cut out of the shell or allowed to dry a bit before removal. Excess moisture must then be removed from the meat by some method of drying, and the resulting copra bagged in sacks for overseas shipment.

Pacific Islands copra was (and continues to be) dried in one or another of three ways: by sunshine alone, by direct "cooking" in the heat and smoke of open fires, or by hot air channeled into large oven-dryers. In the less humid, less cloudy eastern Islands, most native-made copra was sun dried, resulting in a clean and fairly high-grade product. Elsewhere, natives and some of the less well-capitalized foreign planters dried their copra on racks over smoldering husk-burning fires, which produced a dirty and smelly product unsuitable for the manufacture of food or of toilet soaps. High-grade plantation copra was dried on wire-screen racks built in house-sized hot-air ovens. This method dried the copra in about twenty-four hours, several times as fast and much more thoroughly than the sun and smoke methods, with the result that the copra became less rancid. The hot-air-dried copra of the Islands compared favorably with copra produced anywhere else, but the Islands' smoke-dried copra was an inferior product.

Just before 1939 the Pacific Islands were producing annually about one-eighth of the world's one and one-half to two million tons of commercial copra, coming after the Netherlands East Indies, the Philippines, Ceylon, and Malaya. The following tonnages were exported in 1938:

Mandated Territory of New Guinea	73,720 tons
Fiji	33,480
Solomons	22,940
French Polynesia	20,680
Japanese Mandated Islands	13,100
Tonga	12,430
New Hebrides	11,450
Papua	11,250
Western Samoa	11,240
Gilbert and Ellice Colony	4,850
New Caledonia	2,950
Guam	1,660
Cook Islands and Niue	1,300
Eastern Samoa	800
Total	221,850 tons

(Note: exports from West New Guinea were included in the total for the Netherlands East Indies.)

In nearly all these Island polities, copra making had been in previous decades the chief commercial activity, employing more people and touching more lives than any other foreign-dominated enterprise; but there the exact similarities end. In every Island archipelago the copra industry exercised a somewhat different kind of effect on native life, mainly in consequence of differences in the sizes of each area's plantations and in the ways in which production and marketing were carried out. From this point of view there were three main types of producer: native, small planter, and big company.

Native production supplied part of the copra exported from all Island polities, and it accounted for all copra exported from the Gilbert and Ellice Colony, Guam, American (Eastern) Samoa, the Cook Islands, and Niue. Moreover, it accounted for over 60 percent of the copra exported from Tonga, French Polynesia, Western (i.e., New Zealand) Samoa, New Caledonia, Fiji, and the Marshall Islands. In this type of production, native Islanders harvested nuts from their own groves, extracted and dried the copra (by sunning or smoking), and sold it to traders for further marketing. The small trader, usually either an Asian or a Westerner, then either sold the copra to a larger firm for overseas shipment or shipped it overseas on consignment.

The typical small-trader operation became familiar to anyone traveling in the Islands during the decades before World War II: a small, tin-roofed trade store, stocked with lamps, kerosene, matches, cloth, rice, stick tobacco, canned beef and fish, mirrors, hair oil, and so forth—"civilization" set out on rough board shelves in an atmosphere redolent of somewhat rancid copra. Sometimes such copra was paid for in trade or in coin that never left the store. Just as frequently, the copra maker received nothing but a credit against his perennial debt, for no trader would have survived long without offering credit, whether local statutes permitted it or not. Extending credit against future production was termed "native exploitation" by some, but the small trader was just as likely to be exploited by his native customers. Native boycotts had behind them the solidarity of kinship groups, and an unscrupulous or uncooperative trader would not have lasted very long.

A variation of the pattern just described occurred in the Gilbert and Ellice Colony, where the British administration stepped in and helped the natives to set up cooperatives for marketing their copra and for procuring trade goods directly from overseas suppliers, thereby eliminating the small trader. (Needless to add, this "bloody communism" was something less than popular with many Europeans.)

The enigmatic "Chinee" trader and his anything but enigmatic Western counterpart were familiar types on the coconut Islands, but one looked almost in vain for a native trader, and for a good reason. Not that many Islanders did not learn to read and write and calculate; they did, and in some cases with more skill than that possessed by many Western traders. Nor were Islanders inferior in the fine art of abstracting profit from transactions of exchange. But because the values of individual profit making had not yet gone far in most native communities in supplanting the traditional ones of sharing, few native storekeepers were able to keep their shelves filled and relatives satisfied at the same time.

There was one factor in the economics of native production that frustrated the foreign buyer to a distressing degree: in many places the native growers made and sold *less* copra when prices were high. Not so devoted as the foreigners to acquisition for its own sacred sake, they made and sold only enough copra to fill the lamp with kerosene or the pipe with tobacco and worked for the morrow on the morrow.

Copra economy, native style, was for many Westerners the South Seas of memory and romance. It began in the early nineteenth century and in many places persisted up to (and even beyond) World War II. By World War II, however, the small-scale nonnative planter was fast becoming an anachronism. He was independent in name only, for his business was usually mortgaged beyond hope of redemption, and he was utterly dependent on the highly variable world price of copra, with little or no savings to tide him over the lean years. Notwithstanding that predictable outcome, during the previous decades adventurous men had flocked to the Islands, cherishing the dream of a South Seas homestead and excited by the legendary prospects of profits. It seemed such a simple matter: plant the palms, let them grow for a few years, then settle back and count the nuts as they dropped. But the hard fact was that in the twenties and thirties of this century it cost the equivalent of about one U.S. dollar to bring each palm into bearing, and thereafter from twenty to forty to produce each ton of copra. And while the costs were fixed or rising the world market price for copra was subject to wide variation: London quotations on South Seas copra dropped from £39.14s a ton in 1920 to £9.5s at the outbreak of World War II. (These prices included overseas freight charges; the price at out-district island ports averaged about one-half the London quotation.) These figures, probably better than any other index, provided a barometer of economic climate in the copra Islands, and hence for nearly all Island polities.

For the small planter a sustained rise in copra price meant a partial liquidation of indebtedness, usually to the mercantile firm that had lent him cash and extended credit for supplies. It sometimes meant a glorious holiday in New Zealand or Australia (where the traffic in the bar in Sydney's Hotel Usher was nearly as reliable a guide to copra prices as the printed quotations themselves). A sustained drop in price, on the other hand, often meant foreclosure and operation of a plantation by the creditor company, not unusually managed by the former owner now on salary.

Aside from the infrequent trips back home, most small planters led lives of hard work and monotony and loneliness. The corrugated iron roofs of their houses usually covered two or three sleeping rooms surrounded by a wide veranda, with a cookhouse off to the rear. Palms covered all of the three hundred or so acres contained in the average-sized plantation, even extending up to the veranda. A few hundred feet away were the rough barracks of the planter's native laborers, and close to the water's edge stood the drying and storage sheds. Just offshore was sheltered the small launch that linked the plantation with the comparative civilization of the nearest government outpost or trading town.

Day in and day out (except for Sundays), year after year, the planter arose at or before dawn and lined up his fifty or so laborers for the day's work. After doctoring the sores and coughs, he inspected ovens and sheds or struggled with the launch's eternal ailments. He was his own commissary officer, storekeeper, engineer, bookkeeper, and, unless he had been lucky enough to acquire a wife and persuade her to share his island existence, he had to be his own housekeeper, and to doctor himself when fever or dysentery brought him low. His nearest Western neighbor was usually hours or days away by launch or trail; during the one event he could look forward to—the periodic visit of the copra freighter—he was usually too busy supervising the loading of copra and the unloading of stores to do more than enjoy a hurried meal on board. (In recent years, however, with the arrival of home refrigeration and power, he could at least drink his beer cold and tune in on the BBC.)

And even for all his superiority as a "master," he did not possess the authority to enforce discipline over his native employees; only the distant government official could do that. But even controlling his labor force and making efficient use of it was not so difficult as obtaining it in the first place. There was probably never a time in the Islands when native labor was adequate for the foreigners' requirements. Added to that was the increasing tendency of colonial governments to formulate regulations: for limiting terms of indenture, controlling recruiting, specifying food rations, defining housing standards, setting wages, outlawing corporal punishments; in a word, for generally restricting a planter's freedom of action vis-à-vis his labor force. (In the New Hebrides the French government allowed French planters to import Asians for labor, but even there the British planters had to rely on local natives.)

Not the least of the difficulties of the planters—large and small—were the diseases and insect pests that commonly infested their groves and sometimes played havoc with production. The small planter could make little headway against these natural enemies, and even the huge resources of Lever Brothers could not prevail against one infestation that devastated many of their Solomons plantations (long before World War II finished them off).

Clearly, the small planter had no sinecure. Not all of them, however, lived as colorless and unrewarding lives as that depicted above. Near the larger colonial centers (Rabaul, Apia, Samarai, Port Vila, etc.) there were many compensations in the life. Moreover, some exceptional planters, even in far-off and isolated places, surrounded themselves and their families with gardens and books and led generally pleasant lives.

Regardless of their difficulties in material and social well-being, however, nearly all small planters shared some things in common: their fierce individualism in the face of encroaching government controls and big-company absorption, their generally unsentimental attitude toward native welfare, and their increasing insecurity in a world moving toward larger production units and copra substitutes.

Almost a different world was the big-company plantation, comprising thousands of acres of palms and employing a small colony of Westerners plus hundreds of Islanders. Salaried managers directed the day-to-day operations, but directors in Australian, New Zealand, English, and French boardrooms called the tunes.

Big-company plantations were widespread in the Islands. Most of the German ones in Samoa and New Guinea had been conducted along those lines, and big companies had always been preponderant in the Solomons and parts of New Guinea. Some of them, such as Lever Brothers and the Samoan Reparation Estates, were concerned only with production; to others, such as Burns Philp and W. R. Carpenter, production was only one phase of an all-embracing mercantilism.

Lever's Pacific Plantations, Ltd., a branch of the world-encircling Unilever Trust, operated large plantations in the Solomons and Fiji; it survived and apparently prospered despite local setbacks and declining world prices. (Less durable planters muttered darkly of price-fixing, complaining that the Unilever plutocrats in London kept prices low in order to buy more cheaply the copra they needed to supplement their own production in the manufacturing of Lever's shortening and soap.)

Whatever plantation veranda in the British Pacific Islands one happened to be lounging on, the conversation sooner or later got around to "B.P." And notwithstanding the tone of overheard remarks, B.P. did not stand for "Bloody Pirate" (as some hard-pressed colonials often called it) but for Burns Philp (South Seas) Company, Ltd. In the years just before World War II, if one traveled by steamship from Australia to any Island port, or from one Island to another, in all statistical likelihood one traveled in a B.P. vessel. Almost as likely, the largest building in each Island port in the southwestern Pacific was the B.P. store, and much of the copra you smelled in those ports would eventually be carried to market in B.P. bottoms. In its beginning, B.P. was mainly a trading firm, with a network of stores and shipping covering nearly all of the British (including Australian) areas of the southwestern Pacific. Canny management put the firm even with the heavily subsidized German companies there, and, after liquidation of Germany in the area, B.P. raced far ahead of all rivals. In due course the company set up its own plantations and, with loans and credit, supported the efforts of small planters as well: more copra and more settlers made for more freight and merchandizing. Eventually, B.P. acquired the properties of some of its debtors and consequently became a major copra producer in its own right.

Though younger and less far-flung, another British firm, W. R. Carpenter, experienced a somewhat parallel development. Trailing behind these, but still large, were several other English, Australian, and New Zealand companies producing or trading throughout the South Pacific. Similarly, but on smaller scales, a few French mercantile companies operated throughout New Caledonia and the New Hebrides.

However angrily small planters or big companies complained about one another's inefficiencies or monopolies, they joined together as allies in their criticism of plantations run by some of the Christian missions. The Catholic missions in particular went in for copra production to support their missionary endeavors, thereby provoking unprintable comments from struggling lay planters, who claimed that mission plantation laborers worked for nothing or for the privilege of attending mission schools.

For better or for worse, during the four or five decades before World War II, the simple process of obtaining the oil of the coconut—to spread on foreign bread and to bathe mainly foreign bodies—had greater influence than any other factor on the lives of most Pacific Islanders. Indeed, copra had to some degree affected the lives of residents in nearly every Island polity; but it was so dominant an activity in the affairs of some of them that one is justified in speaking of "copra areas." In the following sections of this chapter are told the stories of several of those areas: of the Gilbert and Ellice Colony, where native production predominated; of Tahiti and most other islands of French Polynesia, where native production existed side by side with the foreign small planters; of Western Samoa, constituted like French Polynesia but with a larger proportion of foreign plantations; of the Cook Islands, which were like small-scale Samoas; of the Solomons, the New Hebrides, and coastal eastern New Guinea, where production was mainly in the hands of foreigners. Those were not the only copra areas of the Islands but they were the ones in which most of the inhabitants were affected in their daily lives by world price fluctuations in this commodity. Other copra areas, such as the Lau Islands part of the colony of Fiji, the Marshalls and eastern Carolines, and even Tonga, could with much justification be added to the list; but other considerations have led to the telling of their stories under different headings. The Lau Islands, for example, are thickly planted in coconuts, but as an administrative division of Fiji they were indirectly but significantly affected by the colony's dominating sugar industry. Islanders of the Marshalls and the eastern Carolines had for generations depended upon copra to secure the things that foreigners had taught them to want, but between World Wars I and II an influence over their lives far more important than any single commodity was the colonizing activities of the Japanese. Tonga was also a copra area, but some account of that kingdom's colonial history was given in chapter 9.

The following travelogue through the copra areas begins, quite logically, with the Gilbert and Ellice islands, where production had remained in islanders' hands.

Gilbert and Ellice Islands

The pre–World War II Gilbert and Ellice Islands typify *native*-style copra economy. Owing to the happy circumstance that these islands produced little of interest to commerce except coconuts, and not many of those, most of the natives managed to survive the first century of contact with Westerners by a safe margin, despite the early depredations of whalers and blackbirders. Some of their religious beliefs were changed, as were some of their rules governing kinship and inheritance, but their subsistence techniques remained much the same, because no Western tools or techniques could improve on the consummate skill shown by these islanders in sustaining human life on their specks of land.

The twenty-five atolls comprising these island groups are scattered over thousands of square miles of the mid-Pacific but their total land area is only 180 square miles. They extend above and below the equator; those in the higher latitudes enjoy year-round rainfall, but a few of them nearer the equator suffer periodic droughts, which make native life even more precarious there. Soil is thin at best, and on most islands only coconuts and pandanus will grow naturally. By prodigious effort some root crops have been induced to grow, in some islands only in pits excavated by hand and filled with humus. Notwithstanding all this, there once lived from thirty-one to thirty-five thousand Gilbertese and about twenty-eight hundred Ellice islanders on these infertile atolls, those numbers made possible by the circumstance of there having been on the average about three square miles of fish-filled lagoon for every acre of land. The two peoples making up this colony were much alike in their techniques of extracting a living from land and sea. Nearly every part of nearly every living thing was made to serve a practical purpose, and the natives' artistry in fashioning plant fibers into beautiful and pliable mats has nowhere been excelled. Also, both peoples were expert in the making and handling of canoes, and they were truly as much at home on and in the water as on land.

The Ellice islanders spoke a Polynesian language closely related to that of Samoa—whence, according to legend, many of their ancestors had come. The language of the Gilbertese, on the other hand, was more closely related to those of the Marshall and Caroline islanders, whom the Gilbertese also resembled in physical features: they were shorter and somewhat more darkly pigmented than the Ellice islanders.

For both peoples the most important social units were composed of persons of common descent. And although in both societies a person *could* align him- or herself with the descent unit of either parent (i.e., the choice was potentially ambilineal) the Ellice islanders seemed to have aligned themselves more often with the unit of the father. (I write "seemed" because of some uncertainty about this aspect of pre-Western Ellice society, which was radically transformed by Samoan missionaries before anyone saw fit to describe it.) Differences of social rank were also recognized in both Gilbert and Ellice societies, although the lines were more sharply drawn among the former, to the extent, even, of division into social classes. Moreover, warfare was also more prevalent among the Gilbertese, which led in some places to military conquests and establishment of autocratically ruled political units (which combined or superseded those based on common descent).

Mendaña sighted two of these islands in 1567; other ships contacted the rest of them between 1764 and 1824 and therewith ushered in the destructive procession of whalers, traders, and blackbirders. Although food and fresh water were scarce on the islands, whalers discovered ample compensation in the favors of their comely women, and doubtless left behind many cases of venereal disease. Then came the blackbirders, some of whose atrocities were described in chapter 7. For the natives who survived those onslaughts the next alien intrusion came from Christian missionaries. In 1857 the Reverend Hiram Bingham of the Boston Mission began his labors in the Gilberts, but this field was subsequently turned over to the London Missionary Society, whose first agent, a Samoan, arrived in the Ellice islands in 1861.

In no time at all other Samoan teachers of the Samoa-based London Missionary Society were installed throughout the Ellice islands as paramount authority, usurping leadership from the clan elders and in fact banishing traditional beliefs and practices to such an extent that the whole clan (i.e., descent-unit) system became obsolete. The new beliefs and relationships were based on their versions of the Bible, and most Ellice communities became theocratically reorganized.

In 1888 priests of the Roman Catholic Sacred Heart Mission gained a foothold—soulhold!—in the Gilberts but were unable to do so in the solidly Protestant Ellices. Meanwhile traders had invaded the islands for copra and established shore stations on the larger atolls, but the paucity of arable land kept foreign planters away.

In 1892 Britain's long arm reached out and placed these islands under a protectorate, later transformed into a crown colony. Even the sharpest critic of imperialism must concede the need for such action. Until then these islands were vulnerable to any Western rascal who happened along. Some islands were actually governed by traders, others by beachcombers, others by strong-willed upstart native chiefs with rum-inspired ambitions. With little apparent effort and with a very small staff, the British

administration quickly imposed order and set about to restore the islands
to the islanders. Perhaps it was the slight economic value of these islands
that had kept away all but a few Westerners, and thereby made the task
of governing easier. Or perhaps it was the very small size of the administrative staff, which compelled those officials to allow the islanders to run
their own affairs. At any rate, the product was almost unique in the
South Pacific. Ultimate authority rested with British officials, but as
there were only a handful of them, most of the administration was carried out by native headmen and magistrates. It should not be concluded,
however, that isolation and self-government encouraged these islanders
to revert to their former ways—far from it. The new demands for Western goods were just as compelling here as in other Pacific Islands; the difference lay in the ways they were satisfied.

The Gilbert and Ellice islanders were enabled to earn the money to
buy foreign goods by marketing their labor and their copra. Every year
scores of them went away to work in the phosphate mines on nearby
Ocean Island or on the Western plantations on Washington and Fanning
islands. But because of a government ruling they could remain away only
a year or two at a time and were encouraged to take along their wives.
Thus the break in village life was neither long nor abrupt. Copra, the
other marketable resource, was produced on every island; the colony
exported five to six thousand tons annually, all produced by natives and
with every family sharing in the proceeds. Before World War II one Japanese and two British mercantile firms had agents stationed on some of the
larger atolls, but since they were not natives they were not allowed to
purchase land or even to lease it in parcels larger than five acres. And
even retailing and the buying of copra remained in islanders' hands on
the many islands possessing native trade cooperatives.

Under conditions like these it is little wonder that before World War II
these islands were fast regaining, or surpassing, the number of people
they once had. In 1939 Ellice islanders numbered four thousand and
were on the increase. At that same time, although the twenty-seven thousand Gilbertese numbered several thousands fewer than in precontact
times they were increasing at such a rate that the administration was
moved to resettle hundreds of them upon the nearby uninhabited Phoenix islands.

However attractive one might view the old life of the Pacific Islanders,
untampered and unspoiled, it would require a blindly unrealistic sentimentalist to suppose that the nineteenth-century Islanders could or
should have retained intact their old ways when immersed in alien goods
and ideas. The most that the sentimentalist could sensibly have hoped for
was that the Islanders be left in sufficient isolation to allow them to swallow the new objects and ideas in homeopathic doses. To the extent that
the native patient was not already infected by the earliest alien contacts,

this regimen was being successfully followed in the Gilbert and Ellice islands—that is, before Pearl Harbor changed it all.

In comparison, the therapy of acculturation was differently conceived and only casually administered in French Polynesia.

French Polynesia

Scattered over two million square miles of the southeastern Pacific are several archipelagoes and isolated islands of strikingly varied configurations, from high, craggy mountains to low, flat islets. Tropical temperatures prevail in all of them, but differences in rainfall and soil have resulted in a wide range of vegetation, from verdant profusion to desertlike scrub. Two of these islands were first visited, briefly but calamitously, by Westerners, specifically by Mendaña, in 1595, but a century and three-quarters passed before Western visitors resumed their visits and began to describe these islanders' ways of life. Those descriptions show that despite the dissimilarities of their environments the different native peoples of this region continued to share many features of their common cultural heritage even ten or so centuries after their dispersal from a Tongan-Samoan source. Their differences in environment were of course reflected in what they ate and how they built their houses and canoes, but their languages were closely interrelated, their religious beliefs and practices almost identical, and their societies structured in similar ways (e.g., with ambilineal descent units, stratified social classes, inherited chieftainship, and so forth).

Beginning in 1843 and culminating in 1900, they were all collected into a single, uniformly governed colony, now known as French Polynesia, but the Westernization of the several divisions of the colony differed, in intensity and in kind.

The most famous of the divisions, now known as the Society islands, comprising eight "high" volcanic islands and two atolls, extends some 300 miles along a northwest-to-southeast axis. At the time of its first visit by Europeans, in 1767, its native population numbered about forty-seven thousand to fifty thousand. They were divided into several distinct and sometimes warring political districts but had a common culture, including a common language. Tahiti, the largest of these islands, had some thirty-five thousand inhabitants divided into eighteen districts, which, although uneven in size and population and hence in fighting potential, were nevertheless politically autonomous most of the time. In addition to such political divisions, the whole society of Tahiti (and in fact of the entire archipelago) was a hierarchy of religious and ceremonial privilege derived from inherited rank. In most instances a district's highest ranking individual was also its political chief, but there were several exceptions to that, and several other cases in which a militarily weak district was governed by an incumbent of one of the society's highest-ranking chiefly Titles.

Such was the case in Tahiti's northwestern district of Pare-Arue, in whose well-protected waters the first Western vessel, H.M.S. *Dolphin,* anchored in 1767. During the next quarter century several other British naval vessels harbored there. To the captains of the latter—Cook, Bligh, and Vancouver—every "nation" (which they perceived Tahiti to be) must needs have a "king"; and who but Pomare, the friendly chief of Pare-Arue, was most eligible for that role (especially as he described himself to be so). The *rank* of Chief Pomare (i.e., the religious-ceremonial rank of his inherited Title) was indeed preeminent throughout Tahiti and nearby islands but it required the weapons and other kinds of assistance from Westerners to establish his political kingship, and coincidentally his position as *Christian* king. The final boost to that ascent had been provided by L.M.S. missionaries, whose pioneers landed on Tahiti in 1797. After converting the heathen Pomare (the heir of the original one of that name), and hence by "royal decree" all of his current and subsequent subjects, they attempted to shape the new realm into an independent Calvinist nation, and were on the way to doing so until 1843, when France intervened, not only to establish its colonial rule but to open Tahiti and nearby islands to Catholic missionaries as well.

The native monarchy was permitted to carry on its ceremonies for another four decades, but even before it was officially terminated the indigenous rules of inheritance were superseded by French ones, and Tahitian Mission patterns of governance by French appointees (at the highest levels) and local elections (at the local village level).

French control over the Marquesas was also established in 1843, and by 1900 all of the islands now included in French Polynesia had been annexed and were governed by appointive officials headquartered in Papeete (Tahiti).

Papeete was also the commercial center of the colony. To it overseas vessels carried goods from Marseilles, San Francisco, Auckland, and Sydney, and from it carried away copra, vanilla, and pearl shell for world markets. Schooners, most of them built, owned, and manned by native Polynesians, transported store goods from Papeete to the colony's outlying ports and island produce to Papeete for local consumption or export.

Western entrepreneurs have never been happy about Tahiti and her neighboring Society islands. Attempts to set up large plantations on them have not succeeded: local Polynesians could not be induced to work them, and the Chinese imported for that purpose left them as soon as possible to establish enterprises of their own (e.g., vegetable growing, small-scale retailing, and service occupations, most of which activities they came to dominate). Most of the copra and vanilla, which constituted the Society islands' major exports, were produced by Polynesian householders and sold to Chinese middlemen for overseas marketing; the income was used to buy cloth, kerosene, tobacco, and other such things to supplement the subsistence economy (which in 1939 continued to be the basis of life for most Society islanders).

Numbers of Frenchmen settled in these islands (as civil servants, shop owners, and more or less affluent beachcombers), and they were followed by Westerners from many other nations; but to a degree almost unique in the South Pacific, caste lines between foreigners and natives did not materialize. More than any other segment, the Chinese kept socially to themselves, maintaining their own schools and clubs. But like Westerners, many Chinese intermarried with Tahitians, and their numerous side issue include some of the handsomest people in a population generally noted for its beauty.

Far from Papeete, the Austral and Gambier islands retained much of the old Polynesia (or rather, the missionary-shaped old Polynesia) that had been effaced on Tahiti. A French gendarme, a missionary, and some Chinese storekeepers were usually the only outsiders on most of these islands. Schooners carried their produce (copra, vanilla, coffee, arrowroot, craft-work) to Papeete, and occasionally the more adventurous of their people visited the metropolis, where some of them were caught up in the faster life. In commerce nearly every island had its specialty: Rapa and Rurutu men were the colony's best sailors; the fiber weaving of the Gambiers was unexcelled in southeastern Polynesia; and Tubuai's chief export to Papeete was turkeys!

In the widely scattered atolls of the Tuamotuan archipelago, location, topography, and climate were decisive factors in their peoples' lives. Their great distances from Tahiti, and in many cases from each other, served to maintain many of the local cultural peculiarities that prevailed in times before Western contact. On the other hand, their uniformities in topography (all of them are flat coral atolls) and in climate have severely limited the kind and amount of salable things they could grow—mainly copra, and not very much of that. But although their lands are low and narrow, shallow in soil, and often lacking in permanent water, their lagoons are reservoirs of fish, so that the pre–World War II Tuamotuans led almost amphibious lives. In former days the pearl shell and pearls in those lagoons provided many Tuamotuans with cash incomes, until the beds were exhausted through overharvest. In the thirties, however, the government placed limits on diving seasons and prohibited the use of diving gear, so that the beds began to recuperate.

A different world altogether was that of the Marquesas in 1939. Credible estimates of the population before Western contact of these rugged and isolated islands go up to ninety thousand; in 1939 there were less than three thousand native Marquesans left to wander around among the ruins. Extensive archaeological remains and deserted cultivations bear out early accounts concerning the size and complexity of the indigenous culture; even as late as Melville's day the remnants were complex and fascinating.

In pre-Western times nearly every Marquesan community dwelt in a separate valley, separated from its neighbors by sharp mountain ridges. Feuding was commonplace and cannibalism popular, and more so than in any other Pacific Island society the practice of polyandry (one wife, two or more husbands) was institutionalized. All in all, the Marquesans were a vigorous and in many respects distinctive people, until Westerners appeared on the scene.

The procession of horrors was initiated by Mendaña in 1595; during a week's stay at Fatu Hiva his crew raised three crucifixes and slaughtered two hundred natives. Much later other Westerners arrived, for longer or shorter visits, including the American frigate *Essex,* which based at Nuku Hiva to attack British shipping. (At one point its officers proclaimed U.S. sovereignty over the archipelago. But the *Essex* was subsequently captured by the British and the annexation was never ratified.)

For many years whalers and blackbirders flocked to these islands to refresh themselves, enjoy the favors of their handsome women, and recruit fresh crews for their vessels. Some ports became notorious, even by South Seas standards, for their lawlessness and debauchery, and Marquesans acquired Western diseases and the taste for rum with equally disastrous results. Some chiefs, alarmed at their inability to control the lawless foreigners, petitioned France to move in, and French sovereignty was proclaimed in 1842, after which the decline in population and the erosion of native life became better regulated.

It required several years and many bloody campaigns for the French to subdue all the remaining Marquesans, and official metropolitan interest was never very strong. Once, in 1859, the French abandoned the islands altogether; and when they later set up a new headquarters, at Hiva Oa, it was a mere gesture of sovereignty.

A cotton planting boom inspired by the American Civil War brought other adventurers to the Marquesas; and Chinese, Annamese, and Africans (from Martinique) were imported as laborers. But as in Fiji, the boom quickly passed and the plantations were abandoned although the diseases and drugs introduced by the immigrants remained. (Marquesans proved to be especially susceptible to opium, and little effort was made at the time to halt the trade in it.)

Eventually the whalers and blackbirders and planters moved on. Throughout that dismal epoch the Catholic mission was the only benign influence there, but even it proved incapable of staying the numerical decline and the cultural deterioration, which continued for several decades.

Finally, there is Makatea, a raised-coral ("pancake") island about two hundred miles north of Tahiti. As a source of phosphate and site for a large mining operation its history during the decades before 1939 differed markedly from that of the rest of French Polynesia; something about it is recorded in chapter 13.

Samoa

Rotting on the reef just off the beach at Apia, largest town of Samoa, lies the broken hull of the German warship *Adler,* which was wrecked there in the hurricane of 1889, a stark reminder of the many Westerners' intentions, good and bad, that have been wrecked in this Polynesian archipelago. The Samoans of 1939, sitting cross-legged on their fine mats and whisking flies off their muscular torsos, might well have smiled at the hundred-year impasse they had constructed against the relatively puny outsiders. These indigenes of the islands of Savaii, Upolu, Tutuila, and Manua had driven powerful foreign nations almost to war with one another; they had ruined many official reputations, forced planters and traders into bankruptcy, and divided Western settlers into hostile camps —all this just by remaining exquisitely *Samoan.* And in the process they had taken only what they needed and wanted from the intrusive Western civilization, while increasing their numbers and retaining their pride in the *fa'a Samoa* (The Samoan Way).

In 1939 Samoa presented a markedly different picture from the usual South Seas tableau of a native people cheerfully and unknowingly losing their identity and their heritage in a colonial setting dominated and economically exploited by outsiders. For that reason, Samoa had for many years been pronounced a colonial "failure," and the outsiders' money lost there in commercial ventures and well-intentioned administrative reforms had been nearly matched by the sums spent in official inquiries into the causes of those failures. The causes actually go back many centuries.

The massive islands of this archipelago must have been a welcome sight to the first Polynesians (from Tonga or Fiji or both) arriving there about three thousand years ago. Their descendants came to regard these islands as the best place in the world and The Samoan Way (Samoan custom) the only correct way to live. Those sentiments were nurtured by the ideal environment they dwelt in and by the degree of isolation they enjoyed. That isolation was, however, not complete; their traditions contain many allusions to continuing contacts with Tonga and Fiji, including wars, marriages, and trade. In addition, canoeloads of Samoans colonized several other islands near and far, including probably the Marquesas two thousand miles west.

The indigenous economy of Samoa resembled closely that of other high-island Polynesian societies—growing taro and yams, collecting breadfruit and coconuts, fishing, raising pigs, and so forth—but given the nature of their islands (less rugged topography, richer soils, and more equable climate than most others), it was perhaps easier for them to subsist, thereby leaving more time for the refined arts of Samoan ceremony and politics.

Large extended-family households were their basic residential and subsistence units, each one housed in one or more handsome and well-constructed round or oval houses. During recent centuries all households were grouped into compact coastal communities—true villages; before that some of them may have been inland and more widely dispersed. Crosscutting their households and communities were ambilineal common-descent units (clans), each of which corporately owned one or more of the society's chiefly titles and tracts of land. A person could affiliate with the clan of either parent, but received more important citizenship and land-use rights through paternal ties. The adult members of each clan designated one or more of its members to bear its titles, which authorized the incumbent(s), called *mataʻi,* to head the unit and represent it in the local village council *(fono).* Each clan was centered in one or another of the villages, but because marriage was prohibited between close consanguines, and because a wife usually resided in the village of her husband, some members of a clan, and especially its adult female members, lived in a village other than the one(s) where their clan *mataʻi* resided and where their clan lands were.

Each village was largely autonomous and conducted its communal activities (e.g., land clearing, large-scale fishing, ceremonial visiting, and so forth) under direction of the *mataʻi* of its local clans. But villages were also grouped into districts, generally because of close kinship ties and the occasional need for common action, including common war making. Like villages, each district had its council *(fono);* the members of such councils were, however, not elected to it by their respective villages but rather were those *mataʻi* whose clan titles entitled them to be so. In addition, each village within a district had its traditional role in ceremonials and warfare; for example, one served as the place of assembly for the district council, another as the center for oracles, another furnished leadership in interdistrict wars.

In time there developed larger combinations of districts into two great factions, Tumua and Pule, which encompassed all of Samoa except for the easternmost district of Manua, which remained unattached throughout. Either the Tumua or the Pule faction was alternately ascendant as a result of warfare or intrigue, and the rivalry for gaining or maintaining superiority went on continually. Superiority did not mean force-backed domination as much as prestige and precedence in social-ceremonial affairs, but these latter were the most highly valued goals in Samoan life, and the great families were forever intriguing and warring to push their own chiefly (i.e., *mata'i*) titles ahead.

In Samoa high social position meant title, precedence in ceremonials, and freedom from the activities and responsibilities of everyday life. For the practical side of politics the most highly revered titleholders (the *ali'i*) depended upon their own cunning and that of their principal titleholding spokesmen, called *tulafale* (orators), who not unusually possessed more leadership ability than their affiliated *ali'i*.

In the Samoan polity communalism was the rule, and the individual mattered less as an individual than as a member of a group (e.g., a family, clan, or village) or as the holder or nonholder of a title.

Such was the nature of Samoan society when the first significant Western settlement took place in 1830. In that year the London Missionary Society pioneer, John Williams, arrived from the Society islands and began his fiercely dedicated work. A few beachcombers had preceded him but their influence had been slight. The reception given Williams was anything but hostile: he was immediately adopted by the faction then in ascendance, accorded the high honors due a great sage, and generally assisted in his mission. The rites and cosmogony of the new religion were promptly incorporated into the native one, the Christian God occupying a high position in the supernatural hierarchy; and before many years Samoan converts were spreading the gospel to other islands. Wesleyan, Catholic, and Mormon missionaries arrived somewhat later and secured disgruntled or opportunistic followers of their own, thereby complicating the society's penchant for factional rivalry.

The missions were able to outlaw a few indigenous practices, such as the ceremonial defloration of brides—her virginity having been a source of pride both to her family and her groom—and to add a few new ones, such as strict observance of the Sabbath, but they did not bring about radical changes in native morality or ideology. In Samoa, where religion was less highly institutionalized than in, say, Tahiti, the native mission teachers simply replaced the native priests (such as they were), and the *mata'i,* formerly their clans' intercessors with supernatural beings, simply became deacons in village churches.

Samoans adapted to Western commerce as easily (and as characteristically) as they did to Western religion, choosing those aspects and items that fitted comfortably into the *fa'a Samoa* and rejecting the rest. From the very beginning, Western traders remarked at the lack of awe with which Samoans greeted the appearance of the iron and cloth that had sent Islanders elsewhere into transports of wonder and excesses of acquisitiveness. Samoans made enough copra to enable them to buy a few goods and to place offerings in their church boxes, and that was all. Indeed, there was little incentive for them to acquire more Western goods: to do so would have invited relatives and friends to divide them according to traditional practices of sharing and generosity.

In 1856 the powerful Hamburg firm of Godeffroy and Son established a trading station at Apia, developing it eventually into headquarters for Germany's commercial and political expansion throughout the Pacific Islands. Other companies, British and American, then set up offices and Samoa soon became the most active center of plantation and commercial life in the Pacific Islands. But the Samoans themselves did not succumb to the alien ethic of work and gain, so to assure plentiful supplies of copra for the expanding world markets, Western planters had to acquire land and start their own plantations. And when they learned they could not induce Samoans to work for them they imported Melanesians and Chinese.

By 1870 Samoans had accepted as much of the Westerners' religion and economy as they could comfortably swallow and were well on the way to assimilating it. At that point, however, rivalries among the local Westerners complicated the process.

Throughout the early period of Western contact native Samoan factional strife went on as before. On one occasion a truce between the two major factions succeeded in uniting in the person of one Samoan most of Samoa's most elevated titles, so that there was the appearance at least of a unified realm. Naïve foreigners took this at face value and assumed that it represented Western-style political unification. Then when it dissolved (as it inevitably did), the Westerners attempted to further their respective ambitions by taking sides—the Germans backing the aspirant of one faction and the British and Americans the other. There were the usual angry conferences, the pleas for protectorates, the suspicions of annexation, and the visits of warships, all to the glee of the Samoans, who appeared to relish the novelty of harassing their traditional enemies with modern weapons and trained Western fellows-at-arms. The German side enjoyed the advantage of having more intelligent coconspirators, more able personnel in their trading firms, and stronger naval support nearby. To complicate the issue, a clever rogue of an American, Colonel A. B. Steinberger, arrived on a semiofficial mission, sold out to the Germans, and was established as "premier," until the British and American consuls had him deported. Serious fighting involving nationals of the three powers then broke out and might have led to an international conflict but for a most timely hurricane, in 1889, which wrecked some of the warships preparing for hostilities, thereby drawing the attention of London, Washington, and Berlin to the perils involved.

Jealous of one another's advantage but cautious about wider ramifications, the three powers declared a joint protectorate over the "Independent Kingdom of Samoa," thereby solving nothing but the temporary dilemma of their diplomats. Ten years later, after the admitted failure of that arrangement, Britain withdrew from the Samoan scene, in consideration of concessions elsewhere. Germany and the United States thereupon divided the archipelago, the former taking Savaii and Upolu and the latter Tutuila and Manua, thus recognizing Germany's paramount commercial stake in more highly developed Upolu, and America's naval station in Tutuila's fine harbor of Pago Pago. From that time onward Western and Eastern Samoa went different ways. Copra continued to play important roles in both divisions, but in the American islands it was subordinated to the preoccupation of maintaining a naval base and coaling station there, a development described in chapter 14.

German administrators had very definite ideas about the role to be played by Western Samoa in the grand strategy of expanding German colonialism. First of all, Samoa was to become a rich tropical garden, producing coconuts, fruits, spices, and other things needed in the Western world. Second, the colonial administration there would be required to demonstrate to the rest of the world how Germany, late arrival though she was among the colonial powers, could govern skillfully and justly the native inhabitants of her new dependency.

A vigorous program of agricultural experimentation was undertaken and almost every known tropical crop tried out, with copra maintaining its first place and cocoa and rubber emerging as important commercial supplements. The *Deutsche Handels- und Plantagengesellschaft,* successor to Godeffroy and by far the largest company in the colony, retained its semiofficial status, but the administration dealt tactfully and sympathetically with the large community of non-German planters and traders already established on Upolu. Times were prosperous, although not all the foreigners profited equally. The colonists who flocked to Samoa from Germany, typically with more enthusiasm than knowledge and capital, soon learned that for tropical agriculture to be successful it had to be a large-scale enterprise, unsuited to the small holder. These new settlers joined with other dissidents in the Western colony and expressed their frustrations by criticizing the administration's big business and pronative policies.

The Germans approached the task of governing Samoa with firmness. They informed themselves thoroughly concerning the indigenous culture and shaped their practices accordingly. They promptly did away with the artificial kingship; and although showing respect for village autonomy and for the Samoans' dedication to ceremony, they suppressed all show of disruptive factionalism. Perhaps after a century or two they might have succeeded in weaning the Samoans from title rivalry and political intrigue, but during the few years of their administration they only drove them underground—but not very far underground.

In opposition to the administration's firm hand there developed a native movement labeled *Mau* ("Opinion"), which was led by thwarted

Samoan politicians and evidently encouraged by dissidents in the Western colony. But the solution to this new problem had to be left to the colony's next masters.

In August 1914 a New Zealand expeditionary force occupied Western Samoa without opposition and set up a military administration. Eventually the Versailles Treaty awarded the territory to New Zealand as a Class C mandate, to be governed as an integral part of the dominion in the interest of promoting ". . . to the utmost the material and moral well being and the social progress of the inhabitants. . . ." The League of Nations Covenant of the treaty prohibited slavery and forced labor, liquor and military training, and outlawed interference with mission work and with freedom of conscience and worship. Brave new world!

New Zealand officials approached the task with the best of intentions to carry out the letter and the spirit of the mandate, but their failures were so numerous and so apparent that at one point the government might have been relieved of its mandate had the League of Nations been stronger. In fact, it is improbable that any foreign government could have administered Samoa without some show of force, which, however, was foreign both to the spirit of the League Covenant and to the humanitarianism of the New Zealand government and public of the time.

First of all, the prosperity promised and to some extent realized in Samoa during the German days did not materialize under the new regime. During the first two decades of New Zealand rule copra prices fell off sharply, affecting both Samoans and Westerners. The former, who normally produced about 60 to 70 percent of the copra exports, dried and sold only enough to obtain basic necessities and left most of their groves unharvested.

Western planters suffered even greater reverses. The New Zealand administration had deported all Germans and had taken over their holdings for reparations and set up a company to operate them. Some of the groves were managed directly by government officials, others were leased to New Zealand settlers to operate. The substitution of inexperienced New Zealanders for the seasoned German planters would have had mixed results even in good times and proved to be particularly unfortunate during the postwar depression. Only the largest and most economically managed plantations managed to survive; inevitably, the less successful lessees and other Western settlers blamed their misfortunes on the administration, and managed to infect many Samoans with their dissatisfactions.

In the resulting crisis the noble intentions of the administration were not realized. In one sincere effort to dampen Samoan opposition it was decided to give them a larger voice in managing their own affairs. Thus was established a "democratic," territorywide council, with elected representatives from each village: a body wholly unlike anything the Samoans were accustomed to. For a while the council met in continuous sessions, indulged in typically interminable oratory, and rubber-stamped administration proposals. Meanwhile, back in their villages their "constituents" ignored them and set about to oppose on principle all the reform measures they had approved. At the same time the *Mau* movement surfaced again, this time demanding "Samoa for the Samoans."

Support for the movement came from antiadministration Westerners in the territory and from "native sympathizers" in New Zealand; the latter wrote countless letters to editors, which kept Samoan hopes high by their promise of material aid. The New Zealand government attempted to dissolve opposition by deporting the movement's most active leaders, including its part-Samoan organizer, which of course merely provided the movement with a useful martyr.

Underlying the *Mau* was the conservatism inherent in Samoan life. It manifested itself in a native boycott of things Western: Samoans made little or no copra and traded only with friends, they disobeyed regulations, and they refused to pay taxes. In addition, their leaders composed fine-sounding platforms, demanding autonomy and the end of Western exploitation and control.

At one point in the impasse open hostilities broke out and doubtless would have escalated had not a change of government taken place. Indeed, upon its accession to power in New Zealand, the Labour Government reversed official policy regarding Samoa by interpreting the *Mau* as a legitimate expression of native aspiration and set out to govern accordingly.

Meanwhile, Western enterprise in the territory declined, and it looked as if "Samoa for the Samoans" would become a reality. The New Zealand government undertook to market copra and bananas for their native producers, and did in fact assure some income for them, an operation that froze out the Western middlemen, however. Moreover, Western planters found it more and more difficult to secure labor and to survive in the face of world depression. All but a handful of the indentured Melanesians had been repatriated when Germany lost control, and the importing of Chinese laborers became increasingly hedged about with so many regulations that their numbers dwindled.

The half-castes in the population (Samoan mixed with Western or Melanesian or Chinese) increased in number, thereby providing even more problems for the administration. Some of the mixed bloods were absorbed into the Samoan communities, but many of the part-Westerners attempted to retain the status of their Western fathers, which placed them in the unhappy position of being unwanted by both Westerners and Samoans, and unprovided for by the administration.

While all the above was going on most of the full-blooded Samoans continued to increase in number and to follow their accustomed routines:

garden and grove work on Friday; Sabbath preparation on Saturday; church attendance, hymn singing, and feasting on Sunday; recuperation on Monday; fishing, visiting, and sports on Tuesday, Wednesday, and Thursday; and then begin again. To the Western missionaries they appeared to be devoted adherents and generous supporters of the church, little understanding the doctrines they enthusiastically sang about and ill-prepared to manage their own spiritual affairs. To the Western planters they seemed lazy and undependable, unsuited and unwilling to work, the spoiled darlings of an unrealistic bureaucracy. To many administration officials they remained an enigma, stubbornly resistent to all government efforts on their behalf. To the tourist they appeared a well-formed, gener-ous, and jolly people, living idyllic lives in beautiful surroundings. And to the anthropologist they provided one of the few examples of a Pacific Island people surviving the strong impact of Westernization without los-ing their numbers, their dignity, or their pride in their own ways.

Cook Islands

To state that the Cook islands are *between* Tahiti, Samoa, and Tonga in location is to characterize them in nearly every other respect as well. Their consolidation into one colonial unit, a New Zealand dependency, came about as a by-product of the powers' struggle for control over the more strategic Papeete, Apia, and Tongatabu; the Cook islands were, lit-erally, the crumbs that were left over after the choicer South Seas morsels had been swallowed up. Otherwise, aside from the common Polynesian origins of all Cook islanders, there was little logic in unifying them under a single administration. The northern islands of the colony, low-lying coral atolls crowded with coconut palms, had more geographic affinity with Samoa's coral outliers; the colony's larger, volcanic southern islands had a similar relationship with the neighboring French islands to the east. However, with Germany and the United States occupying Samoa and France all the islands to the east, Great Britain wasted no time in aca-demic geographic argument but took everything in between and handed it in one parcel to New Zealand for safekeeping. That was in 1901.

Long before then British missionaries were at work in both the north-ern and southern islands of this array, quickly transforming its peoples into Protestants.

In their traditional histories many Cook islanders trace their lines back to legendary expeditions from the same Polynesian homeland in the west, but after century-long residence on their separate islands their ways of life assumed some distinctive features. The northern islanders had to adapt austerely to the limiting environments of their atolls, but were not drawn together into a single cultural or political unity. In the larger, more fertile southern islands their peoples developed richer material cultures and more complex social structures, but unlike the Samoans and Society islanders they did not have frequent enough communication with one another to maintain or to forge a common cultural unity.

That unsavory trio—whaler, trader, and blackbirder—left their marks on all of these islands, and, as has been described, the Peruvian slavers nearly depopulated one of the northern atolls. Following those plagues the missionaries appeared. The indefatigable John Williams of the London Missionary Society arrived from the Society islands in 1823 and laid the foundation for an evangelization that was remarkable by any standard. Within a very few years most Cook islanders were converted, some to the point of serving to spread Christianity in heathen islands farther west. In the Cook islands themselves native forms of governance were superseded by mission theocracy: strict blue laws were enacted, night curfews imposed, "adultery" punished, and "immodesty" outlawed.

Meanwhile copra making and trading developed everywhere, supplemented by pearl- and pearl shell-diving in the northern atolls. And when the New Zealand market opened, fruit production became a lively activity in the southern islands.

Annexation of the islands to New Zealand in 1901 further stimulated fruit production, and the principal island, Rarotonga, along with its close neighbors, went over almost entirely to the growing of bananas and citrus fruits. Many Western planters and traders settled on Rarotonga and transformed it into a small facsimile of Apia; but few Westerners moved beyond Rarotonga, and the native residents of the colony carried on as before, producing only enough copra and handicraft articles to purchase Western-made luxuries and to make money contributions to their churches.

Lacking centralized native polities, the Cook islands afforded less opportunity for Westerners to move in and become kingmakers, as they had done with such profit in Fiji and Tahiti (and had attempted to do in Samoa). Nor was New Zealand far enough along in its own economic development to encourage many of its citizens to leave and seek their fortunes in the South Seas. Such factors as these, coupled with their relatively uninviting resources (relative to those of Tahiti, Samoa, and Fiji) may have helped preserve these islands for their native islanders. In addition, the New Zealand government enacted protective land laws that made it impossible, anyway, for nonnatives to acquire more than limited lease rights in Cook island real estate. And although the New Zealand government retained final controls, large areas of local authority were left in the hands of the islanders themselves.

After World War I Cook island economic ties with New Zealand were further strengthened, and political fusion made rapid headway. Elsewhere in the South Pacific, Western settlers, subjects of the colonial powers, were usually the instruments for such fusion, but in the Cooks the islanders themselves played that role. Associations of them were formed to produce and market their cash crops, and more and more administrative responsibility was placed in islanders' hands, but always, it seems, with the objective of encouraging their participation in New Zealand affairs. Unlike the case of Western Samoa, New Zealand's mandated dependency, the colonial alternative of evolution toward independence seems not to have been considered for the Cook Islands before World War II.

Solomon Islands

Tens of thousands of GIs will remember the Solomons for their climate and their coconuts. For sheer cussedness of the former these islands are hard to beat; and when malaria, dysentery, and blackwater fever are added to oppressive humidity and torrential rainfall, it is not surprising that the Solomons were, by Colonial Office standards, no jewel in the crown. And as for the coconuts, they were almost the sole money-earning resource there.

Three hundred and eighty years had passed since Westerners first discovered the fabulous Islands of Solomon, but by 1939 only a few hundred nonnatives, mainly Westerners and Chinese, eked out existences there, and except for colonial officials and missionaries, most of those settlers were in one way or another concerned with copra—producing or buying or transporting it.

Geographically the Solomons compose one sector of the double chain of islands extending from New Guinea to New Zealand. Some of them have fundaments of ancient continental rocks upthrust as massive mountain ranges through which lava has burst to form volcanoes. Heavy rainfall has served to clothe the larger Solomon islands with forests and swamps. Cluttering up the seas between the large islands are numerous small and flat ones covered with jungle and scrub. A few active volcanoes and frequent earthquakes serve to remind visitors that many parts of these islands are still subject to violent physical change.

By 1939 Western-induced cultural changes had been gradual. Back in the hills were to be found natives who had only recently replaced stone with steel, and even those more accessible to outsiders had adopted steel tools, calico, and some Christianity without changing radically their other indigenous ways of life.

Not that all of the archipelago's many native cultures had been alike; far from it. Although most of their subsistence technologies were similar (root-crop horticulture, pig raising, and some hunting and collecting), some of them had become specialists in, for example, catching fish or in manufacturing shell money (which they bartered with neighboring peoples for vegetables). And although most Solomonese spoke one or another of the archipelago's numerous (but widely differing) Austronesian languages, there were also pockets of peoples speaking Papuan tongues. And some of the colony's smaller islands were peopled with Polynesian speakers. In fact, Polynesian genetic and cultural influences were noticeable along the eastern shores of some of the larger islands as well.

The official limits of the British Solomon Islands Protectorate extended north only up to Bougainville, but in terms of genetic classification Bougainville and its northern appendage, Buka, may be grouped with the peoples of the western Solomons—with Shortland, Mono, Choiseul, Vella Lavella, and New Georgia. Together these people constitute the "Black Spot" of the Pacific, their skin color being darker than that of any other Islanders.

As for the social-relational aspects of their cultures, the Solomonese varied widely: in descent-unit structure (in some societies matrilineal, in others ambilineal, and in a few patrilineal); in forms of leadership (in some societies inherited, in others achieved, in still others both inherited and achieved); in the institutionalization of differences in sex or in age; and so forth. In fact, nearly every kind of social system and religious ideology found elsewhere in the Pacific Islands was represented in this one archipelago.

Even the Solomonese stereotype of "natural" ferocity requires some qualification. From the time of Mendaña's first visit in 1567 most native attacks against Westerners were the result of provocation. Mendaña's crew left a trail of blood, and those events seem to have been remembered by many peoples even during the centuries when they were "lost" to Westerners. Whalers used to call in for fresh water and food, and they were not noted for their diplomacy. Then, about 1840, traders began to visit the islands in search of sandalwood, trepang, and turtle shell; and in the usual tactics of their kind they added such refinements as the aiding and abetting of headhunting to curry favor with leaders who could provide good trade. But none of these outsiders made such impressions on the Solomonese as did the blackbirders.

Beginning about 1865 some Solomonese were induced to go to Fiji to work on cotton and coconut plantations. Ten years later they began to be sent in shipload lots to the sugar fields of Queensland. In addition to outright kidnapping, cargoes of them were obtained by offering incentives such as rum and firearms. No notice was taken by Western governments so long as the muskets were used only in local feuding, but when they were turned against Western traders and blackbirders British warships were ordered to shell villages and establish the usual law and order. Recruiting for Queensland was terminated in 1903 after thousands of Solomonese had been sent there; seven years later the recruiting for Fiji was also ended. Before and after that, however, the recruitment of Solomonese for labor within the archipelago continued up to World War II.

As a consequence of the annexation of Fiji, in 1874, and of her continuing campaign against more notorious forms of labor recruiting, Britain consolidated her de facto rule over the central and eastern Solomon archipelago between 1893 and 1899, and a resident commissioner was placed in charge. At that time there were only fifty Westerners residing in the colony—four missionaries and forty-six traders, and not one woman among them. Forty-three years later there were still only five hundred Westerners (officials, missionaries, traders, and planters) and two hundred Chinese traders residing there. Altogether, these foreigners numbered about ninety-four thousand fewer than the Solomonese they were there to employ, Christianize, or generally civilize.

In the first four decades of the twentieth century three kinds of alien institutions impinged on the Solomonese. Foremost was the copra economy, which consisted of labor recruiting, plantations, and trade stores. Second were the Christian missions, at least for about half of the native population. And third was the British colonial government, that awesome institution whose agents carried out censuses, collected taxes, and administered law and order Anglo-Saxon style.

The planters were the last of the three to arrive. Traders had begun buying native-made copra long before, but organized plantation enterprises were started only in 1905, when the British firm of Lever Brothers acquired land in the central islands and laid out cultivations ultimately covering about twenty thousand acres. Shortly thereafter the Australian firms of Burns Philp and the Malaita Company also started plantations. Later on they were joined by the Carpenter Company and a few independent planters, until there were over sixty thousand acres in coconut cultivation, not including the thousands of small groves owned by the Solomonese. Some missions also owned and operated plantations, which were comparable in size to the small-planter ones.

From a native's point of view the main difference between the aliens' plantations was their distance from home. Some Solomonese preferred work near home, but others liked the adventure and glamour of traveling to another island and the identification with a big-company enterprise.

"Government" meant the central Administration headquarters, the jail, and the native hospital, all at Tulagi; the administrative outposts, eight in all; and the annual census and tax-collecting patrols of district officers. The chief official, at Tulagi, was the resident commissioner, a British career colonial officer who was responsible to the British high commissioner of the western Pacific, then with headquarters at Fiji.

The Solomons were generally considered to be unsuitable for Westerners, and no official encouragement was given to Westerners to settle there. In theory at least the administration was pronative, and the officials seemed to have had the best of intentions towards native welfare, although they were ill-equipped in numbers or in facilities to carry out those intentions. And in at least one respect the administrative regulations involved a major paradox: a complex set of rules protected the natives from exploitation and mistreatment by planters, traders, and recruiters, but the head tax imposed on native adult males indirectly impelled nearly all of them to work at least a few years on plantations, there having been practically no other way to earn tax money.

The pioneer attempt to missionize the Solomons was by Catholics and began in 1845, but native hostility forced the Marist priests to postpone their endeavors for fifty years. Next in the field was the Anglican Melanesian Mission, whose work was first directed from New Zealand, then from Norfolk Island, and later from headquarters in the Solomons itself. This enterprising organization depended mainly upon native pastors and dispensed salvation and welfare from the deck of its circuit-traveling schooner, the *Southern Cross*. In due course Methodist, South Seas Evangelical, and Seventh-Day Adventist missions moved in; but by 1939 all the missions together had won adherence from only half the native population.

Those alien institutions—commercial, official, and missionary—influenced the native Solomonese as three distinct authorities and not as a unified Western civilization. The planter hired his labor, the missionary urged his adherence to a set of exotic beliefs and bizarre rules of human conduct, and the official demanded his tax money and his unquestioning obedience to a set of equally bizarre laws that had evolved in a nation on the other side of the world. At times the three sets of demands inevitably clashed, creating dilemmas for the native; and his bewilderment was increased when, all too frequently, he heard the Western "masters" (as they were called in Solomonese pidgin) commit that worst of all colonial crimes: criticizing one another's institution and character within native hearing. The ideological differences between official and missionary were particularly unfortunate; occasionally the wretched Solomonese had to choose between a mild but immediate jail sentence and a drastic but distant Hell.

Most planters, on the other hand, were singularly unconcerned with native civic behavior and native souls, although they had ample opportunity to influence both. At some point in their lives nearly all native youths signed on for a two-year contract to work on plantations, and many of them renewed their contracts for longer terms. Before World War II there were about five thousand of them (5 percent of the whole population) so engaged at all times. The starting age was about seventeen or eighteen; men with families seldom risked leaving their wives for such long periods.

Curiosity about the great outside world was doubtless one incentive for signing on; the need for tax money another. Western recruiters periodically made the rounds looking for new workers and were paid commissions by planters for those delivered; the employers were obligated to repatriate their native employees upon completion of indenture.

Plantation laborers dwelt in barracks and for about fifty hours a week carried out all the unskilled, and some of the semiskilled, jobs. At the bottom of the scale was the raw youngster, probably for the first time wearing a calico *lava-lava* around his loins, whose job it was to scurry up palms monkey-fashion to catch harmful insects. At the top was the seasoned "boss-boy," the veteran of ten to twenty years of plantation work, completely expatriated from his native village. Between those extremes were the coconut collectors and cutters. Each cutter was expected to cut five to six hundred pounds of copra a day, with a small bonus for larger amounts. Wages ranged from ten shillings to several pounds a month, supplemented by an officially approved ration scale of food, a calico loincloth each month, blankets, a mosquito net, soap, and tobacco.

Life at a plantation was completely foreign to Solomonese ways of living. Work was regimented and steady, and the government-backed contract, once entered upon, could not be broken without exceptional cause. Any one plantation would generally employ laborers from a number of different communities, or even different islands, so that the native workers usually had to converse in pidgin. Since there were usually no native communities within easy visiting range and few unmarried native women on the plantations, a worker's life there was abnormal, to say the least.

The only plantation workers who saw much of the civilization they served to support were the few who worked as domestics. The common plantation hands had to learn those wonders secondhand, notwithstanding the airs of sophistication many of them assumed when they returned home. This raises the question: just what effects did work on a plantation have on indigenous Solomonese ways of living?

The "finish-time" native usually returned home with a handful of shillings and a small wooden chest (with the all-important padlock) filled with trade-store knives, pipes and tobacco, cloth, blankets, and so forth, and often a multicelled flashlight (usually with no extra batteries); the use he made of such items provides one answer to the question just posed.

In most Solomonese societies it was possible for a man to rise to fame and influence in his own community by accumulating and distributing material things. Most of those societies possessed some kind of rudimentary "money": durable items such as strings of shell beads or dog teeth. These items were on special occasions worn as ornaments, but they functioned chiefly as repositories of value, having been used in ceremonial exchanges to cement pacts, acquire wives, reciprocate hospitality, and so forth. Some of the commoner types were used much as Westerners use currency (to purchase weapons, pottery clay, and so forth), but the higher "denominations" were reserved for ceremonial occasions.

The Solomonese did not ordinarily collect native money for the mere sake of accumulation; they used it mainly as just listed or to assist young kinsmen to do the same. The older men, who generally possessed most of the native money, were thus by that fact more influential than their juniors. Such was the indigenous practice in most Solomonese societies; in 1939 it still prevailed in many of them, although the influences of plantation work and mission proselytizing had served to undermine it somewhat. For one thing, the importance of younger men was materially enhanced by their plantation work, since their elders at home had to depend upon them for the shillings to pay head tax and to purchase Western goods. And although many young finish-timers continued the practice of distributing their plantation earnings among their elders, to ensure obtaining the native money needed for marriages and ritual exchanges, they returned to their home communities with, typically, less respect for social status based entirely on seniority and native-money wealth.

In yet another way the plantations affected indigenous ways of life. The absence of numbers of young males from their home communities inevitably put more burden on females, and on the very young and the very old, in producing food and maintaining other standards of indigenous life. This circumstance also tended to warp the traditional patterns of courtship and betrothal; few betrothed or married men could have expected their young fiancées or wives to remain faithful during their yearlong absences.

In addition to the kinds of specific consequences just listed, work on a plantation had two more general effects on the Solomonese. First, by bringing together workers from different communities and even different islands, it served to reduce some of the kinds of hostilities that formerly prevailed. That is not to say that all former enemies became friends just from working together: far from it; but enmities were no longer based on ignorance alone. Second, the plantations also provided their workers with some elements (technical skills, beliefs, social values, and so forth) of a shared subculture, including a common language (pidgin).

The effects of missions on indigenous Solomonese ways of life were considerably more direct. Missionaries, unlike most planters, *did* attempt to change native life, and among half of the colony's populace they had succeeded in some respects. The first conversions may have come about through natives' desires to emulate Westerners, but in recent decades that motive came to have less force than the education that was available only in mission schools. In this connection, many Solomonese attributed their caste subordination less to skin color than to Westerners' superiority in economic matters and expected someday to level those differences through schooling. (Remarkably, the inevitable disillusionment of the educated ones did not seem to dampen the hopes of others.) Over the years other Christian conversions were brought about by the desire of young men to break away from the authority of their more tradition-minded elders. The missions frowned on many of the ideas and practices, some of them "heathen," by which men rose to affluence and authority; and they attacked these, directly, by inveighing against them, and, indirectly, by encouraging young converts to ignore them—for example, to disbelieve the supernatural sanctions that helped to maintain the indigenous ways of getting ahead.

Government, the third outside influence on indigenous life, operated principally as a restraint. Natives learned by experience what they should *not* do, but the administration, unlike the missions, did not see fit to advise them what they *should* do or become. Before World War II the Solomonese did not seem to object very deeply (or at least not openly) to the colonial government; even incarceration in the Tulagi jail, although perhaps inconvenient, left no mark of stigma in other natives' eyes. In one respect only was there a grievance: the Solomonese did not understand why Westerners, with all their money, persisted in taxing them for their few hard-won pence.

All in all, the Solomonese did not fare too badly under Western rule, after blackbirding was supplanted by comparatively innocuous plantation indenture and after traders were required to purchase their products at regulated or at least competitive prices. Numerically the population had begun to reverse the decline that accompanied the first introduction of foreign diseases. The missions may have removed some of the pleasures formerly associated with heathen ceremonies, but church attendence also provided rituals that many Solomonese appeared to enjoy. And although the government may have removed some of the *esprit* that had attended warfare and headhunting, there were compensations for those whose villages were no longer attacked and whose heads were no longer taken. Moreover, despite the inroads of foreign plantations they still retained enough of their land to provide an ample supply of food.

Coastal New Guinea

The island of New Guinea sprawls across the top of Australia like a great bird, with its head pointed toward Borneo and its tail toward Fiji. Through the center of its fifteen-hundred-mile-long mass are ranges of rugged mountains reaching heights of seventeen thousand feet. In places the mountains fall away abruptly into the sea; elsewhere they slope gently and provide wide alluvial plains covered with rain forest or swamp. In the interior there are rolling, grass-covered plateaus, but these are isolated by mountains, by belts of limestone, or by wide swamps. A few great river systems (including the Fly, the Sepik, the Purari, and the Morobe) provide some access to parts of the interior, but also create thousands of square miles of swamps.

Added to the island's generally discouraging topography and disconcerting vegetation were deadly anopheles by the billions; large numbers of centipedes, scorpions, and crocodiles; and numerous native peoples lethally hostile to outsiders, including their nearest neighbors. Thus, it is not surprising that even as late as 1939 there remained large parts of New Guinea unvisited by Westerners and little changed by the outside world since agriculture had been introduced several thousand years earlier.

In 1939 most of New Guinea's million and a quarter of known (actually counted or credibly estimated) native inhabitants continued to dwell in small and typically widely separate communities, which ranged in size from less than one hundred to never more than a thousand residents. In many cases two or more communities shared ties of common language, of belief, of practices, and of kinship, but only rarely of common allegiance to one overall chief. Beyond the borders of such ties there usually prevailed deep suspicion of and hostile reaction to all other persons. Except for some enclaves of Austronesian-speaking peoples along the island's coastal fringes, most New Guineans spoke Papuan languages that differed very widely from one another. Wide differences also prevailed in physical type: in stature they ranged from pygmy to moderately tall, in skin color from dark to very light brown, in facial profile from straight to prognathous, and in hair form from tightly coiled to wavy.

And, not surprisingly, the cultural differences among the island's hundreds of distinct peoples were in many respects and in many instances quite wide. All of them practiced horticulture and animal husbandry to some extent, and most of them engaged, at least occasionally, in fishing and hunting and the gathering of wild plants, but there the similarity ends. They differed widely in their social relations (e.g., in the structure of their descent units and in their ways of attaining leadership), in the emphasis they placed on differences of sex and age, in their forms of esthetic expression, and so forth; in fact, in nearly every cultural domain. Indeed, only a huge encyclopedia, which this book is not, could do justice to the cultural diversity that prevailed in New Guinea.

North and east of New Guinea lie scores of smaller islands that have come to be identified with it for Westerners' administrative convenience. Most of these are included within what has come to be called the Bismarck Archipelago: New Britain, New Ireland, New Hanover, the Admiralties, and numerous smaller islands, all of which have had a distinctive recent history owing to their easier accessibility and their suitability for coconut growing. The Admiralties, including Manus island, are the homes of skilled Austronesian-speaking sailors. New Britain is a kind of miniature New Guinea and is well known for its active volcanoes. Clustered around the tail of the New Guinea "bird" are the Woodlarks, Trobriands, and Louisiades, inhabited by accomplished mariners.

Portuguese and Spanish navigators sighted New Guinea in the early sixteenth century but gave it wide berth. During the following century Dutch explorers skirted its shores but passed it up for their more profitable colonies in the Indies. British and French navigators (Dampier, Carteret, and Bougainville) defined parts of its coastal outlines more precisely, but none of them considered it worth colonizing.

The first proprietary move toward New Guinea was made by Holland in 1828, when Dutch suzerainty was established over the western half of the island. But that was only a gesture; although the claim was internationally recognized, for a hundred years thereafter the Dutch did little to consolidate their acquisition beyond establishing small administrative outposts and planting a few coconuts along the more accessible parts of the coast. Natives in the interior continued to go about their Neolithic ways and saw nothing of the outside world except occasional bands of Malayans in search of feathers of birds of paradise.

Coastal natives along the western fringes of the island kept up their age-old trade with the Moluccas, and through them such exotic commodities as dammar, ebony, ironwood, and trepang reached world markets. Also, the Japanese South Seas Development Company, reaching out from Palau, established a trading station on the head of the New Guinea "bird." Missions, Catholic and Protestant, made some headway along the western coasts; and a few converts were won over for Islam through the efforts of traders from Ceram. But the first real stimulus to exploration and development came only in 1932, when Dutch interests organized mineral and oil surveys.

The unclaimed eastern half of New Guinea began to experience the first tentative effects of Western contact somewhat later than did the western half. Fortunately for its natives, the whalers and sandalwooders mainly avoided New Guinea: whaling grounds were too far away and suitable trees inaccessible. Consequently, until about 1870 almost the only Western visitors to eastern New Guinea were explorers and a few Australian traders intent on exchanging their goods for coconuts, pearl shell, and curios. The first recorded shore trade station was set up in 1872 by an Englishman in the Duke of York islands, between New Britain and New Ireland. This pioneer enterprise was quickly followed by agents of the German Godeffroy and Son, operating out of Samoa. At about the same time a Wesleyan missionary began his labors there; and within ten years the Western population of eastern New Guinea and its neighbors had swelled to a total of thirty, mostly concentrated around the northeastern end of New Britain. Most of them were traders, dangerously engaged in bartering their goods for the coconuts and pearl shell of semihostile natives.

Around 1880 traders began to lay out coconut plantations in this area, but throughout the second half of the nineteenth century the local natives fared better than many Islanders elsewhere. In addition to escaping the attentions of whalers and sandalwooders they experienced only a few years of blackbirding, and that of a much milder variety than the scourge that had afflicted parts of the Solomons and the New Hebrides.

During those pioneer days, however, eastern New Guinea was a lawless place, or rather a place of many codes. The few Western planters and traders individually policed their own neighborhoods; even the missionaries were not above fighting (and even killing) hostile natives. Meanwhile some of the traders began to feel out the nearby coasts of the main island, but the missionaries and planters kept to the safer grounds of the smaller islands. And many more planters, mostly German, arrived on the scene.

Although Germany entered the colonial scene late, she made up for it in zeal. The prospect of a South Seas empire to rival Britain's was hugely appealing, and there developed in the Reich a popular agitation to take on new territories. Bismarck's government was at first cool to overseas expansion but the nation's influential merchants changed that.

As more and more Germans appeared in New Guinea and its nearby islands the blunt-speaking and justifiably suspicious Australians warned London and urged annexation, in the interest of Australian security (and commercial advantage?). An official of the Queensland government actually raised the British flag near present-day Port Moresby in 1883, but London promptly repudiated the action. Shortly after, while London and Berlin were exchanging polite disclaimers the government-backed Neu Guinea Kompagnie also raised a flag, this one over northeastern New Guinea and the Bismarck Archipelago. Howls of anger and frustration from Australia finally moved London to assert British sovereignty over southeastern New Guinea and adjacent islands, thereby completing the partitioning begun by the Dutch. From this time onward the three parts of New Guinea—Dutch, German, and British—moved along separate courses; but in one respect the courses were in the same direction, toward copra economy, until after World War I, when the discovery of rich goldfields and the quest for oil led them along separate paths.

Northeastern New Guinea

Included in the German colony were Kaiser-Wilhelmsland (northeastern New Guinea), Neu-Pommern (now New Britain), Neu-Mecklenburg (New Ireland), Neu-Hannover (Lavongai), and the Admiralty islands. Later, by agreement with Britain, the northern Solomon islands of Buka and Bougainville were added, leaving Britain with the rest of the Solomons. Until 1899 administration of the German colony was left in the hands of the chartered Neu Guinea Kompagnie; but the expense of exploration and governing, added to the usual costs of developing new plantations, setting up trade stations, and maintaining interisland and overseas shipping, forced that company to transfer administration to the German Colonial Office. Earlier, an attempt had been made to establish an administrative headquarters for the whole colony on the main island, at Finschhaven and Madang, but malaria and isolation soon induced the officials to locate at Rabaul (New Britain), in the heart of the settled plantation area. (From Rabaul the administrator also governed the German-owned Marshalls, Carolines, Marianas, and Nauru.)

German explorers penetrated far into the interior of the main island, and missionaries fanned out along the coasts, but planters and traders concentrated their efforts upon New Ireland and northeastern New Britain, where they prospered. (Their prosperity, however, was due, not to free-market factors but to indirect subsidy by the German government and by an economically captive cheap native labor force.) Enterprises controlled by large chartered companies predominated, but small independent planters and traders also shared in the increasing profits from copra and pearl shell. When the supply of accessible native labor thinned out, Javanese, Malayan, and Chinese laborers were brought in. The firm-handed government protected the local natives from excessive abuses but otherwise made it clear that the territory was a *colony*, to be utilized for political and economic profit, and not a *trust*, to be administered solely for its natives' welfare.

Upon the outbreak of World War I an Australian expedition landed on New Britain and forced the Germans to capitulate after two days of skirmishing. Then, for seven years the whole territory remained under military rule. The Australians were unprepared for the job of comprehensive administration and maintained, with few changes, the laws and procedures established by the Germans. They even permitted German planters and traders to carry on, under oaths of neutrality, so that commercial life continued as before. During this interim no major efforts were made to open up new areas or start new enterprises, since the international legal status of the territory was uncertain.

In 1920 the territory was awarded to Australia as a Class C mandate, and a year later civil administration was inaugurated. Some changes were then made in the former laws regulating acquisition of land and use of native labor, but the copra economy continued along lines that had been established in German days. The Malays and Javanese were repatriated but most of the Chinese, who had meanwhile become artisans and small traders, remained. The German estates were expropriated and sold and their former owners sent home. Although an effort was made to distribute those estates among smallholders, and particularly returned soldiers, the big companies (including Burns Philp and Carpenter's) eventually gained control of the largest share.

Thereafter, the copra economy spread from New Britain and New Ireland to the New Guinea mainland, and clusters of plantations sprang up around Finschhaven, Madang, and Wewak. In time the area under coconut cultivation reached 265,000 acres, with annual exports averaging seventy thousand tons, over half from New Britain and New Ireland. The worldwide depression of the thirties did not spare New Guinea's copra industry and would have crippled its administration (under Australian rule the territory was required to be financially self-sustaining) if the discovery of huge new deposits of gold in the interior of the main island had not uncovered a new source of revenue. But that is another story, which is told in chapter 13. For the other known and government-controlled areas of the territory copra remained the dominant commercial influence. Within the latter areas there were, as in the Solomons, three major forces active in transforming the previously autonomous and largely egalitarian native peoples into inferior-caste subjects; those were plantation, missionary, and government. The differences in results of those forces, between the territory and the Solomons, were due mainly to the much greater size and much larger population of the former. The more accessible populations of the Solomons had by 1939 become at least partially Westernized, whereas the mountains and swamps and the vast Highland plateaus of New Guinea still harbored tens of thousands of "uncontrolled" natives, including many who were not even discovered until shortly before World War II.

In the years just before World War II half of the total number of the Mandated Territory's forty thousand indentured native laborers worked on plantations, and the turnover was great, especially at the end of the standard three-year term of contract. It can be estimated, therefore, that a large proportion of the total accessible population worked for Western planters at some time in their lives, and the effects of such contacts were like those in the Solomons.

In 1939 the eleven mission organizations active in the territory claimed over 300,000 converts, with annual additions averaging twenty thousand. Here as in the Solomons missionaries launched direct attacks upon the heathen aspects of native life, as well as upon the doctrines and practices of rival missions (see chapter 9). If the extent of their successes were to be measured by the numbers of village chapels, memorized catechisms, elementary schools, and sanitary reforms, then missionaries should be credited with many tactical victories. Also, they had doubtless enlarged the native pantheons of spirits and supernatural powers; but it is unlikely that they had succeeded in transforming many native attitudes or practices vis-à-vis the supernatural, least of all in the sphere of magic, both helpful and harmful.

Government, the third factor of change, had become a very large enterprise just before World War II. It sought to regulate relations between nonnatives and natives, to improve native subsistence economies, and to bring all natives under administrative control. By itself it employed about seventeen hundred natives in its work, and through taxation, patrols, policing, courts of justice, and medical services affected to some extent the lives of all those under administration control. It was staffed by men specially trained for the work and dedicated to the objectives of the League of Nations Mandate. It did, of course, attempt to wipe out native practices regarded as inhumane or inimical to civil order (such as headhunting and feuding); and through its practice of recognizing and appointing native village officials it institutionalized and concentrated native leadership more so than did the native institutions themselves. But it did not, as an organization, attempt to transform New Guineans into Australians, nor even consider them capable of becoming so!

These three agencies of change did not constitute the whole story. Many thousands of natives were employed as stevedores, truck drivers, boat crews, domestics, and so on, and they, more so than plantation laborers, received closeup views of Western civilization. Most finish-time workers eventually returned home, and by carrying their impressions with them served to diffuse those views, however distorted or biased, widely. But more and more native workers tended to remain at the Western settlements, to become detribalized and to work as casual day laborers, thereby earning higher wages and retaining freedom to change jobs, or even to strike.

In 1936 most of the native workers in and around the territorial capital of Rabaul went so far as to unite in a weeklong strike, mainly for higher wages. This unprecedented action stunned the Westerners and while it lasted paralyzed productive and commercial activities. (So far had the natives become civilized!) Quickly, however, the Western planters and businessmen made it clear that, Mandate or no Mandate, Westerners were masters, in both pidgin label and actual fact, and that commerce was supreme. And in this territory, recently enriched through the discovery of vast gold deposits, the commercial future seemed so promising and Western "masters" so numerous that, regardless of published official policy, events were moving toward a Westerners' empire (made possible, of course, by natives' cheap labor).

Papua, meanwhile, with its fewer profit-making resources, followed a somewhat different course.

Papua

The pre–World War II history of the Territory of Papua, comprising the southeastern quarter of New Guinea and its nearby islands in the Coral Sea, falls properly into two periods: from 1884 until 1906 it was administered by agents of the British Colonial Office, since 1907 by those of Australia.

During the first period Papua (or, as it was then called, British New Guinea) did not keep pace with the commercial and agricultural developments pushed by the Germans in the neighboring colony. In fact, Western plantations were almost nonexistent there; and except for some trading, Western economic activity was limited to prospecting. Scores of adventurers underwent epic hardships to find gold, and some of them succeeded in a small way, but a permanent industry failed to materialize because, as one prospector put it, "There's plenty of gold in Papua, but there's too much of Papua mixed in with it."

The main preoccupation of the administration during the first period was exploration and the pacification of "wild tribes"—quite the reverse of the German policy of that era, which was to develop a prosperous and comfortable coastal colony before bringing new areas under governmental control.

The second period of Papua's pre-1939 history was characterized by the active encouragement of Western settlement and the evolution of a more comprehensive native policy. Throughout this period Papua's administration differed markedly from that of its northern neighbor: Sir Hubert Murray and his staff conceived of their task as a balanced course of action between the economic development of some of the colony's natural assets and the trusteeship of native welfare. Toward the first objective they inaugurated a liberal land policy to encourage "persons of means" to settle in Papua and start plantations. Individual adventurers and speculator syndicates were not admitted, but individuals of "substance" and well-capitalized companies were welcomed. There was a minor real-estate rush for a while, but it petered out when it was learned how infertile most of the colony actually is. By World War I, over thirty thousand acres had been planted in coconuts, but the trees did not mature in time to take advantage of the wartime boom in copra prices, as had the older plantations in the neighboring colony; and by the time Papua's copra was ready to be exported the prices were low again. Also, the Australian Navigation Act abolished competitive marketing by restricting Papua's trade outlet to Australian ports (which in fact meant only one vessel a month, to and from Sydney). The shipping situation improved somewhat a bit later, but then the worldwide depression contrived to keep Papua poor in terms of monetary profits from exports.

Meanwhile, thousands of acres of Pará rubber trees were planted and proved well suited to Papua's soil, climate, and type of labor; but the industry suffered from the same economic pains as copra, and not until the late thirties did its prospects begin to improve.

Discouraging as that all was to the planters, it may have been a blessing in disguise for indigenous Papuans (who at the time numbered about 230,000). Freed from pressures to secure land and laborers for Western enterprise, the administration was able to formulate and put into practice a comprehensive but gradual program of Westernization for its native charges. Exploration went on apace, and new peoples were placed under administrative control. Natives were taxed only according to their ability to pay, and all such tax revenues were set aside for native education and medical welfare. And, although the administration favored having natives work for short periods in Western enterprises, no pressure was exerted to make them do so, either by official encouragement or by preferential tax treatment. The administration even advanced to the near-heretical position (according to many Westerners) of assisting natives to set up their own income enterprises to avoid becoming detribalized and disinherited wage-laborers.

Government revenue in Papua was limited by the poverty of the colony and the ridiculously small Australian subsidy (£30,000 to £50,000 per annum), so that the missions were encouraged to maintain native schools. And in this connection, to anyone coming to Papua from the neighboring Mandate Territory and its inter-mission rivalries and mission-planter-government squabbles, the counterpart Papuan relationships seemed harmony itself. For one thing, mission areas in Papua did not extensively overlap. Also, the administration regarded evangelization as an essential substitute for the native religions, which the policy makers perceived to be disappearing willy-nilly.

The effect of all these circumstances was that the cultural changes undergone by the natives of Papua were in some respects just as far-reaching as those experienced in the neighboring Mandate, but those changes were administered in smaller, better regulated doses.

New Hebrides

Between the Solomons, New Caledonia, and Fiji lies the cluster of reefs, shoals, and high islands, including some live volcanoes, that Captain Cook, with singular inappropriateness, named the New Hebrides. To a confusion of topography, tropical vegetation, and native peoples, Westerners have added their own destructive genius, so that in 1939 the archipelago stood unchallenged as one of the unhealthiest, wildest, most mistreated, and most mismanaged spots on earth. According to his tastes, a

1930s visitor to these islands could squat down in a jungle hut and eat roasted yams or, only a few miles away, dine elegantly and swap international gossip with urbane officials in either British English or Parisian French.

Central in the archipelago are Espiritu Santo and Malekula—large, mountainous, forested, and inaccessible. Nearby is tame Efate, with grassland plateaus and gardened coastlands. Lopevi Island is an active volcano, Aore one vast coconut grove, Aneityum a valuable timberland (for more about which see chapter 7). Dangerous reefs and mangrove swamps, insects and parasites, all combine to give these islands a wretched reputation. Malaria and blackwater fever proved fatal to many Western settlers, and natives suffered more than the usual quota of those and other endemic diseases.

Except in some of the smaller eastern islands, where lighter-skinned and straighter-haired peoples lived, most New Hebrideans were dark-skinned, prognathous, and woolly-haired. Original estimates (mostly sheer guesses) of their numbers before Western contact varied between one million and fifty-eight thousand, with most of them in the seventy to one hundred thousand range (McArthur and Yaxley 1968:20). The first authoritative census, in 1967, put the number at seventy thousand, about twenty to twenty-five thousand more than had been estimated in 1939. Given the known occurrences of several devastating epidemics introduced during the times of sandalwooding and labor recruiting, it is certain that the population of these islands had, before 1939, suffered some decline in numbers, but not as sharp as many writers (including myself) had once surmised. (Moreover, comparison between the more credible estimates of 1939 and 1967 indicates a steady increase.)

As in most of New Guinea and the Solomons, the native communities of the New Hebrides were small, politically discrete, and integrated mainly by ties of kinship. Also, as in most of New Guinea and the Solomons, a great deal of effort was spent by New Hebrideans on pigs—breeding, accumulating, and distributing them for wealth and prestige and social influence. But in many New Hebridean societies a pig's value inhered less in the size of its body than in the size and shape of its tusks; the object was to train a boar's lower incisors so that they pierced the jaw and formed one or more complete circles—a pig with a full-circle tusk (or an excised full-circle tusk worn as a bracelet) was the most highly valued object in many New Hebridean societies.

Another distinctive feature of many New Hebridean societies was an emphasis upon secret cults, whose members advanced through a series of masoniclike grades by payments (including tusked boars or tusk bracelets) to those in the next-higher grade. Most of the cults were limited to formally (often brutally) initiated males, but some communities had a female cult as well. In the absence of inherited chieftainship, prestige and privilege in such communities derived from one's position in a cult, and activities connected with cults absorbed most men's lives. And although the cults of each community were entirely local and autonomous, their widespread occurrence and the many similarities between them lent to the archipelago a measure of cultural unity and distinctiveness present in few other parts of Melanesia.

Some ethnologists have drawn attention to Polynesian-like religious elements in several New Hebridean cultures, particularly to myths and rituals associated with local equivalents of the Polynesian god, Tangaroa. It would have been surprising if some stray canoeloads of Polynesian speakers, sailing with the southeast trades, had not reached these shores. But nothing that the Polynesians brought or did could have prepared the New Hebrideans for the visitation of still lighter-skinned men from overseas.

Quirós started the procession in 1606; but Providence and poor map making and navigation spared the islands further foreign visits for 160 years, after which Bougainville, Cook, Bligh, La Pérouse, and D'Entrecasteaux came, and quickly went, in rapid succession. All met trouble, even the usually mild James Cook. La Pérouse's entire party was lost, and probably eaten—the fate of that ill-starred would-be colonist has never been fully discovered.

The next visitations came in 1828, when traders and whalers went ashore seeking sandalwood or refreshment. The southern islands were hardest hit, but none was totally spared. For a period, cheap trade goods (red cloth, axes, knives, beads, tobacco) brought in the sandalwood; and some vessels took along their own logging crews of Polynesians, who succumbed to the local fevers in droves. Then there followed the inevitable clashes between traders and natives, with the usual results; the former had the guns. When sandalwood became scarce and natives reluctant, persuasion was used: kidnapping for ransom, village destruction, and murder. Western-introduced diseases were even more devastating in many places than guns. Here are a few examples (all taken from Tom Harrison, *Savage Civilization*):

— In 1842 a British vessel landed Tongans on Erromango to cut sandalwood. The arrogant Polynesians promptly picked a fight with the local natives, killed sixty of them by gunfire, drove the survivors, including women and children, into caves, built bonfires in the entrances, and roasted the lot. Then the vessel was loaded with sandalwood (no troublesome owners to bother with) and sailed to another unsuspecting island.

— In 1861 one schooner deliberately landed some measles-infected Tanna islanders on Erromango, thereby fatally infecting one third of the population.

— A favorite trick was to capture a community's chief and hold him as hostage until his people ransomed him with sandalwood. Then, instead of releasing the man he would be traded as cannibal fare to another island for more sandalwood.

In some cases, after the natives had supplied sandalwood to a trader he would shoot a few of them and burn their houses to discourage competitors from calling there later on. This stratagem, together with others applied less deliberately, soon moved the natives to suspect that traders and whalers were not, as some of them had earlier believed, the reincarnated Sailing Gods; and after this disillusionment the killing became a two-sided affair.

Into this turmoil moved the missionaries. The London Missionary Society was the first to arrive, in the person of the ubiquitous John Williams. That recklessly self-confident and compellingly dedicated man turned from Polynesia to the New Hebrides in 1839, where he secured immediate martyrdom by walking about unarmed in a place where sandalwooders had left their calling cards. William's murder did not, however, weaken the resolve of his colleagues, who continued their good works by depositing ashore several Samoan teachers, some of whom also achieved martyrdom, as typified in the following account:

In 1853 a Reverend Murray landed several Polynesian teachers on the island of Efate and rejoiced: "When we took the teachers on shore to this most inviting sphere, the joy of the people seemed to know no bounds" (Harrison, *Savage Civilization,* p. 151). Nineteen days after Murray's departure the teachers were all murdered. But, nothing daunted, the mission made another attempt on Efate a year later; result: four teachers and their families killed (and eaten), one dead of fever, another of dysentery.

The Presbyterians were the next to enter the field. The demographic consequences of their evangelization on Aneityum were reported in chapter 7; in other respects, however, they were quite successful, both in converting native survivors and in withstanding the opposition of Western traders (who were shrewd enough to foresee the curtailment of free trade in an area too well missionized).

With diminishing supplies of sandalwood and hence fewer traders the missionaries might have prevailed and brought some order into this anarchy, had it not been for the blackbirders, who soon appeared on the scene. That sordid story has already been told (in chapter 4): how New Hebrideans and other Melanesians were recruited to work on the plantations of Fiji and Queensland; how the commerce in labor became so appallingly ruthless that British warships had to patrol the islands to capture the blackbirders and pacify their vengeful victims (typically by firing a round or two at their villages). No part of Melanesia suffered this evil so intensely or for so long as did the New Hebrides. Thousands of men were taken, mainly by force or false promises, and held for years on foreign plantations without redress. Those who managed to return home brought back with them diseases, firearms, a taste for liquor, and in many cases a cold and enduring hatred of Westerners. The diseases did much damage, the guns (which added efficiency to local feuding) probably did more (obliging traders having seen to the replenishment of ammunition supplies).

It would overextend this chapter by providing more examples of the blackbirders' inhumanities; readers wishing to learn more about them should turn to the works of Corris (1973a, b), Scarr (1968), and Palmer (1871). The latter traveled around the islands in 1869 with (in his words) ". . . the sole object of exposing the deeds that have been perpetrated among the beautiful islands of the South Pacific, by men calling themselves Englishmen, and whose transactions have been invariably carried on under cover of our glorious old flag" (Palmer 1871:vii).

Toward the end of the blackbirding period French and British planters arrived. Large acreages were cleared and planted in coconuts, coffee, and cocoa. Frenchmen from New Caledonia invested in many of the plantations and encouraged more French settlement in the New Hebrides. For a time it seemed that France might even annex the archipelago, but Britain intervened and, anxious to keep out other powers but unwilling to assume sole responsibilities, compromised to the extent of joining France in setting up a joint naval commission to safeguard the interests of their respective nationals. This measure was undertaken in 1887; it proved to be so unworkable that it was replaced twenty years later by an Anglo-French Condominium administration, a slightly more workable, much more elaborate, and distinctly more bizarre system. It "worked" like this:

There was a British Commissioner and his staff charged with safeguarding the interests and curbing the delinquencies of all British subjects, and a corresponding set of officials for the French. Each government maintained its own courts, police force, prisons, currency, weights and measures, and sundry other regulations. In addition, there was a joint condominium staff placed in control of customs, radiotelegraph, and certain phases of justice. The jurisdiction of the Joint Court was mainly limited to questions of land ownership, to cases referred to it by mutual consent of the parties, and to offenses involving native New Hebrideans. The first Judge President, who presided over French and British judges, was, according to the terms of the condominium treaty, appointed to his office by none other than the king of Spain. That worthy was as truly neutral as he was required by rule to be: he understood little French, less English, and of course no New Hebridean vernacular or pidgin; however, none of those deficiencies seems to have been the most serious handicap, because he was also deaf.

Along with such comedy, the condominium had also its tragic side.

France looked after Frenchmen and Britain after British, but only the politically impotent missionaries looked after the natives who had managed to survive a century of Western contact. There were native regulations aplenty, and pages of legal safeguards designed to protect natives from Westerners, but the machinery to enforce those measures was ridiculously inadequate and the loopholes miles wide.

Out of this mess French nationals and French influence emerged dominant. The British regime imposed the usual British restrictions upon its own nationals, regulating their alienation of native land and use of native labor. The French regime, on the contrary, consistently supported French colonization by laws favoring expansion of plantations. The French, but not the British, were permitted to import indentured Asian laborers, and thousands of Tonkinese helped many French plantations to survive and prosper while their British neighbors failed. Also, the French government supported its nationals financially when hurricane devastation or price declines threatened failure. The result was that just before World War II there were 750 French and only 200 British in these islands; several British subjects had given up and left or become naturalized Frenchmen.

For the New Hebridean native it was not so simple: he was not allowed to become French. On the other hand, he could become or remain a Protestant or a Catholic. In fact, the missions seem to have been the only effective, at least partly effective, guardians of native welfare.

SOURCES

General: Brookfield 1972; Brookfield and Hart 1971; Panoff (ed.) 1986.

Gilbert and Ellice islands: MacDonald 1982; Maude 1938.

French Polynesia: Danielsson 1956; Davies 1961; Dening 1980; Hanson 1970; Newbury 1980b; Oliver 1974; Toullelan 1986; West 1961.

Samoa: Davidson 1967; Gilson 1970; Gray 1960; F. Keesing 1934; Mead 1930; Ross 1969; West 1961.

Cook islands: E. Beaglehole 1957; Crocombe 1964, 1971; Ross 1969.

Solomon islands: Belshaw 1954; Bennett 1987; Corris 1973b; R. Keesing 1986; Scheffler 1971.

Northeastern New Guinea: Chowning 1986; Jacobs 1972; Mair 1948; Panoff 1979; Rowley 1958; Sack 1986; Stanner 1953; Wu 1982.

Papua: Legge 1972; Murray 1925; West 1968.

New Hebrides: Adams 1986; Belshaw 1954; Guiart 1956, 1986; Harrison 1937.

CHAPTER ELEVEN

Sugar

The "honey-bearing reed" was merely another souvenir of the fabulous East when Alexander brought some specimens home from India in 325 B.C., but as mankind's sweet tooth developed through the centuries, sugarcane became a factor in international politics, having shaped the course of history in many polities, including three Pacific archipelagoes.

In the period immediately before 1939, world consumption of sugar (raw sugar value) averaged over thirty million short tons annually, and about 60 percent of this derived from sugarcane. Some sugar was used for manufacturing industrial alcohol but it was principally a food, and probably the least expensive of all foods in terms of its cost per calorie.

Sugar passes through five processes before it reaches the consumer in white granulated or powdered form. Initially, juice is extracted by passing the cane through rollers pressed together by powerful hydraulic rams. The juice is then clarified by heating and liming, and the clear liquid is subjected to vaporizing to remove excess water. From the resulting thick syrup raw sugar is crystallized and dried in centrifugal machines. Processing up to this point usually takes place at the locations where the cane is grown; the actual refining of the raw sugar into the final product is nearly always done in refineries near the consumer market.

Sugar is universally such an important item, in peacetime and in war, that most nations strive for self-sufficiency in it by subsidizing domestic production and by tariff barriers. The international sugar picture is further complicated by competition between sugarcane, typically produced in distant cheap-labor areas, and beet sugar, costing more to produce but grown in strategically safer areas nearer centers of consumption.

Australia's sugar, for local consumption and export, was (and is) produced in Queensland. In the nineteenth century Pacific Islanders were imported for labor in the Queensland cane fields, but since 1902 the industry has had to depend upon other workers and has had no direct influence upon the lives of Pacific Islanders.

Not so, however, in Hawaii and Fiji. For several decades preceding World War II the growing of sugarcane was the dominant industry in those two archipelagoes and, directly or indirectly, brought about revolutionary changes in the lives of the indigenous segments of those societies. (After World War I, when Japan seized control of Saipan and Tinian, a comparably large-scale sugar industry was established there; an account of that is given in chapter 14, in the context of other Japanese activities there.)

The effects of sugarcane growing on Island life differed markedly from those accompanying the production of copra. For one thing, cane growing in the Islands was developed by means of tightly integrated mass-production methods. Even within each protected national sphere prices had to be kept somewhat competitive, and profitable operation depended upon installation of expensive machinery kept in continuous use. All that involved centralized control, large capital resources, and assured access to very extensive cane plantings. Under such conditions it was not economically practicable to produce cane, like coconuts, in small scattered groves. In the case of copra, large plantations were able to produce a more uniformly dried product in their large hot-air ovens, but individual growers were also able to produce marketable copra, either by drying it themselves in their own small dryers, or by selling it in lots, however small, to middlemen. In contrast, the technology required to process sugarcane economically enough to be price competitive was complex and costly; estimates were that a sugar mill of the 1930s could not operate profitably on plantation units of less than ten thousand acres.

In their beginnings the sugar industries of Hawaii and Fiji were also conducted on very small scales and included the participation of local islanders as suppliers of cane and as laborers in the Western plantations and mills. However, as the operations increased in scale their Western proprietors had to look elsewhere for more dependable and submissive laborers, and eventually the only direct contribution made by local islanders to the industry was in the form of their land, either by lease or outright sale. In due course scores of thousands of Asians and other foreigners were imported to provide the needed labor, and through the thousands of those who remained as permanent residents the societies of both Hawaii and Fiji were transformed to a revolutionary degree.

Hawaii

From Captain Cook in 1778 to Admiral Yamamoto in 1941, "progress" in Hawaii consisted mainly in the substitution of one form of autocracy for another. Economically, taro and other root crops were replaced by sugar and pineapples; politically, a hereditary ruling caste of Polynesian chiefs was supplanted by a semihereditary ruling caste of Western businessmen. During that era some new lands were opened up and some old ones abandoned. Although the population of the archipelago altered radically in composition, it increased numerically by only one-third: an increase that might well have taken place in time under the old native order without benefit of clergy, mass immigration, industrial paternalism, or medical science.

The Hawaiian archipelago consists of a chain of islands and reefs extending northwest to southeast for sixteen hundred miles. It was formed (is in fact still being formed) by magma flowing up through a weak "hot spot" in the vast Pacific tectonic plate. As the plate moved toward the northwest (at the rate of about 4 inches a year) the underlying magma flowed through the "hot spot," eventually building mountains. Of those that reach heights above sea level the oldest, and hence most eroded, are in the northwest; the youngest (and still volcanically active) island is Hawaii, in the southeast. During the twenty-five million years of their building these islands have also undergone several major changes in sea level and hence of coral formation around their shores.

The eight islands of the chain that were inhabited when Westerners first visited in 1788 contained a large number of distinctive natural zones, the result of differences in topography (from flat coastal plains to mountains up to fourteen thousand feet above sea level) and in rainfall (from under 10 inches annually to over 450). Moreover, the native Hawaiians were at that time utilizing nearly every one of those kinds of zones, even the seasonally snow-decked mountain peaks, where they mined stone for shaping into tools.

Due mainly to their isolation the Hawaiian islands were the last to be settled by Pacific Islanders. That first occurred in about A.D. 750 and by people from the Marquesas, two thousand miles to the southeast. (Evidence for this firm conclusion comes from archaeology and linguistics.) That first landfall was of course accidental, but it was not unusual for canoeloads of Marquesans to take off from their relatively barren islands to escape from their interminable wars or in search of more fruitful lands. Many of those desperate expeditions doubtless ended in the deep but enough of their canoes reached Hawaii for their passengers to survive and reproduce. Some scholars have proposed that the pioneer immigrants from the Marquesas were followed somewhat later by others from the more distant Society islands; it has been recently demonstrated that such voyages *could* have taken place, but not that they did so. In any case, over the course of a thousand years the residents of the Hawaiian islands proliferated and prospered in at least comparative isolation from other Pacific Islanders, and, it should be added, from American Indians as well.

By 1778 the Hawaiians numbered about 200,000 to 250,000, and although they were divided into several distinct politically autonomous districts they shared a common culture, including a single language, similar religious beliefs and practices, and similar patterns of social organization. Owing to the archipelago's wide variety of natural areas and the fairly widespread distribution of communities, there was some localized specializations in subsistence patterns (as, for example, between more-or-less full-time farmers and more-or-less full-time fishermen), but inasmuch as most political districts included a range of natural areas (including inshore and offshore fishing areas, garden lands, and forests) most households could obtain from compatriots what they themselves did not produce. And speaking of specialization, the Hawaiians surpassed all other Polynesians in at least two aspects of technology: in their methods of crop irrigation and in their construction of fishponds (where they not only held fish captive but actually "farmed" them).

The Hawaiians also exceeded all other Polynesian peoples in the evolution of their political organization. Earlier in their history their major political units were, as among most other Polynesians, large ambilineal clans, by which all land was owned, corporately, and over which senior members held sway, as fellow kinsmen and not as unrelated autocrats. In time, however, and with the combining of discrete clans into larger, mainly *territorial,* units (the outcome of conquest and politically motivated marriages), the ties between a chief and most of his people became those of ruler and ruled. In fact, by the time of Cook's visit all of the land of a chiefdom was owned directly by its chief, who distributed feudal-like revenue rights over it to his close relatives and supporters and who appointed bureaucrats to collect those revenues, mostly in the form of food, from the farmers and fishermen residing there. (Usually, the use-rights of the latter were not confiscated with a change of chieftain, but came to be based no longer on irrefutable rights of kinship but on impersonal chiefly concession.)

As we have seen, a potential for social stratification existed in all Polynesian kin systems (i.e., in the priority accorded genealogical seniority), and in some of them two or even three social strata (classes) did in fact exist, even, in some societies, to the extent of the development of a rigid caste line between the highest and lower classes. In Hawaii the stratification became even more hypertrophied, with the emergence of three distinct castes. At the top were the *aliʻi* (nobles), who were themselves further stratified into ten levels, in terms of their genealogical purity (i.e., in terms of their degree of closeness, in line of descent and in birth order, from their respective god-ancestors); the higher one's level the more god-like one was, and hence the more godlike one had to be treated. Among other concomitants, such beliefs encouraged close-in marriage, even between a noble brother and his own sister, whereas within the two lower social classes marriage between consanguines was condemned as incestuous.

Below the nobles was the mass of the people, the *maka'ainana* (dwell-ers on the land). And below the latter and much fewer in number were the *kauwa* (pariahs), who were embued, not with sanctity, as were the nobles, but with defilement (somewhat similar to India's untouchables).

Before Western contact some of the Hawaiian islands became unified under rulership of a single chief, but it was not until after Cook's visit that one chief, Kamehameha, a noble of the island of Hawaii, succeeded by conquest and threat of conquest in subduing all other political units of the chain. It is not possible to weigh how important a role Western ideas about kingship and military tactics may have had in Kamehameha's suc-cess, but they were not inconsiderable. Ironically, while some Western influences were helping to unify all Hawaiians politically, others were serving to decrease their numbers and to transform many of their beliefs and practices, including some that had formerly served to provide super-natural sanction to the authority of chiefs.

The shell of the Hawaiian monarchy founded by Kamehameha lasted until 1893, when it was abolished by, mainly, American planters and merchants, but the fate of the ordinary Hawaiian and his indigenous cul-ture had by then already been sealed.

By 1939 the landscapes of these islands had been transformed. Huge areas that had once been intensely cultivated had been abandoned or given over to cattle or goats. Forests had been cleaned out of sandal-wood. Fishponds were nearly all gone; those remaining bred more mos-quitoes than mullet. Lagoon fishing had become a sport indulged in by nonnative workers on their days off. Deep-sea fishing was carried out mainly by Japanese fishermen in their little sampans, but hardly enough fish were caught to provide hors d'oeuvres for Honoluluans' appetites. Instead of dwelling in dispersed homesteads, most of the islands' resi-dents were cramped together in urban and plantation settlements: Hono-lulu alone contained nearly 40 percent of the archipelago's population.

There was, to be sure, another side to this picture. Tens of thousands of acres barely used in ancient times were producing sugarcane and pine-apples and cattle; and, through stupendous feats of irrigation engineer-ing, whole plateaus had been transformed from wasteland into valuable agricultural land.

Even more striking than the transformation of the land was the change in composition of the population and in ways of living. Instead of the

200,000 to 250,000 Polynesians living there in Cook's time, Hawaii's 1939 population included some 156,000 Japanese, 115,000 Caucasians, 100,000 Filipinos, 50,000 part-Hawaiians, 28,000 Chinese, 6,000 Koreans, and only 14,000 "pure" Hawaiians. And instead of numerous separate Polynesian chiefdoms the Hawaii of 1939 was a thoroughly Westernized society dominated by foreigners. The bulk of island plantations and other businesses, comprising 75 percent of all wage earners, was integrated under the control of a handful of Western businessmen. Government was also an important employer, but aside from engaging in construction (two-thirds of all construction carried out in the territory) and in national defense, most government employees entered into the territory's economic life only as consumers. In addition there were many small enterprises that provided livelihood for several hundred residents, and a few mainland U.S. firms had succeeded in establishing branches there, but only in the face of tough opposition from locally owned firms.

Almost daily, editorials in the local newspapers commented upon the happy state of interethnic relations, and for such a complex racial conglomeration there was in fact a surprisingly small amount of *overt* ethnic antagonism. There was, nevertheless, a distinct class system along ethnic lines in spite of a large number of interethnic marriages. Westerners composed the upper class, and mixtures of Westerners and *ali'i* Hawaiians came next. Then followed, in class-rank order, Chinese, Japanese, Filipinos, and Puerto Ricans. Hawaiians and Portuguese were usually ranked, in local attitudes, according to economic status and were distributed among all but the highest and lowest classes.

Several factors had led to this transformation.

The strategic position of the archipelago was from the very beginning of the colonial era a factor inviting change. Ships from America en route to the Far East and the Antipodes or ships whaling throughout this part of the Pacific dropped anchor in Hawaii's safe harbors, restocked with water and fresh provisions, traded for sandalwood, took on fresh crews, and tarried while their weary seamen caroused ashore and recuperated in the islands' mild climate. In increasing numbers sailors and traders left their ships and settled there. Hawaii also soon attracted the attention of strategy-minded admirals and statesmen of several nations, and men-of-war paid frequent visits.

As a result of all these contacts the native Hawaiians acquired new diseases and appetites for foreign gadgets and ideas. Iron of any kind was clamorously welcomed; textiles, implements, tobacco, and rum were traded for fruit, vegetables, pork, and fish. Through the maladies of civilization—smallpox, venereal diseases, and the rest of that awful inventory—the native population had been reduced by over one-half within fifty years of Cook's fateful visit.

Before a single missionary had set foot in these islands the native institutions and symbols had been already altered, profoundly, by contact with Westerners. One of the first and most important beliefs to go was the power of *kapu* (taboo), a widespread Polynesian concept wherein persons, places, actions, and objects possessed of spirit-derived sanctity had to be kept apart or treated with ritual respect. One of the most awesome forms of *kapu* was publicly flaunted in 1819, when a member of the native monarchy (himself also highly *kapu*) shared a meal with females, an act previously considered to be dangerously sacrilegious for all concerned. At about the same time other Hawaiians began to demonstrate their loss of belief in the traditional religion by destroying their spirit-images, and so forth. (Ironically, it was the native nobility who took the lead in these iconoclasms, thereby destroying the beliefs and practices upon which most of their authority and privileges depended.)

Sandalwood was identified in Hawaii by Westerners in 1790, and by 1805 there had developed around it a lively commerce. For the following twenty-five years the avaricious trade for the wood brought to the islands a vast quantity of trade goods, from beads and billiard tables to completely rigged schooners.

Yankee traders predominated in this commerce. They bartered for the wood in goods or dollars and then shipped it to China in exchange for Oriental goods for the American market. (Measure in sandalwood was reckoned in *piculs* [133 ¹/₃ lbs.], worth on an average ten dollars per picul.) When "King" Kamehameha learned the dollar value of this wood he monopolized the sale of it (it came from forests that had become all "his") to provide revenue for his court. To collect the wood he directed all able-bodied Hawaiians to scour the forests and cut specified quotas for deposit in the royal warehouses. As the wood became scarcer and the king's appetite greater, ordinary Hawaiians had to spend more and more time at this labor, remaining away from their homes for long periods of time; garden work was neglected and food became scarce.

Kamehameha's successor relinquished the royal monopoly by permitting his subordinate chiefs to deal directly with Western traders. However, this move proved even more disastrous, for the traders soon initiated the naïve and greedy subchiefs into the mysteries of the promissory note; this resulted in even larger levies upon the commoners, to meet the demands of the subchiefs' creditors. At one point American warships visited Hawaii to force the officials to pay their debts in sandalwood, or, as it was put at the time, "to protect American Commerce." The commitment of the monarch to pay this debt, which amounted to about $200,000, constituted the first Hawaiian national debt and therewith introduced the kingdom into the company of civilized nations. Further levies were made upon commoners to pay that and subsequent debts, so that by 1830 the supply of sandalwood was all but wiped out.

After the sandalwood trade had peaked there began the era of whaling

ship visits, which continued for several decades and led to the establishment of a number of large, Western-owned mercantile firms that supplied
those and other ships with local and imported goods. Meanwhile, the
newly established commercial centers, such as Honolulu, Hilo, and
Lahaina, lured increasing numbers of Hawaiians away from their rural
homesteads, thereby hastening the disintegration of their indigenous
ways of life.

The missionaries, who began arriving in 1820, changed somewhat the
direction of the disintegration by introducing modes of living better calculated to produce social, economic, and moral values as defined by
Calvinist New Englanders. Agents of the Boston Mission succeeded
fairly quickly in protestantizing most Hawaiians, having been especially
influential among the native nobility. Most of the pioneer missionaries
remained at their labors, but a few turned to agriculture and commerce
or entered the service of the native monarchs, thereby helping in very
large measure to shape the kingdom's economic and social life. (In fact,
some of their very descendants were among the territory's most influential leaders in 1939.)

Sugar succeeded the procession of whaling vessels as the most important factor of change. When Westerners first visited Hawaii they saw
small patches of cane growing near native dwellings, serving both as
windbreaks and as a supplementary food. (In fact, sugarcane grew
widely in the Pacific in times before Western contact; one of the plant's
ancestors, or possibly *the* ancestor, grew wild in New Guinea, whence it
may have spread to Asia.) In any case, the plant had been carried to
Hawaii by one or another of the canoeloads of Polynesian migrants and
when Westerners first arrived there the natives were cultivating and
chewing it for its sweetness, but were not extracting its juice in any
other way.

As early as 1802 a Chinese immigrant set up a simple stone mill in
Hawaii and turned out loaf sugar in small quantities, but this enterprise
lasted for only a year. Not until 1835 did production become established
on a commercial scale; during the intervening years most natives and foreigners were preoccupied with gathering and selling sandalwood and
with supplying the needs of visiting fur traders and whalers. Beginning in
1835, however, many acres were converted to growing cane, owing
mainly to the efforts of some American and British settlers, who foresaw
the need for placing the islands' economy (i.e., *their* islands' economy) on
a firmer basis than could be provided by the declining supply of sandalwood and the uncertainties of whaling. Thenceforth, the eventual financial success of the sugar industry was achieved through a number of measures: technological, managerial, and political. Progress in its internal
development was marked by the following: establishment of land tenure
reforms, procurement of adequate capital, technical advances in cane

growing and sugar extraction, improvement of cane varieties, control of harmful insects, importation of labor, and by the rationalization of the industry into a large-scale, mass-production organization.

Westerners, mainly American and British, pioneered the industry, controlled its operations, and owned most of its assets. On a few occasions some native rulers made attempts to participate, but for the most part Hawaiians neither shared in the ownership nor served as workers in it.

The native system of land tenure was a major obstacle to the industry, as it was to nearly all forms of capitalistic enterprise. As described earlier, when Westerners first arrived these islands were divided into several large chiefdoms, generally two or three to an island, each led by a paramount chief, who held residual title to all lands within his realm. A chief apportioned the land to subchiefs, who in turn reallotted subdivisions among their dependents, and so on down to the native farmer tenant. Theoretically, upon the death of a subject or at the pleasure of the chief, the subject's allotment of land was reallocated by the chief; but in fact generation-long identification of a family with a plot or a subchief with a whole division was confirmed over time, except when one chief conquered another in warfare. In that event the victor sometimes reallotted lands to his own principal followers; but such high-level changes did not usually affect the commoners' tenancy.

Tenants were not bound to the land; they were free to move from the domain of one chief to that of another, but once established anywhere they were obligated to pay fealty in the form of produce and service. Commoners' privileges also extended to use of their chief's forests for building materials and his waters for fishing.

The semifeudal character of Hawaiian land tenure was accentuated as a result of the victories of Kamehameha. After conquering all his rivals he reallocated their holdings among his principal supporters, himself retaining residual ownership of all of them. In addition, he set aside large areas for direct personal use by himself and members of his family. For native Hawaiians this arrangement was merely an elaboration of the traditional pattern and most of them accepted it without demur: they could not do otherwise. For most foreigners, however, that pattern was uncivilized, to say the least. Missionaries characterized it as a barbaric violation of individual rights of fee-simple ownership and were at pains to spread their dissatisfaction among their native flocks. Foreign businessmen objected to it for more practical reasons: their hopes for building fortunes were tempered by the realization that they could not own outright the land in which they invested money and energy. Sugar planters were especially affected, and they began to campaign for reforms.

Missionaries, traders, and planters exerted so much pressure upon the Hawaiian monarch reigning in 1844 that he agreed to wholesale redistribution of land rights along principles of fee-simple ownership. The redistribution, called The Great Mahele, required many years to complete. In the end the distribution was as follows:

— about one million acres were retained by the monarchy for its own personal use;
— about one and one-half million acres were allocated to the Hawaiian government (i.e., "crown lands"—a novel concept for Hawaii);
— about one and one-half million acres were allocated among the other "chiefs" (i.e., the nobility); and
— about thirty thousand acres, in the form of ten thousand separate estates, were allocated to all other Hawaiians (who numbered slightly under 100,000 at the time).

In addition, several thousand acres of prime agricultural and residential-commercial land were awarded to the numerous Western foreigners who had claims against Hawaii's native rulers for one or another kind of service that had been rendered them.

The fact that Hawaiian commoners received so little of their islands' land is of course noteworthy. But just as noteworthy is the speed with which many of them sold their fee-simple titles to foreigners (which they had previously been unable to do).

By the end of the nineteenth century, after another revolution had overthrown what was left of the monarchy, Western foreigners owned four times as much land as all the native Hawaiians, including the once highly privileged "chiefs." Thus, in the words of the historian Gavan Daws, ". . . the great division became the great dispossession" (1968:428).

Cane matures relatively slowly in Hawaii, and a plantation requires a very large financial investment. Outside capital was needed to bring about any considerable expansion, and it was not until the land reforms had been passed that foreign investors, mainly Americans, were attracted. The industry received another fillip as a result of the higher sugar prices during the Civil War; but the most significant increase in capital investment came about after 1876, when a treaty of reciprocity was signed between Hawaii and the United States, admitting the products of each country duty-free into the other and thereby assuring a favorable and expanding market for Hawaiian sugar. Annexation of Hawaii by the United States in 1898 stimulated an even greater movement of American capital into the industry and consummated American domination over it. After that the industry itself built up reserves sufficient to finance its own expansion.

Technical improvements in cane growing and sugar extraction placed the Hawaiian industry ahead of all competitors in operational efficiency.

The local planters were quick to replace ox-drawn with steam-driven vehicles to pull the massive plows required, and large sums of money were spent on developing mechanical methods for harvesting cane. The local mills were also transformed into models of mass-production efficiency.

The cane found growing in Hawaii by the first Western settlers was hardy and immune to endemic plant diseases but not very sweet or highly productive, so it was supplanted by a sweeter variety imported from Tahiti. This newcomer, named the "Lahaina" variety, remained the mainstay of the industry until early in the twentieth century, when it, and the industry dependent upon it, nearly succumbed to a root-rot disease. The day was saved by the development of better varieties resistant to the disease and also with higher sugar content. Meanwhile Hawaii-based botanists kept up a continual worldwide search, along with intensive laboratory experiments, to produce varieties that would combine the desirable characteristics of high sugar content, quantity production, quick growth, brittleness (for ease in harvesting), and resistence to weather, insects, and disease.

Sugarcane requires great quantities of sunshine and water. Hawaii has both, but less than half the good cane-growing lands were so located that they received sufficient rainfall; hence irrigation was required. The amount needed may be indicated by the fact that about four thousand tons of water are needed to grow enough cane for one ton of sugar. On some of Hawaii's plantations the water was obtained via ditches, tunnels, and aqueducts from rain-soaked mountain areas; on others from artesian wells. Some of the systems were quite stupendous: one ditch alone carried sixty million gallons of water daily through a tunnel six miles long. The artesian wells and gravity systems on another plantation supplied three hundred million gallons a day, over four times the amount used in one day in pre–World War II San Francisco.

Hawaiian sugar planters also had to maintain a constant vigil to keep out harmful insects. As new and better cane varieties were introduced the pests that retarded their growth were left behind; but at the same time there were left behind the natural enemies of those pests, the "fleas on the fleas" that kept the pests in check, so that when harmful insects did slip past quarantine they multiplied unchecked and ravaged the crops. For example, early in this century an infestation of leafhoppers destroyed thousands of acres of cane and was finally checked only when small egg-killing parasites were brought in from Australia. Another devastating pest was the cane borer, which was finally controlled by the tachina fly, brought from New Guinea by industry entomologists.

But the most vexing of all the problems that faced the Hawaiian sugar industry was the maintenance of an adequate labor supply. It was just as serious in 1939 as it had been a century earlier. Cane growing still required large numbers of manual laborers. The industry had progressed far past its nineteenth century beginnings, when everything was done by hand, even including human-drawn plows, but some processes, such as weeding and harvesting, had not yet advanced beyond dependence upon manual labor, and in 1939 the Hawaiian plantations still employed about forty-five thousand manual workers.

While the industry was in its infancy it was almost wholly dependent upon native Hawaiian workers, but would never have grown past that infancy if other labor had not been found. The 200,000 to 250,000 Hawaiians of 1778 had decreased to about 70,000 by 1853, and only a few thousand of them were willing to work on plantations. Earlier, many of them had been released by their chiefs to work on Westerner's plantations located on land leased from those chiefs, but even the volunteers among them were not ideal workers. Their way of life had not prepared them for the steady grind of plantation work, and as they knew, their survival did not depend upon wage earning.

Various projects were undertaken to make up for those deficiencies. First, efforts were made to reverse the population decline. Then further efforts were made to engage Hawaiians in the industry by means of incentive systems involving a piecework wage scale. Supplementing those, attempts were made to bring in other Pacific Islanders as plantation workers, the argument having been that these ethnic relatives of the Hawaiians would become quickly acclimated and would blend easily with the Hawaiians. In line with that reasoning some twenty-five hundred Gilbertese responded to the enticements and reported for work, but when they too turned out to be unsuited for plantation drudgery that program was dropped.

Chinese coolies, mostly from the vicinity of Canton, were the next to be imported. Beginning in 1852 and continuing until the Exclusion Act was called into effect by annexation in 1898, about forty-six thousand Chinese had been brought in. Most of these eventually left the plantations and either returned home upon completion of their contracts or remained and established enterprises of their own, including the production of taro and truck crops and the operation of stores and restaurants.

From 1878 to 1913, about 17,500 Portuguese immigrated to Hawaii, mostly from the Azores and the Madeira islands. Some of those who stayed in Hawaii upon completion of their contracts remained at the plantations as skilled workers and foremen.

A much larger influx came from Japan (including Okinawa); from 1894 to 1939 about 180,000 Japanese laborers and their relatives were landed in Hawaii. Some eventually returned home and other thousands of them moved on to the mainland United States, but enough remained in Hawaii to constitute the largest ethnic group there. After the turn of the century, however, their numbers on the plantations steadily decreased.

In 1939 Filipinos were the largest ethnic element still working on sugar plantations; immigration had been continuous since 1906 and over 120,000 had been brought in. Many of them came without their families and returned home upon completion of their indentures.

Numbers of Koreans, Puerto Ricans, Spaniards, northern Europeans, and even Russians were attracted to the islands to work as plantation laborers; but in 1939 the only likely source for additional labor was the Philippines.

From its beginning a hundred years previously the Hawaii sugar industry had moved in the direction of larger and larger mass-production units, and in 1939 it was one of the most highly integrated agricultural enterprises in the world. The reasons for that development were mainly financial. Some degree of integration was present from the beginning. Whereas mainland U.S. plantations and sugar mills had developed as separate enterprises (the individual farmer having sold his cane for sugar extraction), in Hawaii there was no precedent for that kind of relationship and the Western pioneers who established the first plantations had to set up their own mills.

In the early days in Hawaii sugar extraction was slow and simple. Individual stalks of cane were fed into presses that expressed only about 50 percent of the juice, and from this juice sugar was extracted by a process of liming, condensation, and drying, all of which took weeks to complete. The output of a mill was consequently meager and not much cane was required to keep it busy. Later on, technological improvements in extraction speeded up the process, but the new machines were costly and in the interests of economical operation they had to be kept busy. That called for more cane and larger planted areas to be serviced by each mill.

The need for irrigation water was another factor in the trend toward integration, since small plantation units could not capitalize costly irrigation projects. Coordinated efforts, moreover, were required to bring in labor, finance experimentation, combat plant disease and pests, procure supplies, and ship and market raw sugar. And in 1939 that same coordination was required to conduct the campaigns needed to ensure that Hawaiian sugar would receive equitable treatment by the U.S. Congress. Spokesmen for the industry claimed, with what appeared to be some justification, that only through integration could Hawaiian sugar be produced economically enough to compete with other sugar industries producing for the U.S. market.

Basic units in the Hawaiian sugar industry were the plantations. In 1939 there were thirty-eight of them, containing a total of 240,000 acres planted in cane and 510,000 acres given over to forests (for water supply), grazing land (for plantation cattle), and for mills and housing. The 1939 dollar value of all of these plantations was between 155 and 180 millions. Throughout the prewar decade about one million tons of raw sugar were produced annually. During the same decade an average of about fifty thousand workers were employed on the plantations, numerically in the following order: Filipino, Japanese, Portuguese, Hawaiian and part-Hawaiian, other Caucasians, Puerto Ricans, Chinese, and Koreans. With their families these employees made up a total of 100,000, one-third of whom had not been naturalized.

A Hawaiian sugar plantation was an intricate, factorylike organization, with all operations directed toward keeping the sugar-extraction mill working full time. Its general manager had authority not only over all plantation operations but also over the community lives of all employees. Similar patterns of organization and of procedures, as well as similar wage rates, worker prerequisites, and most other details of plantation life, occurred in all the sugar plantations, affording further evidence of industrywide integration.

The dominant position in the sugar industry was held by the "factors," the commercial agencies that controlled the assets and activities of thirty-three of the islands' thirty-eight plantations. The factors dated from the whaling era, when several trading firms sprang up in Honolulu to cater to the needs of the visiting ships; with the decline of whaling in nearby waters they began servicing the plantations. Planter-owners were kept busy managing the day-to-day activities of growing and milling cane. They did not have the time to visit Honolulu when supplies were needed, nor were their knowledge of and contacts with world markets close enough to enable them to sell their sugar profitably under circumstances of increasing worldwide competition. The factors consequently became Honolulu agents for the plantations and went on to extending credit, making loans, procuring labor, arranging shipping, and handling all other business of the industry. Needless to say, ownership of most plantations eventually passed from planter to factor, and by 1939 five of the latter (the "Big Five") owned and managed most of the industry, as in fact they owned and controlled most other phases of the islands' economy, including importing and wholesaling, retailing, interisland and mainland shipping, banking, utilities, hotels, canneries, and some mainland sugar refineries.

Competition did not exist among the Big Five; they were linked by interlocking directorates, by interfamily ties, and, with respect to sugar, by membership in the HSPA (Hawaiian Sugar Planters' Association). The stated functions of the HSPA were the discovery and adoption of new agricultural techniques and labor-saving devices, formulation of a general labor program, and representation (i.e., political lobbying). The most conspicuous part of HSPA activity was its experiment station, expertly staffed and liberally financed, and responsible for some quite remarkable technical improvements in the industry.

In later (prewar) years the Hawaiian sugar industry became the center of heated political controversy. It was attacked as being a despotically paternalistic monopoly that held island economy in bondage, stifling individual enterprise and maintaining labor at the level of peonage. And it was supported by assertions that it had made Hawaii into a productive and wealthy territory, that its employees were well paid and amply provided for with essentials for happy living, and that no other type of organization could have succeeded under the peculiar physical and human circumstances that prevailed in the islands. The correct evaluation lay somewhere in between: the essential fact was that the social values of the United States as a whole had been continually changing, but that the industrial leaders of isolated Hawaii had been unable or unwilling to follow that trend.

The oft-repeated assertion that sugar had made Hawaii what it was in 1939 can be amply documented. For one thing, it had brought about huge changes in the face of the land. The islands' total acreage (about four million acres) had been only slightly altered by Hawaiians before Western contact; patches of taro, sweet potatoes, plantains, small groves of coconut palms, a few fishponds, and widely scattered homesteads were almost lost against the background of forests and grass and wasteland. Mountainous forest land and wide pastures and wastelands still dominated the landscape of 1939, but over 300,000 acres of it had been transformed into cultivation, and of this area four-fifths were planted in sugarcane. On the other hand, it cannot be said that sugarcane had *replaced* native crops; cane did not grow well on the lowlands best suited to the latter and had been planted mainly on forest land, semiarid pasture, and arid land rendered productive by irrigation. In other words, the decline in land devoted to gardening must be attributed to other factors and not directly to replacement by cane.

Much more striking were the effects that sugar had on the composition of the islands' population. Native depopulation was proceeding rapidly even before large-scale sugar production commenced, so that any hastening effect on the process that the industry might have had was indirect. That is not true, however, regarding other changes in the population's makeup. Sugar was directly responsible for introducing nearly 300,000 Asians, about 20,000 Portuguese, and numbers of Puerto Ricans and southern Europeans. Many of these had remained after their contracts terminated, so that they and their offspring constituted the majority of the islands' population in 1939.

Sugar also altered the overall economy of the islands and determined the course of its political history. Half the total working population was employed, directly or indirectly, in the industry. As noted earlier, sugar planters and their allies, acting in the interests of the industry (which of course included their own) broke the native monarchy, secured annexation by the United States, and, publicly at least, were forcefully behind a move for statehood (to give the industry votes in Congress and thereby protect it from discriminatory legislation).

In 1939 the outlook for Hawaiian sugar was as follows. Practically all suitable land was already under cultivation and future increases in production would have to come from the discovery of better canes. Further large-scale import of labor other than from the Philippines was blocked by immigration laws, and most future plantation laborers would have to be recruited from among locally born, democratically educated, and increasingly union-conscious descendants of immigrants. Under those circumstances the search for laborsaving devices, especially for field operations, would have to be prosecuted with vigor. Restrictions on further expansion also came from the side of politics. Worldwide overproduction of sugar, coupled with the prospect of ruinous competition from cheap-labor nations, led the major powers, in 1934, to create several closed-market blocs and to legislate quotas between and within them. One effect of this was to subject Hawaii to decisions by the Federal government as to how much sugar could be produced locally. Clearly, Manifest Destiny had slowed its westward advance.

Hawaii's pineapple industry began much later and fell into the pattern already established by the sugar industry. Pineapples were growing in Hawaii early in the nineteenth century (how they got there is not known) although the natives made little use of them for food. Quantities of the fresh fruit were shipped to the mainland from time to time, and late in the last century Western homesteaders cultivated the fruit for export on a small commercial scale. However, so much of it spoiled during the voyage to the mainland that interest in the project waned for a while. Then an enterprising homesteader, Sanford Dole, whose name has become almost a synonym for pineapples, realized that canning was the answer and secured mainland U.S. capital for a pioneering venture. From that beginning at the start of this century the Hawaiian pineapple industry grew to a point where, in 1939, it was producing 80 percent of the world's canned pineapple, turning out in a peak year a pack valued at sixty million dollars.

The young industry did not go through the long and tortuous career experienced by Hawaiian sugar, but its development was anything but smooth. To sugar-bound Hawaiian businessmen, pineapples were an unwanted foundling left on the doorstep, a potential competitor for land and labor. Because its future was uncertain, no local encouragement was offered it in the form of capital or other aid, and, as just noted, the pioneering capital had to be obtained on the mainland. All that changed, of course, when the profits began to roll in.

The problem of market was also serious at the beginning, and still loomed large in 1939. The American public had to be educated to eating the canned fruit, and that was no mean undertaking in an era not yet advanced to million-dollar huckstering. In some years the overzealous young industry glutted the underdeveloped market and suffered financial setbacks, and even after advertising had established a large public demand, consumption fell precipitously during the depression of the thirties. This uncertain market remained subject to further disturbances as a result of competition from other domestic canned fruits and from canned pineapple imported from nations enjoying reciprocal-trade treaties with the United States.

Land for growing pineapples, on the other hand, turned out to be less of a problem than was earlier feared. It was eventually learned that pineapples grow best in the high, relatively cool plateau lands unsuited for sugar and that they will grow in a variety of rainfall situations. Thus, pineapples did not displace sugar anywhere, or any other agricultural activity for that matter. A good example is the small island of Lanai: formerly a wasteland supporting only a handful of people and a herd of about four hundred cattle, it was bought lock, stock, and barrel by Dole and transformed into thirteen thousand acres of pineapples and a modern plantation community.

Throughout Hawaii laborers who had been brought in for the sugar plantations were already on hand to grow and can pineapple. Since nearly all pineapple operations except harvesting were mechanized, the labor force was relatively small. Notwithstanding that, the industry was confronted with the same problem that sugar then faced: the necessity of obtaining its labor from second- and third-generation citizens educated to expect higher standards of living and better working conditions than their immigrant parents or grandparents had submitted to.

Pineapples no less than sugar were (and still are) vulnerable to pests and diseases. Another set of problems was posed by their seasonality of growth: sugar was harvested throughout the year but the bulk of the pineapple crop matured in the summer and had to be harvested and canned immediately. This caused marked seasonal employment: at the peak of the harvest season field labor had to be doubled and cannery labor quadrupled. Some of that increase was met by employing housewives and school children, and by "borrowing" labor from sugar plantations, but the net result was a less stable labor supply for pineapples than for sugar. Some success was realized in solving the seasonality by chemical measures (i.e., by accelerating and retarding the growth of the fruit, thereby lengthening the harvest season). Meanwhile, efforts continued to develop mechanical means of harvesting.

Many of the circumstances that favored integration in the Hawaiian sugar industry did so for pineapples as well, but since an important part of the latter industry was owned by mainland firms having other interests elsewhere, local integration was not carried as far as with sugar. Nevertheless, except for the plantations and canneries owned by mainland firms, Hawaii's pineapple industry came to be controlled by the same Big Five that controlled sugar, and the pattern of control was similar. However, regardless of ownership, all of Hawaii's pineapple companies voluntarily established production quotas among themselves to limit production to market needs and thereby protect prices.

Whereas a sugar plantation and its mill were physically integrated into a single community (except for the few "adherent planters," who sold their crops to plantations but did not necessarily dwell on them), pineapple plantations and canneries were usually separate, most canneries having been located on Oahu, where casual labor was more readily available to meet the seasonal demand. In 1939 the labor on pineapple plantations consisted mainly of Japanese, Filipinos, and Portuguese; and plantation communities contained much the same facilities as those of sugar—company housing, hospitals, recreation, and so forth.

By 1939 fifty thousand acres of former wasteland and pasture had been converted to pineapple growing; otherwise the industry had had far less effect than sugar in shaping the territory's social and economic life; the dominant patterns had already been drawn when pineapples entered the picture. True, this industry had served to diversify the economy and to stabilize its earnings during years of sugar depression; but the native Hawaiians and their indigenous culture had already been relegated before ever a pineapple was canned.

In 1939 the industry still had room for expansion, provided labor and market problems could be solved, because suitable land was available to the extent of doubling the annual pack.

In 1939 coffee production, in comparison with sugar and pineapples, did not enter importantly in the economic life of the islands nor affect what was left of the native way of life, but it did open up new areas to cultivation and provide livelihood for hundreds of Japanese immigrants who sought escape from what they considered to be the peonage of plantation life.

Coffee growing commenced in 1810 and began to be produced for sale fifteen years later. For a while it was a lively little industry; native Hawaiians grew it by royal decree and paid some of their taxes with portions of their crops. Indeed, until the middle of the century it shared first honors with sugar, but four obstacles edged it out of the race. For one thing, the climate was not ideally suited to its growth. Also, labor requirements were greater than those of sugar, and price fluctuations kept the market unstable. On top of all that a fungus blight played havoc with crops, so that when the American Civil War stimulated sugar production, coffee fell even farther behind. A short-lived boom in the nineties induced some

Westerners to undertake large-scale planting again, but another price decline dropped the industry to the marginal position in which it remained.

During the years just before 1939 the annual coffee crop averaged about 8,500,000 pounds, most of it having been shipped to the mainland for blending with other varieties. The principal growers were Japanese tenant farmers, who eked out existences on submarginal land in the Kona region of the island of Hawaii. These growers sold their crops to small storekeepers, who, typically, held them in debt by advancing credit for fertilizer and store-purchased food. But here again, the Big Five played some role in the industry by means of their financial hold over many of the storekeepers.

In 1939 the coffee picture was changing to the extent that Filipinos were beginning to replace Japanese as growers, while the latter were moving into more profitable jobs.

In the 1930s Hawaii's cattle ranches did not provide even enough meat to satisfy local consumption needs; nevertheless, they were spread out over more acres than all the plantations combined. Moreover, they provided hundreds of native Hawaiians with employment not unsuited to their preferred ways of living.

On the island of Hawaii was located one of the largest cattle ranches in the United States, and throughout the territory as a whole about one-fourth of all the land was given over to pasture, which supported about 120,000 head of cattle. It came as a distinct surprise to visitors beyond the beaches to see typical western cowboy life reproduced on some of the territory's islands.

Native Hawaiians possessed only pigs, dogs, and chickens. The few cattle brought in by Captain George Vancouver in 1793 and presented to the paramount chief of the island of Hawaii were greeted with such curiosity and awe that they were freed and for many years protected from killing by royal decree. As a result, their numbers increased to such an extent that they became a pest to native gardens and to the expanding sugar plantations. In due course three Mexican cowboys were recruited to help herd them, and these men brought with them a way of life that appealed to the natives as plantation agriculture never had. By 1939 nearly half of the eight hundred families employed to herd cattle were Hawaiian or part-Hawaiian; the remainder were Portuguese and Japanese.

The cowboy life, exciting and varied, without the sustained monotony of field labor, corresponded to the Hawaiians' life before Western contact. The dangers of galloping across treacherous, hole-ridden ranges seem to have been enjoyed with the same zest as that shown by their forefathers in racing along in heavy seas after fish.

Though management's paternalism was even more evident in ranching than in the plantations, the lot of ranch laborers was better in some respects. Owners and employees, linked by generations of master-man relationships, were usually on the friendliest of terms, and in this setting the Hawaiians probably had a better chance of survival than in the urban areas to which most of them had moved. The small island of Niihau stood out in this respect.

Niihau was purchased outright in 1863 by a Scottish family that had moved to Hawaii to escape from the stresses of civilization. In 1939 the part-Hawaiian grandsons of those immigrants dwelt on their plantation on the neighboring island of Kauai and permitted no outsider to visit their Niihau property. Niihau's native inhabitants, about two hundred in all, were employed by the owners in herding the cattle and sheep that constituted the small island's main economic resource. Their only link with the outside world was the owners' sampan, which carried in supplies each week. Niihauans were nearly totally self-subsistent; they conducted their own school and church without the help of outsiders, punished their own misdemeanors, and generally managed their own affairs. Even in 1939 the Territorial government exercised practically no jurisdiction over them.

Elsewhere in Hawaii, in addition to the primary industries just mentioned, commercialized tourism provided business opportunities for an increasing number of individuals with modest incomes, thereby adding recruits to the middle-class ranks, which in Hawaii had previously been almost empty.

And finally, the Federal government, though entering the stage late, nevertheless played an important role in shaping Hawaii's economy. Large land and water areas were set aside for military and naval reservations, and their prewar personnel annually purchased millions of dollars of services and supplies. In addition, the Federal government was a big employer of local labor for construction and maintenance projects.

Between 1778 and 1939 the population and culture of the Hawaiian islands had become radically transformed, but no wise observer believed that the current patterns would long endure. The children of the immigrants were being educated in schools that taught ideas about equality and democracy, and these new citizens were beginning to demonstrate impatience with the status and earnings of plantation labor and with the concentration of economic power that limited their opportunities. The time was ripe for unionism, and stimulus from the mainland set it in motion. A battle with entrenched capital loomed unless both sides agreed to compromise, and that word was not popular in the local vocabularies of the time.

The almost absolute authority of big business over island affairs was also being threatened from another direction. Military and naval leaders, and particularly the latter, were beginning to voice their belief that, sugar or no sugar, Hawaii's main function was to serve as a defense outpost. In the view of many military and naval officials, war with Japan was a definite possibility, hence there was increasing uneasiness among them about having a large Japanese-derived populace near Oahu's harbors and air fields. As a matter of fact, anxiety about that situation was a major factor in the prewar recommendation of Congress against Hawaiian statehood.

Still another threat to big business was the Federal government's sugar-quota legislation, which, in the interests of trying to stabilize world sugar production and prices, restricted Hawaii's production to a figure one-sixth below its previous output.

These and other somewhat lesser considerations moved most of Hawaii's different ethnic and economic factions to agitate for statehood, so that Hawaii might have a vote as well as a voice in Congress and thereby keep outsiders, especially mainlanders, from interfering in Hawaii's affairs.

A detailed statistical analysis, fleshed out with numerous case studies, would be required to tell how the native Hawaiians were faring in their homeland in 1939. Suffice it to say that full-blooded Hawaiians constituted no more than 3.4 percent of the territory's total population of about 423,000, and even part-Hawaiians totaled only another 11.8 percent. Moreover, counting full bloods and part-Hawaiians together, their average life span was ten years shorter than the sixty-two years of the total population. And in terms of annual income they stood lower than any other ethnic category except the recently arrived Filipinos.

Such was the destiny, at least up to 1939, of the people who had discovered and populated these islands. Nor did the future hold much promise of a change for them if that future, as many predictors held, were to depend upon their education in the ways of the outsiders; for in terms of numbers of college graduates, they ranked even lower than the Filipinos, whom they outnumbered by about twelve thousand.

Fiji

In 1939 the best vantage point for observing Fiji's transformation from "cannibal isles" to "tropical paradise" was the wide, second-story veranda of Suva's Grand Pacific Hotel. From a comfortable reclining position, a visitor could look inland across the coastal highway onto the green-turfed athletic field and watch Fijians beating their Western "masters" at cricket. If the excitement of watching the match aroused thirst, the observer could call out and be served whiskey and soda by another

dark-skinned fellow, whose smaller stature, sharper face, and straighter hair proclaimed him to be an Indian.

Altogether, an idyllic scene. South and a few yards away the Pacific lapped at the palm-fringed shore. Inland rose a wall of fantastic mountain shapes—surviving plugs and crater rims. Extensive sugarcane plantations, kept productive by industrious Indians, spread out on either hand. And nearby were picturesque villages of loyal and literate native Fijians. Fiji, unofficial capital of all the British South Sea Islands, monument to Western humanitarianism and administrative genius! Or so it seemed to a visitor just off a tour ship.

Away from hotel verandas, Fiji presented a somewhat different picture. By 1939 part of the archipelago was losing much of its South Seas character and was fast becoming a "Little India." Fijian natives still claimed most of the islands' land, and Westerners still drained off most of its productive wealth, but differential birth rates and different work habits were placing the islands' future in the hands of the Indians. This is how it came about.

The Fijian archipelago consists of a western leeward group of massive volcanic islands (including Viti Levu, Vanua Levu, and Ovalau) and an eastern scattering of smaller islands. The original settlers of the archipelago, in about 2400 B.C., came from the west. Over the centuries they developed the kind of culture that has come to be known as Polynesian. And during that era many of them migrated farther east to Tonga and Samoa and probably other smaller islands in between. Then, in about 1800 B.C. there arrived in Fiji other immigrants from the west, carrying a larger component of negroid genes (darker skin pigment, curlier hair, and so forth) along with some "Melanesian" culture traits as well. These new incursions served to alter somewhat the established Polynesian physical types and culture in Fiji, but communication between Fiji and Tonga-Samoa continued, with consequent two-way exchanges of genes and culture traits. Tongans, especially, canoed to Fiji's eastern Lau islands, trading, warring, and sometimes settling down. Much later, after Western contact, a Tongan monarch sent to Lau one of his subchiefs, Maafu, who set up a Tongan hegemony over those islands. Long before those events, however, all Fiji was divided into a large number of autonomous political units, whose relations with one another were characteristically hostile. Within each political unit the extended family was the basic residential and economic unit, and several interrelated families composed a community, mostly in the form of a nucleated village. The father was absolute head of his family, and upon his death the headship passed to his eldest son.

This much of the indigenous social structure of times before and just after Western contact has been documented; beyond that, however, the picture has been clouded by differences among the experts. Some early writers, given more to tidy-mindedness than to close observation, perceived the society of the whole archipelago to have been divided into a number of patrilineal clans *(yavusa)*, which were divided into subclans *(matanggali)*, which were themselves divided into patrilineages *(tokatoka)*. In addition, it was claimed, most clans and all their subdivisions were localized in a single village (solely or with other clans). And to complete the orderly symmetry of this perceived structure, it was held that all the patrilineages within a subclan and all subclans within a clan were ranked according to seniority, and that privilege and authority followed those lines.

Relationships following such a model may indeed have prevailed in that part of Fiji where Westerners first congregated (a small area along the eastern coast of Viti Levu); but subsequent research has shown that clan and village structures were far more varied and complex elsewhere in the archipelago. (Where, for example, segments of single clans and subclans were localized in several villages, and where even the labels for such units were not the same.) Perhaps the most fateful misconception embedded in the model was its notion about land ownership: that all of it everywhere belonged corporately to one or another *matanggali*, and that it was inalienable (even in the event of defeat in war).

Unfortunately, the model just sketched was accepted by Fiji's early colonial governors to be correct, thereby making it the official one whereby the colony was subsequently governed or, despite the best of intentions, comprehensively misgoverned. (Ironically, even the Fijian "chiefs" with and through whom the British administered the colony accepted the official model as their guide.)

A full and accurate description of the structure of Fijian society in pre-Western times would require many more pages than this book will allow. Suffice it to say that the people lived mostly in nucleated villages and that they belonged to patrilineal descent units, which were related to land ownership. Also, it should be added, most villages (which typically were small) constituted autonomous political units, and they shifted their locations from time to time, often but not solely as a result of warfare.

Three native concepts that significantly affected Fijian history were communal *lala*, personal *lala*, and *kerekere*. The first signified the mutual aid expected of all members of a village; the third specified the process of sharing goods among members of a village: those who had not might beg and receive from those who had. Both of these concepts strengthened the communalism of a village. Personal *lala* referred to the tribute exacted by a village's chief from outsiders allowed to settle on unused land associated with the village; as chief he had strongest proprietary rights over that land.

Warfare (more specifically, feuding) was chronic among Fiji's many, typically small, villages; large-scale organized aggression developed only

after native clubs and spears had been supplemented with Western firearms. During the first half of the nineteenth century there developed several great confederations of coastal villages, which proceeded to demonstrate how effectively some neolithic peoples can destroy each other
when armed with firearms. Also, the few Westerners cast up on the
beaches who escaped Fijians' baking ovens added to the bloody aggran-
dizement by serving as military advisers to native chiefs. And for all those
adventures traders eagerly supplied muskets and ammunition in
exchange for sandalwood.

Strongest of all the new confederations was that owing an uneasy alliance to the village of Mbau of eastern Viti Levu. Mbau began as just
another small village and was located on a very small offshore islet.
Through intrigue and warfare its influence was spread to mainland Viti
Levu. Its proximity to the anchorages of the early Western traders served
to spread its influence even wider, so that many Western visitors began to
refer to its chief, Thakombau, as "king" of Fiji, despite the existence of
rivals who, given half a chance, would gladly have eaten him.

Nouveau chiefs of Thakombau's ilk had large responsibilities and
dread power. In each new superconfederation one such chief held temporal power (planning battles and administering civil affairs) and a second
had spiritual powers (directing the priests in their sacrifices and petitions
to ancestral gods and other supernaturals). Some chiefs could call forth
hundreds of warriors to do battle and received tribute from scores of villages settled on their lands. Their households contained many concu-
bines and personal retainers, and their appetite for human flesh kept the
court ovens continually fired.

Such was the scene into which the missionaries first moved, first Wesleyan and then Catholic. The Wesleyans came in the wake of Christianized Tongans, whose newly found missionary zeal armed them with an
additional weapon in their long-seated efforts to extend their influence
over Fiji. From the Tonganized but basically Fijian islands of Lau, the
Wesleyans moved to the larger Fijian islands to the west. They attacked
the native beliefs with zealous recklessness, one of them having courted
death by destroying temples and idols; the fact that so many of them survived may have been due to the frequent visits then being made by British
warships.

When the practical advantages of Jehovah worship became evident,
many ambitious chiefs put aside some of their wives, let their ovens cool
off, and became converts, not realizing at the time that disavowal of their
old gods removed one of the props of their temporal power. For a while
there was fierce warfare between converts and holdouts, but the issue
was finally decided in 1854, when Thakombau acceded to the request of
the king of Tonga and accepted the Wesleyan mission. Shortly afterward
Tonga lent to Thakombau a force of two thousand warriors, who routed

his remaining enemies and extended his power, and that of the mission, over most of Viti Levu.

Meanwhile, planters and more traders were moving to Fiji, acquiring land, setting out coconuts, trading for pearl shell and sandalwood, and entering into native politics. Traders from Salem, Massachusetts were predominant, and the United States designated a consul there. On one fine Fourth of July that convivial gentleman carelessly burned down his home with fireworks and lost a few of his possessions to looting natives. On this and other grounds he presented a huge bill to Thakombau on behalf of the United States, demanding that the "king of Fiji" be held responsible for the action of his subjects. The harassed Thakombau may have been flattered at the implications of the address but he did not have the wherewithal to pay off the claim. In due course this "national debt" doubled and quadrupled, by saltations understood only by the consul, and when American warships were called in to help collect, "King" Thakombau followed the familiar practice of offering his insolvent kingdom to Western powers; but there were no takers at the time.

The world cotton shortage brought on by the American Civil War sent numbers of would-be planters to Fiji and increased the foreign stake in land and local politics. When Fijians proved to be unwilling and unproductive workers in the cotton fields and coconut plantations natives were imported from the Solomons and the New Hebrides, as has been told. Eventually, the blackbirding evils that accompanied this traffic set off the chain of events that induced Great Britain to overcome its initial reluctance and annex Fiji, which took place in 1874. By that time the motley assortment of adventurers, traders, missionaries, planters, and consuls, all intriguing with native factions and competing for land or loot or souls, had created such turbulent conditions that some power had to step in. Since Britain's interests in the region were larger than those of any other nation, and since her New Zealand and Australian colonies were urging strongly, she was forced to extend Her Majesty's sovereignty over what were referred to as "a few more black [actually, dark brown] subjects." The most noteworthy aspect of the annexation was the promise given to the new subjects that their welfare, including especially their titles to their lands, would be vigorously protected for all time to come. Subsequent failure to keep those promises resulted not from a cynical disregard for native rights, but rather from a misunderstanding of those rights, and from the long-range consequences of some day-to-day decisions.

The British government made an evidently sincere effort to guard native interests (insofar as they were understood). At the time of annexation about one-tenth of Fiji's four and a half million acres had already been alienated by Western settlers under conditions confirmed by the government as having been "legal." The remaining nine-tenths were constituted inalienable native lands, which could be leased to nonnatives only with the consent of the native proprietors and of the government. This regulation was designed to protect the Fijians' chief resource, to bind them closer to their native village communities, and to provide them with income from rents. (Sixty-five years later Fijians still retained full use of most of those lands; an additional one-tenth had been transferred and that only by lease.)

Indirect rule was established over those parts of the archipelago still in native hands, where the current native leaders were confirmed in their rank and influence over village affairs. (In fact, the powers of chiefs were legitimated to an extent that the pre-Western, and pre-Thakombau, chiefs had not possessed.) Warfare, cannibalism, and human sacrifice were of course abolished, but for the most part other native affairs were not at first interfered with. Personal *lala,* the tribute paid to a chief, was legalized to a point of importance beyond its traditional scope, and the rights of chiefs were thereby increased. On the other hand, the supernatural underpinnings of chieftainship were undermined by Christianity, and the influence-building rivalry between chiefs and its associated village *esprit* were weakened by official prohibition against "wasteful" intervillage feasts.

A few native rebels appeared from time to time and made pathetic efforts to secure popular backing for reclaiming "Fiji for the Fijians," but the colonial government dealt decisively with them, and most Fijians adjusted easily to the new regime. From an estimated population of about 200,000 at the time of initial Western contact, the Fijians rapidly declined in numbers, but after reaching a low of 82,000 they began a slow recovery that was not subsequently reversed. Meanwhile, most of them continued to live a mainly subsistence economy in their own villages. When the need arose to supplement native-produced things with imports or to raise money for taxes and church, Fijians made copra from their own groves and sold it to traders. In fact, amounts of native-produced copra increased steadily until the depression of the thirties, and the Fijians consistently produced from one-half to two-thirds of the total amount exported. At one point, under government stimulus, they undertook the growing of bananas for export, an enterprise particularly suited to village living. But some of those nice adjustments came in time to be disturbed by new foreign enterprises.

When, during the American Civil War, British textile manufacturers encouraged the production of cotton throughout their South Pacific colonies, men from many lands flocked to Fiji and started plantations, and the local industry flourished for a few years, until Dixie cotton regained its markets. Coffee and cocoa were also attempted by some Western planters but did not meet with success. Nor had copra played the dominant role in Fiji that it had elsewhere in the South Seas. Although it was the earliest plantation crop in the archipelago and continued first in importance in Vanua Levu and on many of the smaller islands, copra had never been produced in large quantities on the main island of Viti Levu, owing to the presence there of a destructive purple moth.

The sugar industry, established there in 1872, was the decisive factor in Fiji's transformation. Within seventy years of its beginnings the annual sugar production had risen to over 125,000 tons, five times the quantity and seven times the value of copra in the late prewar years; that feat was not accomplished with Fijian labor, however. Fijians were found to be unwilling or unsuited to undertake the steady work pace required for cane growing, and since they possessed other resources they did not need to work in the cane fields and sugar mills. For a time the planters were able to make up the labor deficiency by importing natives from the Solomons and the New Hebrides, but all of these were repatriated shortly after Fiji's annexation so that planters had to turn to another source. Through an arrangement with the government of India, Indian laborers were then brought in under contract, with guarantee for repatriation at the end of ten years. By 1916, when the indenture system was abolished, over sixty thousand Indians had been sent to Fiji, and over half of them had elected to remain there when their contracts expired. Meanwhile large numbers of nonindentured Indians had also arrived and settled down as farmers and field laborers.

A decline in sugar prices in 1884 ruined all but the largest sugar operators, so that eventually one company, the CSR (Colonial Sugar Refining Company of Australia), emerged as the sole sugar producer and indeed the largest enterprise in Fiji, representing an investment of over £4,000,000. In 1939 the industry was still entirely dependent upon Indian labor.

The first Indian immigrants served as field workers and mill hands on the Western-owned and managed plantations, living in rough barracks and enjoying no family life because of the absence of Indian women. When free of their indenture contracts, many of them continued to grow cane on small leased plots, and others became traders, domestic servants, or craftsmen. Later, wives began to accompany their men, and Indian families were established. By 1939 there were about ninety-four thousand Indians residing in Fiji, nearly as many as the number of native Fijians and five times the number of all other nonnatives, including Westerners. (Moreover, three-fourths of those Indians had been born in Fiji.) Two-thirds of the wage-earning Indians continued to work in one or another phase of the sugar industry.

The CSR solved the labor problem created by abolition of the indenture system by leasing small plots of cane land to Indian farmers; the company purchased all their cane and advanced capital to them for tools, and so forth, while at the same time retaining control over land use and crop practices. Of the eighty thousand acres in cane in 1939, about 70 percent was cultivated by Indians working as independent farmers or as tenants of the company.

Most of Fiji's Indian immigrants were Hindus from southern India or the Ganges Plain, but a few thousand were Punjabis and Gujaratis. Without question, most of them had bettered their economic situations by going to Fiji. They were industrious and ambitious and generally successful in increasing their incomes and improving their living conditions. They continued to adhere to separate religions (Hindus first in number, then Moslems, then a few Sikhs), but most Indian caste distinctions disappeared in Fiji, along with a number of other social and religious practices disapproved by Fiji's upper-caste colonials. Most Indians looked upon the native Fijians as inferior and primitive, and Fijians held Indians in disdain; consequently, there was very little intermarriage between the two.

By 1939 Indians were increasing in number more rapidly than Fijians. (The annual excess of births over deaths was about four thousand for Indians, twenty-six hundred for Fijians.) They were becoming Western-educated and articulate, and events in India encouraged them to demand larger economic and political stakes in Fiji. They regarded themselves as British subjects and therefore entitled to a far larger voice in governing the colony than they possessed. Most of all, they wanted land. They looked about and saw Fijians owning most of the land in the colony, yet leasing out only a small proportion of it and holding idle all the remainder not required for their subsistence. At the same time, the Indians were compelled to remain satisfied with small, leased plots held under all manner of restrictions.

Here in the South Pacific the British Government faced a dilemma almost as complex as the one they faced in prewar Palestine. Pledges had been given to native Fijians to protect their lands for them; and although the Fijians had not required all their land for current use, their numbers were increasing and hence their need to use more of their land. Yet the Indians in Fiji were also British subjects and could not be kept landless and disenfranchised forever. The government's attempts to dissolve the dilemma were not made easier by the personal preferences of colonial officials for Fijians. Moreover, the whole Western community shared that preference and in addition feared Indian competition in occupations up to then regarded as the domain of Westerners.

One attempted solution was to develop Fijians to the point where they could begin to compete with Indians, both economically and politically, but in this the officials faced the nearly insuperable obstacle of native Fijian custom. If Fijians could only be made to become economic individualists, it was reasoned, they would be better able to survive. But, as was pointed out, even if some Fijian wished to labor and acquire a surplus of worldly goods, his relatives and other compatriots would probably shame him into sharing with them. Also, if he spent his energies in working for his own selfish ends, he would not be able to contribute his share of communal service required by native custom and confirmed by government regulation.

One experiment consisted of cutting a Fijian loose from his communal ties and obligations, either by removing him altogether from his native community and homesteading him elsewhere or by leaving him in his home village and excusing him from the duty to work for the community. In either case, the government then assisted him to become a cash-crop farmer, a capitalist working for himself alone and retaining for himself all his profits. One had to admire the boldness of the experiment; those other social reformers, the missionaries, had rarely undertaken so ambitious a transformation. It remained to be seen how well the experiment would work, or rather how it *might* have worked had not World War II intervened.

Most of the human drama just depicted took place on the main Fijian island of Viti Levu, and to a lesser extent on neighboring Vanua Levu; those two islands were the centers of sugar enterprise and of Indian population. On some of the nearby small islands the copra economy, of both small-planter and native types, still carried on, more or less unaffected by the social dilemma created by sugar. In large areas of Vanua Levu and in other copra areas like Levuka and Taveuni, Western and native planters led lives not unlike those of their counterparts in Melanesia. Many of them supplemented their incomes from copra by growing bananas for New Zealand, which had replaced Australia as the chief market after Queensland protectionists had erected tariff barriers.

Dominating all else in the copra areas was the great god Price. The steady rise in the price of copra, which reached its zenith during World War I, brought prosperity to the Western planters and more gadgets to the native growers. The latter easily survived the price collapse of the thirties, merely giving up trade-store luxuries and returning to the security of subsistence economy and village communalism. The Western planters, on the other hand, fared badly, just as did their brothers-in-travail elsewhere in the South Seas. Indeed, for a while it looked as if the Western planter would disappear altogether from the Fiji scene, leaving the stage to sugar and to the new mining industry then developing on Viti Levu and Vanua Levu.

The gold fever that spread through Melanesia as a result of the rich discoveries in New Guinea in the late twenties also gripped Fiji, and a typical rush followed in the wake of local discoveries in 1932. As such matters usually go, the individual prospectors were eventually supplanted by big companies, in this case backed by Australian capital. Two large mines were developed on Viti Levu and one on Vanua Levu; by

1939 over 108,000 ounces of gold were being exported annually. The ultimate effects of this rich new industry on the colony as a whole were at the time hard to predict: it provided for the government a large source of revenue, second only to sugar, and gave employment to nearly three thousand workers, including the two thousand Fijians who constituted 80 percent of the unskilled labor force. Yet gold runs out eventually, and mining provided only a respite from the colony's Fijian-Indian dilemma born of the sugar industry.

Away to the east of the cane fields, the large plantations, and the gold mines, native Fijian life went on fairly evenly in the smaller, poorer islands of the Lau cluster. In these sparsely populated places the natives continued to grow their own food, producing a little copra to exchange for kerosene, cloth, and other things at the local trade store. Meanwhile they carried on the activities of their kin and village institutions and practiced Christian rites that blended nicely with indigenous beliefs. In retrospect, their most valuable resource was the poverty of their small and isolated islands: nothing in Lau was likely to attract either Westerner or Indian.

Thus, in 1939 there were four Fijis. There was the one of sugar: large, highly rationalized plantations and mills producing wealth for their Western owners and managers and subsistence for their Indian workers, and leaving in its train a basic conflict between Fijian and Indians that dominated political and economic conditions in the colony's two main islands. Second, there was the Fiji of copra: dependent for its survival upon factors of price completely outside local control. Third, there was the Fiji of gold mining: highly profitable to its owners and rich in revenue for the government, but limited in area, in longevity, and in influence upon the course of local events. Last, there was the Fiji of the Lau Islanders: Tonganized and tamed somewhat by Christianity, but far enough removed from the rest of the colony to escape all but the faintest repercussions of the ethnic conflicts that went on there.

SOURCES

Hawaii: Chinen 1958; Crawford 1933; Daws 1968; Embree 1941; Linnekin 1987; Meller and Horwitz 1971; Norbeck 1957; Shoemaker 1940.

Fiji: Chapelle 1978; Derrick 1967; France 1968, 1969; Groves 1963; Knapman 1985; MacNaught 1982; Mayer 1963; Nayacakalou 1955, 1957, 1971; Sahlins 1962; Scarr 1984; Spate 1959; Walter 1978; Ward 1969.

CHAPTER TWELVE

Sea Harvest

Within the cartographers' boundaries of ocean occupied by the Pacific Islands lie thirty million square miles of sea, but the Islanders of 1939 could not rejoice in this statistic because they possessed the facilities for harvesting only a very small proportion of those seas. It is true that food fish and other marine products abound along the reefs and shores of most Islands, enough to supplement the plant diets of many native communities, but the Islanders of 1939 were less able to exploit the open-sea resources than were their ancestors before Western contact.

In 1939, as in pre-colonial times, fishing conditions varied enormously from island to island. The waters of some archipelagoes provided bounteously, while others were a fisherman's despair. At volcanic Mer Island in the Torres Strait, a single throw of a small cast net brought in enough fish for a whole family, while around the southern shores of equally volcanic Bougainville Island, a catch was a memorable event.

In most places with fish the local Islanders displayed ingenuity and skill in catching them. Some were caught with bare hands, others with a wide variety of tools: hooks, throw nets, bows and arrows, spears, dragnets, traps, and weirs. At some places tethered suckfish were used to guide fishermen to larger game; in others fish were captured in a mucilaginous mesh contrived of spider webbing, which was trailed along the water's surface from the tail of a flying kite. In quiet waters poisons were often used to stun the fish and bring them to the surface. Even fishponds were constructed at some islands, but no such artificial devices were required at the many other locations where natural lagoons provided food for the taking.

An event of great importance to many shore communities was the annual appearance of the *palolo*. These reef worms spawn almost exactly one week after the full moon of November; their egg-distended hind portions break off and rise to the surface in the millions, providing a field day for nearby residents, who scooped them up and feasted to repletion.

For Islanders dwelling beside most shores and lakes and slow-moving streams and rivers fishing was and still is a daily food-getting activity, but there were many other places (such as the vast Highlands and montane regions of New Guinea) where the narrow or swift-moving streams harbored few edible creatures and where little or no fishing was engaged in.

Food was not the only product of the sea harvested by the natives of some places. Shells were widely used as ornaments and currency; on many stoneless atolls they were also fashioned into tools. In some places tortoiseshell was highly valued for bracelets and pendants; and in some places shark teeth were lashed to swords and clubs to render them even more murderous.

In many locations the products of the sea brought together shore-dwellers and inlanders to barter and sometimes to fraternize. Special items, such as giant cowries or nacreous bivalves, were traded far inland to areas so remote that residents had no concept of the sea.

The bounty of the sea and the ingenuity of many Islanders in exploiting it was nowhere better seen than on many atolls, whose residents developed impressively rich social and artistic cultures despite their poverty in terrestrial resources. Indeed, a few coconut and pandanus palms plus a lagoon and coral reef were sufficient to permit many communities of atoll dwellers to prosper and proliferate. Or such was the case before foreigners arrived to exploit the marine resources with such rapacity that the former source of economic security became an invitation to demographic and cultural disaster.

Beginning in the eighteenth century the lives of countless islanders were terminated or transformed as a result of foreigners' search for spermaceti and baleen, for pearl and pearl shell, for tuna and bonito, and for turtle and trepang. From these foreign enterprises came necklaces for milady's throat and stays for her corset or flavoring for the mandarin's soup and inlay for his caskets. And from them came large profits for many shipowners and entrepreneurs of New England, Australia, and Japan. But to the Islanders touched by these enterprises came more loss than profit; in return for paltry wages earned as seamen and divers, they had their seas swept clean of whales or their lagoons ransacked of pearl shell, their numbers reduced by kidnappings, and in several cases their health undermined by the dangers of deep diving.

Except for use of their teeth for ornaments and items of ceremonial exchange, whales figured little in the Islanders' indigenous lives, but the presence of whales in the seas around them brought disaster to many island communities. For three quarters of a century Nantucketeers, Sydneymen, and their lesser rivals plowed through the Pacific in search of cachalot and bay right whales, calling at the islands to render oil from their catch and to replenish their stores. Hundreds of vessels used to winter in Hawaii; it is a miracle that its natives survived. Less fortunate were the Marquesans, whose natives never recovered from the onslaught. Other peoples especially hard hit by the visits of whalers and by the rum and disease left by them were those of the Society, Fiji, Ellice, Gilbert, Marshall, and eastern Caroline archipelagoes, as was earlier described. Later, with the shift of whaling to the far northwestern Pacific and the establishment of colonial governments, this scourge was removed from the South Pacific, but the whalers were succeeded in many island locations by another, only slightly less lethal one, in the form of pearling.

Pearl fishing is as old as recorded history, and one of the wonders of the ancient East was the vast pearl fishery that extended from Ceylon to the Persian Gulf. A second, more recent, pearl fishery was located in the Gulf of California, where it was exploited by Spaniards. The third most important of the world's historic pearl fisheries, those of the South Pacific, were known more for pearl shell than for pearls. On nearly every tropical reef in the South Pacific can be found specimens of the mother-of-pearl shells known to commerce: the "gold lip" or "silver lip" pearl oyster *(Pinctada maxima)* and the smaller "black lip" *(Pinctada margaritifera)*. Prize gold-lip shells grow to nearly a foot in diameter and may weigh up to twelve pounds each, but small pearl oysters, containing fewer pearls and better mother-of-pearl, have been more profitable over the years.

The technology of early South Pacific pearl fishing was not complex; the requirements were a small boat, a diver, a weight for descending, a knife, and a net bag or basket. The diver descended to the shell bed, tore off the shell (usually by hand), and placed it in the bag, which was then hauled up to the boat. Shells then had to be opened carefully and cleaned of animal matter and outside coating before being packed for shipment. Before the shallower shell beds were exhausted, naked divers used to descend and work in depths of forty to fifty feet, until air exhaustion forced them to surface. This was the pearl diving of South Seas romance and adventure, and the fictional pictures of it did not have to be greatly overdrawn. Dangers from attacks by sharks, giant eels, rays, and other marine terrors were all very real; and lung collapse or paralysis were the usual prices paid for too long or too deep immersion.

The introduction of diving apparatus made it possible to go deeper, stay down longer, and, of course, get more pearl shell. But these technical improvements soon backfired; the greater volume of shell marketed brought down prices, and many of the best shell beds were exploited beyond predictable recovery. Also, divers' bends and paralysis proved as dangerous as the hazards of naked diving. An even more decisive factor in the subsequent decline of shell diving in the South Pacific was the substitution of other materials for shell in the manufacture of fine buttons, knife handles, and other gewgaws. Nevertheless, fine-quality pearl shell remained marketable, and up to 1939 hundreds of tons of it were exported from the Islands every year.

Nearly every Island colony listed pearl shell among its exports, but the three principal areas of shell fishing were the Tuamotus, Palau, and the Torres Strait. The Tuamotus were the first to attract outside attention, and pearl fishing flourished there as the principal industry until companies using diving equipment cleaned out the beds. The French government then installed conservation measures, which permitted some beds to recover and to provide a regular source of income to native divers. The Palau fishery was developed by the Japanese, who supplemented it with the controlled growing of cultured pearls. The Torres Strait beds began to be worked in 1868. Their extraordinary wealth in pearl shell precipitated a pearling rush, which is described below.

During World War I the marine snail *Trochus niloticus* became valuable because of the success of the Japanese in manufacturing buttons from it. The trochus is conical; the best commercial specimens measure three to four inches in diameter and about three inches in height. In nacreous qualities it is not as fine as true mother-of-pearl, and because of its shape it is not adaptable for use in flat knife handles and inlays, but it possesses other economic advantages. It matures more quickly than gold- or black-lip shell; in addition it grows in shallower water and is consequently easier to harvest and more adaptable to artificial "planting." In short order trochus supplanted true mother-of-pearl as the source of all but the most costly pearl buttons and flat work. Requiring less capital investment in boats and diving gear, trochus fishing tended to remain in native hands more than did pearl-shell fishing, but even so the major profits usually went to the nonnative traders and brokers who purchased pearl shell from native divers and disposed of it in the world's markets.

Trepang *(bêche-de-mer)* is a sausage-shaped sea slug found in shallow tropical waters. When dried to a leathery consistency it is a favorite ingredient of Chinese soups. Trepang fishing has been carried out on a large scale for centuries in the East Indies, and early Western traders in the South Pacific collected it along with sandalwood when they ransacked the Islands for products in demand in China. Later, Chinese and Japanese traders were the principals in drying and marketing trepang, with the Islanders remaining in their usual roles of collectors and laborers. In an average year before World War II several hundred tons of trepang, varying in value up to U.S. $1,500 a ton, were exported from the Pacific Islands.

Sponges, turtle shell, and dried shark fins also entered the trade statistics of the Pacific Islands but the amounts exported were always small.

Much more important were the large tuna and bonita fisheries established by the Japanese in their mandated Islands. After World War I up to forty thousand tons were caught annually and the dried product shipped to Japan. As is described in chapter 14, that industry remained entirely in Japanese hands, even in the manning of the sampans and the drying of the catch. Its principal effect upon the local Islanders was the way it transformed some native communities in Palau, Truk, and Ponape into Japanese towns. The influx of Japanese settlers to man the vessels and factories and shipyards, together with the numerous supportive enterprises, relegated the native Islanders to marginal economic jobs.

The tuna fisheries established by Americans in Hawaii were also manned largely by men of Japanese descent, but their only effect upon the native Hawaiians was to provide them, at typically high prices, with the fish most of them had long since lost the skills and the means to catch. Imagine: Polynesians buying fish caught by Japanese fishermen and sold in American markets! This tableau, however, would surprise no one who examined pre–World War II trade figures and noted that the Pacific Islands, even excluding Hawaii and New Zealand, annually imported hundreds of thousands of dollars' worth of canned fish, principally for sale to Islanders. Few statistics could be more telling with respect to the changes undergone by native fishing in particular or by Island cultures in general.

Summarized, the changes wrought by foreigners' fishing enterprises served to separate Islanders from some of their most valuable resources and, in the process, to subject some of them to new physical hazards, new diseases, new limitations, and new ways of life. Nearly every Island colony had experienced some of those effects; in one, at least, it was the dominant force of change.

Torres Strait

About ten thousand years ago the waters liberated by the melting of the last Pleistocene ice sheets rose and separated New Guinea from Australia by a shallow sea. The higher peaks left uncovered by that sea form the Torres Strait islands, which are surrounded by an intricate complexity of reefs and shoals. Those islands in the west, including Prince of Wales, Horn, Thursday, Moa, Madu, and Mabuiag, are rocky and almost soilless, in sharp contrast to the lush volcanic Murray islands situated in the east and constituting the northern tip of Australia's Great Barrier Reef.

Between these two clusters of higher islands lie some flat coral and sand cays and reefs known as Tutu, Sasi, Burai, Warabu, Guijas, and their equally euphonious neighbors. But all these islands together are only the small visible summits of the far more extensive shoals and reefs that cover most of the surrounding seabed.

Before they were nearly depleted by commercial fishing, these warm, shallow, coralline waters supported a marine life unequaled in quantity and variety elsewhere in the South Pacific. There were great submerged pastures of flawless gold-lip and silver-lip mother-of-pearl, banded trochus, sluggish trepang, horny-plated turtle, and all manner of edible fish, compensating in some measure for the poverty in land resources of most of the area's islands and for the dangerous reefs and the boat-smashing currents that rip through the Strait.

Millennia before the Spaniard Luis Vaez de Torres sailed through the Strait bound from Espiritu to the Indies, these islands became homes for many peoples, whose closest biological and cultural affinities were with New Guineans rather than with those of Australia's nearby Cape York. Nevertheless, before the Western era the Torres Strait islanders regularly visited their Australian neighbors. In fact they served as middlemen between them and mainland New Guineans, their huge canoes having traded far down the Australian coast and up to the estuary of New Guinea's Fly River.

The fertile volcanic soils of the eastern Strait islands provided ample plant foods for their native residents, but that did not weaken their appetites for seafood. And their neighbors on the central coral cays and on the rocky western Strait islands were almost wholly dependent upon seafood.

Throughout the Pacific Islands the sea has always been a better highway than the land, and Strait islanders were great travelers for purposes of trade and warfare. Piracy, plunder-raiding, and headhunting were customary, and these natives developed an organized ferocity and a competence in seagoing savagery exceptional even for that part of the South Seas—a circumstance that came to be grimly learned by the crews of Western vessels trapped on the reefs and shoals of the Strait before colonial law and order were established.

No historian has yet undertaken to number the foreign vessels whose ribs lie rotting in the Strait, but it is known that Spanish, Dutch, English, and Malays all contributed to the graveyard. Now and then coins or decidedly non-Islander skulls have turned up in native villages to recall the times when ships were wrecked and looted and survivors massacred. In its wildest post-Western times the Strait became a byword for dangerous navigation and even more dangerous natives.

The first systematic pearl-shell fishing there was undertaken by a Sydney vessel in 1868. Within ten years over a hundred vessels were similarly engaged and the annual take was valued at more than £110,000. Riffraff from every eastern Australian port flocked to the rich shell beds, and with no effective government control Western skippers and their mixed crews taught the Strait islanders new twists in savagery. Many of the divers were signed-on Islanders from the New Hebrides and beyond; they and their lighter-skinned masters were turned loose on Strait villages to kidnap males for forced diving and females for diversion. (In chronicling man's inhumanity to man it should be duly recorded that many Islanders have freqently and eagerly followed the lead of their Western masters in oppressing other Islanders.) From the very beginning the shell-fishing invaders had the advantage over the Strait islanders by reason of firearms, but their victims did not give up without a fierce struggle, and the blood shed for each season's harvest did not all come from the local natives.

In 1878 the Strait islands were annexed to Queensland and an administrative center was established at Thursday Island. Some of the lawlessness was thereby checked, but for years to come Thursday and its nearby islands were widely known as the "Sink of the Pacific." When the pearl shell thinned out Western divers began to be replaced by Islanders and by Japanese and Malays. Meanwhile, fishing methods had improved: large schooners served as floating bases and supply depots to the fleets of smaller luggers and dinghies, and diving apparatus replaced naked diving. Depletion of shell beds and price fluctuations rendered pearling more economically hazardous; even so, over a thousand tons of pearl shell, worth over £100 a ton, were sold each year as late as 1899. After that, however, pearling fell off year by year and ceased altogether during World War I; but that had the effect of permitting recuperation of the shell beds and led to a postwar revival of the industry that persisted until World War II.

During the interwar years pearling in the Strait became much more orderly. Government regulations protected the beds against exhaustion by strict licensing and by controlling the size of marketable pearl shell. Ownership of the larger companies remained in Australian hands, but pearling operations were carried out on luggers manned largely by Japanese, with a few Islanders and Australian Aborigines serving as crew. Catches were taken to Thursday Island for cleaning, sorting, and crating, and for shipment, mainly to New York and London.

Meanwhile, owing to Japanese initiative, trochus fishing had become very profitable, with Strait islanders able to collect on their own about half of the annual catch (because of the shallower, more accessible trochus beds). Quantities of trepang were also landed at Thursday Island and sold to Chinese traders for shipment to the Far East. Also, Singhalese dealers were on hand to buy turtle shell. In fact, all this varied activity transformed this little port into one of the most cosmopolitan outposts in the world, with the ratios of profits from its enterprises following the familiar descending pattern: first Westerners, then Asians, then Melanesians and Australian Aborigines.

Elsewhere in the Strait the native islanders secured a larger proportion of their marine resources for themselves. Most of the other islands were set aside as native reserves, and under governmental and missionary influence their native residents were assisted in transforming themselves into law-abiding capitalists. They owned and built their own fishing vessels (no more canoes for them!); they conducted their own community affairs according to a strict regimen of blue laws and an exemplary emphasis upon bank savings; they devoted themselves to the rituals of Christianity (mainly Anglican); and they turned out as smart a troop of Boy Scouts as could be seen anywhere in the British Empire.

SOURCES

Whaling: see sources for chapter 3.
Torres Strait: Singe 1979.

CHAPTER THIRTEEN

Mines

Coconuts will continue to grow and trochus to proliferate long after the Islands' deposits of phosphates and metal-bearing ores have been depleted, but in the places where it has taken place mining has had powerful influences on colonial economics and on native life. It began with guano.

The Guano Islands

The discovery that natural soil can be enriched by chemical fertilizers to grow more and better plants led eventually to the pillage of many small Islands scattered over the South Pacific. In 1939 the looting was still going on at the phosphate-rock islands of Ocean, Nauru, Angaur, and Makatea, but the "guano islands" had by then been scraped clean.

Millennia were required to accumulate guano (from Peruvian *huanu*, dung), the powder-dry excrement of seabirds, on the barren coral-capped islands, but it took Westerners only a few years to load it all into ships and transport it to America, Europe, and Australia. The first Pacific guano islands to be exploited were just off the coast of Peru; exploitation of Pacific Islands deposits came a little later, after whalers had discovered them when visiting those islands in search of places to bury dead seamen.

Guano deposits existed throughout the South Pacific, wherever seabirds had lived in sizeable numbers. Millions of boobies and terns, frigate birds and petrels, curlews and golden plovers, and many others of intriguing name and graceful flight, used bare islands as permanent homes or temporary resting places, and by their appetites and their skills in fishing converted part of the marine life swarming about the reefs into tens of thousands of tons of valuable phosphate and ammonium compounds, ready for assimilation by growing plants. On nearly every South Pacific Island some guano can be found, but the famed "guano islands" of Pacific history were those scattered over some four million square miles of ocean between the Hawaiian, Gilbert, Samoan, Society, and Marquesas islands. Some of these, such as Canton, Johnston, and Howland, are barren treeless rocks. Others support dry forests. Still others, such as Fanning Island, are covered with lush tropical vegetation.

Only the southern ones of those islands became permanent homes for humans (in this case, Polynesians) and eventually came to participate in the copra economy. In addition, some of the northern ones served as resting places for seafaring Polynesians, as attested by archaeological remains, but when Westerners first visited them they were inhabited only by seabirds, land crabs, and rats; not even Polynesians were able to make them into permanent homes.

Spanish navigators in the sixteenth century and English in the eighteenth sighted many of the guano islands, but accounts of the American whalers who visited them in the nineteenth century were principally responsible for focusing attention on their rich deposits of guano. In fact, those discoveries were considered so important that the United States Congress, in 1856, passed the Guano Act, allowing Americans to assert the claim of the United States to unoccupied islands in the region for the purpose of taking away guano. Under that act, forty-eight such islands were claimed in due course, but few of these claims survived.

For twenty-five years American companies skimmed off the guano from many of those islands and then abandoned them to the seabirds, and to British companies, operating out of Australia and New Zealand, which gleaned what remained.

The lot of guano diggers was hard and lonely. With natives brought in from Hawaii and southern Polynesia to serve as laborers, the company agent and one or two assistants would remain at the job until the island was skimmed or scraped clean. The richest deposits were located on barren and treeless rocks, with no protection from the heat and glare of the sun. Supplies were taken in three or four times a year from Honolulu, Auckland, or Melbourne; everything that came onto an island and everything that left it, including the thousands of tons of bagged guano, had to be transported through the surf that beat against the unprotected beaches. Ship anchorages were poor or altogether lacking, so that loading was highly precarious. Ashore, tramline tracks were laid out from the guano deposits to the landing beach; some of these still remained in 1939, alongside the temporary shrines of the earlier Polynesian travelers.

With the guano all gone, many of these islands were abandoned and forgotten for decades, until the race for trans-Pacific cable stations and airports again aroused interest in them. Others, with deeper soils and more rainfall, had other fates. A few of the latter were leased to commercial companies and planted in coconuts, by Western managers and laborers from nearby islands. And a few others were converted into homes for permanent settlers from the overcrowded Gilbert islands.

Meanwhile, the quest for fertilizer took a new turn in the islands where, instead of being shoveled off the surface in the form of powdery guano, it had to be crushed out of rock.

The Phosphate Islands

What Pacific traveler has not watched with fascination the nighttime display of phosphorescence stirred up in his vessel's wake? Phosphorus, held in suspension in seawater and diffused over large areas of the world's oceans, comes principally from decomposed marine organisms. In tropical seas marine life is most plentiful around coral reefs, and there phosphatic matter is concentrated. Shallow submerged reefs were ideal platforms for deposit of phosphorus; and when the reefs were exposed, by uplifting of the island or falling of the sea level, some of the phosphates remained on the surface as deposited and other more soluble ones drained down into the softer underlying coral to convert it into calcium phosphate. Such was the origin of some rock phosphate. Other deposits of it originated in bird guano that fell directly onto coral islands, which subsequently submerged and then emerged again. In both cases, however, the harder portions of coral limestone in which the phosphorus or the raw guano were deposited were not affected, so that the usual deposit consists of phosphatic material lodged in pockets (some small, some very large) in the harder limestone. When the phosphate is removed, the remaining limestone is a jagged wilderness of pinnacles and crevasses.

The phosphate itself is highly variable, ranging from metallic hardness to crumbly nodules; it may be gray, brown, or even golden and contain varying intermixtures of lime and mineral impurities. It can be removed from the larger pockets by power shovels after it has been loosened, but much of the mining has to be done by hand: chipping away at the small narrowing pockets that sometimes extend tens of feet deep. Then, before it is shipped and processed, the rock has to be broken up and dried.

Raw phosphate has to be made water-soluble to become available for plant food, and that is done by grinding it and treating it with sulphuric acid, the product of which is the superphosphate used widely to fertilize farms and pastures deficient in phosphorus. Soils differ widely in their phosphate requirements; in Australia, for example, a ton of raw phosphate rock converted into superphosphate will fertilize fifty acres of wheat-producing land.

In the 1930s the world annually consumed between seven and ten million tons of phosphate; without it agriculture as then practiced could not have existed. America supplied most of its own needs, but western Europe, Japan, Australia, and New Zealand had to import, and the last three countries came to depend upon the Pacific Island deposits to supply most of their needs.

Australia's vast wheat industry could not have developed without phosphate, nor could New Zealand's dairying; and the quest for guano and phosphates sent Britishers prospecting to every atoll and island in the South Pacific not claimed by other powers. For a while the search was unproductive, and the Pacific Islands Company of London was reduced to scraping up what the American guano diggers had overlooked. Then, a company chemist had the curiosity to analyze a doorstop of "fossilized wood" brought home by a company agent as a curio from Nauru, an isolated island in the central Pacific. The rock turned out to be very high-grade calcium phosphate, and inquiry turned up that both Nauru and nearby Ocean Island (Banaba) were covered with similar material. Ocean Island was still unclaimed, and it was a simple matter to show the Union Jack there and add it to Her Majesty's Gilbert and Ellice Island Protectorate. Nauru, however, was German, so the company directors had to proceed cannily to obtain mining rights there from an unsuspecting Germany. The trick came off, and the British company began operations in 1900 on Ocean Island and in 1906 on Nauru. The richness of both these deposits turned out to be truly fabulous. The rock was extremely high grade and early estimates of reserves ran to twenty million tons on Ocean and a hundred million on Nauru.

Two major problems faced the company from the beginning: to obtain sufficient manpower for the hand labor predominantly required for mining and to devise measures for loading the rock into ships.

The native islanders of Ocean Island and Nauru were too few in number; moreover, the rents and royalties paid to them for mining leases and for mined rock reduced their incentive to work for the low wages being offered. At Ocean Island the problem was temporarily solved by utilizing indentured natives of the Gilbert and Ellice islands and by importing a few hundred Japanese. At Nauru some Melanesians were tried out as laborers but were later sent home, and the main reliance was placed upon Caroline islanders and Japanese.

Ship loading presented a more difficult problem. Both Nauru and Ocean are raised coral islands of the "pancake" type, whose shores fall away steeply to unfathomed depths save for narrow ledges of fringing reef against which break the full force of the Pacific swells. There is thus no anchorage or protection for ships, and at the start of mining operations all cargo that went onto or off the islands had to be boated through an always hazardous and sometimes impassable surf. Engineers eventually solved this problem by building huge cantilever trestles, which swung out over the reef and conveyed rock either directly into the moored ships, as at Nauru, or, as at Ocean, into boats that lightered it out to the waiting ships.

While Nauru and Ocean Island were being developed, the same British company discovered similar but smaller deposits at Makatea Island, north of Tahiti, and joined with the French in exploiting them. The problems there were overcome in much the same way as at Ocean Island and Nauru, and labor was secured locally and from other islands of French Polynesia, plus some from Japan. Most of Makatea's annual production of about 100,000 tons was sent to Japan.

Meanwhile, the Germans found phosphate on Angaur Island in the western Carolines and began mining there in 1909, with Western managers, Chinese artisans, and natives recruited from nearby islands.

World War I brought about a change in management of the mining at Nauru and Angaur. Nauru was taken from Germany and mandated to the United Kingdom, Australia, and New Zealand. The three governments set up the British Phosphate Commission, which acquired ownership of the original company's interests in both Ocean Island and Nauru and carried on mining as before. The enterprise was financially supported by the participating governments and its output was sold at cost on a quota basis to them, but otherwise it was operated like a private corporation. Chinese were recruited in Hong Kong to take the place of Japanese and Caroline islanders, who were no longer available. Technical improvements were made in mining, crushing, drying, and loading, and by 1939 over a million tons of rock were exported annually, enough to fill all the needs of Australia and New Zealand.

The Japanese took over ownership of the German assets at Angaur and eventually transferred mining operations to a company in which the government retained a large financial interest. Besides working the Angaur deposits intensively, the Japanese branched out to other Caroline and Mariana islands where smaller deposits of guano and rock phosphate were located. In time, some 200,000 tons of guano and rock were annually shipped to Japan, constituting a small but important contribution to Japan's fertilizer-dependent agriculture. Indentured Caroline islanders provided the labor, under the management of Japanese.

All together, the four major Pacific phosphate islands produced only about 8 percent of the world's annual output, but their production was vitally important to Japan, Australia, and New Zealand; none of the three had much domestic phosphate and in terms of freight costs was almost prohibitively far removed from other sources. Added to that, the Pacific deposits were among the world's richest in phosphate content. In sum, these enterprises provided a most fortunate set of advantages: for the companies that operated the mines; for the farmers who spread the refined, and highly subsidized, end product over their fields and pastures; and for the consumers who benefited from it in the prices paid for their bread, butter, and rice. But what about the natives who, one could properly assume, had originally owned the phosphate?

Ocean Island (Banaba), which proved so valuable to its Western exploiters, was previously anything but a treasure to its native Banabans. The few hundreds who dwelt there before Western contact are thought to have gone there from the nearby Gilbert islands, whose people they closely resemble, both physically and culturally. Ironically, this island, which has helped to fertilize millions of acres in other lands, has itself only meager, infertile soil; its native food plants grew only in the narrow coastal belt girdling the coraline hump that composes most of it. In contrast to its poverty in edible plants, the seas around the island teem with fish, which the Banabans obtained in large quantities and by means of several ingenious techniques. There were, however, no means within their abilities to increase the paltry supply of fresh water on their porous and drought-ridden Island. Women had to crawl into caves to fill their shell water containers from shallow pools, and when these dried up (as they sometimes did) some islanders had to emigrate. This decline in numbers was accelerated by the early phosphate operations, so that by 1914 the population had been reduced to about four hundred, one-sixth of the number believed to have been there at the time of first Western contact.

Moreover, where there had once been one homogeneous people, in 1939 there were four. One consisted of the managers of the phosphate operations and the staff of the Gilbert and Ellice Islands Protectorate, which was headquartered there. These Britishers maintained an entirely separate existence; they lived in comfortable bungalows of bachelors' dormitories and during off-hours energetically performed their national rituals of sports and tea. The eight hundred or so Chinese contract laborers recruited in Hong Kong lived in compounds and had little contact with others when not at work. They were not permitted to bring their own women with them and did not have access to native women. Their free hours were spent in truck gardening, theatricals, and gambling; except for an occasional fracas with Gilbertese laborers, they were industrious and "submissive."

To work for a while on Ocean Island was the Great Adventure for most Gilbertese youths, but since many of them brought along their wives and remained for only a year, the change in their lives was not very profound.

To the remaining Banabans, however, the mining operations proved to be revolutionary. Their physical survival was no longer precarious: water was assured them from company supplies, and with the money they received from rents and royalties they were able to purchase enough food and other Western goods. Instead of living in small dispersed hamlets as they formerly had done, they were concentrated in four villages. Their indigenous political organization, based on hamlet and district units and upon a complex ritual, was replaced by a government-imposed system involving native police and the usual colonial-type concern with sanitation and Western concepts of welfare.

One element of the indigenous culture that survived, at least partly, was the sport of fowling. Frigate birds, with great wings out of all proportion to their small bodies, were captured and tamed so that they decoyed other birds to within range of their native masters, who brought the prey down with a kind of bola. In the old days this activity was highly competitive and ritualized and added some excitement to living on this otherwise uninviting place. But like most other zestful things about Banaban culture, the "time-wasting" and "wanton" aspects of fowling succumbed to mission disapproval, leaving the Banabans to entertain themselves with the physical side of the sport.

Nauru, like Ocean Island, is a mass of coral and phosphate, but its fringing coastal belt is wider and its supply of edible food plants larger. Also, natural supplies of fresh water are more plentiful than on Ocean Island, and before the times of phosphate mining the Nauruans were able to supplement ocean fishing with seafood from fishpond reservoirs.

Like the neighboring and culturally related Marshall islanders, the Nauruans before Western contact were divided into several exogamous lineages, but here the lineages were not identified with specific territories; in fact, members of any one lineage might live scattered about in several of the island's distinct political districts. It sometimes happened that one lineage became politically dominant in a district by virtue of the greater number and influence of its members there, but such ascendency was not permanent. Interdistrict feuding was common, but no one district remained dominant for very long.

An unusual feature of indigenous Nauru was its emphasis on individual property ownership, including ownership of land. Inheritance of land was largely primogenitural, with daughters especially favored—not unexpected in this matrilineal society.

Nauruans distinguished three social strata: nobility (persons of inherited or achieved affluence and their close relatives), commoners, and serfs (persons captured in war or accepted as refugees). However, class lines were not rigidly drawn, and it was not unusual for a man of nobility to marry a commoner woman.

Not much more than the above is known about the native culture of

Nauru before Western contact. That culture was only sketchily described by early visitors and had been so overwhelmingly transformed by contacts with Westerners that most of it cannot be reconstructed. Beachcombers and traders started the changes and contributed the advice and the firearms that encouraged stepped-up interdistrict feuding during the first century of Western contact.

In 1888 Germany extended her protectorate over the Marshall islands to include Nauru, and, following the German pattern of colonial rule, the officials encouraged the Nauruans to increase their production of copra, there having been little else readily available for trade.

Phosphate mining changed all that. Native landowners were paid rent for land leased to the mining company and received in addition a royalty on all rock removed. In short order Nauruans became very wealthy by Pacific Islands standards and were able to purchase goods at the trade store without having to earn money by manual labor. Then, after World War I, when the island was mandated to Great Britain, Australia, and New Zealand, the new administration took additional measures to safeguard what they perceived to be the interests of the Nauruans. The usual welfare services were instituted, school attendance became compulsory, and many Nauruans were helped to obtain higher education in Australia. Moreover, they were encouraged to work for the mining company in jobs that were at least semiskilled. In short, the Nauruans material standards of living became much higher by Western criteria, to the extent, for example, that many individuals owned motorbikes and trucks.

Mining operations did not encroach much on the Nauruans' gardens and residential areas, and they continued to dwell in their villages much as before, except, of course, for the usual sanitary reforms. On the other hand, changes took place in some of their social institutions. For example, they were encouraged to "elect" their leaders; these were not infrequently chosen from among commoners on the basis of proven leadership rather than by the traditional criteria of social class and seniority. Another revolutionary change in social relations was the mission-inspired disappearance of polygyny and of most of the practices associated with the indigenous religion.

Nauruans did not have to work very hard to satisfy their needs, including their increasing appetite for Western goods. But as favored wards they became increasingly parasitic upon the administration and the mining company.

Such favored treatment was made possible by the employment of Chinese laborers, who numbered on the average about one thousand and who, like those at Ocean Island, were recruited in Hong Kong for three-year indentures. As at Ocean, the Chinese lived in their compound, entirely separated from the Western managers and the Nauruans. In their womanless exile they worked industriously and submissively, trading with Nauruans for food now and then, but otherwise keeping to their compounds when off the job, with gambling their major recreation.

Inland New Guinea

Hope for gold had spurred on several of the earliest Western explorers in the South Pacific, and substance was added to dreams when Saavedra discovered traces of it along New Guinea's northern coast in 1528. But after fruitless searching, most foreigners in New Guinea turned to the surer profits of trading and planting. But not all of them; a few hopefuls never gave up the search, and as far back as the 1870s there were prospectors trudging through the islands east of New Guinea. Payable alluvial deposits were located on Misima and Woodlark islands and at isolated spots in the interior of the main island, but the indomitables were rewarded for their hardships only enough to keep them hoping. In German (i.e., northeastern) New Guinea systematic searches were undertaken, but had to be given up at the outbreak of World War I.

The first big strike came during the twenties, when prospectors discovered the incredibly rich pay dirt (running as high as £A200 per cubic yard) in the Bulolo River region of northeastern New Guinea's Morobe District. For the first few years it remained a prospector's show, every man for himself, and a few individual fortunes were made in spite of the difficulties attending the whole enterprise. Supplies had to be portered in from the coast through swamps and over ranges, a journey requiring from ten to fourteen days. The supply track led through country inhabited by hostile natives, who added to the miseries of terrain, fever, and dysentery to make the adventure a fatal one for many Western prospectors and their native employees. So hard and costly were work and supply conditions that production had to stay above ten ounces a day to make it worth a miner's while.

When individual prospectors had recovered all the gold dust they could in the Bulolo area with their primitive panning, they fanned out into nearly every range and valley in northeastern New Guinea. Minor rushes also developed in Papua, in the mountains behind Wewak, and even on Bougainville, Guadalcanal, and Fiji, but the Bulolo area retained its lead through the big companies that eventually supplanted the individual prospectors.

Backed by British capital, some of the more foresighted prospectors took over the deposits after crude washing methods had skimmed off the surfaces. Testing proved the existence of deposits that were very extensive but that required modern dredging and crushing methods to exploit. To overcome supply difficulties air transport was introduced; a plane covered the distance from coast to mining area in thirty minutes, as compared with the ten to fourteen days of walking.

From then on everything went by plane: miners and their native employees, lumber, food, heavy mining machinery, vehicles, cows for a dairy, and, of course, beer. In the space of a few years mining centers such as Wau and Bulolo became modern towns, complete with hotels, clubs, and cinemas, an entirely airborne civilization in the heart of a Stone Age wilderness.

By 1939 these gold-mining communities contained about seven hundred Westerners and nearly seven thousand native employees, and gold production, in the peak year, surpassed 400,000 ounces.

Upon the rest of New Guinea the effects of this concentration of people and wealth was galvanizing. Royalties from gold enabled the administration of the Mandate Territory to continue its work energetically throughout the depression years, when a dependence upon a copra economy would have arrested its work of exploration and the extension of government control. The commercial center of gravity shifted so much to the mainland that when a volcanic eruption in 1937 paralyzed Rabaul, the territory's capital, it was planned to move administrative headquarters to Lae, a coastal town nearer the goldfields. The air age ushered in by gold mining brought about scheduled flights to Australia and sliced weeks off ordinary steamship travel time. With all these changes the territory began to attract a new kind of Westerner, one whose customary tempo was geared to the hustle of Western cities rather than to the patient planter life.

The effect of all these things on native New Guineans was to speed up the process of opening up previously unexplored areas to Western influence and control and to provide new experiences for the thousands of New Guineans who worked at the goldfields. The glimpse of Western civilization obtained by natives working on plantations was very limited, compared to what they saw in the modern, more densely populated mining towns. Also, they received more pay than their copra-making cousins, plus closer contact with more numerous Western "masters." Altogether, it was a more exciting and profitable way to earn head-tax money and size up the new Western world. It also provided natives with an unprecedented view of their New Guinea compatriots, since thousands of them were concentrated in camps and campgrounds. Feuding developed among the workers in some camps; fights between those from the Sepik and Markham river areas were particularly bloody.

As copra prices continued to tumble, there were few planters who did not gaze yearningly past their silent groves toward the Morobe goldfields, and many of them made the leap. Some of the more patient and farsighted ones held that gold would someday give out and that the future of the territory (and of themselves) would continue to depend upon agriculture, including a new type of agriculture that was developing in the vast new temperate-climate Highlands of the territory. But before any of those predictions could be put to the test, World War II began in Europe and turned the colonials' thoughts and energies into other channels.

New Caledonia

Through a combination of geological accidents and French design, almost the only feature New Caledonia shares with other South Pacific Islands is its location. Arriving there direct from the coconut belt, the pre–World War II traveler learned with surprise that this island, so near to the New Hebrides and Fiji, had once been the world's largest producer of nickel and chromium. Also distinguishing it from other South Pacific Islands was its bizarre hodgepodge of peoples, consisting of Melanesians, Javanese, Indochinese, and Japanese, along with some of the best and worst natives of France.

New Caledonia extends for 250 miles northwest by southeast and averages about thirty miles wide. The island is rugged; mountain ranges rise to fifty-four hundred feet but are broken in places by deep valleys and large inland plateaus. Erosion has scarred many areas beyond any semblance of orderly topographic pattern, and such areas are practically impassable. The eastern slopes and valleys receive a full measure of rain brought by the prevailing easterlies, with the result that that side has the tropical luxuriance of other Melanesian islands. The western side is drier, however, and is covered with scrub vegetation so that it resembles Australia's outback. In climate, also, New Caledonia differs from islands to the north; the hot season is truly hot and humid, but there is enough seasonal change to render it agreeable and healthful for people accustomed to a temperate climate. And the absence of malaria makes the island even more pleasantly habitable for Westerners.

In 1939 a stroll through Noumea, principal town of New Caledonia and as French as Marseille, would have made it hard to realize that one short century before this island had been inhabited by Stone Age Melanesians. During that century, it is true, some of Noumea's plumbing had not greatly changed, but nearly everything else had done so, and its former indigenous people had been pushed back into reserves in the less coveted parts of the island.

The first census of New Caledonia, taken in 1887, recorded about forty-two thousand indigenes, but by that time their numbers had already been reduced through the familiar processes from a size before Western contact of an estimated eighty thousand, speaking some twenty different Austronesian languages. At the time of Western "discovery," in 1774, the New Caledonians were highly competent horticulturists and resided in nucleated villages. Their clans were patrilineal and exogamous. Warfare was fierce and frequent, and resulted in continual changes in the sizes and compositions of their political units.

Cook's party, the first Westerners to land in New Caledonia, found the indigenes to be friendly and hospitable; but it did not take long for the traders and beachcombers to alter that. Marist missionaries landed there in 1840 and began to pave the way for French annexation, which took place in 1853, almost in the presence of a British warship. So slim was the time margin and so deep the chagrin of the ship's commander that he committed suicide. And well he might; for there, on Australia's very doorstep, was lost an island almost solidly composed of the ores of nickel, chromium, iron, cobalt, and manganese, and many other minerals of rarity and high commercial value.

At first, however, the new French masters were less interested in their island's mineral wealth than in its suitability for penal settlements and ordinary colonization. Colonists were encouraged to go there to produce the sugar, copra, and coffee then needed in France, and land was secured for their plantations by the strategy of engineering native revolts, followed by confiscation of the rebels' territories. During those pioneer days there was also some prospecting for minerals, mainly by Australians, but the chief value of the island to the French government was its distance from France, which made it ideal as a place for undesirables.

From 1860 to 1894 New Caledonia was host to over forty thousand French prisoners; intellectual leaders of the ill-fated Paris Commune of 1871 and Moroccan Arab nationalist leaders shared exile and punishment on the island alongside habitual criminals. Many of the prisoners died on the island; some of them served out their sentences and returned to France; others escaped to Australia or found refuge in beachcombing on nearby Pacific islands; but many remained on the island as free colonists, or served out their sentences as *libérés*. The French government helped the latter to secure farmlands, usually at the expense of native New Caledonians, who were thereby pushed back into smaller and smaller reserves. In time thousands of the colonists' cattles were allowed to graze on the natural pasture, and, with no fences to stop them, they invaded the natives' gardens.

By 1878 the encroachments had become so unendurable that many natives rebelled and massacred whole settlements of French colonists. For a time the native campaigns were carried out so efficiently and ruthlessly that it seemed they might recover most of their homelands. But peace was negotiated and the rebellious natives withdrew to their reserves. That episode had a sobering effect upon the colonial government, and from then on there was at least official recognition of what was perceived to be native rights. Among other things, it became obvious to the colonials that the native New Caledonians could not be induced to labor in the mining enterprises then being developed, which circumstance served to create the colony's principal economic problem, and its major ethnic dilemma.

For a while Western convicts were farmed out to planters and mine operators, but this practice proved to be neither popular nor profitable. The search for labor then turned to Asia, and beginning in 1883 a few hundred Chinese indentured laborers were imported. Japanese were also tried out, but did not prove amenable to the crude living and working conditions. Even a few (Asian) Indians were experimented with, but the hardest working and most docile workers proved to be those recruited in Indochina and Java, and hence those places became the primary sources for labor.

At the turn of the century New Caledonia was the world's largest producer of cobalt, nickel, and chromium. Up to 1939 nickel and chromium remained the economic mainstay of the island, although Canada (in nickel) and Rhodesia (in chromium) took over world leadership in 1905 and 1921, respectively. France and Belgium purchased most of New Caledonia's nickel, and the United States, France, and Australia its chromium. Japan and Germany also took large quantities of crude nickel ore, and during the thirties the Japanese engaged in the actual mining of New Caledonian iron ore to help supply the Japanese market. The Japanese miners, together with compatriots who had earlier settled on the island, became an important element in the commercial life of the colony. In nearly every other respect, however, its economy was bound to France: the island produced things needed in France, was reserved more or less as a market for French products, and was governed by a French metropolitan bureaucracy.

By 1939 New Caledonia had become like no other island in the South Pacific. From its layout and architecture Noumea might have been a coastal town in southern France; and up and down both coasts were sleepy villages reminiscent of Provence. Coffee plantations dotted the landscape, and large tracts of land were set aside for pasturing the colonists' tens of thousands of cattle. Many ore-bearing mountains were scarred by nickel and chromium workings, and sawmills were penetrating the forests where valuable kauri pine timber was being removed.

The composition of the population had been transformed even more than the landscape. The eighty thousand or so natives who had once owned the entire island were reduced in number to thirty thousand, and most of them had been pushed back into reserves where they lived much as their ancestors had done centuries before, supplemented by a few money-earning jobs such as diving for pearl shell, growing coffee and cocoa, and working for foreigners. Their contacts with foreigners, including missionaries, served to teach them a *patois* French along with other externals of Western culture. After it became obvious to the French that they were unwilling or unsuitable for coolie labor, they were permitted to live their own lives and set their own rate of decline and deculturation. After all, they had no effect on the economic life of the colony, which was the concern of its seventeen thousand Westerners and fifteen hundred Japanese, and their fourteen thousand Javanese and Tonkinese laborers.

The economy of New Caledonia was built upon the use of cheap Asian labor in the extraction of nickel, chromium, and iron, and it was an exploitative economy in the classical sense of the term. Chromium ore was mined and shipped direct to overseas markets; in terms of its chromic oxide content some twenty-five thousand metric tons were exported in 1938, composing about 6 percent of world production outside the USSR. The island's chromium mines were owned principally by British interests and were managed locally by British, Australian, and American agents. Except for taxes levied against exported ore, most of the mining proceeds were lost to the colony.

Control over the island's nickel production was also concentrated in the hands of absentee owners, although a few of the nickel mines were owned by local French. Since New Caledonian nickel ore is low grade, it had to be refined one stage before shipping to market. The only refinery and the largest mines were owned by the Société le Nickel, which consequently controlled local production and prices. Some critics held that the Société was owned by the world monopolistic International Nickel Company of Canada; others that it was owned principally by Rothschild and the Bank of Indochina, and that the Société merely had a cartel agreement with International Nickel in connection with price and quota matters. In either case, controls were vested in outsiders and, except for export taxes on ore, the profits did not contribute directly to the welfare of the colony.

Chromium ore was loaded onto freighters at anchorages located near the mines, but nickel ore had to be delivered to Noumea for refining and eventual shipment overseas. In terms of nickel content, some ninety-six hundred metric tons were produced in 1938, about 8 percent of world production outside the USSR.

Mining was largely a matter of makeshift devices and hand labor supplied almost entirely by Javanese and Tonkinese. Most of the mines were at isolated locations and afforded only the crudest of facilities for the laborers, who were compelled by law to serve out their terms of contract. The nickel refining at Noumea was also a makeshift affair, dependent heavily on hand labor.

Parasitic upon the mining industry was an array of smaller businesses (mercantile, service, food production, and so forth). Ownership of the most important of these was concentrated in the hands of a few leading local French colonial families, whose members served also as "directors" of the foreign-owned mining enterprises because of a French law requiring local representation.

Below the upper class of managers, "directors," proprietors, and big merchants was a far more numerous class of Western small farmers and merchants and white-collar workers. Some of this class were the children or grandchildren of immigrant colonists, others of freed convicts. They regarded the island as theirs and fiercely resented the domination of its most valuable resources by absentee owners. They continued to look to France as their cultural homeland, but wished for more autonomy in political and economic matters. But, however poignant a picture they were used to painting of themselves as the mistreated "little men," they did not fare too poorly. To most of them physical labor was as abhorrent as it was to the wealthy, and it was a very poor "little man" establishment that did not have a few native or Javanese domestics and laborers.

The Japanese were latecomers to the island but like their compatriots elsewhere they knew what they wanted and proceeded with energy to get it. Of the fifteen hundred of them domiciled there, the majority were small tradesmen: the "Chinese" of New Caledonia. There was a Japanese store in almost every village, and in Noumea they were to be seen behind the counters of most small shops. Few of these tradesmen had brought wives with them, so many of them lived with native women.

Altogether different, economically and socially, were the local managers of the Japanese iron mine, which was established on the island in the thirties. This enterprise mined and shipped ore direct to Japan and was well advanced toward its annual production goal of a half million tons of ore when World War II stopped operations. In keeping with French law the local "directors" of this firm were all Frenchmen.

The nine thousand Javanese and five thousand Tonkinese living on the Island supplied the muscle and sweat to keep the colony solvent. The latter worked principally in the mines and at the refinery; some of the former also worked in the mines but many of them were indentured to French farmers and worked as field laborers and domestics. Hundreds of these Asians were free residents of the colony, having served out their indentures and elected to remain, but the majority of them were still under three- to five-year contracts. In return for transportation to the colony and guaranteed repatriation upon conclusion of indenture, they had contracted to work in the mines or fields or shops for a few francs a day plus keep. Their employers were backed by government authority, with fines and imprisonment imposed for disobedience.

Living conditions provided for most contract laborers were if anything even worse than those of plantation laborers in the copra islands to the north. Perfunctory inspections of Javanese work camps were carried out by agents of the Netherlands Indies government; but the Tonkinese, being French subjects, had no official champions and occasionally vented their grievances in small and pathetically ineffectual strikes. Caste barriers were erected by the Western masters against these Asians at nearly every point of potential contact: there was no nonsense here about "traditional French democracy." Even the native New Caledonians occupied higher class status in the views of most Westerners.

Over all these classes and factions, with their differing objectives and resources and needs, was placed a colonial governor and a staff of career civil servants. The governor enjoyed autocratic powers and frequently made use of them to discourage tendencies to local autonomy. To advise him and to prepare the budget and levy local taxes there was a fifteen-member General Council, elected by Western residents; because of predominant big-company representation on this council, however, it was identified with the interests of overseas owners and consequently had little time for any "Advance Caledonia" movement. Among other things, this council saw to it that taxes on the mining enterprises remained low and that contract laborers were not "spoiled."

The governor's task could hardly have been an easy one: to contain the autonomous sentiments of the French colonials and to mitigate somewhat, in the name of French democracy, their fierce caste prejudices. And, to make his assignment even harder, there was growing up under his very nose a colony of energetic and resourceful Japanese.

But back to the native New Caledonians, who reacted to all these activities of the foreign interlopers: first with dismay and curiosity, occasionally with hostility, then with coerced resignation and much cold anger.

The issue, as usual, was land. In pre-Western times every area of the island's usable land had been owned by one or another of its numerous patrilineal clans. (That left large areas—swamps, scrub-covered savanna, mountain ridges, and so forth—that were not actively utilized, but even those were identified with one or another clan or group of clans.) In terms of the native technique of land-rotating horticulture, every family required about seven times as much arable land as that under cultivation at any one time. To the land-hungry French colonists, however, "native-owned" land consisted only of areas being used at any one time; thus they had no scruple against confiscating, with or without government assistance, all "unused" land. And in this sense, with the decline in number of natives, more and more land was perceived, or declared, to be "unused," so that by 1939 most of the surviving natives, numbering about forty-two thousand, were contained within officially established reserves that occupied only about one-thirteenth of the island's total land area. And although the survivors had in the meantime become Christianized and conditioned by schooling and other influences to wish for and expect the material and social perquisites of French democracy and civilization, they were left with fewer means to acquire them, a quandry that was doubtless embittered for them by sight of the material prosperity being enjoyed by the numerous foreigners inhabiting their lands. In the words of one historian: "One cannot emphasize too strongly that the basic cause of the clashes and frictions of the past century in New Caledonia is the misunderstanding by European individuals as well as the government of the strength of the relationship between man and earth, the complexity and strength of the Melanesian's attachment to the native soil" (Saussol 1971:230).

SOURCES

Guano islands: Bryan 1941.

Ocean Island and Nauru: Ellis 1936; MacDonald 1982; Silverman 1971; Wedgewood 1936.

New Guinea: Healy 1967; Reed 1943; Ryan 1972; Souter 1963.

New Caledonia: Douglas 1970, 1980, 1982; Doumenge 1966; Guiart 1963; Howe 1977; Leenhardt 1930, 1937; Lenormand 1953; A. Ward 1982.

CHAPTER FOURTEEN

Bases

Every Pacific archipelago has at one time or another been coveted by subjects of foreign powers: some for their land, some for their raw materials, others for the labor or the souls of their native inhabitants. In addition, one other motive that led foreigners to want certain islands has been their locations. For example, Guam's recognized value to Spain lay in its position athwart the galleon route to Manila; Hawaii's situation along a line to the Far East has had an increasing effect on local events; and to many Australians who cared little about copra or gold, New Guinea's primary function was her location as a shield.

It was primarily because of their locations that Britain annexed Fanning, Christmas, Penrhyn, and the Suvorov islands in 1888, to serve as possible stations for the projected Empire Cable (which eventually ran from Vancouver to New Zealand and Australia via Fanning, Fiji, and Norfolk Island). Again, during the 1930s the American and British race for central Pacific airfields singled out pinpoints of land (Johnston, Howland, Canton) that had no value other than location. But these annexations had little effect on Pacific Islanders: only Penrhyn was inhabited, and after annexation no effort was made to utilize it for the proposed cable. In three other cases, however, the factor of strategic location was a dominating influence over the lives of their native inhabitants: in Eastern (American) Samoa and Guam, where the presence of the American Navy shaped their lives in many ways; and in the Japanese

Mandated Islands, where strategic as well as economic considerations seem to have prevailed.

American Samoa

As was already described, the Three-Power Convention of 1899 awarded Eastern Samoa (Tutuila and Manua) to the United States, but indifferent Congresses did not act on the matter until 1926, when accession was formally approved. Since America's chief interest in these islards was in maintaining a naval station at Tutuila's excellent harbor of Pago Pago, the President placed administration of the whole accession in the hands of the Department of the Navy. After that there were the usual official inquiries to define the territory's status, and in 1929 a full-dress commission advocated an organic act, which would have established civil government and U.S. citizenship for resident Samoans; these proposals were not acted upon, however.

Administration by the navy had both good and bad consequences for the native Samoans. The naval governor enjoyed nearly absolute powers, which usually were exercised benevolently but firmly, thereby giving him a role similar to that of their own native chiefs, and hence one the Samoans appeared to understand and respect. On the other hand, a governor's tenure was limited to the navy's conventional duty assignment of two years, which did not allow an incumbent or his staff time enough to master the tortuous intricacies of Samoan politics. Thus, the arrangement did not provide for consistency and continuity in administration.

Throughout the period of prewar navy rule the emphasis was upon maintaining a naval station while ensuring native welfare. There was no official support for foreigners' enterprises; on the contrary, the naval government marketed all native-produced copra (about two hundred tons per annum, the territory's sole export), leaving little scope for the few Western traders still there.

The administration tended to permit Samoans to run their own affairs so long as public order was not interfered with. Unfortunately, disturbances to what most Americans considered to be "public order" were inherent in the native polity, and on several occasions a governor had to interfere actively to settle factional quarrels. Under such circumstances some opposition to the administration was bound to appear sooner or later, and it was only to be expected that the *Mau* movement (described earlier) should spread hence from Western Samoa. Some of the resident Westerners and mixed bloods added their complaints, and newspapers in the United States occasionally published letters from "friends of Samoa" calling attention to the "sad plight of the innocent Samoans under the dictatorial Navy rule." There was then repeated, in miniature, what was taking place in Western Samoa, and the navy's solution was similar to the one later adopted by New Zealand's Labour Party: the *Mau* was officially recognized, and the naval governor even attended its ceremonies (as honored guest), but he never permitted any assumption to be made that actual governmental authority rested in anyone but himself.

By 1939 it appeared, on the surface at least, that the experiments in governing Samoans had been more successful in the eastern than in the western sector of this archipelago. Probing a little deeper, however, it might be argued that paternalistic navy rule had ill prepared the Eastern Samoans for participation in the hard competitive world they would have to face unless they were to remain museum specimens for all time. So dependent, in fact, had they already become upon navy facilities in most aspects of living that the *Mau* formally requested of a visiting congressional commission that the United States set up a trust fund of ten million dollars for the benefit of American Samoa, asserting that generous handouts of this nature constituted the "practice and policy all over the world by all governments"!

Guam

On June 20, 1898, an American cruiser steamed into Guam's main harbor and opened fire on its fort. So isolated was the island that its Spanish governor believed the firing to be a salute and did not learn of the state of war between Spain and the United States until he sent a welcoming delegation to the cruiser. The Spanish officials capitulated immediately and were removed to the Philippines. Because of Guam's perceived potentialities as a naval base, the island was assigned to the Department of the Navy, and a naval officer assumed the governorship in 1899.

During the ensuing forty years Guam's history diverged sharply from that of the other islands in the Mariana archipelago. The process of Westernization, which had proceeded so gradually for 230 years under Spanish-Catholic rule, took some new turnings. On the one hand, the naval administration maintained and even reinforced the regime of discipline and absolutism that had characterized Spanish rule; and although the navy's policy was dissociated from the Catholic Church, it was paternalistic in several other ways. Countering this influence were the up to then unfamiliar theories of Americanism, including social democracy and capitalistic enterprise, which reached the Guamanians through the public (and now secular) schools, and through increasing contacts with American civilians. Some strains did develop out of those conflicting influences, but the trend toward the new remained slow because of the continuing conservatism of the Catholic Church and Chamorro family values. Also, the traditional subsistence and barter system remained firmly entrenched, owing partly to a depression in copra prices and to the scarcity of other money-earning opportunities.

Some consequences of the new regime were visible in the island's settlement patterns. Under the Spanish, church and state had alienated about 500 of the island's 2,090 square miles, and the American administration purchased another 20. On the other hand the administration made it easier for Guamanians to lease government-owned land and encouraged them to resettle in rural areas; as a result, a smaller percentage of the population resided full time in the capital town of Agana. In addition, the administration supervised all land transfers and made it next to impossible for nonnatives to secure land.

During Spanish times a few wealthy Guamanian families had been continually engaged in extending their land holdings: in six cases families owned estates of twenty-five hundred acres and more. During the American era this process was slowed; copra depression, the outlaw of peonage, and increasing emphasis upon money made land by itself an uneconomic investment. At the other end of the scale, the new economy serve to create a class of landless wage earners.

To list a few other changes that accompanied the American take-over: public (secular) schools began to supersede Church institutions as centers of community activities; athletics began to compete with cockfighting for the interest of men; and although older women continued to dress in their Spanish-Filipino style clothing, young women turned to American styles in dress and in coiffures. The mother continued to exercise her traditional authority over her family's religious life, but the previous trend away from matriliny was quickened and was sanctioned by the navy's rule that children take only the surname of their father. American rule also favored individual property rights: the property of parents dying intestate was by law divided equally among all legal heirs. In spite of this regulation, however, family members continued to pool their resources and work as a unit in subsistence matters.

In social relations between the sexes the previous Church-enforced segregation of young unmarried women (tantamount to virgin cultism) began to break down as a result of coeducational schooling and increasing contact with Americans. Marriages still involved interfamily contracts, and divorces were rare, but parental arrangements began to give way to love matches.

The Church continued to maintain an influence over the lives and beliefs of Guamanians, but religious teaching was proscribed in the new and compulsory public schools. In addition, other kinds of contacts with Americans and their irreligious institutions served further to weaken the authority of the Church. The remaining, and generally ultraconservative, Spanish padres did not adapt well to such changes, but it appeared that the more recently installed American priests would speed them up.

It was in the economic field that the naval government's policies contained some basic inconsistencies: on the one hand an emphasis upon development of money economy; on the other a paternalistic protectionism. A prosperous copra industry might have resolved such inconsistencies, but with hurricanes, pests, and poor markets, copra exports were never high or very profitable. Official encouragement was given to the development of other income-earning industries, but, with its high-cost labor and its geographic isolation, Guam could not compete successfully in world markets without subsidy, particularly in view of the excise-tax penalty levied against its copra in the mainland United States. Even without the navy's restrictive regulations against outside industry and commerce, planned as protection for Guamanians, there was little about Guam to attract American or foreign capital to the island. Hence almost the only way most Guamanians could earn money was to work for the naval establishment or its numerous parasitic enterprises, and that did not provide sufficient wage-earning jobs for the many Guamanians who needed money to satisfy their newly acquired wants. Under the circumstances it was inevitable that the older family subsistence and barter economy would continue to prevail, especially in rural areas. Recognizing this situation, the administration sponsored a back-to-the-farm movement and tried to improve agriculture with introduction of new crops and methods.

In political as in economic matters navy rule was benevolently paternalistic and absolute. Whereas in the Spanish era influential Chamorro held high elective and appointive posts, under American rule all high officials were navy officers, and even the municipal authorities were elected or appointed at the discretion of the naval governor of the moment. Democratic reforms might be instituted under one governor and then revoked by his successor; their tours of duty lasted only two years and their discretionary powers were wide. A Guam Congress, consisting of both elective and appointive officials, was established in 1917, but its function was mainly advisory.

In yet another important respect the Chamorro had enjoyed more political rights under Spanish rule: they had been true Spanish subjects and possessed equality with other Spanish subjects before the law. Under American rule they were citizens of Guam, and *nationals* but not *citizens* of the United States; under these circumstances they did not have access to the Federal judiciary system beyond Guam. Consequently, citizenship was one of the major reforms desired by an increasingly articulate faction of the better-educated Guamanians.

Under Spanish rule Guam's upper class consisted of a handful of wealthy, landowning families, who lived Spanish-Catholic lives and mixed socially with the Spanish officials. Navy officials, however, raised some social barriers against all Guamanians, even against those who had emerged as a new upper class of energetic capitalists.

Guam's value to the United States was entirely strategic, a communications point on the way to the Philippines and East Asia. From this point of view it would probably have been easier for the navy had there been *no* Guamanians. But in defense of navy rule it should be added that the number of Guamanians increased from nine thousand to twenty-two thousand during its four decades there, and much of that increase was doubtless due to the medical and public health measures instituted by the navy. (From the vantage point of hindsight, such an increase can be seen to have been an ominous development—a step in the direction of dangerous overpopulation, but when compared with the near-fatal depopulation that had taken place under Spanish rule, it cannot be condemned.) On the other hand, no effective solutions were provided by the naval administration for the inconsistencies between a paternalistic autocratic regime and an awakening appreciation of "democratic" institutions; between a subsistence, barter economy and a desire for things only money could buy. What movies portrayed and schoolbooks promised, limitations of the economy and the form of government denied. That such dilemmas and frustrations produced so few crimes and neuroses must probably be traced to the moderating influence of two centuries of Spanish-Catholic life.

Japanese Mandated Islands

While Spanish soldiers and priests were transforming Tinian, Saipan, and Rota into pious wildernesses, the Caroline and Marshall islands were left to their native ways. The world-dividing Treaty of Tordesillas awarded the Carolines to Spain, but the Spanish made little effort to colonize or Christianize these islands until late in the nineteenth century, after other powers began to display some interest in them. But even Spain did not covet the Marshall islands, and these scattered atolls remained unclaimed until German traders induced their government to establish a protectorate over them in 1885. Before that time all the islands from Palau to Majuro were vulnerable to unofficial agents of the West.

It was an ideal situation for the whalers: no irksome government officials to restrain their exuberance ashore and no missionaries to spoil their fun. The Marshalls received their quota of disease and other disasters, but Kusaie and Ponape were the whalers' first choice. Kusaie, especially, became such a resort for scoundrels that missionaries judged it to be the place *most* in need of salvation. The natives of Truk solved the whaler problem by killing a few of them and thereby escaped being overrun. For a while the Ponapeans also made some difficulties for the whalers but later on proved tractable to everything but kidnapping and seducing the wives and daughters of the *highest* chiefs. Mercifully, this particular kind of scourge ended in the 1860s, when whaling grounds moved far to the northwest.

More enduring and persistent were the traders. In the Marshalls they supplied the weapons that made it possible for some ambitious chiefs to extend their domains by conquest of neighboring atolls. And in the western Carolines traders set up their own domains, until the natives could suffer them no longer and either killed them or destroyed their stores.

The first significant proprietary move by Westerners in the Marshalls was made by the Jaluit Company, a German trading firm with semiofficial connections. The agents of this company succeeded in concluding a trade "treaty" with a powerful chief, which (following the familiar pattern) led a few years later to establishment of a protectorate over the whole archipelago.

Germany's interests in the Marshalls were almost entirely commercial; the protectorate was administered only as a source of copra and pearl shell and guano fertilizer. In fact, for many years after establishment of the protectorate, its administration was in the hands of the Jaluit Company; in return the company was granted several concessions, including a virtual trade monopoly.

During those years Marshallese native affairs were not forcibly disturbed, except to the extent that they interfered with orderly production and trade. The Germans preferred to work through the chiefs and restricted the latters' authority only by prohibiting their feuding and abolishing their right to inflict the death penalty.

Much more far-reaching changes in Marshallese institutions were brought about by agents of the Boston Mission, who with the help of native teachers reached out to nearly every inhabited islet and within a few years succeeded in converting nearly half of the entire population to Protestantism. Jesuits also entered these islands, around the turn of the century, and quickened the race for converts.

The Boston missionaries moved also into the eastern Carolines, beginning in 1852, and met with spectacular success. They were well along toward their goal of transforming these islands into Christian native "states" (under supervision, of course, of the United States) when Spain tardily became aware of her neglected island empire and established a garrison on Ponape, accompanied by the usual Catholic priests. At first the latter made little progress against the well-entrenched Protestants, but the situation changed when some Ponapeans banded together and massacred several of the soldiers. The Spanish punitive expedition that resulted might have depopulated the assassins' districts had not the padres interceded for them. At this display of charity two whole districts went over en masse to Catholicism, leaving the other three to Protestantism. To the American missionaries this defection was even more bitter than the frustration of their political plans, and there was probably some basis for the Spanish charge that the continued hostility toward them from the Protestant districts was due to missionary agitation. Anyway, the American missionary allegedly involved in the agitation was expelled from the island and readmitted only after the customary "vigorous diplomatic representations."

One factor that earlier had led Spain to establish the mark of her sovereignty over the Carolines was the presence of German and British traders there; a crucial point had been reached in 1885 when Spanish and German warships simultaneously raised their flags on one or two islands. The dispute was referred to Pope Leo XIII, who confirmed Spain in her sovereignty but granted free commercial access to the islands to Germany and Britain.

The eastern Carolines continued to prove troublesome to the Spanish throughout their regime, including a series of savage native attacks and bloody Spanish reprisals. Meanwhile, in the central and western Carolines the transition from the neolithic proceeded more peacefully.

Although Palau and Yap were, tacitly, also under her sovereignty, Spain did nothing to tame these islands after the failure of a Catholic mission there in the early eighteenth century. Neither whalers nor Protestant missionaries penetrated that far west, so the only early Western contacts of their native inhabitants were with traders, mainly agents of the British East India Company. One or two of the latter made quixotic attempts to establish British domains, but their efforts led to nothing permanent. The British government displayed only enough interest in the area to dispatch warships to it on punitive expeditions.

After her sovereignty was confirmed in 1886, Spain made a few halfhearted attempts to maintain order, meaning to protect the lives and property of nonnative traders, but most of the latter were British or Japanese, along with a few Germans. The priests, of course, accompanied the Spanish soldiers on most of those order-keeping missions, but few souls are recorded as having been saved.

When the Philippines and Guam were wrested from Spain by the United States in 1898, Germany promptly purchased Spain's other possessions in the region, the Carolines and the rest of the Marianas, added them to her protectorate over the Marshall islands and Nauru, and proceeded to govern all of them in association with her colonies to the south (i.e., northeastern New Guinea, the Admiralties, the Bismarck archipelago, and the northern Solomons). Administration outposts were established on Palau, Yap, Saipan, Truk, Ponape, and Jaluit, and affairs were conducted with small staffs and with seeming efficiency. Although Germany's interest in owning these far-flung islands was doubtless fostered by national sentiments of imperial pride, her method of governing them was mainly commercial—by developing them as sources of raw materials and as markets for German goods. Mission activity was not hampered, but received little positive encouragement; and when all official compulsion was removed from church attendance, many natives "reverted." Native institutions were left alone, except those that obstructed commerce. Copra was the main commercial product, and the supply of it was increased by regulations requiring natives to plant new groves. Pearl shell was also an important trade item, as were native handicrafts and guano. In 1909 a syndicate began the mining of phosphate on Angaur, which possessed reserves of an estimated 2,500,000 tons of some of the highest-grade phosphate in the world.

The Germans administered their islands with research-based insight into native institutions and with tolerant respect for those that did not interfere with all-important commerce. They encountered some native hostility on Ponape but elsewhere matters went smoothly for them.

The instruments of Germany's economic policy were a few large production and mercantile firms, many of which eventually merged with the Jaluit Company. With government support these firms nearly succeeded in freezing out foreign competition from the Marshalls and eastern Carolines, but made little headway in the Marianas and the western Carolines against the strongly entrenched Japanese traders.

The Marshalls, the Carolines, and the Marianas (except Guam) were "entrusted" to Japan by the Peace Conference following World War I in the form of a Class C Mandate, but to most Japanese these islands were deliberately captured prizes of war. If the gentlemen in Geneva wished to make the matter more palatable to themselves, that was acceptable so long as it did not interfere with Japan's firm intention of integrating those islands into her own empire. The written terms of the mandate were kept idealistic, for reasons of international comity and particularly to conciliate President Woodrow Wilson, but Japan's actual objectives were something else. Although not explicitly stated, the islands were viewed by Japan as places in which to resettle some of her surplus population, to produce things needed in Japan, to serve as springboards for further southward expansion, and to interrupt what was perceived to be America's naval threat to that expansion (and possibly to Japan herself). Judging by events, one can only conclude that Japan's overall native policy was to "Japanize" all who could be so transformed and to allow the rest to die out and so make room for more immigrants: no ruthless policy of extermination, but rather a long-range policy of assimilation devoid of any sentimental regard for weaker native peoples (not, however, "assimilation" to a status of equality with the Japanese themselves). In fact, the new wards were considered to occupy a third-class position among the emperor's subjects, lower even than, for example, the Koreans (who at least shared with the Japanese the heritage of East Asian civilization).

After an initial period of naval rule, the government placed the administration of the islands in the hands of civilian officials of the South Seas Government, responsible at first to the prime minister's office and later to the Ministry of Overseas (colonial, not foreign) Affairs. Headquarters was established on Palau, with branch stations on Saipan, Yap, Truk,

Ponape, and Jaluit. A very large bureaucracy was installed, with authority and procedures to cover every phase of life. Officials were civil-service career men, interrelated in a finely graded rank system. Some pretense at native "self-rule" was expressed by the appointment of village "chiefs" and so on, but as more and more colonists poured in and officialdom expanded, the native "chiefs" were bypassed and native affairs were assimilated into the life of the colonial communities.

The terms of the mandate provided for freedom of missionary enterprise, and the administration did not at first interfere except to replace German Protestant missionaries with Japanese. Also, a few American missionaries were permitted for a while to continue their work in the Marshalls and the eastern Carolines. Meanwhile, the religion of the Japanese state began to be promulgated through compulsory schooling, which included inculcation of the state ethical and moral codes and participation in Shinto rituals. Also, for many older islanders the glorification of Japan (a component of the state religion) was promoted through organized tours of Japan.

Economic development went swiftly forward, and before long all foreign interests, including the tenacious Australian firm of Burns Philp, were frozen out of the islands. The entire region was completely integrated into Japan's economy. Saipan and Tinian and subsequently Rota were converted into vast sugarcane plantations. Palau, Truk, and Ponape became centers for large fishing industries. Phosphate mining was accelerated on Angaur and later extended to other islands in the western Carolines and in the Marianas. Bauxite was mined on Palau and manganese on Rota. Trade stores were established throughout, and shipping extended to nearly every populated place. But none of this was done by or for native islanders; the enterprises were owned and managed by Japanese firms, some of them partly owned by the government. Even the labor consisted of immigrant Japanese, Koreans, and Okinawans, except in the mining industries, which employed some Chamorro in semiskilled jobs and many hundreds of Caroline islanders for manual labor.

The only commercial enterprise left mainly to natives was copra production, which continued prosperously throughout the Marshalls and the Carolines and provided the native producers with their income for buying the foreign (i.e., Japanese) goods they had become dependent upon. Indeed, official encouragement was given to copra production in the form of subsidies for new plantings and the construction of drying sheds.

The main source of change in native life was the mass immigration of Japanese and Koreans and of Okinawans (the most numerous). It is debatable whether the industries were promoted to support colonization or colonists imported to service the industries; in any event tens of thousands of them immigrated to the islands and engaged mainly in sugar production, fishing, and mining. As elsewhere in the Pacific Islands, the natives were deemed to be unsuited to the kind of work involved in sugarcane growing or milling, so the employees of that industry were totally nonnative. In connection with fishing, similar reasons could hardly be put forward to explain why natives were excluded, but it so happened that most of the fishing vessels were manned by nonnatives. At each of the main centers there sprang up a rash of small artisan shops, stores, and service establishments. The towns of Garapan (Saipan), Koror (Palau), and Colony (Ponape) were particularly thriving and contained most of the amenities of Japanese small-town life: cinemas, restaurants, beauty parlors, even geisha houses. All such enterprises were owned and run by nonnatives, but natives did have access to them, thereby acquiring new wants and tastes. In other words, despite their third-class status in the Japanese colonial system, the natives were not excluded from participating in the flourishing, and doubtless for them exciting, new life, except to the extent that their small money incomes excluded them.

By 1940 there were some seventy thousand nonnatives dwelling in the territory as compared with fifty thousand natives, and those numbers were diverging steadily and rapidly through immigration of more nonnatives and through an absolute decline in the numbers of natives. By that time, also, large tracts of land had been acquired from native owners and set aside as public domain or leased to industries and individual colonists. So, whether purposefully directed or not, on the basis of statistics alone the trend was toward the disinheritance and extinction of the natives. On the other hand, the Japanese from time to time went to some pains to improve native health and education (even if the latter meant Japanese education). And whether as a direct result of government policy or as an incidental by-product of colonization and commercialism, natives dwelling near the main centers did have direct contact with (though not necessarily full participation in) a more "civilized" way of life. Even those living on the remote out-islands were able to make use of the territory's network of boat services.

But not all of the above generalities applied equally to the 130 inhabited islands and atolls of the territory. In the Japanese Marianas, for example, events took a very special turn.

In 1902 there were only eleven hundred Chamorro living in the Marianas outside Guam, and they were concentrated on Saipan, Tinian, and Rota—many of them only recently returned from "exile" on Guam. In addition, there were some 850 Carolinians dwelling on Saipan and Tinian, having been taken there as laborers or having gone there as result of catastrophes on their home islands.

During the German era their Mariana islands were the least productive part of their protectorate. Despite official encouragement only a few hundred tons of copra were produced there each year, with the immigrant Carolinians doing much of the work; the Chamorro themselves were landowners and less amenable to working for others. One result of German influence, however, was the diversification of native subsistence foods and an increased emphasis upon individual property ownership.

Saipan had been the German seat of administration for the whole group, but it lapsed into such commercial lassitude that after a few years its official agent moved to Yap and thereafter visited the Marianas only occasionally. Saipan and the small islands north of it were devoted mainly to coconuts, and Tinian was used to pasture cattle. In fact, the Marianas proved to be a financial burden to the Germans; nevertheless (or perhaps because of that and their consequent official neglect?) the natives living there increased in number under the German regime. In most respects the native institutions were not interfered with; the Hispanized Chamorro and the less westernized Carolinians went their separate ways, and paternalistic German land laws protected both peoples from disinheritance.

Even during the German era most of the commerce of the Marianas was in the hands of Japanese traders, and overseas trade was almost entirely with Japan.

Under Japanese rule the Marianas were transformed from being the greatest liability to the richest asset of all Japanese Micronesia. A strongly financed company moved in and converted Saipan and Tinian into sugar plantations with the help of subsidies and liberal concessions from the government. Mills were built for crushing sugar and manufacturing alcohol; ultimately thirty thousand acres were placed under cultivation on these two islands and Rota, with an annual production of eighty thousand tons of raw sugar and over 700,000 gallons of alcohol. As mentioned previously, thousands of Japanese and Koreans and Okinawans were brought in as laborers. In the beginning the government lent state-owned land rent-free to the company, which in turn leased plots to tenant householders for cultivation. All such cultivations were subject to company controls in the use of land and planning of crops, and all production was sold to the company at fixed prices. In addition many plots were under direct company management. And about the only role played by natives in this vast enterprise was to lease their lands to the company or to individual colonists.

The Japanese also organized the growing of manioc and coffee, but as with sugar all such activities were in the hands of nonnatives. In fact, the only industry remaining in native hands was copra, which constituted about ½ percent (by value) of agricultural production in the Marianas and only 4 percent of all copra produced in the territory as a whole.

The process of native disinheritance went further in the Marianas than elsewhere in the territory. There is little evidence of calculated mistreatment, but the situation that developed there was just one more example of a slower-paced, native people losing out to better-equipped, more insatiable foreigners.

The Palau islands also became a center of Japanese activity, but of different kinds. To begin with, the Japanese took over the German phosphate mines on Angaur and expanded them into a very large enterprise. In addition, smaller phosphate mines were opened on some neighboring islands, and exports from all of them eventually reached about 200,000 tons a year. The mining was partly government owned; its management and technical staff was Japanese but numbers of Chamorro worked as supervisors and in semiskilled jobs, and hundreds of Carolinians were recruited for unskilled jobs (under circumstances that smacked of forced labor). The Carolinian natives of Angaur itself also worked in the mines, but the wages they received were poor compensation for loss of their best garden lands, which had to be skimmed off to expose the phosphate rock underneath. The phosphate from Angaur and other sites in the territory went to Japan, as did the profits; to pay mining royalties to the native landowners evidently seems not to have entered the heads of any of the government's trustees of native welfare.

During the thirties the Japanese also started bauxite mining on Palau and employed local natives as laborers. But fishing, by far the most extensive industry in the western Carolines, was almost entirely in Japanese hands.

Although the fishing industry was centered at Koror (Palau), fleets roved as far as the Dutch East Indies, and there were smaller shore stations at Saipan, Truk, Ponape, and in the Marshalls. Altogether some 360 vessels engaged in the territory's commercial fishing, with an annual catch of from fifteen thousand to thirty-eight thousand tons of bonito, plus large quantities of tuna, trepang, and trochus. Natives engaged in some collecting of trepang and pearl shell, but the deep-sea fishing was carried out by Japanese, an ironic reversal for natives once known for long oversea voyages and still capable of skillful boat handling and navigation.

Koror, as administrative center of the whole territory, became a thriving Japanese town to which natives enjoyed access (according to their financial means). In the islands near Koror the administration appears to have made some effort to help natives to adjust to the new kind of life. Government-sponsored cooperatives were formed to assist them in production and marketing and purchasing, and many of them were in fact beginning to make fairly satisfactory adjustments to the money economy. But in the southwestern Caroline islands of Tobi, Pulo Anna, and Sonsorol, only a few of their inhabitants had managed to survive the preceding decades of foreign contacts.

The island of Yap has had a peculiar history in several respects. Even though it was continuously under the influence of traders and priests and officials for scores of years, the Yap islanders clung tenaciously to their old culture—more tenaciously, in fact, than to their lives, because Yap's population continued to decline at a steady rate.

Yap itself was for a time the center of diplomatic conflict, but aside from its role as a cable station on the line from Guam to the Far East, it remained underdeveloped commercially. Copra, the main industry, remained in native hands.

There was a colony of Chamorro settlers on Yap, and they, like their ethnic cousins on Saipan, became rapidly assimilated into the local Japanese community (though marginally so), but the Yap natives themselves remained remarkably conservative and apart. Their subsistence economy survived almost intact, and the traditional system of social classes and castes underwent few major changes. Perhaps one obstacle to change was the Yap custom of patrilineal land inheritance. Throughout most of the territory property inheritance had remained matrilineal, and the Japanese masters, in trying to encourage a transition to patriliny, did violence to many other functionally related native institutions. Hence Yap, with its traditional patriliny, provided fewer loopholes for change. In fact, the foreign influence that had most impact upon Yap during the Japanese era came about through the indenturing of her young men to work in the phosphate mines of distant islands.

Truk, with its vast lagoon, had long excited the imagination of voyagers and naval strategists, but under Spanish, German, and Japanese rule it lagged far behind most other islands in the region in commercial development. During the Japanese era, until Truk became strategically important as a naval base, its only importance derived from its fishing industry, which was smaller than Palau's, and from its copra production, which remained in native hands.

Ponape, with its relatively large land mass and extensive, fertile lands, was much better adapted to commercial enterprise than Truk. In addition to basing fishing fleets there, the Japanese attempted to make Ponape the prime agricultural center of the territory. Its agricultural experiment station personnel worked energetically on the development and adaptation of economic plants to island conditions; fibers, pineapples, starches, medicinals, and rice were all tried, but the main cash crop remained copra, with natives and Japanese colonists both producing it.

Subsistence continued to be the basis of Ponapeans' economic life, but more and more of them began to participate in the money economy. This was helped along by changes in land tenure, which were fostered by both German and Japanese regimes. In the process, many of the lands held corporately, by clans, were reassigned to individuals, and native chiefs lost much of their former authority over the goods and labor of their subjects. Beyond that, however, and despite the growth of a large Japanese colony on Ponape, most of the island's natives continued with their traditional forms of prestige-garnering feast exchanges. On the other hand, housing and clothing became increasingly "civilized."

Nearby Kusaie was less affected economically by Japanese enterprises; the major transformation to money economy and several other Western institutions had taken place earlier, under influence of the Protestant missionaries, who had focused their efforts upon this island. One effect of that influence, which was reinforced by Spanish, German, and Japanese regimes, was to undermine almost totally the authority of the Kusaiean chiefs, once among the most absolute in the Pacific. (It is a noteworthy fact that "democratic" Protestantism has enjoyed its most spectacular successes in those island societies that had the most autocratic native governments.)

The paucity of natural land resources in the Marshalls insulated these islands somewhat from some of the foreign influences that destroyed other native cultures located on more fertile islands. The Germans were content to set up trade stores and plant coconuts on a few atolls and left most production of the main crop, copra, to the Marshallese. The Japanese followed suit, and almost the only nonnatives residing there in Japanese times were a few officials, fishermen, and agents of a Japanese mercantile firm.

In former days missionaries had been very active and successful in the Marshalls, and that had been perhaps the most important single factor in bringing about changes in the externals of Marshallese life. Otherwise, the most far-reaching changes took place in the institution of leadership. In times before Western contact the chiefs had authority over all lands and their products, and the Germans actually reinforced that authority in one important way: they levied taxes in the form of copra, depending upon the chiefs to collect the levy and permitting them to retain some of it for themselves. Under the Japanese, however, the authority of the chiefs was greatly reduced: all copra was sold direct to the trader, with only a very small part of the proceeds set aside for the chiefs.

Traders and whalers and missionaries, Spanish and German and Japanese: most of those intruders left their marks on places such as Saipan, Palau, Ponape, and Jaluit. In all these places native life was transformed, sometimes beyond recognition. Yet, a few tens of miles away from the foreign centers were islands in the center of the territory where natives continued to live much as they had done centuries before, except for iron tools and the uneasy knowledge of the presence of a more powerful people and culture not far away. All those out-islands, including Ulithi and Woleai and Nukuoro, made a little copra, collected some pearl shell, and fashioned a few handicrafts to exchange for goods brought by occasional trading schooners, but since there was no immediate Japanese need for their lands or persons they were left for the next batch of foreign masters to transform.

Now to explain my reason for treating the Japanese period of the colonial history of the Mariana-Caroline-Marshall islands under the rubric of
"bases." Unlike the United States, which acquired Eastern Samoa and
Guam solely and *overtly* to serve as bases for ships en route to or from
other strategic possessions (the Panama Canal, the Philippines), Japan's
purposes in seizing and holding Germany's Micronesian islands were
many and relatively complex. The most general of those purposes is
summed up under the term *nanshin,* the concept of a "southward [and
hence maritime] advance," which was counterpart to, and sometimes
counteractive to, *hokushin,* or "northward advance" (onto the Asian
continent). (The United States' concept of Manifest Destiny, with its
westward impulse contained some of the same kinds of emotions and
ideas.) Throughout her history, most of Japan's expansive energies were
directed onto the continent, sometimes peacefully, sometimes aggressively, but the maritime impulse was intermittently also strong, leading
Japanese traders, colonists, and freebooters as far away as Siam. That
impulse revived again in the mid-nineteenth century, when the seclusion
policies of the Tokugawas gave way to the openness and expansiveness of
the Meiji regime. Moreover, this resurgence of interest in *Nan'yō* (the
South Seas) was quickened by realization that the Western colonial powers were leaving very little South Seas real estate to move into.

In the early stages of that resurgence there was nothing like a unified
nationwide view or governmental policy toward the South Seas. For
some persons (writers, adventurers, and armchair romantics) it had
appeals similar to those expressed in the lives of the Melvilles, the R. L.
Stevensons, and the Jack Londons of the West. For others it presented
imagined opportunities for earning fortunes: as planters, traders, and so
forth. Many others, including but not limited to naval officials, were
concerned to acquire bases for screening Japan defensively against potential aggression, especially from the United States, whose growing presence in Hawaii was seen to be especially threatening. And there were
other, generally patriotic but not specifically focused, persons whose
wish was only to see Japan represented in the South Seas in equality with
other powers.

With reference to the matter of *bases,* recent research has established
that the Japanese Navy did draw up contingency plans regarding the
potentialities of the territory for naval-military purposes (as of course the
United States Navy did as well), but the Japanese Navy did not com-
mence to militarize them until late in the 1930s and then more for offensive than for defensive purposes. Sometime before that, however, the Japanese government had closed off their Pacific Islands so effectively from
foreign scrutiny that other governments concluded, quite logically, that
they were up to no good.

SOURCES

American Samoa: Gray 1960; F. Keesing 1934; Mead 1930; West 1961. (See also chapter 10.)

Guam: Souder 1971; Thompson 1947; Valle 1979. (See also chapter 7.)

Japanese Mandated Islands: Hezel 1983; McGrath and Wilson 1971; Peattie 1988; Purcell 1976; Spoehr 1949; Valle 1987. (See also chapter 7.)

CHAPTER FIFTEEN
Losses and Gains

A.D. 1939 signaled the end of an era in the Pacific Islands (see Map 6). By that time every exposed volcanic crust and coral outcrop had been seized by foreign powers, and every Islander had been touched by at least the outer ripples of Western or Asian civilizations: even central New Guinea had seen airplanes overhead. But how to assess the changes that had taken place since Magellan? Obviously, simple comparisons were out of the question, for what yardsticks could be used to compare Honolulu and Auckland with the isolated one-trader atoll or the jungle patrol outpost? The foreign Westerners and Asians had worked through many kinds of agencies and for varying lengths of time, and the island settings of their exploitations were far from uniform. Nevertheless, in 1939 it was possible to draw up a rough trial balance to cover the four centuries of foreign contact and enterprise in the Pacific Islands.

To begin with, it required no great perspicacity to see that foreigners as a whole had usually profited at the expense of the Islanders; but that in itself does not of course condemn all colonial enterprises. Even the most sentimental nativist would have had to agree that New Zealand provided net gains not only for their own fortunate Western settlers, but for the world at large. The great losses sustained by a few hundred thousand Maori could not entirely cancel out the many gains brought about by the transformation of their lands into good homes for millions of foreigners. The pity was that the change had not been accomplished with more

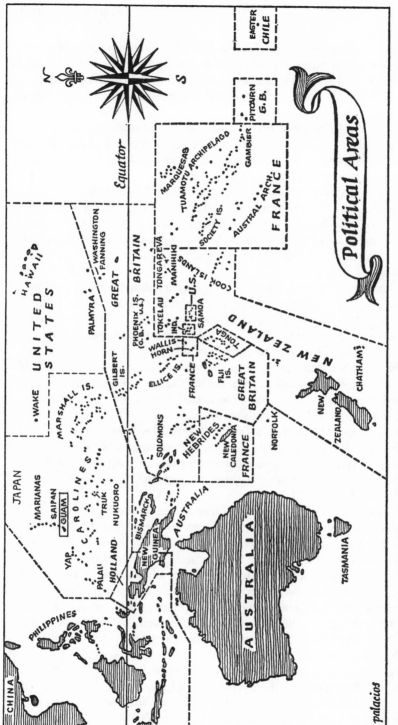

Map 6. Political divisions in the Pacific Islands in 1939 (drawn by Rafael Palacios)

humanity and enlightened administration, for there was actually room enough for Westerners *and* natives. But, leaving aside these special cases, what gains had accrued to the newcomers in the other Pacific Islands?

In 1939 there were some 140,000 Westerners and 540,000 Asians dwelling in the Islands (outside of New Zealand). For a few of those non-indigenes the Islands had brought wealth; for most of them the Islands had provided satisfactory livelihoods, better than they had had in their native lands. Except in Japanese Micronesia, Westerners occupied the highest caste positions and usually gained most economically; but Asians were beginning to narrow the gap by industry and sheer mass.

The greater profits from Island enterprises went not to the settlers but to owners, shareholders, and directors in Australia, New Zealand, Britain, France, Japan, and the United States; and most of the Western "settlers" held to their objective of eventually returning "home" with their earnings.

For mankind at large, the Islands (again excluding New Zealand) provided only limited economic gains; of all Island products only phosphates and, to a less degree, sugar made any significant contribution to the world economy. Copra, nickel, chromium, gold, iron, pearl shell, and fruits, however profitable to their individual producers, were not produced cheaply enough or in large enough quantities to influence world markets one way or another. Even the international powers directly concerned regarded the economic products of their Island dependencies as supplementary rather than indispensable.

Nor, except for Saipan and Tinian, did the Islands have much value as outlets for surplus population. In fact, the principal profit derived from owning islands was strategic; and as events were shaping up in the Pacific in 1939, stock in good naval harbors and airplane runways looked definitely bullish.

But turning now to the Islanders themselves, who did not own shares in Island companies or compete in international rivalries: What had they gained or lost from all this foreign enterprise? Before proceeding, it will be useful to recall that during the centuries before Magella all of the inhabited Pacific Islands had belonged to the Islanders themselves, most of whom went about their various businesses, neither accumulating great riches nor suffering stern deprivations, increasing their numbers and satisfactorily living out their lives according to their own lights. It is true that from them there came nothing to enrich the rest of the world, but neither came there any harm.

Up to 1939 the Islanders' colonial experiences had varied widely from place to place: those of the hybridized and Hispanized Chamorro differed greatly from those of the full-blooded and stubbornly Samoanized Samoans; and those of the naked and "uncontrolled" New Guinean were a far cry from those of the Hawaiian cowboy. Nevertheless, a few similar changes had occurred nearly everywhere.

The Islanders' greatest losses were in their numbers; the population decreased from an estimated 2,500,000 to 3,000,000 in 1522 to 2,000,000 in 1939. Higher death rates accounted for much of this decline: one-sided wars against Westerners, intertribal feuding made more sanguine by foreigners' weapons, and catastrophic new diseases. Lower birth rates were also a factor: disease-induced sterility and infecundity, enforced labor away from home, late marriages, and possibly family instability.

Land and resources were also lost. Even excepting New Zealand, Islanders lost millions of acres of their best lands, along with guano, phosphates, minerals, and other irreplaceables; at the same time, their forests were stripped of sandalwood and most of their reefs of pearl shell. One can, of course, argue that the lost lands were surplus to their simple requirements and the raw materials of no use in their primitive economies, but that rationalization will have no force so long as title to property is not based on usufruct alone. These things were part of their heritage; preserved in trust, such treasures would have provided them with some basis of economic security in the competitive world in which they found themselves in 1939.

Many Islanders also lost their fine skills: their abilities to turn out pleasing arts and useful crafts, their expert seamanship, their capacities for colorful pageantry. But of course it could be argued that there was no use for these skills any more, except perhaps to entertain tourists or to ornament museums.

Turning now to the other side. What had Islanders gained to compensate them for these losses in natural resources and skills?

For one thing, except in the heart of New Guinea, even the poorest household had acquired a steel knife and an ax or adz to lighten the burden of work, which formerly proceeded at a slower, Stone Age pace. Other acquisitions were less useful. Clothes, sewing machines, and other paraphernalia of the mission modesty cult were not required by Island climates, and, if anything, were conducive to sickness. Peroxide, lampblack, rouge, powder, pomade, and perfume satisfied the desire to be fashionable, but were not much improvement over indigenous lime, ashes, ocher, coconut oil, and hibiscus. And among the "gains" one must not forget to mention the rum and twist tobacco, the cans of beef and fish, the hurricane lamp (often without kerosene), the flashlight (often with dead batteries), the Gramophone (often with one record), the heat-radiating galvanized roof under a blistering sun.

Then, too, there were new skills to replace the old lost ones: motor driving (but in their masters' trucks and launches); copra cutting, pearl shell diving, cattle herding; work for the sake of wages to pay taxes, decorate missions, and buy knickknacks. And, of course, there was cricket or baseball or soccer—tame though healthful substitutes for savage pastimes. But most prideful of all acquisitions were reading and writing and calculating, Western or Japanese style: splendid new skills, even though they were hardly relevant to the lives of peasant subsistence and caste subordination that most of them were living in 1939.

Institutional losses and gains were less apparent and harder to measure; notwithstanding this, the changes that took place in human relations were far more significant than any mere substituting of calico for bark cloth.

From the point of view of mission reformers, gains were scored in the apparently improved status of women, in the "legalizing" of matrimony, the "outlawing" of polygamy and adultery, the establishing of virginity cultism; in other words, in a general Westernizing of sexual and family relations. Granting for the sake of argument that those changes *might* constitute gains and that they *may* have generally taken place, it could also be shown that men away from home, working in plantations and mines and ships, could not beget offspring or train children or do their share of family work, no matter how Westernized their morals. And families inevitably lost cohesion when the traditional divisions of labor were disturbed or when mission-trained and commerce-hardened youths challenged their elders' authority.

Yet, with all these modifications, the family as an institution suffered far fewer changes than did the larger social groupings. The outlawing of warfare took away much of the cohesion of native political groupings, and rule by foreign officials frequently resulted in usurpation of political authority by native opportunists who counted for little among their fellows but who were wise in the ways of the new masters. Ties of lineage and clanship were weakened by the trend from communalism toward individualism and lost much of their rationale when the myths that chartered them were forgotten and when the supernatural sanctions that regulated them were ridiculed.

All these changes and their attendant losses in group morale did not necessarily lead directly to mass hypochondria and a general will to die, as some anthropological Cassandras used to assert, but the weakening of traditional ties did create bewildering and unsettling conditions until new equilibriums were established.

In addition to these specific kinds of losses and gains, there were the more comprehensive ones. Islanders in general gained some security of person with the outlawing of feuding. And, although the immediate advantages could not be ascertained, they were given every opportunity to acquire one or another kind of Christian "eternal life." Also, they were brought out of their isolation into contact with larger polities; in the process, however, they were invariably placed in subordinate caste roles, and the more they became assimilated into the new economies, the more vulnerable they were to circumstances totally beyond their control.

But however serious the losses suffered by full-blooded Islanders under foreign rule, their lot was easier than that of the mixed bloods. Most of these latter lived in a caste limbo. Their Western or Asian fathers would not recognize them and colonial society would not accept them; many could and did "revert" to native status, but that too produced its dilemmas.

If the dateline of this audit were 1899, it would have to end on this recital of obvious debits and counterfeit credits, but by 1939 there were beginning to appear some genuine credits as well.

Efforts were being made in some colonies to improve Islanders' health, to provide for their welfare, to protect their remaining lands from further alienation and their labor from abuses. Some administrations were even making moves to return to the Islanders some control over their own affairs. Most hopeful of all, however, was the fact that, save in a few cases, Island populations were arresting and even reversing their numerical declines. With protection against the more vicious forms of exploitation and with time for peaceful and gradual assimilation of some things foreign, it looked as if the Islanders in some colonies might regain some of their indigenous well-being even in Westernized or Japanized societies. But that, as everyone knows, was not to be.

CATACLYSM

CHAPTER SIXTEEN

World War II

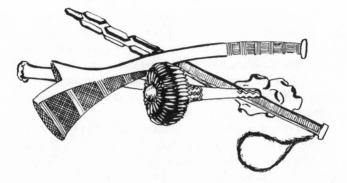

For the Westerners and Asians dwelling or campaigning in the South Pacific, World War II was momentous enough; but for many Islanders, who had nothing to do with its inception and little with its outcome, the war catastrophically disturbed their lives and radically changed their ideas about the world and their places in it.

Signs of war were evident in the Islands long before Pearl Harbor. Abrogation of the Washington Naval Treaty in 1934 marked the end of collective security in the Pacific and turned the Western powers to fortifying their island outposts. The general uneasiness was further excited by the Sino-Japanese War and by Japan's repeated references to *her* South Seas; and Nazi Germany kept the rumors flying by demanding return of her former colonies. Meanwhile the race for island air bases, the search for oil in New Guinea, and Japan's purposeful economic expansion throughout the South Pacific gave the coconut strategists plenty to discuss over their beer.

The three main regions of the Pacific—American Hawaii, Japanese Micronesia, and the Franco-British South Pacific—responded differently to the outbreak of World War II. In Hawaii and Guam there were few visible reactions other than an increasing tempo in military preparations. In Japanese Micronesia we can only speculate about how the news was generally received. In the South Pacific, however, September 3, 1939, was greeted by Western colonials with something akin to enthusiasm. A surge of empire loyalty swept through the colonies, and there was an almost festive air about the various benefits and rallies to raise funds and enlist volunteers. Western residents were of course the principal ones affected, but the contagion also reached Polynesians and Fijians and New Caledonians, who had never lost their keenness for a good scrap.

Local volunteer defense units were formed on some Islands, and many Westerners left plantations and mines and government posts for overseas duty. It was a festival of solidarity and good fellowship, until the hangover set in. The exodus of volunteers from Island enterprises and the mobilization of shipping for war soon had disrupting effects on Island economy. Copra prices rose, but copra rotted in warehouses for lack of ships to carry it to market; and for the same reasons essential imports had to be reduced. Also, production and commerce and administration suffered for lack of personnel. Cooperative shipping and marketing arrangements helped a little, but such arrangements were hampered by the inevitable bureaucratic snafus.

The first severe war crisis came with the fall of France, and the Euro-African drama was repeated on a small scale in the French possessions in Oceania. The Free French movement finally won out in both New Caledonia and Tahiti, although it was a case of principles rather than men, because De Gaulle's representative, the autocratic monk-admiral D'Argenlieu, did anything but endear himself to the colonials. Meanwhile Australia and New Zealand assumed responsibility for the defense and economic survival of New Caledonia and French Polynesia, respectively, and Japanese mining activities in New Caledonia were neutralized by export restrictions.

As Axis power expanded in Europe and Africa and eastern Asia, some islands were strengthened with garrisons from New Zealand and Australia, but these measures did not deter German raiders from potting at Allied shipping. Two raiders caught several phosphate freighters at Nauru, sank five of them, and then shelled the cantilever.

Otherwise it was a quiet, uneventful war, beginning to be tiresome for everyone except the planters who were able to market their produce. And then the Japanese struck.

The extent and progress of the Japanese attack is shown on Map 7; details of the military campaigns need not concern us here except as they affected the South Pacific setting against which they were fought.

The important fact is that for nearly five years hundreds of thousands of Japanese, British, and Americans worked and fought on these islands, shifting native populations, sometimes mixing blood with them, introducing new materials and ideas, and in many places upsetting the fine balance of Island economy and caste relations. But every part of the South Pacific was affected differently.

For Australia and New Zealand the war brought home more emphati-

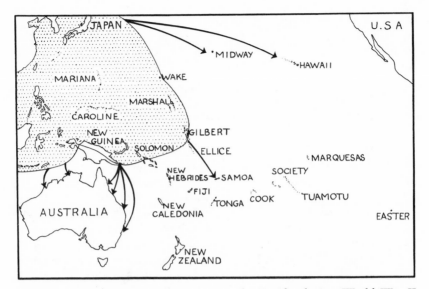

Map 7. Japan's farthest advances into the Pacific during World War II
(drawn by Sheila Mitchell Oliver)

cally than ever before how valuable the Islands were to national security
and how ornamental to national prestige. The need for American support against the common enemy was clearly recognized, and the presence
of overwhelming American forces duly appreciated; but Australian and
New Zealand statesmen hinted that, come the peace, the South Pacific
would revert to being *their* lake. The Anzac pact, concluded in 1944,
contained many fine plans concerning the future security of the region
and the welfare of Islanders, but it also made clear that these islands and
peoples were the concern principally of the two British dominions. The
war also provided tens of thousands of Australians and New Zealanders
with firsthand knowledge of Island conditions; and although most of
them would undoubtedly have reacted in unprintable language to suggestions that they remain in the Islands as colonists, a few felt otherwise. As
for the effect of the war on New Zealand's native people, the Maori participated in no way different from other patriotic New Zealanders.

The first effect of the war on the Mandated Territory of New Guinea
was to demonstrate how loose were the ties between the native inhabitants and their Western masters. The former remained in their villages as
innocent bystanders while most of the latter fled to Papua or Australia.
The few Westerners who remained were either captured by the Japanese
or escaped into the wilderness to serve as intelligence spotters for the
Allied Forces. In sharp contrast to the 1914 changeover from German to
Australian rule, the Japanese seizure of New Guinea marked a complete

break in administration and commerce. Plantations and mines were abandoned and trade ceased. The Japanese attempted to win natives to their side by propaganda, but did not institute any general measures for administration or welfare. For their part, most natives were left to themselves so long as they did not interfere with operations. A few "went over" and a few others evidenced loyalty to the cause of their former Australian masters, but most of them took no sides and returned to their pre-Western pastimes, including some intertribal fighting and headhunting.

The Japanese, however, changed their practices as their military position reversed; in southern Bougainville, for example, native gardens were systematically pillaged, pigs eaten and men impressed into labor gangs and women into pleasure houses for the troops. Elsewhere similar things went on, but these occurrences may have resulted from the pique of individual commanders or from supply difficulties rather than from a general policy of ruthlessness. At any rate, such things did not endear the Japanese to natives; on the other hand, New Guinea proved too large and heterogeneous and politically unconscious to permit any universal manifestation either for or against Japanese or Australians.

Papua suffered far fewer changes than the Mandated Territory. Japanese occupation was restricted to the northeastern slopes of the central ranges running down the peninsula, and even that occupation was short-lived. Civilian government was supplanted by military, but the administration unit was staffed principally with former territorial officials and residents so that there was a large measure of continuity. Also, an official Production Control Board stationed planters back on their properties and kept copra and rubber production up to prewar levels.

Labor was needed to carry supplies, construct roads and airfields, and man plantations, and natives were conscripted by the thousands. At one point the conscript force of Papuan natives numbered two and a half times their normal prewar labor force. As the war moved north, the administrative arrangements functioning in Papua were extended to reconquered New Guinea; the two territories were, in fact, treated as a single unit.

After the main American forces leapfrogged past Rabaul to Manus and Hollandia, it was left to Australians to mop up the bypassed Japanese, and this turned out to be a miserable, tortuous job that was still in process on V-J Day.

Ironically, the Allied "liberators" proved more devastating to native life than the invaders had been. It is likely that the Allies, by virtue of their more massive bombardments, accounted for the larger share of the estimated fifteen thousand natives killed and twenty thousand dwellings destroyed in Papua and northeastern New Guinea during the Pacific campaigns. Also, a dysentery epidemic introduced by Allied troops wiped out many hundreds of natives in one area, and the conscription of native labor, which reached a peak of thirty-seven thousand, severely disorganized many native communities. In some instances the Japanese also resorted to forced labor, but to nothing like the general extent practiced by the Australians. On the other side of the picture, the Australians operated trade stores and hospitals for natives and were not intentionally abusive, and many individual natives made common cause with the Allies and played heroic roles in the conflict.

Copra production and trade came to a standstill in the Solomons soon after Pearl Harbor, and most civilians were evacuated, leaving the few officials and missionaries who chose to remain at their posts. Even after the Japanese closed in on Guadalcanal and Tulagi, some officials managed to avoid capture back of the lines so that a measure of administrative continuity was maintained throughout the occupation. Later, when American forces moved in, control over native affairs remained firmly in British hands, and the British recruited hundreds of Solomonese as laborers for the military forces. Some trade goods were bought by an American government agency and sold to the British for resale to natives, mainly as an incentive for more laborers to work for the military; conscription was not resorted to. Some efforts were also made to revive copra production, but shortages of manpower and shipping interfered, and several plantation areas were used for military installations.

The Solomonese were less affected by the war than were their New Guinea neighbors. Most fighting took place in sparsely populated areas, and only a few thousand natives were in direct contact with either Japanese or Allied troops. Those who worked for Westerners did so voluntarily; and although the youths who normally would have worked on plantations were denied that source of income, actually they did not require cash incomes as there was little to spend it on. Certain other changes were inevitable. Those who did work and come in contact with troops learned new ideas about the value of labor and the relations of castes that augured difficulties for their postwar administrators.

The New Hebrides sheltered three major American bases, two on the island of Efate, and one at southeastern Espiritu Santo. A few Japanese planes sneaked that far south, but otherwise these islands were spared actual combat, save for the quarreling that went on continually between British and French residents. Shipping was somewhat disrupted but copra production flourished; the products went to the United States and Australia. Although imports were difficult to procure, no real hardships were suffered by Western residents, and a few of them made nice profits from the wartime boom. Some natives were recruited to work for the military, and "town" natives on Efate were drawn into the inevitable inflationary spiral; otherwise, most indigenous New Hebrideans were little affected by the war.

For most residents on New Caledonia, on the other hand, war was an experience they were not likely to forget. American troops first landed there in March of 1942 and a few were still there five years later; during most of that period they dominated island life like an army of occupation. French officials held office, but American admirals and generals decided policy in critical spheres of public order, production, and commerce.

The Japanese residents of New Caledonia were promptly interned and shipped to Australia, but rumors continued to circulate about the presence of Axis sympathizers, and few wealthy residents escaped being branded "Pétainist." In fact, the local political situation was complex to the point of comedy. Americans and local residents succeeded in ousting De Gaulle's unpopular representative, D'Argenlieu, and this started a succession of governors sent out from Free French headquarters with the impossible assignment of satisfying both American military demands and the aspirations of the local French residents. Moreover, the government itself was split into factions favoring the several elements of the population.

Meanwhile the local economy boomed with dollar prosperity. Farmers found a ready local market for their coffee and vegetables and meat. Shops and bars sprang up everywhere, and those who couldn't sell things sold services. Imports were limited and supplies for local residents were short, but this did not curb resales to the free-spending Americans. With France temporarily out of the picture, all imports had to come from Australia and the United States. Australia offered to "assume primary responsibility" for ensuring supplies for New Caledonia—and for all other South Pacific areas—but Washington did not go along with this scheme, which contained some all too obvious implications respecting postwar markets. American exporters and their New Caledonian customers also had their private troubles because of Free French purchasing agents in the United States who managed to freeze out the private traders through government-to-government transactions.

Far more serious than any of these semicomic little crises were developments in the mining industry. War needs enhanced the strategic value of nickel and chromium, and New Caledonia remained one of the few accessible sources; therefore, the word went out to United States officials to keep production up. Since British proprietors of chromium mines and companies balked at paying the export fees demanded by the New Caledonian government, shipments were held up for a while. Also, coal for the nickel refining had to be brought from Australia and shipping shortages turned this problem into a continuous crisis. Labor, however, proved the worst dilemma.

The New Caledonian mines and refinery were manned with Indochinese and Javanese imported under indenture, and the industries' technical facilities were so primitive that there was heavy dependence on

masses of hand laborers. In the midst of the emergency the labor contracts began to expire. Under normal circumstances finish-time laborers
would have renewed their contracts voluntarily or have remained as free
workers or have been repatriated. With their homelands occupied by the
Japanese, they obviously could not be repatriated. And few laborers
wished to renew their contract when there existed the alternative of earning, literally, ten times as much by working for the troops. On the other
hand, mine and refinery managers did not wish to lose their laborers, and
in this they were backed by the authorities, both New Caledonian and
American. The upshot was that contracts were renewed unilaterally, and
the American government, official defender of freedom, was placed in
the awkward position of having to support forced labor. Even the Netherlands Indies government had to connive at keeping their own Javanese
subjects under indenture, although a consul was sent out to safeguard
what few rights remained to them. All these events provoked a series of
disturbances all over the island and culminated in a strike centered at
the nickel refinery at Noumea. In the midst of general confusion and
rumors about Communist-inspired insurrections, the French government
stepped in and vigorously suppressed the disturbance by jailing several
leaders and forcing the strikers back to their jobs. Finally, in mid-1945,
when the need for nickel and chromium slacked off and enforced labor
could no longer be justified as a wartime necessity, laborers were freed
and the industries slowed down.

Many New Caledonian indigenes participated in the war by serving as
stevedores and construction laborers and garrison troops, and from their
whoops of enthusiasm as they careened along the highway in trucks, they
seemed to have enjoyed the excitement mightily. Most others, however,
kept to their reserves in the north and saw little of the war save the steady
stream of transport planes overhead.

Wartime Fiji was an active military base and a source of critically
needed sugar and copra. American and New Zealand troops trained and
recuperated there, warships and reserve planes based there, and aircraft
refueled there en route to New Caledonia and Australia. Sugar and copra
exports remained fairly normal despite shipping and supply difficulties,
and some locally produced foods and other supplies were furnished to
the forces. Imports were stringently controlled, but in many other
respects life carried on in a most orderly fashion.

In contrast to the other South Pacific bases, there was never any question about who ran *these* islands; topflight colonial officials were posted
there to administrate the mobilization and, one inferred, to see to it that
the Yanks be kept reminded that Fiji was *British* territory.

Western colonists rallied behind the war effort enthusiastically, and
nearly every Western male of military age was in service. In addition one
of the most picturesque roles in the South Pacific campaign was played

by the battalion of Fijian and Tongan jungle scouts, which had a glo-
riously heroic time harassing the Japanese in the northern Solomons.
Fijians at home also supported the war with service and donations, and
all this strengthened the ties between Westerners and Fijians. With the
Indians, however, it was a different story. With a few exceptions most
Indians were indifferent to the war in which they had so few stakes; nevertheless, except for a strike, their plodding industry kept on producing
the sugar that was needed. Meanwhile the Indians' increasing population
and wealth, and their more articulate agitation for broader political and
economic rights, promised severe headaches for postwar administrators.

For about a year Tonga was also a supporting base for American
troops and an occasional anchorage for warships, but in 1943, New
Zealanders took over the garrisoning and Tonga's active military role
was reduced. Most war activities were restricted to the area around Nukualofa on the island of Tongatabu and did not greatly disturb the life of
the kingdom. Queen Salote reigned, the British consul advised, and
church attendance was only slightly affected by the more diverting activities around the camps. Americans found Tongan girls highly attractive,
but available census figures do not indicate how high.

Soon after Pearl Harbor an enemy submarine tossed a futile shell or
two at Pago Pago, and that was the nearest the fighting war came to
Samoa; but Tutuila and Upolu were important support and communications bases throughout the first half of the Pacific war, and parts of the
central Pacific campaigns were staged through that area.

Tiny Tutuila was overrun by the vastly expanded facilities and forces
stationed there. Civil government was subordinated to that of the commander of the U.S. Marines, and Samoans responded so enthusiastically
to calls for auxiliaries and workers that native community life was thoroughly disorganized.

Western Samoa, with its larger area and population, absorbed the war
impact with less disturbance to normal life. Most Western wives and children were sent to New Zealand, but plantation life went on, and copra
and cocoa were exported in large quantities. There were the usual difficulties in supply, but the New Zealand administration maintained import
controls and kept the other reins of government also well in hand. The
most serious problem faced by the authorities was the perennial one of
trying to govern Samoans made even more ungovernable by dollar prosperity and contact with Americans.

Far, far back of the combat zone were small communications bases—
Penrhyn, Aitutaki, and Bora Bora: "lost islands"—where GIs were exiled
to sit out the war, bored by isolation and make-work, maintaining air-
strips and anchorages for planes and ships that rarely came, and wishing
to be in Guadalcanal or Tarawa or anywhere but in the deadly beauty
and calm of their particular South Sea paradise. (For a poignant and

almost documentary description of one of these outposts, see James Norman Hall's *Lost Island*.)

Outside these militarized islands, the war had little effect other than the universal repercussions of shortages in shipping and supply. Great pressure was put on increase of copra and phosphate production, which brought in dollars and pounds that were largely neutralized by restrictions on imports and by rationing. In fact, some of the outlying islands had to return to subsistence economy. Tahiti's normal tourist trade was interrupted, and the island was insulated, through strict limitations on travel, from "contamination" by Americans based in nearby Bora Bora. The determined De Gaullist governor also ruled French Polynesia's economy and other domestic affairs with the same iron hand, with the result that his jurisdiction became more French and less Polynesian. To the booming copra trade, Tahitians—Westerners and Polynesians—added the manufacture of curios that were sold in PXs all over the South Pacific. Even Seabee artisans were not able to turn out native crafts quite as "authentic" as those mass-produced in Tahiti.

Up nearer the combat zone a communications base was maintained at Wallis Island, where the French administrator feuded continually with the British trader, where copra rotted in the sheds for lack of a vessel to carry it away, and where GIs sat around and worried about contracting encephalitis, which a rumor credited with having emasculating consequences. In the background the local natives kept up their Catholic routines and did laundry for the Americans.

Further north at Funafuti, Americans and Ellice islanders lived harmoniously crowded together on a narrow atoll without apparent ill effects on either group save that of the boredom of the former.

As every Pacific air traveler knew, Canton, Palmyra, Christmas, and Johnston islands were transformed into major air transport stations, but that did not affect any indigenous populations because there were none there to affect.

Tarawa and Makin atolls need no recall even to the shallowest of memories. The Japanese invaders took them soon after Pearl Harbor and killed most of the Westerners who failed to escape. Throughout the enemy occupation, Gilbertese resisted passively (passivity was their only weapon) and were subjected to mistreatment ranging from confiscation of personal valuables to a Japanese retaliatory bombing raid.

British colonial officials returned to the Gilberts with the U.S. Marines and promptly organized a Gilbertese labor corps, which did much useful stevedoring in connection with preparations for the campaign in the Marshalls.

Nearby Ocean Island and Nauru, the phosphate centers, were occupied by Japanese forces early in 1942 and remained in enemy hands up to the end, although American bombers neutralized any value they might

have had for the invaders. Some natives from these islands were later discovered by American occupation forces in the Carolines, where they had
been taken by the Japanese to work.

Vulnerable Guam, cut off from American aid by Japanese Micronesia,
fell into enemy hands soon after Pearl Harbor and was promptly integrated into Japan's South Seas empire, which by then had become one
huge network of bases in support of the southward thrusts.

During the first phase of the Pacific war, before Japan began to be crippled by Allied counterattacks, the Marianas and the Carolines and the
Marshalls were the scene of intensified military and economic activities.
Sugar, copra, and phosphates were strategic war materials and their production was kept going. Gardens were planted to help feed the enlarged
Japanese garrisons and the gangs of coolie laborers imported for military
construction projects. Imports were controlled and carefully rationed,
but there seem to have been no serious hardships at first. In fact, the civilian populations were not seriously inconvenienced during that early victorious period of war enthusiasm.

But later on, when the grim digging-in times came, everything
changed. Supplies became scarce even for the Japanese military; importation of civilian goods ceased almost altogether. Around the main bases,
native lands were confiscated for milit ry purposes and natives were
impressed into labor gangs, some being sent to distant islands. Copra
making ceased entirely, although sugar growing stalled along.

As Japan's military situation deteriorated, less consideration was paid
to natives; but although there were many individual acts of cruelty and
injustice, there is little evidence of a general policy of mistreatment, and
those islands that were distant from the military bases were simply
ignored.

Conditions became much worse after the United States carried the war
to the islands. Men dropping bombs on Truk and other strongholds
could not very well distinguish between military posts and native houses,
and naval bombardments ("Spruance haircuts") unwittingly destroyed
some native life and property.

The Marshalls were first to be wrested from the Japanese; then followed Guam, Saipan, Tinian, and Peleliu; and from these centers American planes continued to blast the bypassed islands until V-J Day.

On the staff of each American island commander were several military
government officers specially selected and trained to maintain public
order and welfare among civilians of liberated and occupied areas. From
the very beginning distinctions were made between ethnic groups in these
areas. Japanese and Okinawan civilians were herded together and
guarded as more or less harmless enemies. Guamanians were greeted as
long-suffering friends and were accorded as much freedom and assistance
as the military circumstances permitted. Natives—Marshallese, Caroli-

nians, and Chamorro outside Guam—were classified as innocent victims of Japanese aggression and prospective wards of the United States. Koreans presented something of a problem, but were apparently defined as rather low-caste allies.

The Marshallese provided good practice for military government, and it was fortunate all around that these islanders seemed good-naturedly amenable and charmingly grateful for all the measures taken on their behalf: the early Yankee missionary efforts paid off here. The natives were fed, clothed, and doctored, and encouraged to restore their "democratic" institutions. Soon a trade program was operating; curios were purchased from natives and goods sold to them, all under close supervision and controlled prices. An English-language school was opened, and it was no time at all before the pupils were loudly harmonizing "Anchors Aweigh."

Circumstances were more complex in the Marianas. All other requirements were subordinated to building and supplying the bases for knocking out Japan, and military government officials had to make do with supplies they could salvage elsewhere. The result was that civilians, even Guamanians, had to exist in makeshift camps on bare rations, and as many as possible were encouraged to work for the military forces.

Basic policies were laid down by the top command and were generally humane and sensible, as were most of the military government officials who administered the policies. A few officers were overzealous or dictatorial or temperamentally unsuited to the job of running others' lives, but as a group they did little harm and much good.

Hawaii, the place where it all started, witnessed few shots fired in anger after that first calamitous morning of December 7, 1941, but the war made a permanent impression upon the land and the people and the institutions of the so-called Paradise of the Pacific.

Hawaii's political separation from the rest of the South Pacific became even more evident between 1939 and the attack on Pearl Harbor. Although neighbors to the south and west were preoccupied with war, there was little change in Hawaii's serenity, except for a gradual increase in tempo of military construction along with some uneasiness about Japan's potential fifth column. This calm made the sneak attack all the more electrifying.

The immediate effect of the blitz was to shock Hawaii almost into hysteria. Fear and rumor ruled, and the much-advertised interracial harmony gave way to suspicion and strife, punctuated with large-scale arrests of aliens. Civil authorities relinquished control to the military; women, children, and tourists were hustled into ships and sent to the mainland. Total blackouts were instituted and the famed bathing beaches were laced with barbed wire as the population nervously awaited the next blows—which, however, never came.

For four years Hawaii was an armed camp. Its war role during that era has become household knowledge; less well known is the effect the war had on the civilian community. The most editorialized change in island life was the sudden and apparently complete transfer of government from civilian into military hands and the extension of government controls over wide areas of living. Movement was restricted, curfew installed, property commandeered. Prices were fixed, goods rationed, jobs and wages frozen, and shipping controlled. Admirals and generals supplanted civilian officials and mobilization was pushed to a degree quite unrealized on the mainland.

Military construction relegated King Sugar to second rank, but, since sugar was a strategic commodity, its production was officially supported. Pineapple production was also maintained and the pack sold to feed the armed forces. The tourist industry as such no longer catered to holiday seekers, but every tourist facility was overtaxed trying to entertain the tens of thousands of involuntary visitors in uniform. Fishing was one of the few major industries to suffer, since the Japanese-manned sampans were tied up for security reasons or were commandeered.

Parts of Oahu's shorelines and cane fields were converted into military installations, but these changes touched only a small proportion of the territory's land and were much less significant than the changes that took place in the population itself.

In addition to the tremendous influx of soldiers and sailors, the government also imported from the mainland tens of thousands of civilian workers, representing a very large increase in the territory's total civilian population and an entirely new kind of resident for Hawaii. Local employees were also mobilized. They were "frozen," without appeal, to their pre–Pearl Harbor jobs and permitted to change employment only by direction; their wages were also fixed. This arrangement was eminently satisfactory to employers: for one thing, it kept workers from transferring en masse to the better-paid government jobs. It was also satisfactory to the military, because it enabled the authorities to requisition laborers from plantations for emergency use on military projects. Needless to say, this arrangement was somewhat less than satisfactory to the workers themselves.

After the initial hysteria in Hawaii interethnic hostility became much less apparent. There was a certain amount of trouble between local hoodlums and transient servicemen, but the predicted clash between Filipino and Japanese workers failed to materialize. Local Westerners and Hawaiians joined up or backed the war as everyone had expected, but it was the Japanese who surprised all the critics. The elders remained on duty and worked doggedly and industriously almost to a man, and their sons enlisted and fought in a manner that was to remove forever any suspicion of divided loyalty.

As the war moved farther west, the military authorities returned controls to civilians and things appeared to move back toward normality, or as normal as they could be in the presence of tens of thousands of transient servicemen and mainland workers. But appearances were deceptive; under the surface there were signs of a major change in Hawaii's basic social structure. Under military government the Western owners and managers of Hawaii's economy did not lose their control over territorial life; the freezing of men to jobs moved some workers to charge the new military masters and the old owner-managers with collusion to protect the status quo. As restrictions were eased, however, there was more and more talk about unionism on the plantations and docks. Resentment against Hawaii's traditional paternalistic system was increased by union-wise mainland workers; and West Coast labor leaders began to turn their attention to this promising new field with the same zeal shown by those other ideologists, the missionaries, who had preceded them by a century and a quarter.

SOURCES

McCarthy 1959; Milner 1957; Morison 1950; L. Morton 1962; Sautot 1949.

CHAPTER SEVENTEEN

After the Battles

World War II unified the South Pacific Islands to an extent never before realized. For a few hectic years nearly every island and atoll was in some measure brought under the jurisdiction of the Allied Combined Chiefs of Staff and their field commanders. But this unification did not long survive V-J Day. Soon after the cease-fire order, the historic tripartite division reestablished itself, with Hawaii moving in one direction, the now "American" Micronesia in another, and the Franco-British South Pacific in a third. Political and cultural distances between the first two regions were of course shorter than they had been before the war; in fact, the cumulative effects of war served to bring all three regions somewhat closer together than they had been before Pearl Harbor, but not close enough to allow the historian to describe them with the same generalizations.

South Pacific

The sudden ending of hostilities aggravated if anything the South Pacific's wartime dislocations. The rush of military groups to clear out and go home was equaled only by the clamor of the Islands' Western residents to get back to their plantations and mines. Valuable military supplies were left to rot and vast war installations to return to jungle. With the military's organization and facilities out of the picture before civil authorities were ready to function, communications and services of all kinds were disrupted. And, of course, everyone but the Japanese was blamed for the confused state of affairs.

Some measure of disorganization, especially in transportation and supplies, occurred throughout the South Pacific, but conditions were progressively worse from southeast to northwest. Tahiti, for example, lacked some of its prewar amenities, but New Guinea's economy was totally wrecked—towns destroyed, plantations overgrown, mines disabled, labor force scattered, and administration confused.

Throughout the Islands there was plenty of money but not much to buy, generally favorable world markets but poor shipping facilities; and in few places were the workers content to return to their old jobs for prewar wages. However, none of these stern realities deterred planners from devising fine programs for the hopeful new postwar world.

Implicit in most of the official blueprints were two warring principles: alongside the recurrent theme of native-oriented, internationally minded trusteeship, there incongruously appeared many not so veiled assertions of national sovereignty and empire.

The trusteeship theme was compounded of several things. In the background was the familiar ethic of humanitarianism that had been increasingly in evidence since the turn of the century. Some memories of the League of Nations mandate system were also present, along with echoes of the Atlantic Charter, of Labour Party socialist policy, and of missionary influence. This theme was definitely pronative and anticommerce in sentiment, and was based upon the premise that government alone could implement postwar plans. Probably the first manifestation of this policy was the Fiji government's appeal to the Colonial Ministry for a substantial increase in the native welfare subsidy. A little later Australia and New Zealand published their agreement to cooperate in carrying out similar objectives, and the theme was again forcefully enunciated by Australia's Herbert Vere Evatt. French officials also made a few tentative pronouncements along those lines, but American authorities were too preoccupied with their new responsibilities in Micronesia to give much thought to American Samoa.

The trusteeship principle was applied most vigorously to the planning for New Guinea's future. The Australian Labour Government made it clear that New Guinea would be administered for the welfare of the natives, with Western residents receiving only secondary consideration and their enterprises tolerated only to the extent that they were harmless to native interests. The usual arrangements were made to pay war damages incurred by Western residents, but the authorities went even further and took the unprecedented action of assuming obligations to pay natives also for their losses in life and property. Basic wages to natives were increased and the indenture system of native labor was liberalized, both pointing to eventual abolition of the system. Also, comprehensive and extremely ambitious plans were formulated for the improvement of native medical service, education, and self-government; and the program for native economic development envisaged a rising standard of living based on improved subsistence economy and supplementary income-earning enterprises for natives. The assumption behind all the planning was that New Guinea natives, given the opportunity, were capable of unlimited "progress."

Similar though less ambitious programs were formulated for the Solomons, and even New Caledonian natives were granted easier access to citizenship privileges. In Fiji native welfare programs simply expanded in the directions already established; and in most other South Pacific dependencies this trend was also evident.

As mentioned above, however, the old signs of national sovereignty and empire also reappeared in the postwar pronouncements and plans. In the dark days of the war, when the colonial powers' resources were thinly spread over such wide areas in the fight for survival, there was much unofficial but not irresponsible talk about jettisoning indefensible island outposts and swapping island territories in the interest of rationalizing measures for security and administrative economy. Suggestions were made, for example, to turn over the Marquesas to the United States, to transfer the Solomons and the New Hebrides to Australia, to amalgamate Eastern and Western Samoa, and to encourage the United States to establish permanent bases at strategic points throughout the South Pacific. The tune changed, however, when the danger passed. It changed so radically, in fact, that responsible American officials had to act with great circumspection to quiet suspicions concerning the intentions of the United States. In numerous acts and statements, the older colonial powers stated their determination to maintain the political status quo in the South Pacific, and these sentiments were epitomized in the arrangements made to redistribute the old mandated territories. When the League of Nations expired, the former mandated territories of New Guinea, Western Samoa, and Nauru were left, de jure at least, without sovereign ties; but their former mandatory governments lost no time in reasserting claim to them under the new label of United Nations Trust Territories. Even Britain, so scrupulous about giving up India and Burma, showed not the slightest disposition to retire from her South Pacific dependencies.

Trusteeship and internationalism versus strategy and empire make for semantic conflict, but the great powers have never been stopped by a mere paradox. Some effort, however, was made to resolve this one when Australia and New Zealand invited the United Kingdom, France, Holland, and the United States to collaborate in establishing a South Pacific commission "to encourage and strengthen international co-operation in promoting the economic and social welfare and advancement of the peoples of the nonself-governing territories in the South Pacific" (excerpt from the preamble to the intergovernment agreement setting up the South Pacific Commission, drawn up in Canberra in February 1947).

The South Pacific Commission headquarters was established at Noumea and an international staff was assembled to engage in research and to act as an advisory body to South Pacific administrations. The commission's functions were, however, restricted to such nonpolitical and nonmilitary matters as economic development, social welfare, education, and health.

While all these policies and plans were being formulated in the rarefied atmosphere of official conference rooms, the nonofficial Westerners with personal stakes in Island production and commerce began to reassert their views on the way islands should be run. Now, with the Japanese threat out of the way, they turned their attention to the new menace of government planners seemingly intent upon destroying the Island world they knew before the war. The governments were accused of liquidating Western enterprise in favor of giving the natives freedom and help "they could not use and, in fact, did not want." These critics were alarmed at the danger to their personal interests and laid much of the blame to the plotting of leftists in and out of government. And in some instances they believed their fears realized by the rash of native strikes and nativistic movements that broke out after the war.

Those outbreaks took many forms. A general restlessness and impatience with prewar living standards and caste institutions was the inevitable result of the disturbances and the flood of new things and ideas brought on by the war. New Guinea natives, for example, were bound to draw conclusions from seeing their Western masters flee before the Japanese. And, there and elsewhere, time gaps in administration, contacts with troops, breakdowns in services, and a thousand and one crises affecting every phase of old life all contributed to uncertainty and unrest. Then, too, many Islanders were becoming aware of events and ideas and standards in the rest of the world through means of education and their increasing literacy.

Nativist manifestations varied from mild cynicism about Westerners' superiority to sullen and organized movements against White colonialism. In New Guinea there were some nasty local incidents against the authorities; in the Solomons a few ambitious native leaders managed to organize such a strong and ramified anti-Western movement, the so-called Marching Rule, that the authorities had to send a destroyer to "show the flag" and then round up the ringleaders with police force. This movement followed the familiar pattern of the "Cargo" cults of former days, and there was evidence from some of its slogans that leftists among the Allied troops may have helped to touch it off.

The best publicized of all these movements was the Western Samoans' petition to the United Nations for more self-government and for consideration of the reunion of Western and Eastern Samoa. A United Nations mission duly visited Western Samoa and came back with a recommendation that the Samoans were not yet prepared for complete autonomy, but should be given more control over local affairs. Meanwhile the New Zealand government adopted its own plan for changing Western Samoa from a Mandate to a Trust Territory; the administrative changes did not go quite as far as the United Nations plan suggested, but a few reforms were effected and a few titles changed so that agitation was quieted for a while.

In the meantime, American civilian critics of the navy's rule in American Samoa moved the president to set a date for transferring administrative responsibility to the Department of the Interior and to ask Congress to extend citizenship and an organic act of government to the Eastern Samoans. (The question of union between Eastern and Western Samoa was too intricate for the statesmen to cope with.)

Postwar restlessness showed up in the Cook islands in the form of demands for more political rights and for a larger share in economic gains. The native membership of the Cook Islands Progressive Association became more aggressive in their tactics to control local industrial affairs, and they were said to have received encouragement and support from leftist elements in the New Zealand longshore unions. Other factions of native workers organized an officially sponsored union, and the two opposing groups engaged in jurisdictive strife and strikes against shipping in the best longshore-union tradition. Even Tahitians organized into "syndicates," but these were mild affairs and were not taken very seriously. More significant, for Tahiti, was the action taken by several Tahitians to keep officials from disembarking from the ship that brought them from France, their object being to remonstrate against having metropolitan French colonial officials sent out to fill jobs that Tahitians were capable of filling. The governor vigorously put down the "revolt" and demonstrated that France, at least, would not tolerate any weakening of central authority if she could help it.

In New Caledonia the impatience with prewar ties took a different form. Westerners, rather than natives, sought to gain a larger measure of control over local affairs and even pressed for power to subordinate the metropolitan-appointed governor to the will of the locally elected General Council. Back of this movement was the wartime experience of managing their own affairs while cut off from France. Back of it also was the desire of the less affluent Western residents, who constituted the majority, to nationalize the principal local industries and so ensure the profits from local enterprises did not all end up in the pockets of absentee owners overseas. Another goal was to secure greater freedom to develop beneficial commercial ties with Australia and New Zealand.

Postwar stirrings also ruffled the calm of Fiji's community and there even occurred a mild strike among Fijian mine workers, but Fuji's principal postwar ailment was her chronic Indian problem. Indians continued to outbreed Fijians and Westerners, and, with their increase in numbers and in political experience and emboldened by events in India, they sharpened their demands for political suffrage. Having alienated Westerners and Fijians by holding aloof from war activities, they made themselves even more unpopular by carrying off a paralyzing strike against the sugar industry. Even optimists began to despair of a solution to Fiji's perennial problem.

The birth of Indonesia left temporarily undecided the fate of Netherlands New Guinea. The Hague Round-Table Conference of 1949 postponed the handling of this knotty problem in an effort to negotiate the larger issues of Indonesian autonomy, meanwhile leaving the Dutch in control pending final settlement, in 1950, of western New Guinea's sovereignty. Judging from actions and speeches in early 1950 it became evident that neither side would surrender its claims without a fierce political battle. And to the student of the Pacific Islands it seemed probable at that time that the natives, unaware of the issues and unable to articulate their own wishes, if, indeed, they had any, would neither be seriously considered nor systematically consulted in this matter of who their masters would be.

While all these more or less local factors were shaping events in the postwar South Seas, world economic conditions were also exerting their influences. Copra and cocoa prices rose, bringing prosperity to those Island communities that could market their products. The need for nickel and chromium slacked off, but the renewed demand for gold and oil pressed the operators and explorers to heroic exertions to reestablish mining and test drilling in New Guinea. Interest was awakened in fishing, and American and British experts laid plans for huge ocean-sweeping fishing enterprises. Enthusiasm developed for other industries as well, for growing of tea and rice, and for establishing tourist facilities; and the whole tempo of communications was speeded up by the extension of civil air travel between the principal centers.

In the presence of all this ferment and ungovernable change, of all these clashes of interest and differences in objective, only the most deluded escapist would have chosen the postwar South Seas as a haven of calm and continuity.

American Micronesia

Immediately after V-J Day the new American rulers of Micronesia had to take on the tremendous task of occupying and administering the numerous bypassed and far-flung Caroline islands in the face of rapid demobilization and general disintegration of all communications and supply facilities. And when the surrender parties put ashore at places like Truk and Ponape and Koror they found unbelievable want and devastation among both Japanese and natives.

After interning and shipping away all Japanese military personnel, the next significant move undertaken was to repatriate all Japanese and Okinawan civilians, and then to return to their home islands all islanders who had been displaced during the war. This move assuredly simplified the administrative task and removed the cause for probable future difficulties comparable to the Indian problem in Fiji, but the precipitous way the operation was carried out caused many heartbreaks; some Okinawans had spent most of their lives in the islands and had acquired native families, which were broken up by the move.

As for the remaining Micronesians, few were starving but most needed medical help; many of their structures and all their boats were destroyed; their life savings, invested in Japanese banks and postal savings, were gone; their standard of living depressed, livestock killed off, lagoons and reefs depopulated of fish by bombardment; their gardens and groves threatened by pests introduced during the war years; their sources of income vanished. And now they were faced with the painful necessity of starting out from scratch to adjust to a new set of masters and rules—their fourth in fifty years.

Unlike the Australians in New Guinea and the British in the Gilberts, the American Naval Command possessed no reserves of precedent and experienced personnel with which to govern their new wards. Guam was administratively separated from the rest of the islands and governed approximately as before, but Saipan, Rota, the Carolines, and the Marshalls posed new and tough problems. Inexperienced officers were stationed on isolated islands and ordered to repair the devastation, heal the sick, rehabilitate the economies, reconstitute and govern native communities, adjudicate quarrels, enforce American-type rules of law and order, and educate their charges for roles in the new age. And, while all this was supposed to be progressing, bases were being dismantled, personnel (including military government personnel) were being shipped home, transport was disrupted, supplies reduced to a trickle, and the whole governing organization demoralized by the lack of any official objective or long-range administrative program for Micronesia. Under these circumstances, Micronesia did not recover stability and prosperity overnight, but that was no fault of the well-meaning but harassed officers who had to cope with these difficulties on the spot.

The world became poignantly acquainted with the exodus of "King" Jude and his Bikini people to make way for the atom-bomb tests of Operation Crossroads. The lives of other Micronesians were less dramatically affected, but few escaped altogether the consequences of postwar disruptions; and although no one died of hunger, few regained their prewar standards of living during the first two postwar years.

The nadir was reached in the early months of 1946; after that some constructive policies were formulated and gradually implemented. Naval officers were required to attend a university course in colonial administration before undertaking Island assignments. Relief goods were sent where critically needed and a start was made in commercial distribution through government-subsidized trade stores that eventually dotted the area. Copra and pearl shell and curios began to trickle in.

All this was done by military government officials working on a day-to-day basis, still waiting for a long-range policy and understandably reluctant to proceed with any fundamental measures without a green light from Washington.

The turning point for America's captured islands of Micronesia came in April 1947, when the Security Council of the United Nations approved a trusteeship agreement for the territory and designated the United States as administering authority. In its clauses guaranteeing the rights and welfare of the native inhabitants, this trusteeship agreement was almost identical with those approved for New Guinea, Nauru, and Western Samoa; but, unlike those others, it entitled the United States to close off parts of the area for security reasons.

The trusteeship agreement helped point out the general direction, but it did not set the course. That was left for Washington to quarrel over. The ensuing controversy might have been entertaining had it not involved the welfare of thousands of unconsulted Micronesians. The policy battle lines were drawn between military and civilian departments of the government, specifically between the navy, which controlled the islands, and the Department of the Interior, which wanted to govern them. The navy based its claim on the essentially *naval* security and functions of the Islands and upon the continuing need to service the Islands by naval transport and communications. The Department of the Interior based its claim on the rights of civilian Micronesians to be governed by civilians. Navy defended its ability to govern civilians by pointing to Guam and Samoa; Interior attacked the record of Guam and Samoa. This war of memoranda was enlivened by shots from the sidelines; both Navy and Interior had their unofficial protagonists who fought the issue back and forth on the editorial pages. Some critics, with little confidence in either Navy's or Interior's capacities for governing, proposed a new executive agency to administer all of the nation's dependent territories.

Various drafts of organic acts were submitted to Congress setting forth charters for governing the Trust Territory, Guam, and Samoa. An

Organic Act for Guam was passed by Congress in 1950, giving Guamanians United States citizenship and some local autonomy, but similar bills for Samoa and the Trust Territory were not acted upon. Without waiting for Congressional decision, the executive branch agreed upon a piecemeal transfer of administration of the islands from the navy to the Department of the Interior; this transfer began with Guam, on August 1, 1950, and was in due course followed by Samoa and the Trust Territory.

Meanwhile, although official indecision may have retarded recovery somewhat in the Trust Territory, the Micronesians did not sit about and starve while waiting for Washington to make up its mind. Subsistence living improved and even commerce picked up, with increasing amounts of copra and pearl shell being exported and more goods being imported. Phosphates were mined and sent to Japan to stave off a disastrous fertilizer shortage there, but arrangements were made to reimburse Micronesians in some measure for the loss of this valuable resource. In general, final objectives were still undecided but immediate problems were cared for.

Guam's rehabilitation proceeded more swiftly than Saipan's or Koror's or Ponape's, but even five years after Hiroshima, Agana was still filled with rubble and many Guamanians continued to dwell in camps far from their own villages and farms.

Guam also came in for its share of the spotlight, and numerous official visitors urged changes in the traditional order. It was generally recognized that some change was inevitable if Guamanian economy was to adapt to the presence of the large defense establishment there. It looked as if copra economy was out: Guamanians would in the future probably derive most of their income from working for the military. It also seemed obvious that their increased contact with mainlanders would sophisticate them to the point where more self-government must be granted.

As in the South Pacific, postwar events in American Micronesia were influenced by the paradoxical principles of trusteeship and nationalism; by praiseworthy concern for native welfare; and by sincere respect for the aspirations of the natives, provided, of course, they did not conflict with national interests. Otherwise, the South Pacific parallel did not carry through. There were no Western colonials in American Micronesia to criticize government practices, and from most indications there would not be any for many years to come. Finally, there had not yet appeared in Micronesia a protest against Western rule sufficiently organized to be labeled an autonomy movement. Guamanians had their complaints and expressed them volubly; but even had there been a sentiment of extremism (which was unlikely) Guam's postwar prosperity was not conducive to demonstrations of independence. And as for the rest of the natives of American Micronesia, they had so far had too little opportunity to size up their new Western masters. Regarding this, an informed observer of the Pacific Islands of 1950 could only have predicted: Give them time!

Hawaii

Postwar Hawaii was dominated by the struggle between big business and organized labor. After V-J Day most of the mainland personnel who had served during the war returned home, military construction activity subsided, tourists began to trickle in again, and, on the surface at least, Hawaii appeared to be returning to normal. It was a slightly altered normalcy, to be sure: the permanent military establishments were bigger than before the war, and air traffic brought the territory nearer to the mainland and gradually quickened the pace of life; but otherwise life seemed to drift back to *aloha*-ism. Scratching below the surface, however, revealed anything but peace and contentment.

The conflict lines between big business and labor were actually forming before the war, but wartime events postponed the real battle. In other ways, however, war provided an advantageous setup for the West Coast union organizers who appeared in due course to direct labor's campaigns.

Longshoremen and sugar workers were the first to strike, and these initial work stoppages were long and costly affairs; they ended in compromise, however, and did not permanently cripple the territory's economy as some observers predicted they would. Even so, for a while it looked as if organized labor were winning; but then there occurred a tactical mistake. Union leaders threatened to extend the work stoppage to public utilities, and that threat to the security of everyday life, to ordinary things that affected everybody, aroused the community much more than did the somewhat distant events in the fields and on the wharves. Against a popular indignation, enflamed by a group improbably called "We the Women of Hawaii," the union leaders had little chance, and the tide of labor's popularity and power began to ebb.

Later on, by the time the pineapple workers got around to demonstrating, big business had the situation well in hand and this strike ended in failure for the unionists. Big business won these first skirmishes by virtue of its superior organization and enormous resources, but it also possessed strong allies in the whole community and in the character and conditions of the workers themselves. No matter how small a stake they may have had in Hawaii's riches, most residents not employed in manual-labor jobs tended to identify themselves with the owning and managing classes. This lineup was certainly not peculiar to Hawaii, but it was strengthened there by the ethnic situation and by the territory's shortage of intellectuals and disinterested liberals. There was also some possibility that such militant unionism may have been too rich for the blood of the workers, who were mostly Asians with agelong conditioning in subordinate roles. Also, with boom times past, many workers became concerned for their security, especially when they observed management's increasing interest in mechanization.

At any rate, big business survived successfully the first test of strength, and Hawaii settled back to beautifying its facade for the swelling tourist trade.

CHAPTER EIGHTEEN

Epilogue

This narrative ends at the year 1950. Needless to say, the trends of events depicted in it did not terminate there nor always remain on the same courses.

By 1988, when this book's revision was written, most of the Islands' residents had remained, or become, citizens of politically independent nations. Recent events have demonstrated, however, that common citizenship in an Island nation did not necessarily guarantee political equality. And an Island nation's political independence was in nearly every case circumscribed by indispensable *economic* dependence: in the form of grants or loans by foreign governments or of financial infusions by foreigner-controlled enterprises (including vast new mining operations, exploitative lumbering, foreigner-manned offshore fishing, and a proliferation of air transport into and within the region). Moreover, those and other activities were accompanied by far-reaching changes in Island residents' lives, including massive population movements—from rural to urban, island to island, and island to elsewhere. (In 1988 there were, for example, more Samoans in Hawaii and California than in American Samoa; more Niueans in New Zealand than in Niue.)

However, merely to chronicle all those and other large-scale postwar changes in Island societies would require another lengthy book. And several more books would be needed to provide an adequate sample of the effects of those changes upon the lives of individual Islanders. Information about such matters is accumulating space, but it must await the efforts of other, less superannuated, writers to collect and collate. Several ongoing periodicals contain articles on post-1950 Pacific events, e.g., *The Journal of Pacific History* (Canberra), *Journal of the Polynesian Society* (Wellington), *Pacific Studies* (Laie, Hawaii), and *Journal de la Société des Océanistes* (Paris). Another such periodical soon to appear is *The Contemporary Pacific* (Honolulu).

Bibliography

Adams, Ron
   1986   Indentured Labour and the Development of Plantations in Vanuatu—1867–1922. *Journal de la Société des Océanistes* 42:41–63.

Alkire, W. H.
   1977   *An Introduction to the Peoples and Cultures of Micronesia.* 2d ed. Menlo Park, Calif.: Cummings Publishing Co.

Amherst, Lord, and B. Thomson
   1901   *The Discovery of the Solomon Islands.* 2 vols. London: The Hakluyt Society.

Beaglehole, Ernest
   1957   *Social Change in the South Pacific: Rarotonga and Aitutaki.* London: George Allen & Unwin.

Beaglehole, J. C.
   1966   *The Exploration of the Pacific.* 3d ed. Stanford: Stanford University Press.

   1974   *The Life of Captain James Cook.* London: The Hakluyt Society.

Beaglehole, J. C., ed.
   1955   *The Journals of Captain James Cook on His Voyages of Discovery.* Vol. 1. Hakluyt Society Extra Series no. 34. Cambridge: Cambridge University Press.

   1961   *The Journals of Captain James Cook on His Voyages of Discovery.* Vol. 2. Hakluyt Society Extra Series no. 35. Cambridge: Cambridge University Press.

   1967   *The Journals of Captain James Cook on His Voyages of Discovery.* Vol. 3. Hakluyt Society Extra Series no. 36. Cambridge: Cambridge University Press.

Bellwood, Peter
   1979   *Man's Conquest of the Pacific: The Prehistory of Southeast Asia and Oceania.* New York: Oxford University Press.

Belshaw, Cyril
    1954 *Changing Melanesia: Social Economics of Culture Contact.* Melbourne: Oxford University Press.

Bennett, J. A.
    1976 Immigration, 'Blackbirding,' Labour Recruiting? The Hawaiian Experience 1877–1887. *Journal of Pacific History* 11 (1): 3–27.

    1987 *Wealth of the Solomons: A History of a Pacific Archipelago, 1800–1978.* Pacific Islands Monograph Series, no. 3. Honolulu: University of Hawaii Press.

Berde, Stuart
    1979 The Impact of Christianity on a Melanesian Economy. *Research in Economic Anthropology* 2:169–187. Greenwich, Conn.

Berndt, R., and Peter Lawrence, eds.
    1971 *Politics in New Guinea: Traditional and in the Context of Change— Some Anthropological Perspectives.* Nedlands: University of Western Australia Press.

Bligh, William
    1792 *A Voyage to the South Sea, Undertaken by Command of His Majesty, for the Purpose of Conveying the Breadfruit Tree to the West Indies, in His Majesty's Ship the* Bounty. *Including an Account of the Mutiny on Board the Said Ship.* 2 vols. London: G. Nicol.

Bougainville, L. A. de
    1772 *A Voyage round the World. Performed by Order of His Most Christian Majesty, in the Years 1766, 1767, 1768 and 1769.* Translated by J. R. Forster. London: J. Nourse and T. Davies.

Boutilier, J. A.
    1985 " 'We Fear Not the Ultimate Triumph': Factors Effecting the Conversion Phase of Nineteenth-Century Missionary Enterprises." In *Missions and Missionaries in the Pacific,* edited by Char Miller, 13–63. New York: The Edwin Mellen Press.

Boutilier, J. A., D. T. Hughes, and S. W. Tiffany, eds.
    1978 *Mission, Church and Sect in Oceania.* Lanham, Md.: University Press of America.

Brady, I. A.
    1975 "Christians, Pagans and Government Men: Culture Change in the Ellice Islands." In *A Reader in Culture Change,* edited by I. A. Brady and B. L. Isaacs, 111–146. Cambridge, Mass.: Shenkman Publishing Co.

Brookes, J. I.
    1941 *International Rivalry in the Pacific.* Berkeley: University of California Press.

Brookfield, H. C.
    1972 *Colonialism, Development and Independence: The Case of the Melanesian Islands in the South Pacific.* Cambridge: Cambridge University Press.

Brookfield, H. C., and Doreen Hart
1971 *Melanesia: A Geographical Interpretation of an Island World.* London: Methuen & Co.

Brown, Paula
1978 *Highland Peoples of New Guinea.* Cambridge: Cambridge University Press.

Brown, R. G.
1977 "The German Acquisition of the Caroline Islands, 1898–9." In *Germany in the Pacific and the Far East,* edited by J. A. Moses and Paul Kennedy, 137–155. St. Lucia: University of Queensland Press.

Bryan, E. H., Jr.
1941 *American Polynesia: Coral Islands of the Central Pacific.* Honolulu: Tongg Publishing Co.

Buckley, K., and K. Klugman
1981 *The History of Burns Philp, the Australian Company in the South Pacific.* Sydney: Burns Philp & Co. Ltd.

Carrington, Hugh, ed.
1948 *The Discovery of Tahiti: The Journal of George Robertson.* London: The Hakluyt Society.

Chapelle, Tony
1978 Customary Land Tenure in Fiji: Old Truths and Middle-aged Truths. *Journal of the Polynesian Society* 87:71–88.

Chinin, Jon J.
1958 *The Great Mahele: Hawaii's Land Division of 1848.* Honolulu: University of Hawaii Press.

Chinnery, E. W. P.
1924 The Natives of South Bougainville and Mortlocks (Taku). Canberra: *Territory of New Guinea Anthropological Reports, nos. 4 and 5.*

Chowning, Ann
1986 The Development of Ethnic Identity and Ethnic Stereotypes on Papua New Guinea Plantations. *Journal de la Société des Océanistes* 42:153–162.

Colwell, James, ed.
1914 *A Century in the Pacific.* London: C. H. Kelly.

Corney, B. G., ed.
1913 *The Quest and Occupation of Tahiti by Emissaries of Spain during the Years 1772–1776.* Vol. 1. London: Cambridge University Press.

1915 *The Quest and Occupation of Tahiti by Emissaries of Spain during the Years 1772–1776.* Vol. 2. London: Cambridge University Press.

1919 *The Quest and Occupation of Tahiti by Emissaries of Spain during the Years 1772–1776.* Vol. 3. London: Cambridge University Press.

Corris, Peter, ed.
1973a *William T. Wawn: The South Sea Islanders and the Queensland Labour Trade.* Honolulu: University Press of Hawaii.

1973b *Passage, Port and Plantation. A History of Solomon Islands Labour Migration 1870–1914.* Melbourne: Melbourne University Press.

Crawford, D. L.
1933 *Paradox in Hawaii.* Boston: Stratford Press.

Crocombe, R. G.
1964 *Land Tenure in the Cook Islands.* Melbourne: Oxford University Press.

1971 "The Cook, Niue and Tokelau Islands: Fragmentation and Emigration." In *Land Tenure in the Pacific,* edited by R. G. Crocombe, 60–90. Melbourne: Oxford University Press.

Crocombe, R. G., ed.
1971 *Land Tenure in the Pacific.* Melbourne: Oxford University Press.

Cumberland, K. B., and J. W. Fox
1962 *Western Samoa: Land, Life and Agriculture in Tropical Polynesia.* Christchurch: Whitcombe & Tombs.

Danielsson, Bengt
1956 *Work and Life on Raroia (Tuamotus).* London: Macmillan & Co.

Davidson, J. W.
1967 *Samoa mo Samoa: The Emergence of the Independent State of Western Samoa.* Melbourne: Oxford University Press.

Davies, John
1961 *The History of the Tahitian Mission, 1799–1830,* edited by C. W. Newbury. Cambridge: Cambridge University Press.

Daws, Gavan
1968 *Shoal of Time: A History of the Hawaiian Islands.* Honolulu: University of Hawaii Press.

Dening, Greg
1980 *Islands and Beaches: Discourse on a Silent Land: Marquesas 1774–1880.* Honolulu: University Press of Hawaii.

Derrick, R. A.
1967 *A History of Fiji.* 2 vols. Suva: Government of Fiji, Printing & Stationery Department.

Douglas, Bronwen
1970 A Contact History of the Balad People of New Caledonia, 1774–1845. *Journal of the Polynesian Society* 79:180–200.

1980 Conflict and Alliance in a Colonial Context: Case Studies in New Caledonia, 1853–1870. *Journal of Pacific History* 15:21–51.

1982 "Written on the Ground"; Spatial Symbolism, Cultural Categories and Historical Process in New Caledonia. *Journal of the Polynesian Society* 91:385–416.

Doumenge, François
1966 *L'homme dans le Pacifique Sud: Étude geographique.* Paris: Musée de l'Homme.

Dunmore, John
1965 *French Explorers in the Pacific.* 2 vols. Oxford: Clarendon Press.

Ellis, A. F.
1936 *Ocean Island and Nauru.* Sydney: Angus & Robertson.

Ellsworth, S. G.
1959 *Zion in Paradise: Early Mormons in the South Seas.* Logan: Utah State University Press.

Embree, J. F.
1941 *Acculturation among the Japanese of Kona, Hawaii.* Menasha, Wis.: American Anthropological Association.

Faivre, Jean-Paul
1953 *L'Expansion française dans le Pacifique: 1800–1842.* Paris: Nouvelles Editions Latines.

Firth, Stewart
1977 "German Firms in the Pacific Islands 1857–1914." In *Germany in the Pacific and the Far East,* edited by J. A. Moses and Paul Kennedy, 3–25. St. Lucia: University of Queensland Press.

1982 *New Guinea under the Germans.* Melbourne: Melbourne University Press.

Force, R. W.
1960 *Leadership and Culture Change in Palau.* Fieldiana Anthropology 50. Chicago: Chicago Natural History Museum.

Forman, C. W.
1982 *The Island Churches of the South Pacific: Emergence in the Twentieth Century.* Maryknoll, N.Y.: Orbis Books.

France, Peter
1968 The Founding of an Orthodoxy: Sir Arthur Gordon and the Doctrine of the Fijian Way of Life. *Journal of the Polynesian Society* 77:6–32.

1969 *The Charter of the Land: Custom and Colonization in Fiji.* Melbourne: Oxford University Press.

Gallagher, R. E., ed.
1964 *Byron's Journal of his Circumnavigation 1764–1766.* 2 vols. Cambridge: Cambridge University Press.

Garrett, John
1982 *To Live among the Stars: Christian Origins in Oceania.* Geneva: World Council of Churches.

Gassner, J. S., trans.
1969 *Voyages and Adventures of La Pérouse.* Honolulu: University of Hawaii Press.

Gifford, E. W.
1929 *Tongan Society.* Honolulu: Bishop Museum Bulletin 61.

Gilson, R. P.
1970 *Samoa 1830–1900: The Politics of a Multi-Cultural Community.* Melbourne: Oxford University Press.

Goldman, Irving
    1970 *Ancient Polynesian Society.* Chicago: University of Chicago Press.

Grattan, H. C.
    1963 *The Southwest Pacific to 1900: A Modern History. Australia, New Zealand, the Islands, Antarctica.* Ann Arbor: University of Michigan Press.

Gray, J. A. C.
    1960 *Amerika Samoa: A History of American Samoa and Its U.S. Naval Administration.* Annapolis: U.S. Naval Institute.

Groves, Murray
    1963 The Nature of Fijian Society. Review of *Moala: Culture and Nature on a Fijian Island* by M. D. Sahlins. *Journal of the Polynesian Society* 72:272–291.

Guiart, Jean
    1956 *Un siècle et demi de contacts culturels à Tanna (Nouvelles-Hébrides).* Paris: Société des Océanistes.

    1963 *Structure de la chefferie en Mélanésie du Sud.* Paris: Musée de l'Homme.

    1986 La conquête et le déclin: les plantations, cadre des relations sociales et économiques au Vanuatu, ex Nouvelles-Hébrides. *Journal de la Société des Océanistes* 42:7–40.

Gunson, Niel
    1978 *Messengers of Grace: Evangelical Missionaries in the South Seas: 1797–1860.* Melbourne: Oxford University Press.

Gunson, Niel, ed.
    1978 *The Changing Pacific: Essays in Honour of H. E. Maude.* Melbourne: Oxford University Press.

Hall, James Norman
    1944 *Lost Island.* Boston: Little, Brown & Co.

Hanson, F. A.
    1970 *Rapan Lifeways: Society and History on a Polynesian Island.* Boston: Little, Brown & Co.

Harding, T. G., and B. J. Wallace, eds.
    1970 *Cultures of the Pacific: Selected Readings.* New York: Free Press.

Harrison, Tom
    1937 *Savage Civilization.* New York: Alfred A. Knopf.

Healy, A. M.
    1967 *'Bulolo': A History of the Development of the Bulolo Region, New Guinea.* Canberra and Port Moresby: New Guinea Research Bulletin no. 15.

Hempenstall, Peter
    1977 "Native Resistance and German Control Policy in the Pacific: The Case of Samoa and Ponape." In *Germany in the Pacific and the Far East,*

edited by J. A. Moses and Paul Kennedy, 209–233. St. Lucia: University of Queensland Press.

1978 *Pacific Islanders under German Rule.* Canberra: Australian National University Press.

Hezel, F. X.
1978 "The Role of the Beachcombers in the Carolines." In *The Changing Pacific: Essays in Honour of H. E. Maude,* edited by Niel Gunson, 261–272. Melbourne: Oxford University Press.

1983 *The First Taint of Civilization: A History of the Caroline and Marshall Islands in Pre-Colonial Days, 1521–1885.* Pacific Islands Monograph Series, no. 1. Honolulu: University of Hawaii Press.

Hilliard, David
1974 Colonialism and Christianity: the Melanesian Mission in the Solomon Islands. *Journal of Pacific History* 9:93–116.

Hogbin, H. I., ed.
1973 *Anthropology in Papua New Guinea. Readings from the Encyclopaedia of Papua and New Guinea.* Melbourne: Melbourne University Press.

Howard, Alan, ed.
1971 *Polynesia: Readings on a Culture Area.* Scranton: Chandler Publishing Co.

Howe, K. R.
1977 *The Loyalty Islands: A History of Culture Contacts, 1840–1900.* Honolulu: University Press of Hawaii.

1984 *Where the Waves Fall: A New South Sea Islands History from First Settlement to Colonial Rule.* Pacific Islands Monograph Series, no. 2. Honolulu: University of Hawaii Press.

Howells, W. W.
1973 *The Pacific Islanders.* London: Weidenfeld & Nicolson.

Inglis, John
1887 *In the New Hebrides: Reminiscences of Missionary Life and Work.* London: T. Nelson & Sons.

Jacobs, Marjorie
1972 "German New Guinea." In *Encylopaedia of Papua and New Guinea,* edited by Peter Ryan, 485–498. Melbourne: Melbourne University Press.

Jennings, J. D., ed.
1979 *The Prehistory of Polynesia.* Cambridge: Harvard University Press.

Journal de la Société des Océanistes, vol. 25
1969 *Les Missions dans le Pacifique.* Paris: Musée de l'Homme.

Kawharu, Hugh
1971 "New Zealand: Salvaging the Remnant." In *Land Tenure in the Pacific,* edited by R. G. Crocombe, 129–145. Melbourne: Oxford University Press.

Keesing, F. M.
  1934 *Modern Samoa*. London: George Allen & Unwin.

Keesing, Roger
  1986 Plantation Networks, Plantation Culture: The Hidden Side of Colonial
        Melanesia. *Journal de la Société des Océanistes* 42:163–170.

Kelly, Celsus, ed.
  1966 *La Austrialia del Espiritu Santo*. 2 vols. Cambridge: Cambridge Univer-
        sity Press.

Kennedy, P. M.
  1977 "Germany and the Samoan Tridominium, 1889–98: A Study in Frus-
        trated Imperialism." In *Germany in the Pacific and the Far East*, edited
        by J. A. Moses and Paul Kennedy, 89–114. St. Lucia: University of
        Queensland Press.

Knapman, Bruce
  1985 Capitalism's Economic Impact on Colonial Fiji, 1874–1939. *Journal of
        Pacific History* 20:66–83.

Korn, S. R. D.
  1978 "After the Missionaries Came: Denominational Diversity in the Tonga
        Islands." In *Mission, Church and Sect in Oceania*, edited by J. A. Bouti-
        lier, D. T. Hughes, and S. W. Tiffany, 395–422. Lanham, Md., Uni-
        versity Press of America.

Lamb, W. K.
  1984 *The Voyage of George Vancouver, 1791–1795*. 4 vols. London: The
        Hakluyt Society.

Langness, L. L., and J. C. Weschler, eds.
  1971 *Melanesia: Readings on a Culture Area*. Scranton: Chandler Publishing
        Co.

Laracy, Hugh
  1976 *Marists and Melanesians: A History of Catholic Missions in the Solo-
        mon Islands*. Honolulu: University Press of Hawaii.

Lātūkefu, Sione
  1974 *Church and State in Tonga: The Wesleyan Methodist Missionaries and
        Political Development, 1822–1875*. Honolulu: University Press of
        Hawaii.

  1977 "The Wesleyan Mission." In *Friendly Islands: A History of Tonga*,
        edited by Noel Rutherford, 114–135. Melbourne: Oxford University
        Press.

Laval, Honoré
  1968 *Mémoires pour servir à l'histoire de Mangareve, ère chrétienne, 1834–
        1871*. Paris: Société des Océanistes. Musée de l'Homme.

Lawrence, Peter
  1971 "Introduction." In *Politics in New Guinea: Traditional and in the
        Context of Change—Some Anthropological Perspectives*, edited by
        R. Berndt and Peter Lawrence, 1–34. Nedlands: University of Western
        Australia Press.

Leenhardt, Maurice
   1930 *Notes d'Ethnologie Néo-Calédonienne*. Paris: l'Institut d'Ethnologie, University of Paris.

   1937 *Gens de la Grande Terre*. Paris: Gallimard.

Legge, J. D.
   1972 "Papua-European Enterprise to 1942." In *Encyclopaedia of Papua and New Guinea*, edited by Peter Ryan, 880–882. Melbourne: Melbourne University Press.

Lenormand, M.
   1953 L'évolution politique des autochtones de la Nouvelle-Calédonie. *Journal de la Société des Océanistes* 9:245–295.

Lessa, W. A.
   1975 *Drake's Island of Thieves: Ethnological Sleuthing*. Honolulu: University Press of Hawaii.

Linnekin, Jocelyn
   1987 Statistical Analysis of the Great Mahele. *Journal of Pacific History* 22:1–2.

Lundsgaarde, H. P., ed.
   1974 *Land Tenure in Oceania*. Honolulu: University Press of Hawaii.

McArthur, Norma
   1968 *Island Populations of the Pacific*. Honolulu: University of Hawaii Press.

   1974 *Population and Prehistory: The Late Phase on Aneityum*. Ph.D. dissertation, Australian National University.

   1978 "And, Behold, the Plague Was Begun among the People." In *The Changing Pacific: Essays in Honour of H. E. Maude*, edited by Niel Gunson, 273–284. Melbourne: Oxford University Press.

   1981 *New Hebrides Population 1840–1967: A Reinterpretation*. Noumea: South Pacific Commission Occasional Paper no. 18.

McArthur, Norma, and J. F. Yaxley
   1968 *Condominium of the New Hebrides: A Report on the First Census of the Population, 1967*. New South Wales: Government Printer.

McCall, Grant
   1976 European Impact on Easter Island: Response, Recruitment and the Polynesian Experience in Peru. *Journal of Pacific History* 11:90–105.

McCarthy, Dudley
   1959 *South-west Pacific Area: First Year—Kokoda to Wau*. (series on *Australia in the War of 1939–1945*). Canberra: Australia War Memorial.

MacDonald, Barry
   1982 *Cinderellas of the Empire: Towards a History of Kiribati and Tuvalu*. Canberra: Australian National University Press.

McGrath, W. A., and W. S. Wilson
   1971 "The Marshall, Caroline and Mariana Islands: Too Many Foreign Precedents." In *Land Tenure in the Pacific*, edited by R. G. Crocombe, 172–191. Melbourne: Oxford University Press.

MacNaught, T. J.
   1982   *The Fijian Colonial Experience: A Study of the Neotraditional Order under British Colonial Rule prior to World War II.* Canberra: Australian National University Press.

Mair, Lucy
   1948   *Australia in New Guinea.* London: Cristophers.

Marcus, G. E.
   1980   *The Nobility and the Chiefly Tradition in the Modern Kingdom of Tonga.* Memoir 42. Wellington: The Polynesian Society.

Masefield, John
   1906   *Voyages of William Dampier.* 2 vols. London: E. Grant Richards.

Maude, H. E.
   1938   *Report on the Colonization of the Phoenix Islands by the Surplus Population of the Gilbert and Ellice Colony.* Suva: Government Press.

   1964   Beachcombers and Castaways. *Journal of the Polynesian Society* 73:254–293.

   1981   *Slavers in Paradise: The Peruvian Labour Trade in Polynesia, 1862–1864.* Canberra: Australian National University Press.

Mayer, A. C.
   1963   *Indians in Fiji.* London: Oxford University Press.

Mead, Margaret
   1930   *Social Organization of Manu'a.* Honolulu: Bishop Museum Bulletin 76.

Meller, Norman, and R. H. Horwitz
   1971   "Hawaii: Themes in Land Monopoly." In *Land Tenure in the Pacific,* edited by R. G. Crocombe, 25–42. Melbourne: Oxford University Press.

Métraux, Alfred
   1937   The Kings of Easter Island. *Journal of the Polynesian Society* 46:41–62.

Miller, Char, ed.
   1985   *Missions and Missionaries in the Pacific.* New York: The Edwin Mellen Press.

Milner, S.
   1957   *The United States Army in World War II, the War in the Pacific: Victory in Papua.* Washington: Department of the Army.

Mol, J. J.
   1964   Race Relations, with Special Reference to New Zealand: A Thoughtful Discussion. *Journal of the Polynesian Society* 73:375–381.

Morison, S. E.
   1921   *The Maritime History of Massachusetts, 1783–1860.* Boston: Houghton Mifflin Co.

   1950   *History of United States Naval Operations in World War Two.* Vol. 5, *The Struggle for Guadalcanal, August 1942–February 1943.* Boston: Little, Brown & Co.

Morrell, W. P.
1960 *Britain in the Pacific Islands.* Oxford: Clarendon Press.

Morton, Harry
1982 *The Whale's Wake.* Honolulu: University of Hawaii Press.

Morton, L.
1962 *The United States Army in World War II, the War in the Pacific: Strategy and Command—The First Two Years.* Washington: Government Printing Office.

Moses, Ingred
1977 "The Extension of Colonial Rule in Kaiser Wilhelmsland." In *Germany in the Pacific and the Far East,* edited by J. A. Moses and Paul Kennedy, 288–312. St. Lucia: University of Queensland Press.

Moses, J. A., and Paul Kennedy, eds.
1977 *Germany in the Pacific and the Far East.* St. Lucia: University of Queensland Press.

Murray, Hubert
1925 *Papua of Today.* London: P. S. King & Sons.

Nayacakalou, R. R.
1955 The Fijian System of Kinship and Marriage. *Journal of the Polynesian Society* 64:44–45.

1957 The Fijian System of Kinship and Marriage. *Journal of the Polynesian Society* 66:44–59.

1971 "Fiji: Manipulating the System." In *Land Tenure in the Pacific,* edited by R. G. Crocombe, 206–226. Melbourne: Oxford University Press.

Newbury, Colin
1980a The Melanesian Labour Reserve: Some Reflections on Pacific Labour Markets in the Nineteenth Century. *Pacific Studies* 4:1–25.

1980b *Tahiti Nui: Change and Survival in French Polynesia 1767–1945.* Honolulu: University Press of Hawaii.

Norbeck, Edward
1957 *Pineapple Town, Hawaii.* Berkeley: University of California Press.

Nowell, C. E.
1962 *Magellan's Voyage Around the World.* Evanston: Northwestern University Press.

Oliver, D. L.
1955 *A Solomon Island Society: Kinship and Leadership among the Siuai of Bougainville.* Cambridge: Harvard University Press.

1973 *Bougainville: A Personal History.* Honolulu: University Press of Hawaii.

1974 *Ancient Tahitian Society.* 3 vols. Honolulu: University Press of Hawaii.

1988 *Return to Tahiti: Bligh's Second Breadfruit Voyage.* Honolulu: University of Hawaii Press.

1989   *Native Cultures of the Pacific Islands.* Honolulu: University of Hawaii Press.

Oram, N. D.
1971   The London Missionary Society Pastorate and the Emergence of an Educated Elite in Papua. *Journal of Pacific History* 6:115–132.

Palmer, George
1871   *Kidnapping in the South Seas: Being a Narrative of a Three Months' Cruise of H.M. Ship* Rosario. Edinburgh: Edmonston & Douglas. Reprint. Penguin, 1973.

Panoff, M.
1979   Travailleurs, recruteurs et planteurs dans l'Archipel Bismarck de 1885 a 1914. *Journal de la Société des Océanistes* 35:159–173.

Panoff, M., ed.
1986   Les plantations dans le Pacifique Sud. *Journal de la Société des Océanistes* 42.

Parnaby, Owen
1964   *Britain and the Labour Trade in the Southwest Pacific.* Durham, N.C.: Duke University Press.

Patterson, George
1882   *Missionary Life among the Cannibals: Being the Life of the Rev. John Geddie, D.D., First Missionary to the New Hebrides.* Toronto: J. Campbell & Sons.

Peattie, Mark R.
1988   *Nan'yō: The Rise and Fall of the Japanese in Micronesia, 1885–1945.* Pacific Islands Monograph Series, no. 4. Honolulu: University of Hawaii Press.

Purcell, D. C., Jr.
1976   The Economics of Exploitation: The Japanese in the Mariana, Caroline and Marshall Islands, 1915–1940. *Journal of Pacific History* 11:189–211.

Ralston, Caroline
1978   *Grass Huts and Warehouses. Pacific Beach Communities of the Nineteenth Century.* Honolulu: University Press of Hawaii.

Reed, S. W.
1943   *The Making of Modern New Guinea.* Philadelphia: American Philosophical Society.

Ross, Angus, ed.
1969   *New Zealand's Record in the Pacific Islands in the Twentieth Century.* Auckland: Longman Paul.

Rowley, C. D.
1958   *The Australians in German New Guinea 1914–1921.* Melbourne: Melbourne University Press.

Rutherford, Noel, ed.
1977 *Friendly Islands: A History of Tonga.* Melbourne: Oxford University Press.

Ryan, Peter, ed.
1972 *Encyclopaedia of Papua and New Guinea.* 3 vols. Melbourne: Melbourne University Press.

Sack, Peter
1977 "Law, Politics and Native 'Crimes' in German New Guinea." In *Germany in the Pacific and the Far East,* edited by J. A. Moses and Paul Kennedy, 262–287. St. Lucia: University of Queensland Press.

1986 German New Guinea: A Reluctant Plantation Colony? *Journal de la Société des Océanistes* 42:109–127.

Safford, W. E.
1902 Guam and Its People. *American Anthropologist* 4:707–729.

Sahlins, M. D.
1958 *Social Stratification in Polynesia.* Seattle: University of Washington Press.

1962 *Moala: Culture and Nature on a Fijian Island.* Ann Arbor: University of Michigan Press.

Saussol, Alain
1971 "New Caledonia: Colonization and Reaction." In *Land Tenure in the Pacific,* edited by R. G. Crocombe, 227–247. Melbourne: Oxford University Press.

Sautot, H.
1949 *Grandeur et Décadence du Gaullisme dans le Pacifique.* Melbourne: F. W. Cheshire.

Scarr, Deryck
1967 *Fragments of Empire: A History of the Western Pacific High Commission 1877–1914.* Canberra: Australian National University Press.

1970 "Recruits and Recruiters: A Portrait of the Labour Trade." In *Pacific Islands Portraits,* edited by J. W. Davidson and D. Scarr, 225–252. Canberra: Australian National University Press.

1984 *Fiji: A Short History.* Sydney: George Allen & Unwin.

Scarr, Deryck, ed.
1968 *A Cruise in a Queensland Labour Vessel to the South Seas, written by W. E. Giles.* Canberra: Australian National University Press.

Scheffler, H. W.
1971 "The Solomon Islands: Seeking a New Land Custom." In *Land Tenure in the Pacific,* edited by R. G. Crocombe, 273–291. Melbourne: Oxford University Press.

Sharp, Andrew, ed.
1968 *The Voyages of Abel Janzoon Tasman.* Oxford: Clarendon Press.

1970 *The Journal of Jacob Roggeveen.* Oxford: Clarendon Press.

Shineberg, Dorothy
   1967   *They Came For Sandalwood: A Study of the Sandalwood Trade in the South West Pacific 1830–1865.* Melbourne: Melbourne University Press.

   1971   *The Trading Voyages of Andrew Cheyne 1841–1944.* Canberra: Australian National University Press.

Shoemaker, J. H.
   1940   *Labor in the Territory of Hawaii.* Washington: Government Printing Office.

Shuster, D. R.
   1982   State Shinto in Micronesia during Japanese Rule, 1914–1945. *Pacific Studies* 5:20–31.

Silverman, M. G.
   1971   *Disconcerting Issue: Meaning and Struggle in a Resettled Pacific Community.* Chicago: University of Chicago Press.

Sinclair, Keith
   1980   *A History of New Zealand.* London: A. Lane.

Singe, John
   1979   *The Torres Strait: People and History.* St. Lucia: University of Queensland Press.

Souder, P. B.
   1971   "Guam: Land Tenure in a Fortress." In *Land Tenure in the Pacific,* edited by R. G. Crocombe, 192–205. Melbourne: Oxford University Press.

Souter, G.
   1963   *New Guinea: The Last Unknown.* Sydney: Angus & Robertson.

Spate, O. H. K.
   1959   *The Fijian People: Economic Problems and Prospects.* Suva: Government Press.

   1979   *The Spanish Lake.* Canberra: Australian National University Press.

   1983   *Monopolists and Freebooters.* Canberra: Australian National University Press.

Spoehr, Alexander
   1949   *Majuro: A Village in the Marshall Islands.* Fieldiana Anthropology 39. Chicago: Chicago Natural History Museum.

   1951   The Tinian Chamorros. *Human Organization* 10 (4): 16–20.

   1952   Time Perspective in Micronesia and Polynesia. *Southwest Journal of Anthropology* 8:457–465.

   1954   *Saipan: The Ethnology of a War-devastated Island.* Fieldiana Anthropology 41. Chicago: Chicago Natural History Museum.

   1957   *Marianas Prehistory: Archaeological Survey and Excavations on Saipan, Tinian, and Rota.* Fieldiana Anthropology 48. Chicago: Chicago Natural History Museum.

1978 "Conquest Culture and Colonial Culture in the Marianas." In *The Changing Pacific: Essays in Honour of H. E. Maude,* edited by Niel Gunson, 247–260. Melbourne: Oxford University Press.

Stackpole, E. A.
1953 *The Sea Hunters: The New England Whalemen during Two Centuries 1635–1835.* Philadelphia: Lippincott.

1972 *Whales and Destiny: The Rivalry between America, France, and Britain for Control of the Southern Whale Fishery, 1785–1825.* Amherst: University of Massachusetts Press.

Stanner, W. E. H.
1953 *The South Seas in Transition.* Sydney: Australasian Publishing Co.

Stanton, William
1975 *The Great United States Exploring Expedition.* Berkeley: University of California Press.

Sullivan, I. L. G., ed.
1940 *The Maori People Today.* London: Oxford University Press.

Thompson, Laura
1945 *The Native Culture of the Mariana Islands.* Honolulu: Bernice P. Bishop Museum Occasional Papers 11.

1947 *Guam and its People.* Princeton: Princeton University Press.

Thomson, Basil
1894 *The Diversions of a Prime Minister.* Edinburgh & London: Blackwood & Sons.

Toullelan, Pierre-Yves
1986 Plantations sans planteurs: les cultures spéculatives dans les Établissements Francais de l'Océanie. *Journal de la Société des Océanistes* 42: 139–151.

Tung, Shur-Liang
1984 The Rapid Fertility Decline in Guam Natives. *Journal of Biosocial Science* 16:231–239.

Valle, Teresa del
1979 *Social and Cultural Change in the Community of Umatac, Southern Guam.* Guam: Micronesian Area Research Center, University of Guam.

1987 *Culturas Océanicas Micronesia.* Barcelona: Editorial Anthropos.

Vayda, A. P., ed.
1968 *Peoples and Cultures of the Pacific.* Garden City, N.Y.: Natural History Press.

Wallis, Helen, ed.
1965 *Carteret's Voyage round the World 1766–1769.* 2 vols. Cambridge: Cambridge University Press.

Walter, M. A. H. B.
1978 The Conflict of the Traditional and the Traditionalized: An Analysis of Fijian Land Tenure. *Journal of the Polynesian Society* 87:89–108.

Ward, A. W.
  1982 *Land and Politics in New Caledonia.* Canberra: Australian National
        University Press.
Ward, R. G.
  1969 Land Use and Land Alienation in Fiji to 1895. *Journal of Pacific His-
        tory* 4:3–26.
Wedgewood, Camilla
  1936 Report on Research Work in Nauru Island, Central Pacific. *Oceania*
        6:359–391.
West, F. J.
  1961 *Political Advancement in the South Pacific: A Comparative Study of
        Colonial Practice in Fiji, Tahiti, and American Samoa.* Melbourne: Ox-
        ford University Press.
  1968 *Hubert Murray: The Australian Pro-Consul.* Melbourne: Oxford Uni-
        versity Press.
Whiteman, D. L.
  1983 *Melanesians and Missionaries: An Ethnohistorical Study of Socio-Reli-
        gious Change in the Southwest Pacific.* Pasadena: William Carey Li-
        brary.
Williams, F. E.
  1977 *'The Vailala Madness' and Other Essays.* Edited and with an introduc-
        tion by Erik Schwimmer. Honolulu: University Press of Hawaii.
Wiltgen, R. M.
  1979 *The Founding of the Roman Catholic Church in Oceania, 1825 to
        1850.* Canberra: Australian National University Press.
Worsley, Peter
  1957 *The Trumpet Shall Sound: A Study of 'Cargo' Cults in Melanesia.* Lon-
        don: MacGibbon & Kee.
Wu, D. Y. H.
  1982 *The Chinese in Papua New Guinea, 1880–1980.* Hong Kong: Chinese
        University Press.

Index

Admiralty Islands, 44, 161, 163–165, 258
Africans, 144
Agana (Guam), 94, 232
Air transport, 79, 214, 220–222, 229, 263, 273
Aitutaki Island, 45, 262
Alexander the Great, 174
Alkire, W. H., 91
Ambrym Island, 27
American Micronesia. *See* Trust Territory of the Pacific Islands
Americans. *See* United States and Americans
American Samoa. *See* Samoa, Eastern
Aneityum Island, 96–98, 169
Angaur Island, 6, 65, 216, 237–238, 241
Anglicans. *See* Missions
Anglo-French Condominium, 172–173. *See also* New Hebrides Islands
Annamese, 144
Antarctica, 38
Anzac pact, 257
Aore Island, 169
Arrowroot, 51
Atiu Island, 45
Australia, European discovery of, 41, 44
Australia and non-Aboriginal Australians, 46–47, 51, 61, 66, 68, 71–74, 76–79, 137, 164, 175, 202–203, 209–210, 214–217, 219, 225, 256–261, 269–270
Australian Aborigines, 209–211
Australian Dependencies. *See* Nauru Island; New Guinea, Northeastern; Norfolk Island; Papua; Torres Strait Islands
Austral Islands, 143
Austronesians, 13

Bacon, Roger, 36
Baker, Rev. Shirley, 121

Baker Island, 79
Balboa, Vasco Nuñez de, 36
Banaba. *See* Ocean Island
Bananas, 64, 199, 202
Bases, military-naval, 229–230, 233–234, 242, 244, 248
Bauxite. *See* Mining
Beachcombers, 53–54, 223
Beaglehole, John, 42
"Big Five" (of Hawaii), 187, 191–192. *See also* Hawaiian Sugar Planters' Association
Bikini Island, 274–275
Bingham, Rev. Hiram, 139
Birds, 11, 162, 212–213, 218
Bismarck, Otto von, 60–61, 70, 163
Bismarck Archipelago, 70, 161. *See also* Admiralty Islands; Lavongai Island; New Britain Island; New Ireland Island
Blackbirding. *See* Labor recruiting
Bligh, William, 45, 142, 170
Bonin Islands, 79
Bonito. *See* Fishing, commercial
Borabora Island, 43, 262
Boston Mission. *See* Missions
Bougainville, Louis Antoine de, 44, 50, 162, 170
Bougainville Island, 44, 57–58, 79, 164–165, 204, 220, 258
Boutilier, James, 118
Boyd, Benjamin, 66
Britain. *See* Great Britain and the British
British Dependencies. *See* Canton Island; Enderbury Island; Fiji Islands; Gilbert and Ellice Islands Crown Colony; Nauru Island; New Hebrides Islands; Ocean Island; Pitcairn Island; Solomon Islands; Tongan Islands
British East India Company, 51, 236
British New Guinea. *See* Papua

Index

About the Author

Douglas L. Oliver is emeritus professor of anthropology at Harvard University and the University of Hawaii. Educated at Harvard and the University of Vienna, he has been concerned with the Pacific Islands since 1936. He has carried out field research in New Guinea, the northern Solomons, and the Society Islands and has written more than a dozen books on the islands of the Pacific. He is a Member of the National Academy of Sciences and a Fellow of the American Academy of Arts and Sciences. He and his wife, the Australian anthropologist Margaret McArthur, now live in Honolulu, where they continue writing.